Praise for *THE REASON FOR FLOWERS*

"*The Reason for Flowers* is an extraordinarily good book. It covers the subject with thoroughness and scientific accuracy, working it (as flowers deserve) into history and culture, and is written with poetic sensitivity."
   —Edward O. Wilson, University Professor Emeritus, Harvard University

"*The Reason for Flowers* is a riveting account of the science, history, and culture surrounding blooms since the dawn of humankind."
   —*Science News*

"Humans often use flowers as decorative accessories. But in this book, Stephen Buchmann, a professor of ecology at the University of Arizona, explains that they also serve other, more urgent purposes."
   —*Time*

"Buchmann, a prolific and ardent pollination ecologist, peels back the petals to reveal fascinating aspects of floriculture. . . . Intensely researched, well paced, intricately detailed, and delightfully accessible, Buchmann's exploration of this trove of living sensory delights is a boon to both casual and committed flower lovers."
   —*Booklist*

"With a subtitle that serves as a swift, sweet summary, [Stephen Buchmann] compresses the cultural and natural history of flowers into a few hundred graceful pages. . . . A volume that is like a Eurail Pass that will carry you through gorgeous terrain you will want to explore in more depth."
   —*Kirkus Reviews*

"Accessible . . . well-researched."
   —*Library Journal*

"Do flowers need a reason? In *The Reason for Flowers*, Stephen Buchmann reminds us that flowers exist for more than just beauty and fragrance. They are miniature chemical factories, wireless signal stations, inspiration for artists, and—of course—sustenance for the most important creatures living on the planet. In short, flowers run the world. Stephen Buchmann is a gifted storyteller and an inquisitive scientist who is intrigued by the dazzling and intricate world of flowers. Thanks to this delightful new book, you will be, too."

—Amy Stewart, *New York Times* bestselling author of *Flower Confidential*

"Here, we discover through our captivating guide just how interdependent flowers and people are: from ancient burials to modern ikebana, to chefs and edible blooms, to Monet's wisteria and flower gardens, to jasmine and rose attar in classic perfumes, to Shakespearean sonnets and the Rolling Stones. *The Reason for Flowers* is a fascinating tapestry of floral inspirations. Buchmann draws inspiration from bees and other pollinators that bring every third bite to our tables as he crafts stories of their sex lives from the field."

—Mark W. Moffett, author of *Adventures Among Ants*

"Stephen Buchmann is to plants and their pollinators as Jacques Cousteau, Sylvia Earle, and Carl Safina have been to the oceans. He opens our eyes to wondrous worlds we have never seen before. This world-renowned explorer of nature's inner workings will delight you while unobtrusively edifying you at the same time."

—Gary Paul Nabhan, W. K. Kellogg Endowed Chair in Sustainable Food Systems, University of Arizona

"Aesthetically, flowers enrich our lives and symbolize our emotions, but they are of even greater importance to us in their functions in nature. In this attractive book, Stephen Buchmann brings to life for the interested reader the many facets of flowers' existence and their interplay with insects and other animals, informing us well about how they evolved and the roles that they play in our world."

—Peter H. Raven, President Emeritus, Missouri Botanical Garden

"*The Reason for Flowers* is a gardening book and more. Buchmann entertains with particulars of the patriotic gardens of Washington and Jefferson, and those of Asia and ancient Rome. We learn how our most beloved flowers came to be, along with new oddities like the black petunia. Every gardener and flower-lover will want this book."

—Carrie Hulburd, President, Columbine Garden Club
(GCA chapter) of Phoenix, Arizona

ALSO BY STEPHEN BUCHMANN

The Forgotten Pollinators
(with Gary Paul Nabhan)

Letters from the Hive: An Intimate History
of Bees, Honey, and Humankind
(with Banning Repplier)

Pollinators of the Sonoran Desert: A Field Guide
(with Nina Chambers and Yajaira Gray)

Pollinator Conservation Handbook
(with Matthew Shepherd, Mace Vaughan, and Scott Black)

The Conservation of Bees (coeditor)

Honey Bees: Letters from the Hive: A History of Bees and Honey

The Bee Tree
(with Diana Cohn, illustrated by Paul Mirocha)

THE
REASON
FOR
FLOWERS

~

Their History, Culture, Biology,
and How They Change Our Lives

STEPHEN BUCHMANN

SCRIBNER
New York   London   Toronto   Sydney   New Delhi

For my late parents, Jane Marie and Stanley Buchmann

And to my life partner, Kay Richter

SCRIBNER
An Imprint of Simon & Schuster, Inc.
1230 Avenue of the Americas
New York, NY 10020

First Scribner trade paperback edition February 2016

SCRIBNER and design are registered trademarks of The Gale Group, Inc.,
used under license by Simon & Schuster, Inc., the publisher of this work.

For information about special discounts for bulk purchases,
please contact Simon & Schuster Special Sales at 1-866-506-1949
or business@simonandschuster.com.

The Simon & Schuster Speakers Bureau can bring authors to your live event.
For more information or to book an event, contact the Simon & Schuster Speakers
Bureau at 1-866-248-3049 or visit our website at www.simonspeakers.com.

Manufactured in the United States of America

3   5   7   9   10   8   6   4

Library of Congress Cataloging-in-Publication Data

Buchmann, Stephen L., author.
The reason for flowers : their history, culture, biology, and how
they change our lives / Stephen Buchmann.
pages cm
Includes bibliographical references.
1. Flowers. I. Title.
SB404.9.B83 2015
635.9—dc23
2015017169

ISBN 978-1-4767-5553-3
ISBN 978-1-4767-5554-0 (ebook)

CONTENTS

PART IV

Flowers in Literature, Art, and Myth

PART V

Flowers in the Service of Science and Medicine

PREFACE

Most open by dawn's first light or unfurl their charms as the day progresses. Others unwrap their diaphanous petals, like expensive presents, after dark, waiting for the arrival of beloved guests under a radiant moon. We know them as flowers. They are nature's advertisements, using their beauty to beguile and reward passing insects or birds or bats or people willing to attend to their reproduction. The beauty of their shapes, colors, and scents transforms us through intimate experiences in our gardens, homes, offices, parks and public spaces, and wildlands. Importantly, flowers feed and clothe us. Their fruits and seeds keep the world's 7.2 billion people from starvation. Flowers represent our past along with our hope for a bright future.

Before recorded history, all cultures collected, used, and admired flowers not only for utilitarian purposes, but for their elusive fragrances and ephemeral forms that, ironically, symbolized recurring vigor and even immortality. They have enthralled and seduced us, exploiting entire civilizations to enhance their sex lives and spread their seeds. We give and receive flowers as tributes, and to commemorate life's many triumphs and everyday events. Flowers accompany us from cradle to grave. As spices, they flavor our foods and beverages. We harvest their delicate scents, combining them into extravagantly expensive mixtures, for perfuming our bodies to evoke passion and intrigue. Some yield a woven textile for every purpose, like the valuable fibers surrounding cottonseeds that began their development inside the ovary of a fertilized flower.

Flowers inspired the first artists, writers, photographers, and scientists, just as they do today on street corners, in florist shops and farmers' markets, in books, paintings, sculptures, and commercial advertising. They moved online with ease. Arguably, because of the sustaining role they undoubtedly played in the lives of our hominid ancestors, we might not be here if there were no flowers, a love affair, begun early. Once captivated by them, I observed nature's infinite palette of garden blooms and California wildflowers in the chaparral-clothed canyons near my boyhood home. The honey bees I kept visited flowers for their rewards of nectar and pollen. The bees fed upon the pollen and converted the nectar into delicious, golden, thick honey I drizzled atop slices of hot toast at breakfast. As a child, finding and observing bees of all kinds on wildflowers became my passion and quest across California's wildlands. The bees showed me the way, leading to a lifelong dedication to flowering plants.

As a pollination ecologist, and entomologist, my professional career has focused on flowers and their animal visitors. Using 35 mm film and making silver gelatin prints of blossoms has been an abiding interest since my teenage years. Today, I carry a 35 mm digital camera and close-up lenses to photograph flowers and their pollinators. (I have selected some favorite floral portraits and included them in this book.) Having written books on bees, I knew a different kind of book must follow, one that traces humankind's fascination with and use of flowers for every imaginable purpose and delight, since prehistory across all continents and cultures. There is much that we fail to appreciate in flowers, especially the roles they play in human affairs. Why do they make us happy and lift our spirits? Many people insist they heal our bodies and minds.

You are about to undertake a journey into the secretive world of flowers, animals, and humanity. I want you to see and smell like a hungry bee, and a hummingbird, but also like a plant breeder, flower farmer, importer of cut blooms, or a floral biologist. Together, we will explore the industry and economics of the global production, distribution, and sales of container plants and cut blooms. As you join me, consider keeping a single flower or a colorful bouquet close by, as your botanical muse along our shared path of discovery.

PART I

SEXUALITY AND ORIGINS

A bee-pollinated cactus blossom

CHAPTER 1

Attracting Attention

A flower's fragrance declares to all the world that it is fertile, available, and desirable, its sex organs oozing with nectar. Its smell reminds us in vestigial ways of fertility, vigor, life-force, all the optimism, expectancy, and passionate bloom of youth. We inhale its ardent aroma and, no matter what our ages, we feel young and nubile in a world aflame with desire.

—Diane Ackerman, *A Natural History of the Senses*, 1990

The Stargazer lily
(*Lilium* sp. hybrid)

What Am I?

Here for you to identify is a living organism, much loved and admired. Having no say in the matter, millions are bought and sold, removed from

3

their natural habitat for the pleasure of the buyers, living fast, dying young, without offspring—then discarded without a second thought. Sometimes they enjoy a better fate, free to live outdoors, reproducing prolifically, enjoy full life spans, their beauty on display for all to see.

The smell of this organism is a hauntingly sweet fragrance, once inhaled, never forgotten. The appearance is dramatic. A long, tumescent rod, topped by a broad, gray-purple tip oozing a clear, sticky liquid, juts suggestively from the center of a yellow, starlike throat. Surprisingly, this phalliclike structure is a female, not a male, organ. The viscid tip evolved to catch and hold pollen grains—dustlike particles that are the male essence. Surrounding the long rod, six yellow-green arms project from the starlike mouth, the bulging, orange packages at their tips ready to split wide-open to release sperm at just the right time.

A hermaphrodite, with male and female parts united in one body, it is capable of having sex there within, though preferring to mate with others, especially nonrelatives. The largest and most spectacular part of this body consists of the two pinwheel-like whorls surrounding the sex organs, one on top of the other, outlined in white and shaded from white to pale pink to a deep almost-purple-pink hue, their surfaces spotted with raised, red dots. Below, where the whorls join the green stalk, is an ovary, containing eggs waiting to be fertilized. Lacking legs or wings, this regal-looking organism is grounded—unable to move during its entire lifetime—and thus dependent upon animal intermediaries. If its concentrated appeal is able to reach out, it is the bees or perhaps other animals that transport its sperm helping it to reproduce. Earthbound and immobile, it casts a gaze upward, to the stars, as it whispers a name sending a message of fanciful dreams, optimism, and unlimited possibilities. What am I?

A *flower* of course, but more specifically a Stargazer lily. The Stargazer, which came to market in 1978, is the result of many years of crossbreeding efforts by the eccentric genius lily-breeder Leslie Woodriff, who wanted a beautiful, fragrant, spotted lily that would hold its blooming head proudly high, unlike any other horticultural lily of the time.

Florist-shop product it may be, but the Stargazer is nonetheless typical of all flowers—which is to say that even though a breeder tinkered with its genealogical stock to make it a crowd-pleaser in the human market-place, its structure, appearance, and smell are ultimately all about attract-ing the pollinators it needs to reproduce. *Outcrossing* instead of *selfing* (self-pollination) prevails among flowering plants. Mating with nonrelatives increases genetic diversity by spreading favorable and subsequent genes through the population, thereby enhancing the fitness of the next generations of plants.

To achieve that outcrossing, flowers broadcast a powerful message to potential pollinators. Flowers are perhaps a little bit of everything, but they are, in essence, the sex organs of the plant. They need sexual favors to spread their sperm and have their eggs fertilized. Natural selection has made them into some of nature's most successful advertisers. Their petals act as living billboards, deploying an extraordinary array of shapes, sizes, color palettes, and scents to communicate the treasures awaiting their sexual enablers. Texture matters, too. They may have matte or glossy finishes, smooth or hairy surfaces, depending on the preferences of the animals they need to attract.

Although we humans have come to love looking at and experiencing flowers in our own way, their petaloid messages were not meant for our eyes or noses. Instead, they have been beckoning for millennia to the tiny insect aerialists that became the first fliers on the planet, taking to the air during the Devonian age, which began over 400 million years ago. The two trajectories combined in a later age and have had a long and fascinating history that is by no means finished now.

The Evolution of Flowers

Plants have not always had flowers. Certain plants, the angiosperms, "invented" flowers and never turned back. They chose wisely. (As I hope is obvious, this is anthropomorphic shorthand for a complicated set of biological processes, for the plants did not make decisions; they tried everything, and natural selection [survival of the fittest] ensured that their genes were the result of the most successful "experiments" and were reproduced.)

Flowers evolved from small leaves that bunched together at the stem tips. When they changed later and took on roles that were very different from those of their leafy progenitors, they lost their green color and began developing into the petal and bract structures we now recognize within flowers. These were their come-hither beacons and perfume dispensers, which changed over time. As traits and their gene frequencies within populations varied, they were inherited one generation to the next, creating the best available fit of flower to animal. These "matchups" are known as floral mutualisms, forms of tug-of-war, a give-and-take whereby flowers and their pollinators are mutualists in a coevolutionary endeavor that does not cross the line into antagonism. Bees prefer sweeter nectar and choose flowers with more sugar. Gradually, in their descendants, flowers with richer nectar prevailed. This is also brinkmanship. If flowers offer too little, the bees won't come; too much and they've wasted precious energy. Flowers and insects are mutualists, but they are first and foremost looking out for themselves, satisfying their own needs.

Since flowers don't get around much—unless they're in a wedding bouquet or a high-school-prom corsage—they found ways to have sex with other plants. Not a fling or an affair, but the real thing. The animals that fly from flower to flower, along the way dispersing each flower's sperm (in the form of pollen) to other flowers, enable plants to go on virtual dates with each other, and to reproduce. Pollinators afford a wonderful solution to their mobility handicap, and one that nature began to put into action over 100 million years ago, when the earliest flowering plants came into being.

The Flower Revealed

To understand the true meaning of flowers you need to be familiar with a few terms for the floral parts. The natural objects we call flowers might call on you to have a fresh-cut flower nearby as you read. Let the blossom be your guide. A lily flower would be ideal, which is why I open the chapter with the Stargazer. It's readily available, with parts big enough to be seen without a magnifying glass, and it's not coy about sharing the secrets of its sexuality. Although other common flowers such as roses, carnations, peonies and chrysanthemums share the same basic anatomy, they are perhaps too ruffly. Parting those floral skirts to get at what lies beneath might be a bit challenging to the amateur botanist voyeur. So let's consider the simple lily, a big, brash beauty.

As mentioned, it is a hermaphrodite. Starting from the top of the flower, we see that long, tumescent rod, the female sex organ. It's called the pistil (or carpel), and it has three sections. The first part you see, consisting of the style (the slender stalk) and the stigma (at the tip), rises straight up and out of the third part, the ovary, found below the petals. Floral styles can be short and squat or, as in the Stargazer, long and thin. The stigma at the tip is moist or gooey to catch and hold the pollen that

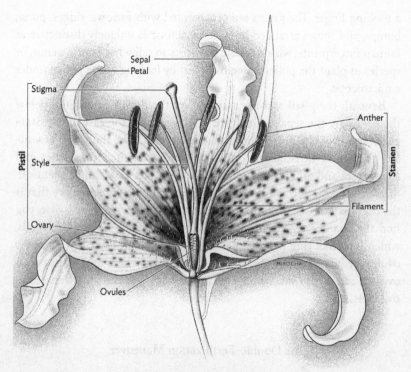

A cutaway illustration of a Stargazer lily,
with labeled parts, by artist Paul Mirocha

come to it courtesy of a hungry pollinating animal, or perhaps a passing breeze.

Sprouting from the floral base, and surrounding the stalklike part of the pistil, are the stamens. Rising on their own long, slender stalks, called filaments, they emerge outside the swollen green ovary. Depending on the flower, there may be a few or many. The Stargazer has six stamens. Atop each are two structures that look like conjoined hot dogs. These are the anthers, containing thousands of dustlike pollen particles. As the flower matures, the anther walls peel back and release their precious cargo. Microscopic in size, and spherical or football-shaped, the pollen grains are yellow or orange, but, depending on the plant, may also be red, green, blue, purple, white, or nearly black. They're covered with an oily coating that makes them stick together, so that they cling to pollinators—or to a probing finger. The grains are ornamented with furrows, ridges, pores, bumps, and spines arranged in patterns almost as uniquely distinctive as human fingerprints, which enable botanists to tell what family, genus, or species of plant the pollen came from just by looking at the pollen under a microscope.

Beneath the pistil and the stamens are the flower petals, and below the petals are the sepals, which are often green. In the case of the Stargazer, however, the outer whorl of what appears to be the petals is actually the set of three sepals, for in some flowers, including lilies and amaryllises and orchids, the sepals and the petals look almost identical. Sitting immediately above the sepals is the enlarged green ovary that is the bottom part of the pistil. If you cut through the ovary crosswise, you find the chambers containing the Stargazer's ovules—its future seeds, which look like tiny peas. Depending on the plant, there can be many ovules, or just one, but regardless of how many there are, within each ovule is an embryo sac, which contains the egg and the other reproductive cells.

The Double-Fertilization Maneuver

This weird-sounding reproductive action is so unique to angiosperms—the flowering plants—that it is one of the traits used to characterize and identify them. It's called double fertilization because it involves not one but two sperm cells, one that fertilizes the egg, and the other to help form the endosperm, the starchy tissue that feeds the developing plant embryo. Fertilization begins when the pollen grains land upon the gooey stigma, the tip of our lily, after which things happen quickly. Each pollen grain swells up, nearly ready to burst, until it germinates, and one part of it sends a thin tube down the floral style, probing its way toward the ovary, while the other part, a generative cell, travels down the pollen tube. Finally, after several hours or a few days, as the cell approaches the embryo sac of the ovary, it divides into two sperm cells—ready to play their roles in double fertilization. The chromosomes from one sperm cell fuse with the egg cell that will develop into the tiny plant embryo found within every seed. The chromosomes from the second sperm cell fuse with different cells inside the embryo sac, developing into the endosperm.

Floral Rewards:
What's in It for the Birds and the Bees?

For fertilization to occur, outside pollinators are enticed to visit flowers. But there has to be some reward for the pollinators—and some way of advertising that reward—or else they won't bother to visit the blooms.

So, flowers fulfill many needs for their animal visitors. For bees as well as some other pollinators, flowers are cafés and rest stops, offering a rich abundance of food. They can also be rendezvous sites for pollinators to find each other and pair up. For predators, including crab spiders, ambush bugs, and mantids, wildflowers and garden blossoms provide ready-made perches from which to hunt their prey. Many insects seek out flowers for the warmth they find inside. This is especially true in arctic and alpine regions. The parabolic-shaped petals of these flowers not only warm the heat-seeking creatures but also speed up the development of ovules within flower ovaries. The remaining floral rewards consist mainly of nest-building materials and sex pheromone precursors in the case of some bees and butterflies. Floral oils, for example, can be eaten, but some tropical bees also turn them into protective linings for their brood cells. Fragrances produced by orchids and other sources are the pheromone-like precursors harvested by male orchid bees and used in their aerobatic courtship and mating rituals.

Of course the single most important reason insects and other animals visit flowers is to feed. Within flowers, they find nutritious food for themselves or their larvae. The adults of most flower-visiting insects seek food only for themselves. This gives them the energy they need to fly or stay warm. But other insects, including bees and certain specialist wasps, bring the pollen back to the hive or solitary nests, where the protein-rich grains feed them and also provide nourishment to their developing brood.

Flowers produce four types of rewarding food substances to draw the pollinating animals, hold their attention, and keep them coming back for more. These foods are nectar, pollen, floral oils, and the edible body tissues of some flowers.

Nectar is the sweet but watery liquid secreted from glands located near the base of the petals of most flowers. A high-energy food, nectar oozes up from hidden nectar glands into crevices deep inside most flowers, but can sometimes be produced elsewhere within flowers or from buds and leaf bases. Nectar is a high-energy, liquid food usually hidden from view. The sugars reward bees, wasps, flies, butterflies, moths, birds, and bats, but to reach those low-lying pools of nectar they have to brush up against the stamens, causing pollen to stick to them—ready to be transmitted to the next flower they visit. Floral nectar is a blend of three sugars—sucrose, glucose, and fructose—but may contain other minor sugars. When the pollinators eat and digest the sugars in the nectar, they get the energy they need to fly, or to stay warm in the cold. Certain social bees, such as honey bees, bumble bees, and stingless bees, are able to turn the nectar into the sugary "fossil fuel" we know as honey, which can be saved for the future. Honey bees visit their waxen cupboards to reclaim this stored energy during cold winters as well as periods of inclement weather.

Nectar, while an important fuel food, is not as critical for bees as the pollen that they obtain from flowers. They can't live without it nor feed their young. Pollen contains from 5 to 60 percent protein, all of the essential amino acids, diverse lipids, and antioxidants that bees need. It's not so easy to get at those nutrients, however. Pollen grains, tiny as they are, are actually supertough. Imagine them as hard-walled Ping-Pong balls with a nutritious liquid center. Their outer walls are a biopolymer, a natural plastic. These walls are so resistant to chemical attack that we find pollen grains fossilized in 100-million-year-old sediments. But that doesn't stop the bees, which use a special trick to eat the otherwise indigestible pollen. They extract the pollen interiors with a combination of osmotic shock, which causes the grains to swell up and burst, and enzymes from within their digestive tracts, which break them down further allowing their nutrients to be absorbed. Once eaten, the undigested outer walls of the pollen are defecated by adults and their larvae. Looking at this waste product, we can perform a bit of forensic scatology to tell what types of pollen the bees ate, thereby knowing what plants they'd visited. I know this probably doesn't do a lot for you, but it's exciting for bee scientists such as myself.

Just as an aside: While pollen is the ideal balanced natural diet for bees, it may cause problems for mammalian digestive systems. Those who buy bee-collected pollen from health-food stores face a possible food-allergy risk because this pollen may come from ragweed or other allergenic plants. So, you might want to sparingly test a few pollen pellets before heaping them on your breakfast cereal. Honey is a different matter, however, since it contains only the faintest trace of pollen and may actually benefit hay-fever sufferers.

Another category of food offered to pollinators is super-high-energy floral oils contained within exotic flowers in the world's tropical rain forests and deserts. These oils, which are used by specialist bees in the genus *Centris*, come mostly from flowers in the tropical family Malpighiaceae. These flowers bear unusual secretory glands on their undersides. Beneath a protective skin covering, like a blister you might get from gardening without gloves, the secretory glands contain oils with unique chemistries that are sought out by bees. Female bees land on the oil flowers and take up a four-legged stance. If you could slow down the rapid action, you'd see the bees raking their front legs across the oil glands. Their legs have broad, flattened scraper hairs that rupture the oil blisters and transfer the oils to the mats of thick hairs, almost like scrub brushes, on their back legs. When they fly home, they mix the floral oils they've collected with pollen, often from other kinds of flowers, creating a nutritious "bee bread" for their hungry larvae. The oil has another use, too. Some bees enzymatically convert it into a slow-hardening wall coating for the underground chambers, the brood cells, where the bee larvae grow and mature into adult bees. Other chemicals in the oil may protect the developing bees from the ravages of soil-borne bacteria and fungi. Nest-building materials may also come from the flowers that grow on the tropical *Clusia* tree. Its flowers are a sticky mess because they have glands that ooze tacky resins that attract pollinating bees, which harvest the resins for use in their nest-building.

Perhaps the strangest floral rewards of all (at least in terms of their presentation and later use) are the essential oils—terpenes and similar chemicals—produced by specialized orchids, e.g., *Stanhopea*, *Coryanthes*, and *Gongora*. These orchids produce no edible rewards—not a trace of pollen or nectar for their bee pollinators, the emerald-green or cobalt-blue beauties known as euglossines. Since these orchid bees are native only to the neotropical forests—from southern Sonora, Mexico, to the rain forests of the Amazon basin—you may not have had the pleasure of seeing one of these living jewels. The male orchid bees, never the females, visit the orchids, and while they are paying their floral visit, the bees probe for nectar that isn't there, and for pollen that does exist, but is so securely shrink-wrapped inside testicle-shaped packages (known as pollinia) that it is unavailable to them. But during the bees' search for food, the orchid flower, whose shape has been molded by millions of years of fine-tuning, maneuvers them into exactly the correct position for the bright yellow pollinia to be glued securely to their bodies, ready to be carried to the next flower they visit. Practicing a bit of thievery of their own, the bees scrape assiduously at the scent-producing tissues on the orchid blossoms, which they stash inside hairy glands within their enlarged, hollow hind legs.

After days, weeks, or months of collecting these fragrant substances, the male orchid bees form *leks*. These are display areas where one or more males put on a show for choosy females. An example of this kind of courtship in birds is the prairie chicken, also known as the sage grouse. The male birds puff out their breasts, call, and strut their fancy tail feathers in front of females, who choose their eventual mate based on the best performance. We think much the same thing happens in orchid bees. Male orchid bees flash their colors, buzz loudly, and puff out little clouds of sex pheromones—the fragrances they liberated from the orchids, which they have turned into *aphrobesiacs*, or at least that's what we think is happening. We don't know quite a few things about the orchid/bee pollination arrangement, but our best guess is that the bees somehow modify, mix, or blend the purloined orchid scents for use in their own mating rituals.

Versions of this orchid/pollinator arrangement occur around the world, especially in tropical rain forests. Typically, the orchids advertise that pollen or nectar is present when, in fact, most of these offerings are a sham—just clever advertisements. Pollinators are invited in, only to end up branded with bright yellow pollen sacs, glued on, for their trouble. They must go elsewhere to satisfy their hunger or sexual lust. In the world of flowers, what pollinators see is not always what they get. The guiding principle of caveat emptor in human commerce applies equally for animals visiting flowers.

The last of the food rewards offered by some groups of flowers are food bodies on the flowers themselves. At the tips of thickened petals called tepals are protein-rich, knobby structures that sap and rove beetles like to eat. A familiar garden flower offering this reward system is the eastern and western spicebush (*Calycanthus*). Small beetles are attracted by the dozens to their wine-colored blossoms. Beetles can't resist and force their way through the maze of fleshy petals and down past the stamens. Spicebush blossoms offer no nectar but feed their beetle visitors with pollen and with these small, whitish food bodies. The beetles are in no hurry to leave. They feed, mate with abandon, and defecate, before taking flight in search of the next blossom.

Fragrance:
Perfuming the Out-of-Doors

Scent production that sends fragrances wafting through the air is a powerful way for flowers to advertise their presence to the creatures they need for their pollination. So it won't surprise you to discover that among their other talents, flowering plants are master chemists, scenting the air with their aromatic petals and other floral parts.

Floral scents are usually produced at the time the flowers first open, and the intensity of the fragrance will vary depending on the time of day. In general, flowers tend to release the maximal amount of scent in hot, sunny midday weather.

You can do an experiment yourself to verify this. If you come across a kind of flower that you remember as having a scent, but you find that, upon a casual first sniff, you can barely smell anything, clip some of its petals and put them in a clean, small jar with a lid and leave it in a sunny window for an hour or two. When you come back, open the jar and sniff. The flower's scent should now be concentrated and easily detected.

Not every flower effects its perfume alchemy in daytime, however. Flowers release their scents when their pollinators are most active. As gardeners who have created so-called moonlight gardens know, certain blossoms—e.g., jasmine, moonflower, queen-of-the-night cactus, sacred datura, and other nocturnal bloomers—release their sweet essences onto the night breezes. Both the queen-of-the-night cactus and the datura's large, white blossoms are visited by fast-flying hawk moths that follow the floral odor plumes to the flowers at sunset and into the night. Also, some temporal rhythms in scent production have to do not with the time of day but with the age of the flower. Fresh, young blossoms quickly peak in their scent production, when their stigmas are most receptive. As the flowers age and eventually wither, their fragrance production drops until it eventually stops.

The nature of the different floral aromas broadcast by flowers is related to the types of pollinators they're trying to entice. For example, let's take a look at—or rather a sniff of—a potted African *Stapelia*. If you've ever owned one of these and had it bloom on your kitchen windowsill, you may remember that until you finally realized the smell was coming from your houseplant, you went looking high and low throughout the kitchen for whatever had died—a mouse? a rat? whaaaaat?! Plants such as *Stapelia*, and its relatives among the African milkweeds, as well as skunk cabbage and the voodoo lily, depend for their pollination on carrion flies. These flies, which normally feed on dead animals, are attracted to the nitrogen-containing aminoid compounds released by carrion during decomposition. In 1885 Berlin physician and chemist Ludwig Brieger, a man with a good nose and a keen sense of humor, gave these pungent molecules the evocative names by which we know them today—putrescine and cadaverine. These are the source of the unpleasant and unforgettable smell of death. Putrescine also plays a role in giving urine its distinctive scent.

Remarkably, natural selection enabled flowers to develop and make the same fetid-smelling compounds that carrion releases. I find it fascinating that these carrion flowers are able to tap into the smell of death, evolving in a way that they, too, could produce putrescine and cadaverine and use them to advertise their presence to the carrion flies they need to achieve their sexual unions.

Each pollinator has its own preferences for scents, and is associated with certain flowers that evolved to adapt to those preferences. Butterflies prefer the light, sweet aromas emitted by phloxes, *Polemonium*, and similar flowers. Working the night shift, settling moths and large, fast-flying hawk moths are attracted to blossoms such as jasmine, which have heavier, almost sickeningly sweet fragrances created by benzyl acetate and linalool (among a hundred other compounds). Flowers pollinated by bees have lively and sweet but somewhat fainter scents. Think of the scent of snapdragons, wild peas, *Penstemon*, or foxgloves. Often these flowers are found in the same area, where their use of similar chemical components to entice their bee pollinators makes for an economy and efficiency that suits all parties in the interaction. In addition to colors and shapes, flower-specific scents help pollinators find the same floral species. This is mutually beneficial to flowers since their pollen is moved to unrelated individuals of the same species, not wasted on the wrong blossoms. Floral fidelity, but to different individuals within a plant species, works for both partners.

Among the vertebrates and their flowers, the situation is quite different. Most of the pollinating vertebrates are birds and bats, and except for vultures and condors, most birds have an extremely limited sense of smell. So hummingbird-pollinated flowers, for example, are essentially scentless. These vivid red flowers, including *Salvia*, *Hibiscus*, and *Penstemon* to name a few, may look lovely in your living room, but they won't do anything to lend it a pleasing aroma—something to keep in mind when you see beautiful bouquets of tubular, red flowers in the florist shop.

Bats, however, are among the vertebrates that enjoy floral scents. Flowers attract neotropical nectar bats for pollinating visits with batlike chemical-messenger odors, either sulfurous or fruity. Most bat odors don't do anything for me, but I do enjoy some of the fruitier scents in some bat blossoms. A favorite scent not just of the bats but of mine is from the lofty saguaro—often growing seventy feet tall, a columnar cactus and the state flower of Arizona. Pollinated by nectar-loving bats at night and cactus bees by day, the saguaro has a floral aroma that reminds me of the lovely mild fragrance of a ripe honeydew melon. The bats seem to enjoy the smell as much as I do, greedily lapping up the saguaro's dilute but abundant nectar as they spread cactus pollen around.

Most animals have a strong response to smell, which can play a major role in their reproductive life. But some researchers have suggested that flowers today are losing their fragrances due to climate change, and that this will disrupt links in pollination and affect our food supply. This, like so many other concerns about global warming, increasing levels of UV radiation, and other climate-change effects, should be explored more thoroughly by environmental scientists before it is too late for flowers, pollinators, and us.

Tactile Messages:
Pollinators Read Micro-Braille

Smell matters to most pollinators and so, too, do tactile sensations. The nature of surface textures has a lot to do with which plants attract which pollinators. Some floral petals are smooth even when viewed under an electron microscope. Others are noticeably hairy, with a soft matte finish. Many are thick and waxy. Others have unique microscopic layers and other features that produce a characteristic visual effect that attracts the targeted pollinators. An extreme example of a plant with reflective petals, their surfaces almost as shiny as those from a high-gloss wax applied to a prized automobile, is the buttercup, the genus *Ranunculus*, with about six hundred species. Its glossy petals are shinier than most others in the plant world, so shiny that if you hold a buttercup under your chin, it will reflect its yellow glow onto your skin—as you may remember from your childhood, when lore had it that if your chin turned yellow, it meant you liked butter. Bees, like children, are drawn to the specular reflections and highly directional sheen of buttercup petals.

Recently, it was discovered that bees, and likely other pollinators, are able to discriminate between flowers, or between adjacent microscopic surface textures within the same flower, solely on the basis of touch. Using the sensitive sensory cells on their legs and mouthparts, bees can differentiate between the subtle surface textures of leaves and flower petals. In one experiment, petals from different blossoms were dried and sputter-coated with gold atoms (to eliminate any possibility of color, odors, or other conflicting stimuli). Honey bees and bumble bees were trained to associate a sugar reward with one surface type, either bumpy or smooth. After a few trials, the bees clearly and easily discriminated between the petal surfaces by using only cues in their microscopic surface textures.

Electricity: Do Bees Get a Charge out of the Flowers They Visit?

Imagine a highly charged bumble bee landing on a flower, then sensing the flower's electrical condition—and possibly being able to draw useful information from it. This isn't science fiction. In spring 2013, researchers at the University of Bristol's School of Biological Sciences published a paper describing their discovery of a previously unknown flower-to-bee signaling modality: electrical signals.

We've known since 1929 that plants have electrostatic fields. Plants and their flowers are both literally and electrically grounded, which means that flower petals and pollen grains have weak, typically negative, electrical charges. We also know that every object flying through the air, whether it is a Boeing 787 Dreamliner jumbo jet, a baseball, or a bumble bee, acquires a strong positive electrostatic charge from friction with the air. A bee might be carrying a charge as high as 450 volts. The waxy surface cuticle of the bee's body helps hold on to the charge, which discharges and dissipates slowly. So what happens when our positively charged bee lands on a negatively charged blossom? What kinds of interactions might occur between these electrical opposites? Can the bee sense patterns and changes in the flower's negative charge, somehow using that information to its advantage? Conversely, could flowers be using their electrical charges to advertise their food supplies to the bees?

Working with Professor Daniel Robert at Bristol, Dominic Clarke and Heather Whitney detected patterns in the electric fields on the sexual parts and petals of certain flowers and speculated that the bees might be able to detect those patterns and use them as guides to the flowers' stores of pollen and nectar—much in the way that bees use ultraviolet-light patterns on flower petals to lead them to food (as you'll read about below).

By placing electrodes on the stems of petunias, the Bristol researchers discovered that when a bee lands on it, the flower's charge changes for several minutes. From my own research on electrostatic charges on flowers and bees, especially buzz-pollinated ones, it seems plausible to me that by leaving this "electric footprint" when they land on a flower and feed, bumble bees and other bees might passively be "labeling their empties"— so that the bee, and its hive mates, would not make the mistake of returning to the same flower too soon. After all, why bother with a flower you just visited, likely one already emptied of its nectar and pollen, when you can quickly move on to virgin territory? I agree with the Bristol researchers that it makes sense that bees might be using the electrical signals naturally present on flowers or left by the bees themselves.

I'm reserving judgment, however, about whether these electrical differences can be actively produced by flowers, perhaps fine-tuned for bees, until other behavioral studies are completed. But nature has unending surprises, so almost anything seems possible.

Flowers blush. It may seem remarkable to say this, but it's true. Many flowers change colors after they are pollinated. This physiological shift happens because of a pH change from basic to acidic within their petals, possibly triggered by pollination or subsequent fertilization. In other flowers, colors often change with age, transitioning from a young, rewarding bloom (rewarding to a pollinator, that is) to an older, senescent one. In lupines, a white spot at the base of the banner petal blushes pink as they age. In the Mexican paloverde, a small legume tree that grows in the Sonoran Desert around my home in Tucson, Arizona, the uppermost petal, the banner petal, turns from yellow to a bright red. In red-hot pokers (*Kniphofia*), the flowers start out a brilliant red then become yellow close to the end of their lives, when they are no longer secreting nectar. Many garden or wildflowers show similar color changes. Unlike demure, young human female blushing beauties, flowers tend to do their blushing toward the later stages of their lives. These floral color changes are their way of shouting out their new status as they move from floral adolescence into maturity, senility, and finally death. The yellow to red shift is the most common signal to pollinators that the flowers are no longer rewarding, but others may use different colors as their signal. Whatever the colors, the flowers might as well be holding up a sign that reads NO FOOD HERE, PLEASE MOVE ALONG.

This is an efficient arrangement for both partners. The color-shifted flowers have already been visited and likely fertilized. Further bee visits would be wasted on them. For bees it means that they can learn quickly whether the next flower is likely to contain nectar or pollen, which allows them to become more efficient foragers, visiting flowers that are rewarding while skipping those that aren't. As you'll read below, most bees don't register the color red, so although the shift to red make these flowers more visible to humans, it may lessen or somehow change their visibility to passing bees.

A Colorful Come-Hither:
Painting with Pigments and Light

Color is one of the main signaling strategies flowers use to beckon their pollinators. Floral colors also serve as filters, selectively attracting specialist pollinators to certain blooms while eliminating others. For many of those pollinators, the brighter the better, which must be why floral colors, especially those created by the petals, are among the most highly saturated colors found in nature. Technically speaking, saturation is the strength of any given color in relationship to its own brightness. The purest, most highly saturated colors are of one or a few close wavelengths and contain almost no white light (the combination of all wavelengths), while unsaturated colors appear faded or washed-out because white light has diluted the colors. Saturated colors can be equated with their perceived intensity.

The colors of a flower are determined by the interaction between light (from either the sun or the moon) and the floral pigments inside its petals. Air spaces and fluid-filled vacuoles within the petals also play a role. The pigments are of at least three types—carotenoids, betalains, and flavonoids (which include the red- and sometimes blue-reflecting pigments, the anthocyanins). When these pigments interact with light, they absorb certain wavelengths and reflect others. Those that they reflect determine the colors that we see. For example a red rose is red because its various colorful anthocyanins selectively absorb blue and green light from the sun, while reemitting the red light that hits its petals. A deep blue larkspur (*Delphinium*) is blue because delphinidin, an anthocyanin within its tissues absorbs red and green wavelengths but reflects blue. While the anthocyanins tend to produce red and blue colors, carotenoids are responsible for the oranges and yellows (as well as some of the reds) we see in various flowers, and also in carrots and tomatoes. Betalain pigments produce some of the most highly saturated and beloved reds of all, as in certain cactus flowers. You also know the betalains from common garden beets, *Portulaca* blossoms, amaranth stems, and the prickly pear cactus.

More Colorful Than a Rainbow: A Hidden World of Invisible Floral Colors

Think of the last rainbow you watched as it winked briefly into view before evanescing into the vapor. Its brilliant colors ranged from red to orange, yellow, green, blue, indigo, and, finally, violet. The reds are at the longer-wavelength side of the color spectrum, with violet at the opposite, short end. However, that part of the rainbow you are able to see occupies only a small middle portion of the wider electromagnetic spectrum, with light continuing beyond red into the infrared at the far end of that spectrum, and ultraviolet at the opposite end. Human beings cannot see colors in the infrared or, as we'll discuss below, in the ultraviolet.

Like us, birds and insects and other animals are capable of sensing only part of the electromagnetic spectrum. That much—the fact of being limited—we have in common. Yes, bees and people both have trichromatic vision, which means we each detect and respond to three main color regions due to three types of sensory cells, but which three color bands is where we differ, and that in turn means that those regions of the visual spectrum we see, and how we process them, differ. The result is that what bees view of their world differs greatly from what we see. For example, bees are not capable of seeing either red or infrared light. Therefore bees (and most other insects, too; except perhaps for the Asian honey bee *Apis dorsata*, a few butterflies, and buprestid beetles) are red-blind; for them, the brilliant red flower colors we have been talking about might as well be black, the absence of colors. But their lack is a signal, too, as we discussed, because it allows them to focus on the more visible—and more rewarding—flowers.

While bees, including the familiar honey bees and bumble bees, don't see the infrared part of the spectrum, they as well as ants, wasps, and other insects do see ultraviolet colors. The sensory regions of their eyes allow them to sense ultraviolet light at wavelengths measuring between three hundred and four hundred nanometers. (For us, these UVA longwave and UVB shortwave wavelengths fall just below our visual detection limit—though they do have an effect on us, since these are the ranges that can give us a sunburn, tan us, or lead to skin cancers.) That wasps, ants, and bees can sense the presence of ultraviolet light was first noticed by the great naturalist Sir John Lubbock in 1877, during his observations on British ants; and that flowers reflect ultraviolet light was proven photographically and discussed in a 1922 article by Americans Frank Lutz and F. Richtmyer.

Humans—except for infants less than three months old, whose crystalline lenses within their eyes have not yet stabilized—are generally unable to see the ultraviolet patterns visible to bees and other flower-visiting insects. However, we can get around this handicap by a bit of scientific sleight of hand, commandeering the technology inside special cameras, sensors, and filters to give us at least a sense of what the bee's eyes can see.

If we took one of these devices, say an ultraviolet-sensitive camcorder, and went on a field trip to a colorful meadow or local garden, how would our favorite flowers look as we aimed the camera at them? Would we even recognize them as the same flowers?

Panning around the garden with our newfound bee vision, we discover that bright yellow flowers are excellent places to look for the ultraviolet floral patterns that we can't ordinarily see. Of these, members of the large and common sunflower family (Asteraceae) give us particularly vivid displays of the UV signposts we're looking for. So let's consider one of them—the familiar black-eyed Susan (*Rudbeckia hirta*), which is abundant throughout the eastern United States.

Without bee vision what we would see are long, narrow yellow petals

A sunflower relative (*Bidens ferulifolia*) in visible light (human view, left)
and ultraviolet light, as seen by insects, on the right

surrounding the dark brown center of the sunflower "face." Bees, however,
see something quite different. Though they do see the dark brown center, they don't see the petals as a homogeneous yellow color. Instead, the
bottom portion of the petals, the part closest to the center, looks "dark"
to a bee because it absorbs UV light while also reflecting yellow. In contrast, the uppermost portion is reflecting yellow plus a little or a lot of UV
and looks bright. What this combination of yellow and UV wavelengths
actually looks like to a bee we don't know, but insect neurobiologists call
the resulting color *bees' purple.* The dividing line between bees' purple and
plain yellow appears about halfway along the length of the petals. Viewed
in its entirety, the sunflower face has two rings of different colors surrounding the dark brown center, making for a dramatic bull's-eye effect,
and turning the flower into a gigantic signaling unit, all the better to catch
the attention of bees, butterflies, flies, and beetles. Many yellow flowers
have ultraviolet-enhanced bull's-eye patterns similar to that found in the
black-eyed Susan or the *Bidens* above.

But other flowers have non-bull's-eye patterns created by ultraviolet light that vary in ways that also speak eloquently to their pollinators.
When we turn our techno-gaze upon the lowly marsh marigold (*Caltha
palustris*), an herbaceous plant of temperate, wet woodlands, we see thin,
wavy, dark UV-absorbing lines radiating outward on the petals. These
UV-absorbing markers, set against their reflective leafy backgrounds, help
direct bees to nectar produced but concealed from direct view in crevices
at the petal bases.

I have studied an Arizona plant, the Mexican yellow-show wildflower (*Amoreuxia palmatifida*), which may be the world's UV champion. Reflecting 90 percent of ultraviolet wavelengths from their large, curved orange petals, these flowers are highly saturated color beacons of amazing intensity, living signposts beckoning to its bees. How could any bee resist dropping in for a closer look? *Amoreuxia* flowers are visited and buzz-pollinated by carpenter bees, bumble bees, and a few other smaller native bees.

A visit to an orchid fancier's greenhouse reveals many other examples of floral patterns created by ultraviolet light. Orchid flowers, especially those of the neotropical *Oncidium*, have broad lower lips that reflect large amounts of UV light, signaling fast-flying *Centris* bee pollinators in their neotropical forests.

Lights, Camera, Fast Action

Imagine a bumble bee flying low over an alpine meadow in riotous bloom somewhere in the Colorado Rockies. Looking down, it sees hues of green and brown vegetation punctuated by highly attractive points of saturated light. Those lights popping in and out of view across its visual field indicate single flowers or clumps of plants in bloom. The bee takes notice. Bees in flight can detect objects much better than we can when we are in rapid motion. In fact, researchers Peter Skorupski and Lars Chittka have recently demonstrated that bumble bees have the fastest color vision of all animals. These bumble bees see the world almost five times faster than we do and can therefore make extremely fast decisions about how to respond even to moving objects while they themselves are in rapid motion, flying at 15–20 mph. They, and likely other bees, can easily navigate through shady bushes to find food, escape predators, or apprehend potential mates midair.

They can do all this even though they see almost no details from far away. Unlike us, bees have to be extremely close to objects to make them out with any clarity, because from even a medium distance they see only a fuzzy image. In fact, bumble bees and honey bees can't recognize that a colorful object is a flower until they are almost upon it, perhaps four inches away. Smaller bees (and other pollinators, too) possess even more limited vision and have to be closer yet to see and differentiate objects, including flowers. So forget those wondrous "mosaic" or kaleidoscopic views of the world that all insects supposedly have. This fantasy idea about insect vision, which has been perpetrated by movies, television, and magazines, is incorrect.

That said, the speed of bees' vision is remarkable because a huge amount of processing is going on every second inside a bee's tiny but powerful brain. The salt-grain-size neuropile (brain) of the familiar western honey bee, *Apis mellifera*, houses 960,000 neurons and a staggering number—10^9—of neural synapses. We, the brainy, naked apes, have 85 billion neurons to our credit, with synapses totaling 10^{15}. Sounds like a lot, but remember that they are housed within a brain that is *1.2 million times larger* than that of our flower-visiting honey bee.

To get an idea how the bee's vision benefits from all that neural power within the bee's brain, imagine a honey bee flying into a movie theater, then pausing to watch a Hollywood blockbuster. Watching a movie is nothing more than fooling the brain into thinking that a series of individual static images (frames, as they're called in the language of cinema) projected rapid-fire onto the screen is in seamless motion—which is similar to what happens when you riffle through the pages of a flip book. Behavioral scientists call this phenomenon flicker fusion, and the frequency at which these flashing images become smooth, fusing into a steady image for the observer, is the flicker-fusion rate, which is a function of how rapidly visual signals are processed by the brain and seen in our mind's eye. For people, the flicker-fusion frequency is considered to be sixteen hertz—an image flashing on and off sixteen times every second. For bees and flies, their flicker-fusion rate is higher, by almost twenty times, an amazing three hundred times per second. A bee watching a fast-moving, action-packed thriller would probably wonder what all the fuss was about and be bored out of its mind by the slowly changing still images flashed on the big screen. (That is, if it could see as far away as the movie screen—which it can't.)

The reason for this digression into the physics and physiology of bee vision is that what bees see has had a powerful impact on why flowers look the way they do. From the distant past to the present, bees and other insects, along with a few birds and bats, have been the primary selective (natural-selection) forces causing wildflowers to have the diverse palette of colors that they do. Flowers signal to insect and other visitors—via food rewards, color, shape, size, texture, scent, etc.—and the animals respond. If everything goes right, bees and other insects carry away the precious pollen grains, acting as go-betweens for the plants they visit. The stronger the floral attraction and the more frequent the visitation, the higher the survival and reproductive rate of that flower, and its descendants.

Today's wildflowers and flowering garden plants have colorful blooms to attract, guide, and hold the attention of bees and other pollinators. But they haven't always looked the same. The world of big, bold, colorful, and lavish flowering plants or cut flowers from the florist's shop that we experience today took a long time to develop, with painstaking breeding trials. So in the next chapter we will go back into geological time, long before the arrival of modern humans, and of many of the insects currently on the planet, to the origin of the earliest flowering plants and their blooms. We will discover when angiosperms first experimented with showy flowers, and how that evolutionary experimentation was encouraged when diverse pollinating creatures began noticing and using them for food, rest stops, and more. We will explore an ancient world of flowers trapped and preserved within golden amber, and others that were compressed into stone, leaving faint carbonized residues of their former glory. This is the story of the first flowers on the planet—known to us today only as the rarest of fossils.

CHAPTER 2

Flowers and Their Ancestors

Sacred-thorn-apple blossom
(*Datura wrightii*) near Tucson

Other than being outdoors, watching bees visiting flowers, my favorite haunts are natural history museums. Whether I'm strolling the dark, musty-smelling behind-the-scenes research and storage areas that most never get to see, or gaping at the dazzlingly well-lit high-tech exhibits in modern exhibition halls, natural history museums are spellbinding palaces to me.

Nose pressed against glass display cases, or body craning forward at the guardrails, I jockey with kids and fellow grown-ups for the best viewing position, not allowing age, size, or adult decorum to interfere. We peer at exquisite slabs of Paleozoic marine animal life, such as the stalked crinoids topped by their featherlike calyxes, looking more like plants than their near relatives the sea stars, and—my favorites—the segmented trilobites, those phenomenally diverse and successful marine arthropods.

We're awestruck by the spectacles of life in the next era, the Mesozoic—exquisitely mounted skeletons of giant sauropods, and toothy carnosaurs standing on hind legs with mouths agape in reconstructed ferocious poses. But wait, something is missing from our image of Mesozoic life-forms. Where are the slabs of fossilized flowers dating from that time, perhaps some magnolias or water lilies? Did I overlook them in the neighboring botanical exhibition hall?

No, I didn't miss the fossilized flowers—because they *weren't* there. Although a few major US and European natural history museums have fossilized flowers, they rarely put them on public display. The *Tyrannosaurus rex* dinosaur fossils, or the mammals taken from Rancho La Brea— the dire wolves, the giant ground sloths, the saber-toothed cats—steal the show from them every time. On the "wow factor" scale, fossilized flowers don't rate. Even the blackened fern fronds, horsetails, and the bark impressions of giant club mosses attract more interest from difficult-to-please museumgoers. So at the museums that do house them, fossil flowers are stored locked away inside cabinets in back rooms that only the occasional researcher might venture into.

Before There Were Flowers

Before we get to the earliest flowers, and the fossil evidence establishing their existence, we should look briefly at what came before the flowering plants. We now think that the first flowers appeared perhaps 130–160 million years ago. For hundreds of millions of years before that there were many forms of vegetation—but without flowers. About 472 million years ago (in the mid-Ordovician period of the Paleozoic era) the earth began greening up. The monotonous browns, blacks, and whites of terrestrial rocks and soils gradually gave way to the colors of plant life. Living in and near water, the earliest plants, including the one-celled algae known as diatoms and then multicellular, branched, filamentous algae, established their beachheads. Eventually a living, green biofabric, the plants developed, blanketing vast expanses of the earth's surface. Mat-like at first, those earliest colonizers of the land—algae, liverworts, and mosses—began growing taller in their competition for light and space, and evolved into plants similar to the ferns and horsetails we know today.

By the Devonian period, beginning about 419 million years ago (mya), vast forests of plants released airborne spores to reproduce. They depended upon the wind or, rarely, water currents to move their gametes.

Spreading across equatorial continents (Eurasia, North and South America, Africa, Antarctica, India, and Australia) that made up the supercontinent Pangaea, these new plants took over the land so completely that they "terraformed" the planet. Their predominance brought the vast climatic changes and oxygen enrichment of the atmosphere necessary to sustain future animal life.

Animal life, during the Devonian period, also known as the Age of Fishes, consisted largely of the ray and lobe-finned fish that swam the oceans and lakes, and vast numbers of insects that flew through the air. Our distant ancestors, the first four-legged vertebrates, were just beginning to crawl ashore.

To conjure up a vision of this tangled, forested world, perhaps you can call to mind colorful dioramas in natural history museums that depict prehistoric scenes. The diorama created by French artist Édouard Riou portrays a scene from the Carboniferous period (359 to 299 mya), which I saw on a visit to the Chicago Field Museum when I was a teenager. It was so vivid an evocation of the plant and insect life in that ancient time that it made me feel I'd been transported back in time. It further inspired me to become a field biologist. Exotic as the scene was, some of the early plants depicted in similar paintings—brilliant green carpets of squishy mosses, horsetails and ferns of many types, flattened liverworts and hornworts growing on rocks, fallen logs, and earthen banks—would be familiar to anyone with a naturalist mind-set on a leisurely hike through a hardwood forest somewhere in Wisconsin or Arkansas.

Nonetheless, a walk through a forest today would not prepare you for what it might be like to pay a time-traveling visit to one of those ancient forests. The club mosses and horsetails of today are small, only a few inches to several feet tall. But in the Carboniferous and Devonian periods many were enormous, and you would have walked around and under the towering giants, some with trunks and crowns towering a hundred feet overhead.

You would probably also have noticed the abundant pollen- and spore-feeding insects. Scavenging insects and other arthropods found a readily available food supply in the spores of ferns, seed ferns, and their allies. Later, they would have fed on the pollen grains and exudates from the gymnosperms, which you'll read about in the next section. This was happening as long ago as the Permian period, 298 to 252 mya, and we have the smoking gun to prove it—pollen grains preserved inside the guts of fossilized early insects such as xyelid sawflies, a type of primitive plant-feeding wasp, rock crawlers, web spinners, and others. Palynologists (scientists who study fossilized and modern pollen grains) can often look at the pollen those early insects ate and identify which plants the pollen came from.

Gymnosperms: The Naked-Seed-Bearing Plants

Before we meet the earliest true flowers, another vitally important group of plants must be mentioned, which also appeared on the earth sometime during the early Devonian period. Those ancient plants, including many still with us, are the gymnosperms, literally the plants with "naked seeds," which is the hallmark of their evolutionary history—the characteristic that distinguishes them from their spore-bearing predecessors, and their flowering descendants. The seeds are naked in the sense that, unlike the seeds of most flowering plants, they are not embedded inside fleshy fruits.

You will certainly recognize at least one kind of still-extant gymnosperm—the evergreen conifers. Pines, spruces, firs, larches, and tamaracks are all conifers, and we find these trees not just in our forests, where they cover many millions of acres across the temperate regions of Canada, the United States, and Eurasia, but also in our backyards.

Conifers, like other gymnosperms, reproduce not via air- and waterborne spores, but by seeds. Each tree produces cones of both sexes—small, male, pollen-bearing cones that are so unobtrusive that most people don't even notice them (unless they have a pine-pollen allergy), and the large, female pinecones that we all know. The reproductive act begins when the male cones shed their pollen into the wind. Most of the vast number of pollen grains wafted through the air die before reaching their mark. A lucky few, however, will be captured by a sticky pollination droplet on the surface of a large female cone, then pulled inside for sex. Conifer sex happens slowly; fertilization and development often taking several years. When this is finally complete, the female cone falls from the tree, its prickly scales opening wide to release the naked seeds—the pine nuts—to the ground, where some will germinate and take root.

Planted along streets and in gardens across America is another of the gymnosperms, the exotic-looking ginkgo (*Ginkgo biloba*), which was introduced two hundred years ago from its native Chinese homelands. With its elegant, fan-shaped leaves, which turn a brilliant yellow in the fall, the ginkgo has been admired and reproduced in Asian art and jewelry for centuries. Its history on the planet is traceable not in centuries, but in hundreds of millions of years, with evidence for its existence going back 270 mya, based on fossils found in two small regions in Zhejiang Province in eastern China. Unlike the conifers, which have male and female cones on the same tree, the sexes are separated on the ginkgoes. Male trees release their pollen into the wind, and fertilization occurs using the same pollination droplet mechanism by which conifers reproduce. It's easy to tell the male from the female trees because after fertilization the females drop their nuts, which are so rancid smelling their odor has been compared to that of vomit. Although in this country people ardently select against the female ginkgo trees, in China the females are valued for their "stinky nuts," which are popular both as a traditional food and for their purported medicinal uses.

Another extant order of gymnosperms is the cycads (Cycadales), many of which bear a resemblance to the palm tree, though they are unrelated. *Zamia*, the common Florida plant known as the Florida coontie, is the only genus of cycad native in the United States. Cycads are typically wind pollinated, but others are also pollinated by beetles, including weevils and leaf beetles, that are attracted to the edible pollen grains—another possible link to the flowering plants.

In my travels, one special place makes me believe I've been transported back to the late Jurassic period. A three-hour drive down the escarpment starting from Canberra in the Australian Capital Territory, on the way to the popular Pebbly Beach with its mobs of food-mooching eastern gray kangaroos, there is a towering forest of spotted gums (*Corymbia maculata*). This tree, from the eucalyptus family, is a comparatively late arrival and would not have made an appearance in any Jurassic scene. But the bizarre understory of the forest gives me the chills. In all directions, are millions of dark green cycads—more than you'll ever see in any other single place. The scene is so eerily reminiscent of another era that I almost expect to see an ankylosaur raise its head, contentedly chewing away, with cycad fronds dangling from its mouth.

Being in this place near the Australian coast makes me dream of the time before flowering plants achieved dominance over the land, when the gymnosperms were still in ascendance, and they and their ancient insect partners were taking the first trial steps along adaptive paths that would lead them to where they are today. We don't know a great deal about those early insects, but recent discoveries are beginning to give us a tentative idea of how they lived.

Earth's First Pollinators

In 2012 scientists published information about amber from Lower Cretaceous sediments (110–105 mya) in the Basque region of northern Spain that contained some interesting surprises—tiny female insects laden with hundreds of pollen grains they must have acquired while feeding. The insects are thrips, which today's gardeners are familiar with as straw-colored, millimeter-long garden pests found in roses and other blooms. But long before they began to consort with angiosperms, thrips were likely pollinating the gymnosperm ancestors of flowering plants, as the thrips from Spain reveal. Analysis of the pollen grains covering their bodies suggests that the pollen was likely derived from either a cycad or a ginkgo tree. This is possibly the first *direct* evidence of insect pollination from the distant past.

But as we now believe, based on speculative but persuasive recent findings, insect pollination may go back further still. In 2009, Dr. Dong Ren of the Capital Normal University in Beijing, China, published an intriguing report about fossilized scorpion flies that were found in sediments dating from 167 mya. No one had suspected that insects from this ancient lineage had anything to do with pollination because the scorpion flies we know today (aka hanging flies) are either carnivorous or scavenge upon dead insects. However, on the basis of their appearance, Ren and his American colleagues speculate that the scorpion flies were indeed pollinators in ancient times. Their looks are certainly suggestive. Most notable are their long beaks, some of which were half as long as their bodies. What were they doing with such long mouthparts? The scientists who found them suggest that the scorpion fly used its siphonlike proboscis to probe and feed upon the nectarlike juices of seed ferns, conifers, and ginkgolike and other ancient plants. Regrettably, a close examination of the fossil slabs reveals no telltale pollen grains on the flattened scorpion-fly bodies. We have no definitive forensic clues as to their last meals. But their unusual feeding tool kit certainly supports the idea that they were pollinators. So, if this hunch is correct, and the dating of the sediments in which they were found is accurate, the discovery pushes animal pollination further back, almost 50 million years earlier than previously thought, into the late Jurassic, instead of the early Cretaceous period.

Recently my belief that various types of flies and beetles were the only pollinators to visit the early gymnosperms was forever altered. Butterfly lacewings have been preserved in 165-million-year-old fossils from Liaoning Province, China. I was lucky to be one of the first to see the actual fossils at the Smithsonian Institution. They are the size of the palm of your hand, with siphonlike mouthparts and vivid eyespots on their brown-and-black wings. They are relatives of the aphid-eating green lacewings familiar to gardeners.

What a thrill it would be to see them flying and foraging, I thought as I looked at these amazing fossils. Smithsonian Institution paleontologist Conrad Labandeira believes that the butterfly lacewings were pollinators of extinct gymnosperms. Candidates for their attentions may have included the male parts of *Welltrichia* (an extinct gymnosperm with flowerlike organs), and the female organs of *Williamsonia* (extinct gymnosperms resembling cycads).

Darwin's "Abominable Mystery"

In July 1879, just three years before his death at age seventy-three, Charles Darwin wrote a now-famous letter to Sir Joseph Hooker, then director of the Royal Botanical Gardens, Kew, in London, in which he referred to the origin and spread of the angiosperms as an "abominable mystery." It was long believed that what was troubling Darwin when he wrote his letter was the lack of fossil evidence for the angiosperms during the early Cretaceous period (100–135 mya). During Darwin's lifetime, few fossils of flowering plants had been discovered from that era.

Recently, however, a detailed historical analysis by Harvard botanist William E. Friedman has completely reframed our understanding of what was troubling Darwin. It wasn't the scarcity of Cretaceous fossil evidence that concerned him; had there been many more such fossils, he would still have been confounded because, according to Friedman, what "deeply bothered" Darwin was the highly accelerated pace of evolution that culminated in the appearance of the first flowering plants. Darwin was a devout believer in the notion that *natura non facit saltum*—nature does not make a leap. But the seemingly abrupt appearance of flowering plants in the early Cretaceous period, followed by the highly accelerated diversification of flowering plants in the mid-Cretaceous, seemed to him to be far too rapid. This led him to years of speculation that there might have been a missing island or continent where the pre-Cretaceous evolution of flowering plants had occurred—a sunken Atlantis, as it were.

Later, Darwin came to believe that, if the rapid diversification of flowering plants in the mid-Cretaceous era was in fact a real phenomenon, it might be explained by coevolutionary interactions between pollinating insects and angiosperms that were so successful they hastened the pace of evolution beyond what was typical for plants and animals. Trying to account for this seeming exception to his belief in long, slow, gradual evolution was extremely important to Darwin, for he felt that if any species "had started into life at once, the fact would be fatal to the theory of descent with slow modification through natural selection"—and would provide support for a creationist's view of life.

Although Darwin's "abominable mystery" was not about the whereabouts of Cretaceous-period fossil evidence for flowering plants, the scarcity of such fossils during his lifetime probably exacerbated the mystery of what we might think of as the missing links. If we look at the "fossilization lottery," we can see that flowers, with their soft expanses of petals, are bound to lose out to plants with tougher parts more likely to be fossilized. Woody stems and tree trunks, leathery leaves, pinecones, and the hard seeds of many fruits are usually what's preserved in the fossil record.

Although flowers on a stem rarely fossilize, certain conditions did make that happen—flash floods or mud or ash flows that swept up everything in their path, burying the plants and preserving them for eons in sediments where we can still trace their carbonized outlines. Amber (fossilized resins) is an even better preservative. Some of the most complete examples of fossil flowers and early flower pollinators are found in amber. The golden gem of the ages, amber was formed from sticky plant resins that hardened over time and contains an amazing record of the insects and plants of hundreds of millions of years ago.

Fortunately, thanks to discoveries that have been made since Darwin's time, today's paleobotanists (students of ancient botany—not geriatric botanists) have a more complete fossil record of life on earth. Looking at the many flowering plant fossils that date back to different eras and have been found all over the globe, we can examine and trace the nuances of their evolutionary history—while acknowledging that we don't yet know everything about them.

Trapped in Clay, Entombed in Amber

Some of the most amazing fossil flower discoveries have been made on American shores. In the 1990s thousands of tiny, exquisitely preserved flowers were discovered in clay pits in New Jersey—pits that had been mined to make bricks since the early nineteenth century. The flowers found in these Cretaceous-period clay and amber deposits are about 90 million years old. Known as charcoalized fossils, they are made entirely of carbon, and their preservation is astonishingly good, revealing every detail of the flowers' anatomy, down to the cellular level, and much about their pollination requirements as well.

How the blossoms were preserved in such detail isn't entirely clear. One possibility is that they fell into the dead leaves on the forest floor and were caught up in a flash fire that roared across the ancient landscape, quickly charring the leaf litter and turning the blossoms into some of the most perfectly complete yet discovered. Flowers preserved in sediment are typically mere carbon ghosts of themselves. Even when such a rock slab is brightly lit by a fiber-optic lamp and viewed under a stereo microscope, you are likely to see an incomplete, perhaps one-half, flower, folded in on itself so that its petals and shape are hard to make out. A painterly reconstruction of the original flower for a museum diorama or a line drawing for a scientific publication is quite a challenge, requiring use of your imagination to bring this flattened object to life.

No such act of the imagination is required to visualize the fossil flowers from the New Jersey clay pits as living organisms. Looking at these diminutive flowers, which average only one-tenth of an inch in diameter, we can see anthers, stamens, petals, stigma, style, and basal ovary (the latter three forming the carpels), nectaries, and what may be scent-producing glands, and enough details that we can also identify the family groups to which the flowers belonged. Descendants of these flowers that have survived to the present age include members of the blueberry or heath families, the magnolia family, and the laurel and witch-hazel families.

Nectar-producing glands present on the fossils of these miniature flowers tell us that they were attracting pollinators with their sugary-sweet secretions, just as flowers do today. We can also see, on some of the fossils from the ancestors of the blueberry family, detailed evidence of exactly how pollination occurred. Tetrads of pollen grains—each tetrad consisting of four pollen grains permanently joined to each other—were clumped into larger groups that were united by sticky filaments called viscin threads. Thus when a pollinator visited one of these plants and brushed against this gooey clump, the clump would stick to it, and the pollinator would end up transporting not just one grain but a tangled glob of grains to the next flower. This was, and is, an effective means of pollen transport, which made it more likely that at least a few of the grains would find their mark. Today, azaleas and rhododendrons have pollen grains held in bondage similar to those in the blueberry ancestors.

Amber oozes from the trunks of resin-producing trees, hardens, and becomes fossilized under the heat and pressure of layers of clay sediments. It holds an important part of our fossil record. Thousands of species of plants and animals that would otherwise have remained unknown to us are exquisitely preserved in amber and are easier to see than those preserved in clay—though flowers locked even in amber may have their details obscured by opaque areas within the golden nugget, or by bubbles, soil, or other debris.

Deposits of amber are found all over the globe, with particularly rich deposits in the Baltic area and the Dominican Republic, where enterprising merchants and artisans fashion it into jewelry—all the more unique (and much more rare and expensive) if it has a plant or animal fossil, an inclusion, entombed within. The most common of the flowers to be found in the Dominican and Mexican ambers are those of the resin-producing trees themselves—*Hymenaea courbaril*. Imagine the delicate blossoms dropping from the branches, tumbling and bouncing against the lower tree trunk, finally getting stuck in freshly oozing patches of *Hymenaea* resin, then being trapped as more gooey resin flows over them. Come back in 15 to 20 million years, excavate the sediments, and voilà!—exquisitely preserved flowers, with every detail clearly visible. Fragile petals, fat anthers atop slender filaments, they're all there.

Much-older amber, dating to the early Cretaceous, is found in Burma, now Myanmar. Burmese amber has been traded for nearly two millennia, originally with the Chinese, and then, beginning in the nineteenth century, with Europeans. One of the most venerable of the Burmese mines, known since at least the first century AD, is located in the Hukawng Valley and dates to 105–100 mya. Some of the amber from this area contains early insect pollinators and exquisite fossil flowers, including one perfectly preserved specimen of a small flower. Perhaps the most extraordinary discovery from this amber mine, made in 2006, is of a beelike hymenopteran—*Melittosphex burmensis*—that dates back to the middle Cretaceous, about 100 mya. There have been other discoveries of stingless bees in amber—including *Proplebeia dominicana* specimens from mines in the Dominican Republic, which have been dated to roughly 20 mya, and several from the Baltic amber 45 million years old. *Cretotrigona prisca*, from New Jersey amber, has a minimum age around 65–70 mya—but the one from the Burmese mine is by far the oldest fossil superficially similar to a bee. It had branched hairs that are associated with pollen capture by modern bees, but there is no proof in the fossils that this protobee gathered pollen.

Although it would be extraordinary to find a fossilized bee or other insect pollinator inside a fossil flower, caught—literally—in the act, we have something close. Fossilized bees and other pollinators have been found with flower pollen clinging to their bodies or inside their guts. With a bit of forensic sleuthing, we can establish what flowers they were visiting just before their untimely demise, which can give us invaluable information about the flowers themselves. For example, the stingless bee *Proplebeia dominicana* in amber has played a significant role in our understanding of the origins of the orchid family, which had long been shrouded in mystery because there are no fossils of orchids. The mystery began to be unlocked in 2007, when orchid massulae were found clinging to the body of a stingless bee caught in 15–20-million-year-old Dominican amber. Here was a true example of pollen transport frozen in time, a glimpse into the history of orchid flowers and their bees. Using this evidence and extrapolating from what they assumed to be a relatively constant rate of orchid evolution, the Harvard researchers who discovered the pollen-bearing bee used a molecular clock-dating approach to arrive at a speculative late-Cretaceous date for the first appearance of orchids. If that's true, then the earliest orchids coexisted with long-extinct dinosaurs.

The First Flowers

For decades botany textbooks used flowers such as *Magnolia grandiflora*, with its gloriously large (as befits a plant named grandiflora), fragrant, white blossoms as the archetypes of primitive flowering plants. Botanists, paleontologists, and others with a serious interest in such matters long believed that the first flowers, at the start of the Cretaceous, were big, even by comparison with today's flowers. But we were all wrong. What we now know from fossil evidence is that virtually all the oldest flowers (including the earliest magnolias, when they eventually came along in the mid-Cretaceous) were puny runts.

Over the years many contenders have appeared for first true flower in the fossil record. Some of these were eventually reclassified as nonflowers, while others were dated more accurately to a later geological time. Right now, the best and most unambiguous contender for the title of first true flower is *Archaefructus sinensis*, described in 1998 by Ge Sun at Jilin University and David Dilcher of the University of Florida. *Archaefructus* was found in Yixian lake-bed deposits in Liaoning Province of northeast China. Dating from the lower Cretaceous age, its scientific name means "ancient fruit from China."

In an evolutionary rather than a poetic sense, perhaps we should consider *Archaefructus* as the mother, the Eve, of all living flowering plants. Because the fossil slabs that contain these flowers also contain small fossil fish, we speculate that the plants may have been aquatic or semiaquatic, growing in shallow lakes, extending their leaves, thin stems, and flowers above the water's surface. The small size of the *Archaefructus*—it was only about eight inches tall—and its ability to flourish in both kinds of habitat may have given it an advantage over long-lived but slow-growing and less adaptive woody trees, allowing it to spread rapidly, colonizing new areas far from where it originated.

The *Archaefructus* had deeply lobed, finely branched leaves similar to those of modern buttercup or carrot, but flowers without petals or sepals to advertise their presence to passing lakeside insects—not exactly good candidates for winning any ribbons in a local flower show. We don't yet know whether *Archaefructus* bore its small, unisexual flowers on long stems, or if the stem was itself part of the flower stalk. The fossils reveal that the plants had unfertilized ovules within the ovaries—which, following pollination and fertilization, would have become fertile seeds housed within a fruit similar to the woody pea pods found in today's legumes. This characteristic—seeds enclosed within an ovary that becomes a dry or fleshy fruit—is one of the defining characteristics of the angiosperm. In fact *angiosperm* in Greek means "vessel" and "seed." The entire female anatomy of the flower—stigma, style, and ovary—constitutes the carpel. Along with the double-fertilization maneuver described in the first chapter, the seed-bearing ovary is what makes an angiosperm an angiosperm.

Archaefructus seems to belong to a long-extinct plant family unlike anything currently known. The closest (albeit not very close) living relative to *Archaefructus* is a water lily. While it may not have been earth's first true flower, *Archaefructus* is the oldest flowering plant we know about.

Is Bigger Better?—and Other Evolutionary Questions

Flowers kept developing for the 130 or more million years of their existence on earth. Every few million years they varied in size, shape, color, scents, edible rewards, and reproductive morphology as the different species came and went. Their interactions with the ancestors of modern flower-visiting insects, many of them now extinct, also shifted—which resulted in further refinements in the flowers, and in changes to the insects themselves.

One major trend we see when we examine the fossil record is that flowers gradually increased in size. The modest-size *Archaefructus* and those carbonized pip-squeaks from the New Jersey clay pits were typical of flowers during the Cretaceous period, when they ranged from 0.04 to 0.23 inches in diameter, and their pollinators were similarly diminutive. Flowers didn't just get larger, they became brighter, showier, and more fragrant. Bigger, more colorful petals helped make flowers more visible against the green background of leaves, better able to attract and hold the attention of pollinators. The scent-producing glands on their petals perfumed the air, to entice hungry insects to the blossoms. Bigger blossoms also contained more stuff—greater numbers of anthers and therefore greater quantities of pollen, as well as nectary tissues producing more of the nectar needed by flower-visiting insects.

All these coevolved features made flowers more attractive to their animal go-betweens, which helped flowers compete more effectively. Plants that are more frequently pollinated leave behind more seeds, reproducing more prolifically and spreading their genes more widely—which every plant and animal lineage does if it survives into future generations. Flowers just did it extraordinarily well.

Mutations among the early flowers resulted in ovules that were more enclosed and protected, giving the developing seeds a better chance at living long enough to fall to the ground and grow into new plants. In many early angiosperms, we see their evolutionary experimentation with reproductive organs, too. Some were unisexual plants with both male and female parts, while on other plants the male and female parts appeared on separate blossoms. Flowering plants also tried various genetically based breeding systems and population sex ratios during their long histories. Flowers weren't prudish about their sexual contrivances.

In the earliest days of flower life on earth, small beetles and flies predominated as pollinators, and the small flowers they pollinated were relatively open, accessible to all. Bees arrived on the scene a bit later (witness those stingless bees in amber), and they, too, were small. Later, diverse and highly specialized morphologies began to evolve in flowers. They became bigger and more complex, with some of them hiding their nectar and pollen deep inside tubular-shaped blossoms so that they were no longer handed out freely. In response, flies and bees as well as moths and butterflies began evolving longer proboscides, and they used different foraging techniques to reach the hidden nectar and pollen, coming back again and again to the flowers to search for the precious substances, thus maximizing the flowers' pollination strategy. From the fossil record we see that the pistils didn't just get longer and more tubular, but also larger, which allowed pollen pickup and delivery by bigger insects, and eventually by bats and, later still, hummingbirds. Flowers and their visitors were already engaged in a mutualistic dance—a dance that goes on to this very day.

Early Visitors to Flowers:
Beetles, Flies, Bees—and More

Beetles and flies, early pollinators of flowering plants, belong to extremely ancient lineages and were around long before there were true flowers. If we use the number of currently known species as our criterion for success and we exclude bacteria, beetles are by a wide margin the most successful living animals on the earth. Taxonomists have identified roughly four hundred thousand species of beetles worldwide. In what may have been an apocryphal exchange, responding to clerics who asked if anything could be learned about the Creator from studying the natural world, the late British geneticist J. B. S. Haldane was reputed to have said, "The Creator, if he exists, has a special preference for beetles." The evidence would suggest that the Creator also liked flies, which played a key role in the pollination of early flowering plants and are very much with us today.

So how did primitive flowers entice their pollinators? A few examples will show nature's ingenuity, which will be further explored in the next chapter.

Early angiosperms such as the water lily and the magnolia deployed multiple strategies for attracting flies and beetles. Not only did they have floral structures that mimicked those of the gymnosperms the insects had long been familiar with, but they had some special signals of their own. Using internal starch reserves as energy to heat up their flowers, they emitted pollinator-enticing scent compounds that made these flowers more alluring from farther away. Another possible advantage of the heat may have been to fool a female fly into thinking that she'd landed on a still-warm mammalian carcass on which to lay her eggs.

Although modern versions of the water lily and magnolia no longer deploy this heat-producing strategy to lure their pollinators, it still works for the common houseplant *Philodendron*, or "elephant ears." In its homeland in the New World rain forests, scarabs and other beetles pile into the *Philodendron*'s flowers to feed and mate during the heating phase. Once mature, these mild-mannered plants burst forth with a dramatic phallic-looking, white spadix wrapped inside a green sheath. Over several days, the cream-colored spadices become noticeably hot to the touch, up to 57 degrees Fahrenheit above ambient temperatures. If you have a *Philo-*

dendron in your collection of houseplants, you can see—and touch—this floral example in your home.

Another form of beetle pollination that has come down to us from ancient times is called *mess and soil*—a term that, for me, conjures up riotous images of wanton feeding, copulating, and defecating; orgies taking place inside each flower, which is exactly what is happening. The western spicebush, *Calycanthus occidentalis*, still makes use of this reproductive strategy. Even from a distance the spicebush is enticing, as I remember as a graduate student at UC Davis, roaming the Napa Valley foothills and their shiny green, serpentine rock outcrops where it flourishes. Its dark green foliage is set off by crimson flowers that emit a potent fragrance something like the aromas of the wines I often tasted at the Beringer, Nichelini, and Franciscan wineries.

Peering into a spicebush blossom often reveals a dozen or more slender, black-pointed-tail rove beetles, or black-and-brown, short-winged sap beetles. At the tips of the innermost spicebush petals are small, whitish food bodies, decoys that lure beetles to their feeding frenzies while keeping them at a discreet distance from the plants' tender private parts. Sure, the munching beetles inflict some damage, but in frolicking about, they become dusted with pollen grains that get a free ride to the next beetle orgy a flower or two away—preferably on a neighboring spicebush. The same thing was happening in the Mesozoic, as we can see from chewing marks in fossils of the ancient gymnosperms and earliest flowering plants.

First Bee Visitors to Flowers

Bees have been on the planet for a long time. Exactly how long we still don't know. The Burmese amber protobee fossil from about 100 mya is the oldest evidence we have of early bees or their ancestors. But today we view stingless bees as the culmination of eons of social evolution, and we feel sure that the oldest amber bees must have been preceded by ground-nesting bees that were solitary—the problem being that we have no fossil proof of their existence. All we know is that certain bees, similar to the modern stingless bees we know today, became highly social and also lost their stingers while adopting other defensive strategies—such as biting and chemical warfare—instead.

Stingless bees, like their ancient ancestors, live in tropical forests. Walk along any forested path in southern Mexico, Costa Rica, Panama, or Brazil and you find housefly-size black or orangish stingless bees such as *Trigona, Tetragonisca,* or the larger, striped *Melipona.* They seek out plant resins, saps, and gums—they hoard them, and you can find them scraping away at oozes and rot areas on tree trunks, and visiting resin-producing flowers such as *Clusia.* Combs, presses, and rakes on the legs of the females collect pollen from the flowers during their visits, and afterward, when the females groom themselves, they wet the pollen with saliva or regurgitated nectar, which forms a moist pellet of pollen that adheres firmly to the concave surface of their hind legs for the journey home. They do the same thing with resins, so that irregular blobs of the substance stick to their hind legs on their way back to the logs in which they live. Pollen is food for the adult bees and their young, and the resins are used to caulk up any fissures in their homes, to disinfect their nests against pathogenic bacteria and fungi, and to defend against ants and other enemies.

Remarkably, the bees have somehow developed ways to prevent themselves from getting stuck in the resin—perhaps with a resin solvent?— but once in a while they become hopelessly fouled in the sticky goo, and some of them end up fossilized in the amber treasured by collectors and scientists alike.

Small bees, beetles, and flies were not the only pollen eaters in ancient times. The 50-million-year-old mid-Eocene oil shales of Messel, south of Frankfurt, Germany, contain exceptionally well preserved fossils of larger animals such as bats, which have huge amounts of pollen in their stomachs. Just like certain living bats, the Messel bats must have visited flowers to feed on their pollen and nectar, moving pollen from flower to flower, pollinating them.

Today: Flowers Everywhere

No matter where we go—wandering through alpine meadows, strolling along the paths in a botanical garden, or picking our way through our own home gardens—we come across displays of brilliant flowers. Yet never do we pause to wonder why the monotonous greens and browns over the long expanse of time before flowers arrived on earth gave way so suddenly—abruptly enough on the evolutionary scale to cause Darwin great concern—to an earthscape where flowers became nearly ubiquitous.

The answer to "Why flowers?" is that their evolutionary strategies were highly adaptive. From their simple and miniaturized beginnings the angiosperms developed an extraordinarily diverse set of biological innovations and "learned" to rely on a seemingly infinite variety of means of reproduction. Flowering plants come in just about every life-form imaginable, from tiny floating duckweed to the tallest rain-forest emergent trees, from columnar cacti to prostrate shrubs, and they can flourish in most climates. Some tree species live for thousands of years, capable of enduring withering droughts and freezing winters. Flowering plants also excel at chemical warfare. They ooze, drip, and volatilize chemicals that inhibit the germination of unrelated plants below them.

One of the most valuable contributions to this 130-million-year-old success story is double fertilization, which ensures that each flowering plant seed comes with its very own "survival space suit," or onboard starchy or oily food reserves. These stored nutrients get the young seedling up out of the soil, where it can start making its own food from sunlight, carbon dioxide, and water.

Also critical to the success and spread of the flowering plants is the diversity of their reproductive strategies. Some use wind or water to move their pollen around, while the vast majority enlist myriad hungry insects, some birds, a few bats, other mammals, and a lizard or two as their pollinators.

The versatility of the flowering plants, their double fertilization, and mutually rewarding, coevolutionary dance with pollinators are all factors in having made them one of the most successful forms of life on the planet—organisms that have the ability to colonize almost every terrestrial environment, from arid deserts to shallow marine waters along the coasts of the North Pacific, from lowland rain forests to mountaintops where they can be found above the tree line. Flowering plants are survivors.

In the next chapter we will return to the flower-visiting animals, this time to take a look at the living descendants of those we've glimpsed here in the fossil record. We will explore the animal visitors to flowers, focusing on intriguing and often bizarre examples of the sexual relationships between them, and providing case histories of colorful blooms and their guests. We'll tour the diversity of volant insects that feed on and pollinate flowers, from tiny thrips to beetles, flies, wasps, ants, bees, butterflies, and moths. We'll examine generalist blooms that welcome all comers, and superspecialized mutualisms such as those between yuccas and their moths, figs and their fig wasps, and bucket orchids that force their pollinators, the metallic green-and-blue orchid bees, to swim out of the pools that collect inside the bucket-shaped petals of its flower. We'll watch the workings of various trap flowers, such as Dutchman's-pipe, which lure flies down the throat of its curving tubes, where they are held in captivity for a day before being released, dusted with pollen, to repeat the experience at the next flower. There are wonders such as the solitary oil-baron bees and bees that turn themselves into living tuning forks to harvest pollen. Among the animals with backbones, we follow the foraging lives of specialist hummingbirds, sunbirds, honeycreepers, and nectar-feeding Arizona bats, charismatic honey possums and elephant shrews in South Africa, along with a remarkable lizard, a pollinating, nearly fluorescent green-and-red day gecko on the remote island of Mauritius in the Indian Ocean. All these animal visitors play vital roles in the life cycles and remarkable stories of flowers.

CHAPTER 3

The Pollinators

A honey bee visits a lyreleaf jewelflower
(*Streptanthus carinatus*)

Two years ago I witnessed an extraordinary example of a natural embrace between a flower and its specialist pollinator. On the steep slopes of a rain forest of abundant but often hidden flowers, I stood overlooking the Caribbean terminus of the Panama Canal in the Republic of Panama. Bees, wasps, butterflies, and flies flew past me in the forest understory. A pair of blue-crowned motmots called, adding to the din of other birds and wailing cicadas. In the distance, a troop of black howler monkeys bellowed. The local gardens and forest edges overflowed with brilliant orange and red *Heliconia* blossoms, and flamboyant hummingbirds streaked past my head between their sips of nectar.

My longtime friend and fellow melittologist Dr. David Roubik and I were here as orchid and bee experts to help make the Disneynature feature film *Wings of Life*. Dave had allowed the producer and film crew to temporarily invade his private rain-forest enclave. Although I'd worked with dozens of independent-film producers, this was my first big Hollywood-style production, complete with line producer, dolly and jib operators, focus-puller, grips, and various assistants. For our shoots, as many as twenty people were on location.

For one scene, we needed a few bucket orchids. They grew in the nearby forest, but it would have been impossible to find in time, so we ordered several plants from a Panama City orchid man. Luckily, he had rare bucket orchids that had large flower buds the day before our shoot. Orchid flowers come in a phantasmagorical array of shapes, colors, and sizes. They epitomize the notion behind my favorite Aussie expression that "flowers like to tart themselves up." The delicate *Coryanthes* (*C. panamensis*) orchids had survived a jolting five-hour drive west from Panama City. Dave and I removed the plants from the Land Rover and lashed their rounded pseudobulbs—with delicate, palmlike leaves—to the base of a buttressed tree. We watered them, then waited overnight like expectant fathers. Would the three precious buds on their slender stalks open into normal flowers? Would male orchid bees from the adjacent forest follow their scent and find the blooms?

At 7:00 a.m. the next morning, Louie Schwartzberg, our Hollywood director, peered over my shoulder smiling. Another expectant father. "Where are the bees?" he asked. "We need to stay on schedule and begin filming." I mumbled that the flowers were only partially open and not yet releasing any scent. Louis walked away only to return a few minutes later. My heart sank. Were the plants damaged from their long ride? By 9:00 a.m., the wait was over. Before our eyes two gorgeous, fist-size yellow blossoms slowly opened, then filled their bucket basins with slimy drip-tip secretions. Dave Roubik stood beside me with a knowing smile. The flowers were now fully open and they smelled great, spicy but subdued cinnamon with a ripe orange burst tucked inside. Now, we waited.

As if on cue, from the forest edge came a half dozen brilliant green, metallic blue and red orchid bees, male *Euglossa*. They hovered in midair downwind from our orchids. One after one, they alighted, then scraped at the petals, gathering the orchids' scent chemicals. Then, doing a methodical, quick shuffle hovering in the air, they transferred the fragrances into the slits on their swollen hind legs. The compounds would attract females later in their lives. One bee slipped on the flower's rim and fell into the pooled liquid inside the orchid's bucket. This "accident" had been the orchids' pollination strategy all along. The bee struggled and moved its legs and tried to crawl through the slippery trough. After several minutes it reached a tiny floral step, a platform serving only for a bee on its way through a narrow passageway to freedom. While holding the bee in a grip at the portal, the orchid glued two pollen packets (pollinia) precisely onto the bee's back. The little bee peered out, flailing with its front legs. We could not know in advance how long the bee would be held in place by the orchid turnstile. My best, uneducated guess was that this would take only five or ten minutes.

Two hours later, the bee stopped moving. Was it dead from exhaustion? This couldn't be happening. Louie was clearly troubled. Keith Brust, our director of photography, looked concerned. Maybe Louie could have the CGI (computer-generated imagery) artists work their animation magic so we wouldn't need an actual bee emerging from the orchid's stranglehold. Surprising us all (except Dave) the little bee that could gave a mighty push and freed itself from the orchid's viselike grip. While the cameras rolled, the bee flew off, carrying two golden pollen sacs on its back. Everyone breathed a sigh of relief. Our money shot was in the can, as directors are fond of saying. That day we earned our Hollywood stripes as orchid bee wranglers.

Orchids and Their Bees

Most orchids are mistresses of deceit. Like the bucket orchid, the majority of the world's estimated thirty thousand orchid species secrete no nectar and lack accessible pollen grains to entice and feed their bees. Instead, orchid pollen grains are shrink-wrapped inside globose packets— by pairs, fours, and sixes. These pollination bombshells are then glued to their pollen carrier. The sperm-filled pollinia usually get attached to a nutritionally challenged or sex-starved bee. With great precision the flower "knows" what it is doing. It also uses only a specific part of an insect's body, where its sperm packets cannot be removed by the pollinator. Pollinia are then moved to the right part of the next orchid on a future flower visit by the bee or other pollinator. The pollinator is searching, always searching, and the orchid has evolved so that lights and bells go off in the insect's brain when it smells or sees an orchid of a particular kind. The evolutionary strategy is not to waste pollen on the wrong type of orchid, but it is also the product of an eerie foray into the mind of an animal by a plant. Like the bucket orchid, many other orchids have evocative and mysterious fragrances. In turn, male orchid bees have scraper hairs along with special storage glands inside their legs to gather up the floral chemical treasures.

A male *Euglossa* bee spends every day for weeks or months gathering up and storing fragrant chemicals inside pouches almost like a cowboy's saddlebags on his hind legs. These aromatic treasures come from tropical orchids with tongue-twisting names such as *Coryanthes*, *Gongora*, and *Stanhopea*. Some members of the *Philodendron* family (Araceae), including *Spathiphyllum*, also offer bee-enticing odorants. In the absence of flowers, males collect the smelly resins from oozing tree wounds, fungi, a few non-orchid flowers, or even animal excrement. Once the correct mixture of chemicals is acquired within their hind legs, the bees use them to attempt to dominate—as alpha males of many larger animals often do—a site to which females arrive for mating. For the orchid bee, it is a perch site on a tree or woody, upright stem in the forest.

The orchid bees' mating rituals have been described as bizarre, but are really quite low key and even a bit pedestrian. They wait for hours for their potential mate to appear and occasionally interact with other males, mostly to show who's who and maintain their territorial positions. Males of each species form a loose group of males that constantly vie to copulate with females. Such "dance ensembles" are known as bee leks, but are hard to find and observe. These orchid bees position themselves a few feet off the ground on tree trunks and then spend many hours performing a stereotyped behavior. A perching male will buzz loudly to fan its wings, visibly lifting slightly off the tree on the tips of its legs. The males apparently release small puffs of their leg chemicals into the air, which they have carefully removed from a hind leg and put on their "wing comb" or the wings themselves, or another part of their body, depending on the kind of orchid bee. The smells and possibly the place, along with the movements or colors of bees, get the attention of both males and females of a single bee species. Most important, it attracts virgin females.

Sometimes male *Eulaema* bees engage in extensive "jousting matches" in which these insect knights circle head-on at each other, going round and round for many minutes. Perhaps they are sizing up each other, not unlike rival bull elk during the fall rut. After the jousting match plays out, one male, presumably exhausted by having to hold a flight pattern for hundreds to thousands of times, while narrowly avoiding full head banger jousts with its rival, teeters off into the forest. The females do no such acrobatics, nor are they duped to find a male where they were expecting food or a flower (male perches are never near flowers). A female lands on the perch beneath the male, copulation takes place, and almost before the coupled pair hits the ground, the female is back to her foraging and nesting activities, and the male continues as ever. We know the female mates only once, but who knows what these orchid-perfume-besotted bee knights are up to. . . . . We look back in time to the 1960s to find out.

Male orchid bees are easily fooled. In 1964, Mrs. Calaway Dodson, the wife of an orchid biologist, was sitting inside her hotel room in Manaus, Brazil—the gateway city to the Amazon—applying her favorite perfume. The perfume contained a trace of cineole, which smells like crushed *Eucalyptus* leaves. On that fateful morning, the window was wide-open and the humid tropical air ebbed and flowed into the room. A brilliant green male *Euglossa*, a bee that had followed the alluring scent trail from the nearby forest, entered the room, where it investigated the open perfume bottle. Dodson called to her husband, who came to identify the mysterious intruder. Dr. Dodson determined that the bee was attracted to the flowerlike scent, then watched it collect the fragrance just as if the perfume were a real orchid blooming in the tropical forest. The rest is history. Soon, dozens of orchid floral scents had been extracted and chemically analyzed using gas chromatography and mass spectrometry. Surprisingly, cineole is a common ingredient in many orchids, as well as other flowers.

A pivotal field test of the chemical by another orchid biologist, Robert Dressler of the Smithsonian Tropical Research Institute (STRI), took place at Panama's Cerro Campana. Putting out cineole and other synthetic orchid baits, Dressler was soon enveloped in a quietly buzzing swarm of two hundred orchid bees, aerialist living jewels. The bees did not harm Dressler, since male bees have no stings. Instead, they were interested in collecting the cineole to enhance their own sex appeal. STRI tropical ecologist David Roubik has set out blotters soaked in various orchid fragrance chemicals in unbroken monthly surveys since 1979, perhaps the longest-ever-insect-population census. The presence of three forest preserves within a day's drive of his Panama base makes the census possible. Some bees have increased in abundance, but on average he encounters fifty or so hovering orchid bee males at one time, or from three hundred to seven hundred bees in a typical four-hour morning's census, and fifteen to thirty species in a day. Only male bees are attracted to the chemical baits. Only twice, after surveying nearly a half million bees, says Dave, has he seen females. The females do the usual "bee behavior" foraging for pollen and drinking nectar from blossoming trees and tropical wildflowers, and they do occasionally take a sip of salt from an animal source. The other strictly female bee thing they do is collect nesting material, almost always sticky resins but also mud and some vertebrate feces. It is advantageous for them to be as picky in selecting these materials as in selecting their food and that of their offspring, not to mention their mates. Female orchid bees have ways of assessing "good genes" in their prospective mates, which explains why all this jungle pickiness takes place.

It is not unusual for bee biologists or ecotourism operators to use synthetic chemical baits to attract flamboyant male orchid bees. This is a crowd-pleasing demonstration from Mexico through Brazil. You might be lucky enough to find one of the attracted bees carrying a bright yellow backpack of orchid pollinia from an earlier floral encounter. As different orchids package their pollinia in various shapes and sizes, you can learn to discriminate between a *Lycaste* and a *Catasetum* pollinarium based on the number of packets, their shape, size, and whether they have stalks attaching them to the adhesive patch clinging to the bee. Synthetic orchid chemicals are applied to pieces of blotter paper or sponges at chest height on trees from 8:00 a.m. until noon, preferably along a ridgetop. If there is a bit of a breeze, and any bees are nearby, they'll arrive a few minutes after baiting starts. If you visit or live near a Costa Rican, Panamanian, Ecuadorian, or Amazonian rain forest, give it a try. It's mesmerizing to be the pied piper for a throng of brilliant metallic euglossine bees. Unlike birds, they have few common names, but some could easily be fashioned. For instance, Hanson's red-tailed blue bee or Dodson's fire bee or Dressler's brassy two-tone. The imperial bee of Panama holds court in the rain forest, and ignites our fascination.

Beetles as Pollinators

Orchid bees may appear to be flashy celebrities visiting extravagant orchids, but most pollination goes on without notice or fanfare. We met smaller flower-loving beetles in chapter 1 as they munched on white food bodies, the modified petal-like tips of blossoms of the western spicebush (*Caly-*

canthus occidentalis). Many blossoms have adaptations catering specifically to members of the order Coleoptera. Rove and sap beetles are attracted to flowers with fruity odors and colors that mimic ripe fruits. Dozens of beetles pile in and begin to feed on loose pollen and the protein-rich food bodies. While eating and defecating, males and females pair up, mating with abandon. Once the food is gone, they clamber out, flying to the next pollen party, unknowingly carrying the pollen on their bodies.

For beetle flowers, the main strategy is to be redundant; that is, to have lots of spare parts. If a few of their succulent petals or stringy stigmas are devoured, plenty are left for pollination and fertilization. Their ovules are ensconced below, out of harm's way from the clamoring beetles and their chewing mouthparts. Our room-trashing beetles are typically those found visiting *Magnolia-* and *Annona*-type blossoms, which are beetle-pollinated-only flowers. It's a common floral ploy. Botanist Peter Bernhardt reviewed the scientific literature in 2000 and found that thirty-four families of flowering plants contain at least one species pollinated exclusively by beetles, and an additional twenty-two families have species pollinated by a mix of beetles and other insects. Peter also brought to my attention a nineteenth-century cartoon by the French caricaturist J. J. Grandville (1803–47). This entertaining antique image shows a group of partying beetles sitting inside a poppy flower smoking opium.

Why is this relevant? Some of our favorite garden blooms, including the Asian poppy (*Papaver orientale*), are beetle-pollinated and all came originally from the Middle East. Visit Israel in March and you will find the hairy scarab beetles *Amphicoma* and *Anthypna* copulating inside those poppy flowers as well as the blooms of crown anemones (*Anemone coronaria*), giant orange buttercups (*Ranunculus asiaticus*), pheasant's eyes (*Adonis*), and even one of the wild tulips that gave us some of our showier garden hybrids. What do these flowers have in common? Most make lots of stamens and many tiny ovules, and those beetles really go for orange-crimson petals with black centers. In South Africa, members of the iris family host over eighty kinds of monkey beetles (another group of scarabs), which hold orgies inside gaudy red, orange, or cream-colored, scentless flowers. At first glance, most beetles seem unlikely pollinator candidates. After all, their bodies are hard, smooth, and shiny. Their wing covers—the elytra—are smooth, usually without the hairs needed to hold and transport pollen. Most flower-pollinating scarabs, and other species such as the beautiful jewel beetles (Buprestidae), do, however, sport thick hair tufts on their legs and undersides. This is the architectural result of insect pollen-foraging strategies.

Not all beetles are vandals. A large number, mostly scarabs and jewel beetles, treat their flowers with respect. The flowers also provide a "cruising zone," a rendezvous site for lusty males that visit flowers in rapid succession, searching for mates. Often, intense, prolonged fights occur among males for access to virgin females. Male and female beetles may remain en copula on the same flower for hours as the female placidly eats pollen.

Those Flirtatious Flies

Flies get universally bad press (far worse than beetles). Almost everyone believes that the fly that just executed a perfect six-point landing on his or her plate of Aunt Emma's prizewinning potato salad is carrying a few billion drug-resistant deadly plague-causing bacteria. Some flies do tote around a few nasty microbes, and others are blood-feeding offenders, including certain female mosquitoes, which transmit life-threatening diseases. However, most flies are benign, even helpful. I'd go as far as saying flies are essential to our well-being and survival.

The order Diptera, the familiar insects we know as flies, is old and diverse. Worldwide, there are an estimated 160,000 species. Of these, roughly 10,000 fly species in at least 71 of 150 dipteran families routinely visit more than 550 kinds of flowers. The predominant flies that frequent flowers are hoverflies and flower flies (syrphids), horseflies (tabanids), and carrion and flesh flies (muscids and calliphorids). There are also highly specialized, long-tongued flies such as the odd-looking humpbacks (Acroceridae) and the long-tongued and elegant tangle-vein flies (Nemestrinidae). Flies are the second most important pollinators of flowering plants, after bees. Even female mosquitoes pollinate blooms. Yes, they are seeking vertebrate blood, but they like nectar and pollinate while visiting the small, green flowers of the northern bog orchids (*Platanthera obtusata*) for their sugar-rich nectar.

In Arizona and Sonora, I locate flower-visiting flies by triangulating on the high-pitched whine of bee flies (Bombyliidae), whose long-tongued, fuzzy females resemble miniature bumble bees on stilts. In Africa, there are weird horseflies (Tabanidae) with tongues 0.8 to 1.6 inches long. The real champion of exaggerated mouthparts is the tangle-vein fly *Moegistorhynchus longirostris*, with its 3.3-inch-long tongue compared to its 0.4-inch-long body. It is a floral-nectar specialist, visiting the flowers of at least twenty species in the iris (Iridaceae), geranium (Geraniaceae), and orchid families.

Flower flies (Syrphidae) are my favorites. Syrphids are colorful, diverse, and fascinating flower visitors, insects that are fun to watch. Flower flies, including the familiar "H-bee," or drone fly (*Eristalis tenax*), live in most habitats. Their females visit blooms to sop up pollen grains whose protein allows them to develop their egg clusters. Drone flies are so hooked on eating pollen they are innately attracted to the color yellow. A fly presented with a yellow piece of paper touches it with her proboscis. Many of the world's more than six thousand flower fly species are brilliantly colored, patterned in brown, black, yellow, and white. Because of their bold stripes, black and yellow aposematism (warning coloration), and their hovering or darting flight maneuvers, they are often mistaken for stinging bees or wasps by their predators and people alike. That cream-colored stalk of bear grass (*Xerophyllum tenax*) blooming on a mountain in Oregon or Washington may be pollinated by over twenty different hoverfly species.

Still don't like flies or think we could get by without them? If no wriggling fly maggots lived in rotting plant debris on the ground or in cultivated cacao plantations, the world would be without chocolate bars, delectable bonbons, or cocoa powder! Cacao trees (*Theobroma cacao* and other species) bear tiny, whitish-pink flowers that emerge directly from their trunks as small clusters. Female midges (*Forcipomyia*) no bigger than the head of a pin find their way, likely by scent, to the tiny blooms, seeking nectar and pollen food and transporting some grains to other blossoms. Five to eight months later the tiny florets have turned into football-shaped fruits containing the large seeds that are fermented, roasted, and finely milled for the delicious concoctions that chocoholics crave.

Trapper Blossoms and Their Catches

Certain blossoms incarcerate their flies overnight. In graduate school, I would drive along Highway 128 south of Lake Berryessa in the Napa Valley and adjacent hills. Here, tall oak trees were festooned with vines. These climbing vines, native to California, are perennial woody vines in the Aristolochiaceae, or Dutchman's-pipe, family. Their flowers are unusual. Some call them birthworts, as the sacklike flower reminds some people of the shape of a fetus. *Aristolochia californica* blossoms are almost two inches tall, hollow, and bent in half, looking like miniature, fat tobacco pipes. Thin, parallel, purple lines run from pedicel to the floral opening of these mostly greenish flowers. Three paired, brownish-yellow lips flare open at the entrance to the cavelike floral interior. The blossoms remain open for four or five days before withering. Walking past living curtains of hundreds of draping *Aristolochia*, I always noticed their distinctive lemony scent, produced inside their flared lips.

On the first day they open, the citrus aroma, and possibly their color, attracts minute flies. Fungus gnats (family Mycetophilidae) alight on the floral lips and walk inside. About a half inch from the base of the flower is a deep purple band. This is nectary tissue, and the temporarily imprisoned flies drink nectar from its glistening droplets, sometimes depositing eggs. Above, the anthers release their powdery yellow pollen. Translucent green tissue around the uppermost region of the flower acts as a window that attracts the flies. On the first day the *Aristolochia* stigma is receptive and pollen is released. By the second day the glandular hairs forming the nectar ring have dried up, and the pollen-dusted flies exit the now senescing flowers.

Aristolochia californica offers a relatively mild treatment of its fly captives, unlike the forced one- or two-day internment used by various aroids, including almost two hundred species of voodoo lilies (*Amorphophallus*), the dragon arum from Europe, or the Sumatran *A. titanum*, the world's largest flowering stem (it's a maypole supporting thousands of itty-bitty flowers), with a stalk up to nine feet tall and a powerful stench to match, which attracts carrion-feeding flies. Technically, *A. titanum* is a collection of many smaller flowers. Its grand architecture is really a huge version of the lowly skunk cabbage and philodendrons mentioned previously. Inside the flowers of *A. titanum*, also known as the corpse flower, are complex, downward-pointing hairs, which gradually lose their turgidity, allowing the flies to escape. With them the small flies carry their dusting of pollen on the second day of the flowers' life history. Dutchman's-pipes such as *Aristolochia californica* seem to be an early stage in this continuum from always-open and accessible blooms, to the traps of *Amorphophallus*, which imprison their flies for long periods.

Carrion Flowers of Borneo

A world away, I encountered the world's largest flower, which is also fly-pollinated. I traveled with friends, and we had been driving from the coastal city of Kota Kinabalu within Sabah, East Malaysia. We visited tourist locales including Mt. Kinabalu, Poring Hot Spring, the Mesilau Nature Park, and a nearby butterfly farm and insect zoo. But we were after a different rain-forest treasure, the famous *Rafflesia arnoldii*, one of thirteen to fourteen *Rafflesia* species unique (endemic) to Indonesia and Malaysia.

Rafflesia arnoldii is a stupendous flower, unlike anything else you will ever see. Surprisingly, the main body of the plant is entirely hidden. It is a parasite of another plant and grows internally. Inside host vines of the genus *Tetrastigma* in the grape family (Vitaceae), the parasitic monstrose flower and its host live only in undisturbed rain forests. *Rafflesia* is a flowering plant without leaves, stems, or roots and no green chlorophyll pigments. Almost funguslike it extracts nutrients from its host's woody vines. Over a period of up to ten months, a bulge forms on the vine and the round, cabbage-size flower buds appear. After this long gestation-like development, the flowers open, but remain viable for only a few days. The immense single flowers are often three feet in diameter and weigh a hefty twenty-four pounds each.

This was the holy grail of floral biology for me. Sure, I'd read about *Rafflesia* in books and seen photographs. But, experiencing them firsthand in the wild was different; it had been high on my bucket list. We had just passed the small village of Tambunan. Out of my peripheral vision came a fleeting glimpse of something big and red. "Look at that!" I sputtered, bringing our rental car to a skidding stop in the roadside gravel. What, a painted *Rafflesia*? Sure enough, in front of a small wooden house was a sign crudely painted with the likeness of the crimson giant. Advertising pays. I said, *"Selamat pagi,"* bidding a hearty good morning to the Malay woman greeting us from the doorway of her home. I negotiated in rudimentary Bahasa Malaysia language for a tour. Were any giant, stinky flowers (*Bunga Patma*) nearby? Could we perhaps visit and photograph them? My heart was pounding with excitement. I paid the fee of a few Malaysian ringgits, bid her a hearty *"Terima kasih,"* and our trio of hopeful flower-gawkers was off on our quest. Her agile, ten-year-old son ran us down a forest path leading away from their home.

Behind a low wooden fence lay our prize. I stepped over the low fence and sat next to one of the two wide, maroon flowers. My breaths came rapidly. *Rafflesia arnoldii* at last! They were two feet across and ten inches tall, leathery tough and otherworldly. They looked like something from the set of a Hollywood 1950s science fiction B movie. Each flower had five broad, flattened arms like a fat starfish. The central disk was surrounded by an incurved thickened bowl. An eight-inch hole led into the darkened interior. Inside were dozens of strange reddish spikes and many anthers, with their slimy, white secretions. Intensely reddish brown, its disk was interrupted by hundreds of irregular creamy patches dotting the entire flower. The smell wasn't too bad. Yes, it did smell a bit like over-ripe roadkill, but its deathlike stench was less intense than I'd anticipated. Well, maybe these two flowers were a bit older, not as fresh and appealing as they might have been.

There doesn't seem to be detectable heat production within *Rafflesia* blossoms. The long-distance lure for the flies must be their death-and-decay odor plume, and once the insects are close, the blotchy red and white colors and surface texture take over, mimicking the corpse of a large animal. Limited field research has been conducted on the rare, giant flowers, and their separate males and female blossoms which require carrion flies to move pollen from flower to flower. The main pollinators are carrion (bluebottle) flies of the genera *Lucilia* and *Chrysomya*. Mostly female flies obtain dorsal loads of viscous liquid pollen perhaps by visiting male *Rafflesia* flowers. Pollen-laden flies next visit the female blossoms, where they must squeeze inside a groove where the pollen contacts stigmatic areas. No nectar rewards are offered to the flies, only the false promise of a rotting corpse, delectable juices, and a place to lay their eggs.

Waspish

Let's examine wasp/flower relationships. Naturalists in the Victorian period were the first to notice that wasps and flies are often found at the same flowers because these two, dissimilar groups of insects appreciate similar odors and color patterns. Sometimes very different animals pollinate and share the same flower. Flowers that appeal to flies and wasps usually lack sweet perfumes and seem dull to our eyes (greenish or brownish, or sort of iodine). Nonetheless, the relatively stinky and icky-colored blossoms offer nectar in large, accessible drops we know are rich in amino acids (the building blocks of proteins). What particular group of insects pollinates most of these "in-between" flowers?

Brown's peony (*Paeonia brownii*), in the northwest portion of America (Idaho, Oregon), offers nodding brown cups with yellow rims. Its odor seems almost acrid, and it has big nectar glands that produce lots of dilute sugars and amino acids. When it first blooms, after the snow and ice retreat in April, the most important pollinators are fat, long-tongued flies (*Criorhina caudata*). You can easily mistake them for small bees, and their hairy coats carry hundreds of peony pollen grains from flower to flower. The flies, though, are fickle. By mid to late April they'd rather visit blooming balsamroots and delphiniums. Is the peony bereft of pollinators? No, the slack is taken up by at least six kinds of wasps that emerge late in spring. They aren't very hairy and carry far fewer pollen grains than can bees, but they make up for reduced pollinating capacity in their sheer numbers. A single peony flower may be visited by three hungry wasps at the same time.

Based on fossil and DNA evidence, we suspect that one group of small wasps (the pemphredonines) were likely direct ancestors of all hunting wasps and our modern vegetarian bees. We like to think of true wasps as winged hunters of caterpillars, beetles, or flies—carnivores. While wasps are easily observed drinking nectar from various flowers, most don't mess around with pollen. Under the microscope you find that the hairs on a wasp's body are straight shafts, while bee hairs are branched, hooked, almost feathery to both gather and hold pollen grains. The branched hairs make up the fine fur coats that many bees wear, which also keep them warm on cold days. Think of bumble bees, which often are out foraging on dreary days.

If few wasps have a mutualistic dance with flowers, then few flowers also attempt to attract and reward these meat eaters. In Europe and North America, figwort (*Scrophularia*) flowers, cup-shaped, brownish blooms, are visited by social wasps, including native and introduced yellow jackets (*Vespula*). In my Tucson front yard are beardtongue (*Penstemon*) blossoms visited by fast-flying bees and masarid wasps. Elsewhere grow passionflowers (*Passiflora*) or helleborine orchids (e.g., *Epipactis*), visited frequently and pollinated by wasps. Springtime brings blooms of fritillaries (*Fritillaria*) to Turkish hillsides. It's reported that British gardeners are upset when their *Fritillaria graeca* blooms. The brownish flowers smell like rancid meat, and *Vespula* wasps come to investigate. It seems that wasps visit brown or green flowers, many of which give off "green-leaf volatiles," the same chemicals released by plants when being attacked by aphids or caterpillars. Perhaps this is another form of chemical mimicry and floral larceny, which may attract a predator to rid the plant of one of its pests.

The awkward generalization that wasps do not specialize upon flowers has a few exceptions. In North American and African deserts we find a family of flower-loving wasps, the masarids (Masaridae), with long, charming clubbed antennae. Females feed their offspring pollen, not animal fare such as paralyzed spiders, beetles, or caterpillars. The large, slender, brown or black-and-yellow wasps visit native wildflowers including scorpionweed (*Phacelia*), eagerly gathering up pollen and nectar. Masarids construct nests of pebbles, resin, and mud, then stock their nests with pollen and nectar like most bees. A truly nonconformist wasp.

Everything's topsy-turvy in Australia. In the woodlands and bush of this drying continent a group of bizarre orchids depend entirely upon the libido of male wasps for pollination. The females are wingless and expect their males to feed them nectar during their mating flights. These flowers sport lip petals that resemble the bodies of female ichneumon and flower wasps. Hundreds of females mimic Australian orchids with iodine-colored flowers. The plants possess evocative common names because the weird flowers resemble tongues (*Cryptostylis*), spiders (*Caladenia*), birds (*Chiloglottis*), and hammers (complete with movable hinge—*Drakaea*). The male wasps, a bit randy, search the shrubby expanses for receptive females, but pounce on the orchid flowers instead, trying to copulate with them. Botanists and floral biologists call this type of pollination pseudo-copulation. Television audiences are enthralled with nature documentaries featuring the wasps and orchids as the males hang on, not giving up easily with their floral surrogate mate.

Beautiful Klutzes

Let's move now from the bizarre and unusual wasps to the sublime but often overpraised butterflies. Certainly butterflies (largely the diurnal Lepidoptera) are icons of beauty. One often watches with pure joy as those sprites flit their way erratically across a blooming meadow. Since antiquity, butterflies have delighted people everywhere. In modern times they appear on every imaginable object as decorative elements and are widely used in advertising and corporate logos. The butterflies have a special meaning to us. The Greek word *psyche* means "life," "breath," or "human soul," and we find it in modern English words such as *psychology*. Psyche, as a Roman demigoddess, was represented as a fair young maiden with the wings of a butterfly, not unlike Tinker Bell in the Walt Disney version of J. M. Barrie's 1904 play *Peter Pan*. Many cultures find inspiration in the butterfly's metamorphosis from a lowly crawling caterpillar into the pupal resting stage and finally its glorious emergence and flight into the world as a brightly colored, winged adult butterfly or moth.

Ancient Irish and Mexican/Guatemalan folklore holds that butterflies were souls of the recently deceased. This soul-like depiction was also used in the Oscar-nominated 1983 American and British film *El Norte* (not to be confused with the 1994 Rob Reiner film of a similar name). Today we can appreciate the winged beauties at hundreds of commercial butterfly houses. In captivity, their chaotic flights are restricted and calmed. They slowly and methodically visit flowers, fruit baits, and sugar-water feeders. We can watch their behavior up close. They even land on our noses and fingers. In Africa, one particular mountain butterfly will land on you if you are wearing something red.

But large butterflies don't always make the best pollinators; they can be beautiful pollen klutzes. Pollen doesn't stick easily to their broad, dry, and scaly wings. They are also too leggy, standing up high and rarely contacting anthers or stigmas when they feed from open-topped sunflowers and similar blooms. Even the monarch butterfly and milkweed pollination story is a bit of a stretch. Monarch and queen butterflies (*Danaus plexippus* and *D. gilippus*) lay their eggs under milkweed leaves, and their larvae are ravenous. However, adult monarch butterflies, while nectaring at blossoms of native milkweeds (*Asclepias*), are not dependable pollinators. Their skinny legs rarely slip into the floral grooves, a complex floral mechanism in *Asclepias*, with just the right orientation. Either their legs don't get stuck temporarily (remember orchid bees at bucket orchids), or they aren't strong enough to pull themselves free. Small butterflies are sometimes found hanging dead from the parasols of milkweed umbels, which become death traps. Larger bees and spider wasps (Pompilidae) usually pollinate the milkweeds. Their legs acquire chains of milkweed pollinia.

One group of tropical butterflies, however, are truly pollen specialists. The steamy forests of Costa Rica and Panama are home to a partnership between tropical butterflies and unusual flowering vines in the gourd and pumpkin family (Cucurbitaceae). Here, *Psiguria* and *Gurania* vines dangle low to the ground and present strange flowers that attract brightly colored butterflies known as zebra, tiger, or postman longwings (*Heliconius*). In the same forests, *Heliconius* also visit the genera *Psychotria* and *Palicourea*, of the same plant family as coffee, for nectar and pollen. Together, those butterfly blooms have long, tubular, usually bright orange corollas. In the morning, the butterflies search for flowers that, once located, occupy much of their time, as they drink nectar and acquire large dollops of sticky pollen. Those tropical vines lodge their oily pollen at the bases of the butterfly tongues, making them efficient pollinators.

Photographs of longwing butterflies with their comical big pollen loads always make me smile. They remind me of people with milk mustaches. After acquiring their pollen, longwings often steep their pollen in pools of nectar, allowing amino acids and proteins to leach into the nectar. The resulting nectar smoothie is an ingenious feeding method not used by other butterflies. Added pollen nutrients in their diets allow *Heliconius* adults to live for as long as nine months, much longer than the average two-week butterfly life span. Of course, not all butterflies visit only flowers. Many visit bird or mammal dung, or even carrion, for liquid nutrients. Especially in the tropics, you may come across dozens of male butterflies "puddling" together at damp roadside mud. Here, they gather essential mineral nutrients—a kind of nectar of mother earth. The minerals are subsequently passed to the females during mating as nuptial gifts.

Wings in the Dark

The less familiar members of Lepidoptera, the moths, fly mostly at night. The diversity of form, color, behavior, and lifestyle of the world's magnificent moths far exceeds that of their much-beloved diurnal relatives. In the United States, about seven hundred kinds of butterflies can be found, compared to an estimated ten thousand of moths. Most of them lead secretive lives, and many, without fanfare, remain nameless and unknown to science. Only a few moths cause direct mischief and economic loss, such as the few caterpillars that actually eat woolen fabrics in our clos-

ets, or those attacking row crops such as corn, and the budworm defolia-
tors of our forest. Yet, perhaps because of their largely secretive, nocturnal
habits, the only moth we think we know (or like) is helpless, the long-
domesticated silk moth (*Bombyx mori*) of China. Caterpillars of the silk
moth eat only mulberry leaves, and the adults, like those of many moths,
eat nothing at all. . . . We need to view moths in an entirely different light
to truly appreciate these marvelous insects.

My favorites are the sleek hawk moths or sphingids (Sphingidae). I
appreciate them not only for their swept-back wings and fighter-jet look,
fast flight, and aerobatic maneuvers, but their intriguing feeding relationships with the blooms they visit. One of the best places to watch "hummingbird moths" are isolated patches of angel's trumpet or sacred datura
(*Datura*) along mostly dry creek beds in southern Arizona. The blooms
of *Datura wrightii* are delightful. The greenish-yellow buds rise above the
leaves, unrolling and expanding at sunset to become nearly twelve-inch-
tall and six-inch-wide goblets in less than thirty minutes. Immediately,
the lush sweet scent of the blossoms commands your attention. From afar,
the moths are noticing it, too, flying in to drink the dilute sweet floral
nectar. It has been claimed that the *Datura* nectar is spiked with night-
shadelike poisons, thereby drugging its floral visitors. Common sphinx
moth visitors include the omnipresent white-lined sphinx (*Hyles lineata*)
and the somewhat rarer tomato or tobacco hornworms (*Manduca sexta* or
M. quinquemaculata). You may know their hornworm larvae as the ravenous cigar-size, green caterpillars with their thorny tails, defoliating your
tomato plants. The larger *Manduca* hover and drink with extended six-
inch proboscides (the correct plural term for the Latin name for "tongue"),
but the smaller *Hyles* dive headfirst into the floral tubes to reach the nectar
with their shorter tongues. All depart from the flowers with a light dusting of pollen grains on their tongues and legs—unless they are duped by
porch lights, bug zappers, or candles, coming to an untimely early death.
Tragically, outdoor security lights have spelled the end of night for these
insects as much as they have for us.

Growing nearby may be a rare and glorious look-alike blossom, possibly part of a mimicry complex among flowers to lure the same moths.
On only a few nights each year, the brilliant white blooms of *La reina de
la noche* (*Peniocereus greggii* and *P. striatus*) top the cryptic gray and skinny
stems of this rare Sonoran cactus. They bloom during the hottest time of
the year when little else dares to flower. Some chemicals in the queen's

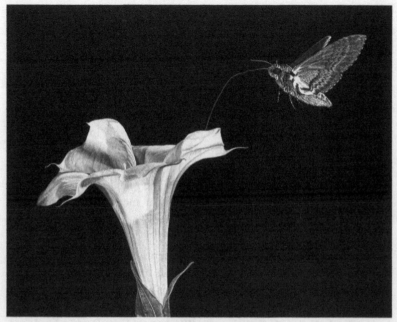

A hawk moth (*Manduca sexta*) approaching an angel's trumpet blossom
(*Datura wrightii*) for nectar

fragrance are shared with that of jimsonweed (*Datura*)—including benzyl alcohol and linalool, part of the odor mimicry suite, and there is a hint of wintergreen, the compound known as methyl salicylate.

Fat *Manduca* moths visit and pollinate *Peniocereus*, but their visits are more infrequent than those to *Datura*. Early the next morning, as the heat and sunlight cause the blossoms to close forever, metallic green sweat bees and honey bees swoop in for the remaining pollen and nectar.

Darwin's Prediction

In 1862 naturalist Charles Darwin (1809–82) made a famous prediction about a special duo, a flower and its moth. Growing as newly grown curiosities at Kew Gardens near London and in the greenhouses of Victorian elite plant collectors were magnificent new arrivals from Madagascar, including the star or comet orchids (*Angraecum sesquipedale*) and other fanciful blooms. Darwin was a serious student of orchids. He was sent a live plant by the great orchid collector James Bateman (1811–97) before 1862. Darwin examined the big, waxy-whitish flower and noted it had a long spur that contained a few drops of nectar within its tip. That nectar tube was nearly a foot long. In a letter to Joseph Hooker (then director of the botanical gardens at Kew), Darwin remarked, "I have just received such a Box full from Mr. Bateman with the astonishing *Angraecum sesquipedale* with a nectary a foot long—Good Heavens what insect can suck it." Darwin predicted that there must be an insect, likely a hawk moth, with a great proboscis, long enough to reach far into the depths of the spur to extract nectar, somewhere undiscovered on the island of Madagascar. The problem was that no such long-tongued insect, moth, or other visitor had ever been found in Madagascar, and especially not at star orchid blooms in the wild.

Many people, including his fellow scientists and orchid collectors, believed he was wildly wrong, but Darwin held firm to his prediction. From his other observations of form and fit between bloom and pollinator, research and original observations that became his now classic 1862 book, *On the Various Contrivances by Which Orchids are Fertilised by Insects*, he believed his ideas about star orchids were correct.

Sure enough, after his death and more than twenty years after Darwin originally made the prediction, a large hawk moth (*Xanthopan morganii praedicta*) was discovered in Madagascar. Latin scholars and etymologists will note the subspecies *praedicta* in the moth's name. Science requiring extensive and costly fieldwork takes a lot of time. Darwin predicted the missing moth pollinator, but field observations and photos of Madagascar hawk moths sucking nectar from this comet orchid, and related species, began to appear only in the 1980s. Research has continued and we now have videos of these elegant big moths feeding at their star orchids.

Moths with Tentacles?

Across the deserts of the southwestern United States, they stick up like white candelabras, hundreds of massed creamy-white flowers pointed skyward. They are the blossoms of yuccas, or Spanish bayonets, used by landscape architects, and favorites of painters, photographers, and hikers. Fresh blooming stalks are the resting places of a small but essential group of moths. Find a tall yucca stalk in bloom and give it a sharp whack. If you are observant, you may notice a few 0.4-inch-long white moths freed from their floral hideaways. These are the yucca moths (especially the genus *Tegeticula*), which are obligate specialists on yucca blossoms and will use nothing else. The female moths have bizarre elongate mouthparts called tentacles. Once inside a yucca flower she scoops up masses of the sticky pollen with those tentacles and forms it into a ball. The same tentacles carry the pollen "meatball" to the stigma, then jams it home. This is one of the few cases of active, one could almost say deliberate, pollination in nature. Even bees don't go to such extremes for their flowers.

Why are only female yucca moths such passionate pollinators? After providing stud service to the *Yucca* flower the *Tegeticula* moth turns around and lays her eggs deep inside the ovary. The *Yucca* plant is trading sex (pollination) for food, some of its own developing seeds. Remarkably, not all the munched seeds are destroyed by the feeding caterpillars. University of Arizona researcher Judie Bronstein and her students discovered that the tiny *Yucca* embryos are hidden within the thickened rims of the black, triangular seeds and escape destruction. The bright pink caterpillars tunnel and eat their way through the thin centers of the seeds stacked like poker chips. The larvae are doing the seeds a favor by scarifying them so rainwater will penetrate more quickly when they drop to the ground and are ready to sprout.

Recently, we've learned that senita cacti are also pollinated *deliberately* by a different moth, *Upiga virescens*. This insect, along with yucca moths and some female fig wasps, is the only known example of an active, purposeful flower pollinator aside from us human plant breeders.

But It's Still a Bee-Pollinated Planet

We've already glimpsed the secret lives of orchid bees and their remarkable host flowers, but we now turn to the lives of their more widespread, less glamorous relatives, who outnumber them by the thousands. Other than the masarid wasps and a few butterflies and flies, bees are the only insects that visit flowers to actively collect pollen as the sole food for themselves and/or their developing brood. Bees also carry nectar back to their nests. It's kept inside their stomachs, while they carry the pollen grains on their legs or occasionally on their thoraxes. Leafcutters and related bees (Megachilidae) may also have Velcro-like aprons on the underside of their abdomen, while some of our spring mining-bees (Andrenidae) have pollen-carrying hairs on their hind legs. With the exception of a few tropical stingless vulture bees that ingest protein from carrion and dung, almost all of the thousands of bee species are strictly vegans.

Bees are world-champion pollinators because of their ancient specialization upon flowers (70–100 million years ago, according to the earliest fossils), and their ability to learn and manipulate complex floral signals, shapes, colors, and odors. Moreover, they can fly, sometimes for miles, to their foraging sites. They also have finely branched hairs coating much of their bodies. The interstices catch and hold the pollen grains. With other hairs and leg parts modified into combs and scrapers, they quickly and efficiently groom themselves, packing the nutritious pollen onto their fluffy hind legs or undersides. Bees recover most but, fortunately for the plant, not all the pollen on their bodies. Many plants deposit pollen where the bees can't reach it or forget to look for it. Less than 1 percent of the grains become lodged between leg bases, under tongues, or on a narrow stripe down the bees' backs. The refugee pollen resides in those safe sites and is carried from flower to flower. This is essential for flowering-plant reproduction. For millions of years plants have been hiding their pollen on bees in places where they can't groom it off, where it remains until accidentally brushed onto the receptive stigmas of flowers.

Most of the world's twenty thousand described bee species, like ants and their wasp ancestors, are ground nesters. Bees are often mistaken for wasps. The habitats where bees prefer to live, and where we find their highest diversity, are the sandy, well-drained soils of deserts and savannas of the world. Tropical soils are too wet most of the year, so the social bees living there nest inside trees, sealing their nests with fast-drying and water-repellent resins. In any given habitat about 10–20 percent of the bee species are specialist cavity nesters in broken, pithy stems (such as elderberry or dried blackberry canes), small cervices, or vacant beetle galleries in wood. If you have a wooden deck at home, you may know that carpenter bees (*Xylocopa*) use their powerful jaws to excavate galleries in wood. Most wood-nesting bees, however, aren't able to dig their own tunnels. Ironically, they depend on the life cycles of flower-visiting beetles, especially long-horned (Cerambycidae) and jewel beetles (Buprestidae). The beetle grubs burrow and eat their way through tree trunks and branches. When the grub changes into a winged adult, it chews an escape hole, leaving its former nursery to female leafcutter and mason bees, which move in and begin nesting.

Most bees are floral generalists that visit many different species of flowers for pollen and/or nectar. In deserts, these specialist bees predominate. They include cactus-loving bees, mallow bees, and sunflower specialists. Some confine their shopping to one closely related group (a genus) of wildflower or shrub species.

A common misconception about bees is that they are all social, live in populous colonies, and make honey—the whole Winnie-the-Pooh scenario. In fact, there are only eleven species of true honey bees (*Apis*) and but one widespread honey-making bee (*Apis mellifera*), which evolved in the Oriental region (it later spread on its own to Africa and Eurasia and later everywhere else, thanks to us). The tropics have over five hundred species of stingless bees (meliponines), and they hoard enough honey to make honey harvesting (beekeeping) by humans worthwhile. About forty-seven species of bumble bees (*Bombus*) live in the United States, with some two hundred fifty species worldwide. They are also social honey-makers but store only a few teaspoons of honey, so digging up their nests isn't worth their defensive (and painful) stings. They are perhaps loved by their enemies for their brood, while their flower-visiting behavior is what makes them ever so important to plants, other animals, and people.

Some flowers protect their pollen from pollen robbers and other insects that make poor pollinators. About 6 percent of the world's more than 350,000 known flowering plant species play this hide-and-seek pollen game with bees. Pluck a tomato flower from your vegetable garden and examine it with a loupe. The central part of the flower is a bright yellow "cone" of five anthers encircling the female pistil. Each anther tip has holes, the apical pores. This is the only way the small, light, and dry pollen grains can escape. Imagine the flower is a botanical saltshaker. Tomato flowers offer only pollen. No glands ooze sweet nectar. Tomatoes aren't the only crop plants to make saltshaker flowers. Blueberries, cranberries, chilies, eggplants, and kiwis have them as well, but blueberry, cranberry, and chili flowers also secrete nectar.

Female bumble bees, and a few other bees, seek out flowers that have perforated anther tips. One of my favorite activities is to sit quietly near a nightshade (*Solanum*) or partridge pea (*Senna*) patch in the Sonoran Desert. Before sunrise female bees begin arriving to forage for pollen inside these nectarless flowers. A bee lands on a flower near me. She bites into the anther cone with her jaws (mandibles) and curls into a C shape with her thorax covering the anther pores. I hear a funny sound, like someone giving me the raspberry, but it's coming from the bee. The bee is emptying the anthers with her sonic vibrations! The comical sounds I hear are an ancient pollen-harvesting technique used by bees around the world on this kind of blossom, called buzz pollination. The bees are living tuning forks. Using the powerful flight muscles inside their midsections, the muscles that power the wings in flight, they contract them with wings held flat and unmoving over their backs. The sound and vibrational frequencies are about three hundred to five hundred cycles per second (Hz). If you're a musician, you know these sounds to be in the range of the musical notes A or middle C.

Buzz flowers cater to a specialized group of bees in the know. Ordinary bees and other insects cannot extract the pollen grains from these blossoms. The bees' sonic buzzes get the pollen grains bouncing into each other inside the anthers. The pollen grains reach their escape velocity and stream forcefully out of the anthers by the hundreds of thousands in a few tenths of a second. Measurements of buzzing bees reveal they impart 30 g (1 g is equal to acceleration due to gravity at the earth's suface) to the pollen inside the anthers. By comparison, fighter pilots can withstand about 9 g-force with training and by wearing a special pressurized anti-g-LOC suit. An untrained person typically blacks out and loses consciousness, due to blood loss from the brain, at only 5 g.

You can put buzz pollination to use in your daily life. If you grow tomatoes in a home garden and you don't have bumble bees around, try this. Get the appropriate A or C tuning fork, an electric toothbrush, or a new commercial product called the VegiBee. This novel device is essentially a modified electric toothbrush with some clever marketing. Now, you are the sonicating bee as you move from tomato flower to flower. Your reward will be tasty, homegrown tomatoes a few weeks later. It's quite an accomplishment. You can do what commercial honey bees can't. They aren't equipped to buzz pollinate or don't learn the behavior needed to sonically harvest pollen from porose anthers.

Bee Economics: Every Third Mouthful of Food

Wild pollinators, including leafcutter, mason, stingless, digger, sweat, and bumble bees, along with the wasps, beetles, flies, butterflies, and others we've heard about, all contribute to modern agriculture, literally every third mouthful of food we eat or drink. In the United States, annually about $3 billion of agricultural productivity is made possible by the foraging and pollinating activities of unmanaged wild insects visiting flowers of more than 125 American crops and about 1,400 worldwide. Managed honey bee colonies contribute the remainder of the approximately $10–$15 billion annual US total agricultural production. In the tropics, the stingless bees are the rising stars in pollination. Their colonies are smaller, forage freely but in a smaller range, are less heavy and also easier to manage, and are now being propagated and moved to different crops.

To balance our pollinator portfolio and not become entirely, and dangerously, reliant upon the ecosystem services of one introduced insect, the European honey bee, researchers have domesticated and developed new agricultural pollinators from a bevy of natives and one introduced bee. In the 1930s farmers in Utah noticed that they had some new livestock in their buildings, literally living inside the wooden beams and roofs of their barns. Eurasian immigrant bees had arrived and were spreading fast. The new bees were alfalfa leafcutter bees (*Megachile rotundata*), and they took up residence in nail holes and crevices in weathered lumber.

Alfalfa farmers were quick to notice that these small, black, housefly-size bees were supremely efficient pollinators of their major crop, alfalfa. They started drilling and hammering holes in their barns like mad. Given a choice, honey bees don't preferentially visit alfalfa blossoms, but the diminutive leafcutter bees pushed alfalfa yields from 198 pounds of cleaned alfalfa seed per acre to an astounding 2,000 pounds per acre. Today, alfalfa-seed farmers buy five-gallon buckets, each containing about ten thousand leafcutter bee cells, for about $100 from bee brokers or bee ranchers in Canada. They deploy them on mobile trailer shelters among the blooming expanses of their alfalfa fields. The leafcutter bees live inside paper straws or prefabricated Styrofoam boards. These alien bees make possible the nearly $5 billion annual value of the US alfalfa crop. You may not realize the importance of alfalfa seed grown into alfalfa plants and used for hay as livestock fodder. These and other bees help put meat on our tables as well as adding delicious fruits and many edible seeds to our diets.

A native bee of the Pacific Northwest is the blue orchard bee (*Osmia lignaria*), or more colorfully, BOB. These industrious bees visit and pollinate the blossoms of many tree fruits in the rose family. The bees are especially fond of sweet cherry blossoms for their pollen and nectar. A few dozen female BOBs living in cardboard straws and small shelter boxes within an orchard can do the work of an entire honey bee hive containing up to thirty thousand bees.

Bumble bees are the pollinator of choice for pollinating greenhouse tomatoes and green peppers around the world. My favorite farming operation to visit is a three-hour drive from my home. Here, north of Willcox, Arizona, four hundred acres are under glass, an immense tomato factory. EuroFresh Farms, a formerly Dutch-owned facility (now operated by NatureSweet), hydroponically produces one of every six tomatoes on the vine clusters sold in US markets. Workers ride electric carts on rails to harvest the tomatoes, then electric tomato trains bring the ripe fruit to the sorting and packing house. None of this could happen without bumble bees (*Bombus impatiens*) to buzz pollinate and set the crop. Bumble bees are raised by insectary companies in other states, then flown and driven to NatureSweet farms. The bees are licensed for their pollinating services per cubic yard, and the spent colonies are traded out every few weeks for fresh younger colonies.

European honey bees are the de rigueur pollinator for the majority of today's agricultural crops. They can be raised and the colonies divided at will to produce more bee colonies. Since the 1860s and the Civil War era, beehives (known as Langstroth hives) have been used by beekeepers. Their interchangeable-frame technology enables apiculturists to easily extract honey, along with managing and inspecting their bees. The commercial migration of a million or so of our 2.5 million beekeeper-managed honey bee colonies follows the American bloom, mirroring the seasonal progression of crops and wildflower blooms across the nation. Most commercial beekeepers don't earn their living from the backbreaking labor needed to produce honey. Instead, they lease their Lilliputian livestock to agricultural growers. Today, the primary imperative in commercial beekeeping is to get your eighteen-wheel semitrailer truckloads (carrying about four hundred hives each) to Southern California in February, just ahead of the ephemeral almond bloom. Beekeepers no longer reward growers with a five-gallon bucket of tasty honey for allowing them to place their bees on nectar-rich croplands.

Pollination contracts are signed a year in advance, and the money is good. For the California almond-bloom gold rush, beekeepers rent their hives to almond growers for $150 or as much as $200 each. Each year there is an increasing shortage of available honey bee colonies, caused by colony collapse disorder (CCD), neonicotinoid insecticides (neonics), mites, diseases, and other factors. The hives rest four to a pallet and are placed one or two per acre, for just two or three weeks during the hasty almond bloom. With 890,000 acres of prime agricultural land planted in bearing almond orchards, this is indeed big business in bees. Honey bees pollinate most of the world's agricultural crops. Honey bees, however, are too often credited with pollinating buzz-pollinated crops, including blueberries and cranberries, which are largely pollinated by wild bumble bees, unbeknownst to the growers, who pay for leased honey bee pollination services.

Whirring Wings

If you live in North America, you may have witnessed the incredible flights and flower visits of those tiny marvels the hummingbirds (Trochilidae). Weighing only 0.07 to 0.70 ounces (a penny weighs just 0.08 ounce) and beating their wings at up to two hundred times per second, they are the only birds able to hover, fly backward, or upside down. With their diminutive size and outlandish metabolism, they constantly need energy, the sugar rush they get from floral nectar. To be able to sleep and not perish at night from starvation, they tune down their metabolism and become torpid, their heartbeat and breathing slowing down. Each morning, breaking their nighttime torpor, they go in search of new flowers to power their flight and sustain their lives.

In Sonoran Desert washes we find spectacular red-bloomed plants visited by hungry migratory and resident hummingbirds. Chuparosa bushes (*Justicia californica*) are visited by numerous *chupamiel* ("honey sippers," poetically in Spanish). On adjacent hillsides, hundreds of coach-whip-stemmed ocotillos (*Fouquieria splendens*) point skyward. Beginning in March, for a month, their branch tips burst forth in riotous torchlike, red blooms. The plants are eagerly patrolled and defended by territorial male

Anna's, black-chinned, and rufous hummingbirds, while the females try to sneak in for an unmolested drink.

These bird blossoms share several common features. First, they are brightly colored, in the case of chuparosa and ocotillo, brilliant red. Flowers visited by hummingbirds can also be yellow, orange, or other colors. Their nearly odorless flowers are thin and tubular, perfectly adapted to the fit of the narrow, long beak of a hovering hummingbird, but provide no place for a bee to land. The flowers are reinforced with strong veins to resist the "poking" bills. The scant pollen is usually deposited in small patches on the crown of the bird's head or at the base of its bill. The flowers that hummingbirds visit are attuned to their visitors' energy needs. These flowers produce abundant but weak nectar, usually 17–25 percent total dissolved sugars. Hummingbirds need to drink often. When these feisty, little birds aren't sipping nectar, they are chasing down tasty fruit flies and other small insects around flowers, providing essential proteins and fats in their diets. In North America, at least 130 flowering plants are dependent upon various kinds of birds for their reproduction.

You can predict in a science-based way what kind of pollinator might drop in to visit any flower just by looking at it and paying attention. Taking note of a flower's color, shape, food rewards, and type of scent will go a long way toward predicting what animal (or wind or water) might pollinate a wildflower, or a flower in your garden. In the past this has been called the pollination syndrome approach. Applied to our ocotillo blossom above, it reveals a high likelihood that a tubular red, orange, or yellow blossom with abundant but dilute nectar and no scent will attract hummingbird visits but hardly any from bees, butterflies, or bats. The pollination syndrome concept has, however, been controversial among academic floral ecologists. I find it to be a wonderful and evocative entrée into "thinking like a pollinator" and understanding flowers.

Around the world, we find many other bird-pollinated flowers. True, hummingbirds are confined to our western hemisphere, but if you take a holiday to Hawaii, you might glimpse vibrant-colored birds with long, curved beaks, bills that fit certain blooms. These birds and blooms are found nowhere else. Hawaiian honeycreepers (Drepanididae, related to canaries) were once abundant in all Hawaiian forests, with 51 species. Today, due to forest destruction, predation from feral imported animals, and avian malaria, a dozen species are already extinct, with another fourteen imperiled.

Of these birds, perhaps emblematic of the group is the scarlet-colored 'I'iwi (*Vestiaria coccinea*), the third most commonly observed honeycreeper. The 'I'iwi has a sharply down-curved bill like most of the honeycreepers, an adaptation for probing into its preferred blossoms in search of nectar. The flowers are modified so that when the birds drink, a tiny amount of pollen is dusted onto their foreheads and transferred to the next flowers as they feed. The 'I'iwi is a spectacular sight when perched or feeding on the brilliant blue flowers of opelu (*Lobelia grayana*) at the Waikamoi Preserve on the island of Maui. Among the floral hosts of the honeycreepers are 125 species of lobelioids in six genera, e.g., *Clermontia, Cyanea, Lobelia*, and *Trematolobelia*. Several species of those genera are extinct on certain islands and endangered on others. All have curved floral tubes that closely fit the beak curvature of the various honeycreepers. If you visit Waimea Canyon on the island of Kauai, you can watch at least three different honeycreepers (including the 'I'iwi) gorging on nectar in the bright scarlet bowls that bloom on the Kauai bottlebrush tree (*Metrosideros waialealae*). It's a cousin of eucalyptus and myrtle.

Traveling down under, you find other beautiful birds with a sweet beak for nectar. During a stay with my family in bushlands near Canberra, Australia, I fondly remember hearing and seeing a noisy friarbird (*Philemon corniculatus*) feeding on nectar from the stout, curved, red, orange, or purple blossoms of *Grevillea* species. Here, we find abundant honeyeaters, sunbirds, Australian chats, and various colorful lorikeets, the latter a group of true parrots. You may have visited a zoo, such as the St. Louis Zoo, and had the pleasure of watching and feeding surreal rainbow lorikeets, enjoying them lap up sugar water from a cup with their brushy tongues.

In all, about 170 honeyeater species (Meliphagidae) are found throughout the Old World section of the Pacific basin. The family is extinct in Hawaii, but 70 species live in Australia proper. The dominant pollinating passerines (perching birds) in Australia belong to the honeyeaters, sunbirds (Nectariniidae, one tropical species but charming), thornbills (Acanthizidae), and silvereyes (Zosteropidae). None deliberately eat pollen. Pollen eating is restricted to true lorikeets (7 species in Australia and about 55 species through the Pacific basin).

The sunbirds are small songbirds, including about 132 species, more common in Africa and tropical Asia than in Australia. In the Republic of South Africa, you might be rewarded with visits of brilliant yellow, purple, and green, metallic-plumed sunbirds such as the variable sunbird

(*Cinnyris venustus*) feeding from flowers of cape honeysuckle, or from aloes in Tanzania. Arborescent forms of aloes, the tree aloes, are favorites of sunbirds across much of southern Africa. Other nectar-feeding birds from tropical islands in the Indian Ocean, the western Pacific, subtropical Africa, and back in Australia are the charming little passerines the white-eyes (Zosteropidae). Although insectivorous, they can be found feeding on flowers for nectar. One, the mountain black-eye (*Chlorocharis emiliae*) is frequently encountered feeding at *Rhododendron* blossoms on the slopes of Mt. Kinabalu, Sabah, Malaysia.

In almost all flowers pollinated by birds the stickiest pollen is deposited on the base of the bill (as in many hummingbirds), while the "drier," less greasy pollen (usually in the form of lobed or spiny pollen grains) is deposited between the feather barbules on the bird's forehead or breast. The main exception is the African bird-of-paradise plant (*Strelitzia reginae*), routinely planted as an ornamental in Orange County, California. In their native African homelands birds alight on the massive orange and blue blooms to sip nectar. The perch isn't a good one. Rather, it evolved to make the birds' feet slip. As the birds try to retain their grip, the sticky, white pollen clumps end up between the birds' toes. Well, it doesn't happen this way in the California gardens because the local nonadapted birds don't know how to work the flowers. Most of the pollen stays put, and these garden ornamentals rarely produce fruits.

Nectar Bats, Honey Possums, and Elephant Shrews

Something strange is happening at hummingbird feeders across southeastern Arizona. A few decades ago, bird-watchers living in Portal, Arizona, dutifully filled their hummingbird feeders with fresh sugar water every evening, to be ready for the early-bird hummingbird onslaught the next morning. By morning, however, their feeders were always drained dry. What was going on? The same thing has been happening in Tucson since about 2006. Who were the thirsty and mysterious nocturnal marauders?

They're bats! These intelligent animals had learned a new foraging trick and seem to be able to communicate the location of feeders to other bats in their roosts. Why spend a lot of energy flying many miles looking for cactus blooms when you can rob from sugar-water feeders conveniently supplied by birders? Each summer the bats dependably return to raid the bird feeders from about mid-August until early October. Two species of nectar bats, the southern long-nosed bat and the Mexican long-tongued bat (*Leptonycteris yerbabuenae* and *Choeronycteris mexicana*) are migrants to southern Arizona from regions farther south in Sonora, Mexico. Along US and Mexican flowering-nectar corridors the nectar bats roost by day in caves and mines, then by night forage dozens of miles to feed upon the sweet nectar of agaves (also called century plants) and columnar cacti.

Charismatic nectar bats have pointed faces like sleek greyhound dogs—unlike most bats. They also have long—up to half their body length—brush-tipped tongues. Watching them feed at the broad panicles of agaves, or the goblet-shaped, white flowers of saguaro, is awe-inspiring. What happens in the blink of an eye has been slowed down with high-speed cinematography in recent television documentaries. In less than one second, the bat hovers at the blossom and thrusts its entire head and neck into the bloom. Backing out of the flower, its fur is coated with pollen, later groomed off and eaten. Interestingly, these bats do not forage alone but in

A Mexican long-tongued bat (*Choeronycteris mexicana*) drinking nectar from flowers of a century plant (*Agave p. palmeri*)

groups of dozens. Wave after wave come to the melon-scented saguaro or coconut-like Palmer's agave (*Agave palmeri*) across the Sonoran and Chihuahuan Deserts of Arizona, New Mexico, and northern Sonora, Mexico. Both kinds of flowers offer copious amounts of nectar and lots of tasty pollen. Each saguaro flower may have as many as four thousand anthers and up to a teaspoon of nectar.

Just because you're not a bat and can't fly doesn't preclude flower-visiting in your feeding repertoire. A small but diverse group of wingless but adept climbing mammals routinely visit flowers for nectar and pollen. Perhaps the most amazing nonflying mammal to visit flowers is the honey possum (*Tarsipes rostratus*). An Australian, toothless marsupial, it is only 3–4 inches long and weighs about half as much as a house mouse. These animals have a long snout and tongue to reach into their favorite blossoms. The tongue is tipped with brushlike cells. Mostly nocturnal, they climb into the leathery foliage to reach the nectar contained inside the intricate, tall blooms of *Banksia*, *Adenanthos*, and *Calothamnus*. The honey-possum homelands are restricted to the heaths and shrublands of Western Australia.

In the Karoo region of South Africa, rodent pollinators, including two gerbils, visit the African lily (*Massonia depressa*). Rodent pollination in the southern hemisphere was first recorded on *Protea* shrubs (relatives of the Aussie *Banksia*). Also in South Africa, long-nosed cape rock shrews (*Elephantulus edwardii*), also known as elephant shrews because of their long noses, lick the nectar of the African pagoda lily (*Whiteheadia bifolia*) and pollinate its nondescript, small, green flowers. Within the southern hemisphere, there could be as many as fifty-nine species of nonflying mammals, rodents, that visit almost a hundred different plants for their sticky snacks.

Lizards in Your Begonias?

Well, not begonias, exactly, but a few flowers are visited by reptiles, lizards in fact. It happens most often on islands where pollinators are few and colonizing plants evolved in association with hardy animals that had the opportunistic eating habits required for survival under harsh, insular conditions. While the dinosaurs of the Cretaceous period may have watched early bees buzz by 65 to 100 million years ago, scientists now have examples of living flowers pollinated by lizards, of all things. The remote island of

Mauritius in the Indian Ocean is a distant twelve hundred miles from the southeastern coast of Africa. Once the home of the flightless dodo bird, Mauritius has plenty of other botanical and zoological oddities.

Many strange flowering plants live there and nowhere else. Several Mauritian plants have highly unusual nectars. One is truly bizarre. A kind of bellflower without a better common name, *Nesocodon mauritianus* has bloodred nectar. Two other endemic Mauritian species have red and yellow nectars. Even a nonchalant weekend gardener would recognize sanguineous nectar as peculiar. All floral nectars are colorless, right? What possible function could colored, or fluorescent, nectars have? Several Swiss researchers think they have the answer. Found nowhere else, cliff-loving day geckos (*Phelsuma ornata*) on Mauritius are regular visitors to the bellflowers and mallows, and their blooms. The colorful red and yellow nectars in these accessible flowers seem to function as honest signals to the geckos. The climb is worth the effort since sweet nectar is present. Additionally, the nectar may contain bitter chemicals meant to keep away omnipresent nectar-robbing ants, while remaining tasty fare for the lizards. Around the world, as many as sixty plants species, belonging to fourteen families, may have colored nectars.

Living on the Poor Knights islands near New Zealand are other lizard pollinators. Duvaucel's gecko (*Hoplodactylus duvaucelii*), New Zealand's largest native gecko, is a regular flower visitor. It feeds on Poor Knights flowers including ngaio (*Myoporum laetum*), the Poor Knights lily (*Xeronema callistemon*), with its large, red bottlebrush floral clusters, and the glorious red-flowered myrtle pohutukawa (*Metrosideros excelsa*). These twelve-inch-long geckos climb the plants in search of their abundant sweet nectar. Curiously, Duvaucel's gecko has evolved modified throat scales in response to its new flower-loving (anthophilous) behaviors. These are believed to be an adaptation to better catch, hold, and disperse pollen grains, in much the same way that bees evolved branched hairs, differentiating from the unbranched, simple hairs of their wasp ancestors.

Most of the lizard pollinators are geckos and are expert climbers, just like those little, nonflying mammals the pollinating honey possums and elephant shrews. Climbing skills, not wings, give these animals access to a new banquet of flower foods. It is not too surprising to learn that a few lizards raid flowers for nectar and may become semidependable pollinators. On some islands of the Seychelles, in the Indian Ocean, certain geckos (*Phelsuma*) visit rare palms including the "coco de mer" (*Lodoicea maldivica*), which produces the largest nut on the planet (its shell can be carved into a drinking bowl), and the mature fruit looks surprisingly like the lower half of a nubile woman (perhaps at least in the mind of a lonely sailor). It's hard to believe that each huge fruit (weighing in at sixty-six pounds) is produced by a thirsty lizard, and/or the wind, playing Cupid.

Man as Pollinator

It isn't just lizards, beetles, bees, and the tropical breezes that pollinate palm trees. People pollinate palms, too, and they have been doing so for millennia. Humans, or at least winged deities, as pollinators are figured in a twenty-five-hundred-year-old bas-relief carved into an Assyrian temple wall and now owned by the British Museum in London. The technique for pollinating date palms is something of an anachronism. Yes, it has been mechanized, but orchardists haven't changed the technique, invented three to seven thousand years ago. Today, just as their fathers and grandfathers did before them, in villages across Iraq, Iran, Syria, and Egypt, adolescent boys climb date palms (*Phoenix dactylifera*). Kids pollinating date palms anywhere is no fun. Date-palm fronds and trunks have curved and brittle spines that easily break off into unprotected flesh. With a curved, short metal knife the boys cut away the tough outer sheath (spathe) protecting the delicate receptive female flowers within. They cut off the tips of the flowering stems and carefully insert branches of pollen-laden male flowers they brought with them. Those laborious actions are repeated for each branch on the female trees and for every tree in the tall date-palm orchards. Pollen from the male blossoms fertilizes the female flowers. The delectable sugary dates follow months later.

Although not climbed by armies of barefoot young boys, the many acres of Medjool Date Palms, familiar to Southern California drivers zooming through the Mojave Desert cities of Indio and Twentynine Palms, are still pollinated by hand by farmworkers climbing on skinny wooden ladders into the feathery crowns of the tall palms.

It's a logical progression. People can and have learned to become pollinators, too. By necessity, we have learned to pollinate flowers to produce foods and bring their special beauty into our lives. Humans learned to pollinate flowers in antiquity, in the case of date palms and likely other agricultural crops, to increase yields. Sometimes in the past, entire cultures have forgotten how to do it, forgotten the secrets of hand-pollinating flowers, assuring yields and seeds for future plantings. For modern, especially Western, cultures, people fulfilled pollinator roles following the realization of flowering-plant sexuality by England's Nehemiah Grew (1641–1712), the binomial and plant sexual classification system of Linnaeus (1707–78), and the marvelous book and copper-plate flower engravings of Germany's Christian Konrad Sprengel (1750–1816). A big jump in the use, spread, and appreciation of garden hybrid roses and numerous lilies followed soon after. Irishman Arthur Dobbs investigated the garden tulip and hand-pollinated them around 1750. This amazing man was also a North Carolina landowner and former governor, a neighbor of Jonathan Swift's, the discoverer of the Venus flytrap (*Dionaea muscipula*), and ardently dedicated to the search for a Northwest Passage through the Canadian Arctic.

We can think of the last two hundred years as a frenzied time of people hybridizing different things, or creating new varieties of garden and cut flowers. Surprisingly then, even with the popularity of gardening, few modern American gardeners know how to make the simplest crosses, or even how to pollinate squash or zucchini blossoms in need of pollen when the right bees (*Peponapis* or *Xenoglossa*) aren't around.

Later in this book, we will learn the origins and extent of plant breeding. The corporate and academic plant breeders and agronomists today make carefully controlled crosses between parental plants. They bag flowers to isolate female blossoms and to collect and store their pollen. Sometimes they shoot DNA-laden gold particles into the nuclei of leaves or tissue-culture plantlets to bypass the sexual process, creating new strains or hybrids. Today, in places in China women climb high into apple trees, brushes and pollen in hand, and provide a workforce of human bees. Their lands are now poisoned with insecticides and too few honey bees or wild bees are left to pollinate the flowers that can become fruit. That is one explanation of this peculiar plight. Another, perhaps equally likely, is that nobody considered the self-infertility of apple clones. A given clone is compatible only with certain other varieties and cannot produce a single seed or fruit from its own pollen.

Closer to home, I'm willing to bet that gardeners might learn new tricks and try their hand at being bees and other pollinators. Indigenous North American farmers and some recent Hispanic immigrants living in the southwestern United States have not completely abandoned or forgotten their ancestral gardening ways. Get out your VegiBee or old-fashioned artist's brush for cucurbits and other vegetables. Try creating your own blue rose or fancy tulip, something that hasn't arisen in nature.

Out of necessity, curiosity, and our innate drive to create and manage beauty, with almost godlike manipulative powers in the case of modern plant breeding, we *are* pollinators. Begun in the Fertile Crescent countries seven millennia ago with date palms, and longer for the cereal crops, our matchmaker talents with the flowers of agricultural plants continue into modern times, kept alive by seed-saving farmers. Throughout the history of *Homo sapiens* we have been and are on-again, off-again pollinators, intermittent go-betweens in the world of flowering plants. Curiously, we do something that flower-visiting insects, birds, bats, and others won't do, or can't do. We collect, multiply, and hoard the plants we love for the unique beauty of their flowers, to ornament the land around our homes, our interior living and work spaces, and, of course, each other.

PART II

GROWING, BREEDING, AND SELLING

A trio of gerbera daisies (*Gerbera* spp.)

CHAPTER 4

Pleasure Gardens Ancient and Modern

Inner petals of a rose (*Rosa* sp.)

It's early October and across the Eastern Seaboard and adjoining states the annual fall planting race is off and running. Spreading like a wave from the eastern to western coasts of America and Canada, the planting urge advances along with the chill in the autumn air and the changing leaves. Old-timers are consulting their calendars and thumbing well-worn copies of the venerated *Old Farmer's Almanac*, looking up suitable planting days and checking weather forecasts. All are digging up their flower beds to stuff in tulips, daffodils, crocuses, and other popular bulbs.

Once the daytime highs hit sixty degrees Fahrenheit or a bit lower, this seems to be the right time to add bulbs, ensuring colorful blooms the following April, May, or June. The same autumn rituals also occur in gardens across Western Europe. Bulbs, tubers, and corms add fresh, new spring colors, a vibrant rebirth after the long, cold monotony of winter whites and naked brown branches. It's all a bit ironic when you consider the history of hunting and gathering.

Ten thousand years ago our distant ancestors used sharpened and fire-hardened digging sticks of wood for planting and harvesting wild, edible bulbs. People living around the Mediterranean still eat the bulbs of the wild relatives of our grape hyacinths (*Muscari*), and tribes in Oregon still think that slow-baked blue quamash (*Camassia*) taste like sweet potatoes. Today, we use cherished worn garden trowels to put domesticated bulbs into the soil to feed our sense of the aesthetic, creating the seasonal yet ephemeral beauty of flowers.

We live in an era in which most of us appreciate a seasonal bed of ornamental flowers without feeling it's a waste of land that should have been used to grow more food. It wasn't always that way, and some prominent cultures on this planet still don't see much value in a garden of the pretty but inedible. Where and how often did our species stop gobbling roots and shoots long enough to think, "This would look nice growing around my hut?" Which cultures and civilizations were the earliest to encourage flower hunting and growing for their own sake, and what have we inherited from them? We'll soon find out.

Out of Africa

Our primate ancestors foraged for flowers and fruits as part of their omnivorous diets. No doubt our own sweet-tooth preferences began with these flower- and fruit-munching ancestors. We can reasonably imagine our hominid ancestors of 6 million years ago pausing by a patch of scented and colorful flowers, gently picking one, and sucking out its sweet nectar just as children do today with Japanese honeysuckles.

The use of digging sticks may predate that of stone tools, but because they are less durable, they did not leave a record. Sticks were widely used in Mesoamerica to dig out underground roots and flower bulbs, poke out burrowing animals, or search for tasty insect larvae. While these sticks remained in use by the Kooris of Australia well into the twentieth century, Europeans, Asians, and Africans replaced them with the hoe and their draft-animal-powered plows.

Did the invention of digging tools open the door to agriculture first, and gardening later? I believe it did. Hunting and gathering were gender-skewed in early nomadic cultures. Women were frequently the gatherers of all plant materials for food, medicines, clothing, cordage, and containers. Women typically prepared plants and animals as food, so it is almost assured that the first farmers and gardeners were women.

Cultures that never invented, or borrowed, agricultural technology never created ornamental gardens. Examples of such nongardening societies include, but are not limited, to the !Kung people (San) of the Kalahari Desert, the Kayapó of Brazil, the Australian Kooris, and pastoralists such as the Maasai (or Masai) of Kenya and Tanzania. No culture with agriculture develops pleasure gardens unless the collective belly is full. Estimates range widely, but perhaps these people ate as many as five thousand calories per day. Modern dieters take note: consuming two thousand calories per day, a supposed "ideal" food intake, is based upon our largely sedentary, couch-potato society, one that does not chase down and kill ferocious, large animals. People do not waste limited arable land on beautiful but needless luxuries (flowers) unless they are well fed at the moment and their granaries are full. Fertile soil is a precious resource not to be wasted on potted pretties.

With the advent of agriculture by the world's earliest civilizations in the Fertile Crescent region between the Tigris and Euphrates Rivers, these cultures had time left for relaxation and more creative projects. Plants with attractive flowers were grown first as crops (flax, chickpea, lentil, and bitter vetch) in the Fertile Crescent. However, the earliest and most important food crops were wild grasses domesticated in the region (emmer wheat, einkorn, and barley), all of which have nonshowy, small, wind-pollinated flowers. Both grain grasses and legumes were likely planted in rows, making them easier to tend and harvest. This may have been the forerunner of linear gardens or border designs.

To be clear, we need to contrast what seems to be a universal human appreciation of flowers in extinct hunter-gatherer societies versus what happened once small camps became villages, then cities with flourishing early civilizations. An interesting similarity exists between the Kooris in Australia, who never developed agriculture, and some of our Amerindian tribes that domesticated a few species (corn, tobacco, beans, and squash). Both isolated cultures have wide-ranging myths and tales about animals but few if any flower myths or stories. A few traditional peoples spoke about the origin of flowers that are strange looking (red-flowered mistletoes and red waratah bouquets), or vegetable foods (tropical water lilies). These and other nonagrarian societies speak of red flowers as signifying spilled blood, understandable in nomadic hunting cultures. In contrast is the compelling history from ancient to modern times of civilizations repeatedly using agricultural knowledge to support gardening for pleasure. First we must ask ourselves, What makes us want to grow a lily in a pot?

One way to think about our attraction to the beauty and gestalt of flowers is to consider what may have occurred in our distant hominid past. Flowers and fruits are not so unlike in how we perceive them. Both open flowers and ripe fruits have bright colors (saturated yellows, orange, reds, blues) making them stand out from the contrasting but homogeneous backdrops of green leaves or brown soils. We see and smell them from a distance. We easily associate their shapes, colors, and scents with gustatory experiences and pleasure. When we bite into fruits or flowers, their sweetness fills our mouths, and soon other flavors take hold. Some flowers smell just like ripe fruits, and vice versa, because they have overlapping scent and flavor chemistries. This may explain why we, as a species, are highly attracted, perhaps innately, to flowers even though they are not usually nutritious or a satisfying meal.

Some psychologists and anthropologists insist that flowers produce immediate and long-term effects on human emotions and social behaviors and may even enhance memory formation. This has been demonstrated in controlled studies, as we'll explore later. It's perhaps not a stretch to realize that flowers may also target their beauty and charms at us, not just insects, birds, or bats. Plants may be seducing us to do their bidding, making us serve their sedentary sex lives. In the distant past, insects unknowingly selected for those flowers that were colorful, the showiest and most rewarding. Over the last four centuries, the artificial evolution of flowers via human meddling in plant affairs has changed many wildflowers into domesticated gardening favorites. Artificial selection was rapid because the emerging sciences of economic and reproductive botany helped define plant geography and sexuality. However, human selection and the placement of flowering plants in urban gardens are much, much older.

The World's Oldest Gardens

The most ancient civilizations of Assyria, Babylonia, and Sumeria, along the Fertile Crescent (about ten thousand years ago), had gardens, likely lavish ones, for their ruling elites in their palaces and temples. Recorded historical details about these gardens are mostly wanting, so we must rely upon meager evidence later interpreted by archaeologists following their excavations. At Tell Hassuna, downstream from the ancient city of Nineveh, on the river Tigris (modern Iraq), there are deposits of layer upon layer of agricultural discards. Similar finds have been excavated at Tell Halaf, Arpachiya, and other sites. Their agricultural plantings may have included small yard or kitchen gardens. Even the warlike Assyrians enjoyed and created gardens. Inscriptions tell of Assyrian king Tiglath-Pileser I (ruled 1114–1076 BC), who conquered foreign lands, then returned with cedar, likkarin, and algum (sandalwood and cypress) trees, establishing a sort of early botanical garden with trees from faraway lands.

In the *Epic of Gilgamesh*, the oldest work of literature that has survived (engraved on clay tablets in cuneiform found at Kuyunjik), is a detailed description of an idealized sacred vineyard. It could also have been a garden. The epic poem describes a landscape garden or parklike area, including a cedar mount and sanctuary where the gods dwelt.

The use of flowering plants in Egypt reaches into remote antiquity and continues fervently to the present day. Since the days of the pharaohs, the Egyptians were skilled herbalists, using plants in gardening, bouquets and garlands, flavoring foods, and in flower-based perfumes, cosmetics, and medicines. A carved ivory panel on a casket from the king's tomb shows the boy king Tutankhamun and his queen holding floral bouquets in a stylized setting.

In a hot, dry climate such as ancient Egypt's what could feel better than sitting in the shade of a large sycamore fig (*Ficus sycomorus*) growing at the center of one's walled courtyard garden? However, let's first consider those large gardens associated with temples such as those at Karnak or Luxor. They must have been truly spectacular, based on the detailed and elaborate paintings found on tomb and temple walls. We also know some details about the private gardens of wealthier Egyptians. They cultivated formal gardens harboring ornamental plants along with a few edible, fruit-bearing kinds. Trees were planted in tidy, straight rows and flowers arranged in square beds or along straight borders. A rectilinear geometry prevailed, as illustrated in the colorful tomb paintings.

An amazing Egyptian garden was created by Nebamun, a scribe for King Thutmose IV (c. 1400 BC), who lived in ancient Thebes. He constructed his courtyard garden around existing large trees. His tomb paintings reveal two date palms towering over his pink, mud-brick house. In many homes of this period the garden predominates and the house is often reduced to a portico. In the tomb of Nebamun (c. 1380 BC), a wall painting shows a fish pond with floating water-lily flowers. Nearby is a flowering border with associated trees: sycamore, carica figs, and fruiting date palms. Hathor, the sycamore goddess, is shown carrying figs to accompany Nebamun into the afterlife.

A splendid Theban residence garden was that of Ineni, a master builder for King Thutmose I (1528–1510 BC). The tomb walls were not expansive enough to reveal the entire garden layout, but Ineni made certain there was a hieroglyphic accounting of its splendor: 170 date palms; 120 dom palms; 73 sycamore figs; 12 unidentified vines; 31 persea trees (*Mimusops laurifolia*); 2 moringa trees; 16 carob trees; a Christ's-thorn (*Paliurus spina-christi*); 10 tamarisk trees; 2 myrtles; and a few others. Whomever Ineni enslaved, they must have been kept busy watering those plantings using the shaduf, a ceramic pot affixed to a long pole attached to a stand and pivot point. Shadufs are still commonly used today across the Egyptian countryside for raising water. Numerous tomb paintings suggest that the ancient Egyptians adored their flowers. We find the scented, blue and white water lilies (*Nymphaea*) in their pools. Much later, the Egyptians acquired the pink-and-white Indian lotus (*Nelumbo nucifera*) by trading with the East. The borders of herbs at the gardens' edges included cornflower and opium poppies. Also depicted is the mandrake, whose showy yellow fruits would have complemented the blue of the cornflowers and the crimson poppies. This pattern of yellow, blue, and red was a popular herbaceous border in these ancient gardens.

Several exotic (nonnative) plants from distant lands were purposefully brought to Egyptian gardens. The pomegranate tree provided lush red flowers as well as tart, juicy fruits. Other trees included the persea tree and the Egyptian garden favorite, the sycamore fig. Somewhat later, olive trees were added, as seen in garden paintings. Ancient royals such as Queen Hatshepsut had a taste for exotic flowering plants. She brought one type of incense tree to her temple garden at Deir el-Bahri. Some pharaohs demonstrated horticultural interests, such as the far-ranging expeditions of Thutmose III in Asia Minor. Unfortunately, we have few records of what the presumably lavish gardens associated with most Egyptian royal palaces may have looked like.

The Egyptians also had sufficient space to plant small herb gardens. Fragrant chamomile, with its small white and yellow flowers, was commonly grown and was used to anoint the mummified body of Rameses II.

From a trash dump excavated at the sacred animal necropolis at Saqqara, numerous medicinal herbs, now grown for their attractive flowers, have been found. These include acacia, apricot, basil, chrysanthemum, Egyptian plum, flax, pomegranate, and ashwagandha (*Withania somnifera*). Yes, the ancient Egyptians were master gardeners, but they had serious competitors a continent away, and each knew nothing of the other's existence.

Early Chinese Gardens

The earliest gardens in China are as old as the most ancient Egyptian gardens. The significance of flowers in Chinese culture is reflected in names from antiquity, such as *hua*, the word for flower. The ideal garden became a "timeless paradise" as a retreat for scholars and hermits alike. Among the most cherished flowers grown in Chinese gardens since antiquity are chrysanthemums, gardenias, forsythias, magnolias, pinks, rhododendrons, roses, and wisterias. The earliest Chinese monograph on the chrysanthemum dates from the start of the twelfth century. Many of the cultivated flowers of China are tree flowers, such as peach, plum, camellia, magnolia, and tree peony. At this same time in the West, there was little more than the rose. Flowers of peach, chrysanthemum, lotus, peony, magnolia, and tiger lily have been grown in Chinese gardens since at least 800 to 1000 BC, as early as the Chou Dynasty. The rest of the flowers we've come to associate with Chinese gardens were already in widespread use by AD 1000 in the Song Dynasty. Indeed, domesticated garden blooms have a long association with Chinese culture, mirrored in its rich arts and literature traditions. China's floriculture and agriculture contributed ginseng, the camellias, azaleas and rhododendrons, mulberries, the persimmon, rice, tea, and all the various kinds of *Citrus* fruits to the rest of the world.

A favorite place among my travels is the faithful replica of an ancient, yet relatively late in China's long history, private garden. The Lan Su Chinese Garden ("garden of awakening orchids") in downtown Portland, Oregon, encloses a full, walled city block. This garden reproduces a tranquil and contemplative environment with its replicated home, courtyard gardens, and a scholar's study. It is modeled after a Chinese Ming Dynasty (1368–1644) home in Suzhou, a city in Jiangsu Province. Here, are still pools, carved and natural limestone rocks, flowering trees, water lilies, colorful carp, pebbled walkways with inset mosaic art, and dividing stone walls.

Asian gardens are more meditative and less reliant on big, bold blooms than are gardens devised by Western civilizations. Here, flowering plants are understood as beautiful even when they are barren, appreciated equally for their leaves and stems. The use of nonflowering elements is seen especially in the ways Chinese gardens use decorative rocks and boulders. The large, water-eroded boulders in some Chinese gardens are the famous Taihu stones from the lake of the same name. They are gnarled, full of jagged holes, and said to look like goblins or strange beasts. Mostly, they seem to represent distant, ragged mountain vistas. Nothing exactly like the Taihu stones appears in other gardens around the world. Wealthy Chinese went to great efforts to dredge them out of lake bottoms or to "repurpose" them from older gardens.

The Lan Su garden re-creation represents a spiritual utopia for a wealthy Chinese family of this era. This soothing place, with every detail masterfully designed, allowed the family to escape the worries of everyday life. Here, they could meditate and rest, becoming refreshed and energized by connecting with a stylized version of nature. A visit to Lan Su always has a profoundly calming effect on me, makes me slow down and take notice of minute and graceful details of this confined and scripted version of idealized nature from ancient China. Digital camera in hand, I pause and compose tranquil scenes through the viewfinder.

Masterful examples of Chinese public gardens are found in the West Lake region of Hangzhou, or the imperial family compound and retreat at Chengde, north of the Great Wall. Other famous garden sites are the Yuyuan gardens in Shanghai, or the Shi Zi Lin, the "stone lion grove," in Suzhou. In Shi Zi Lin we find an elegant, small courtyard with typical elements used in many Chinese gardens of this period. This little landscape contained carefully set mosaic pavements of shiny black and white stones, a raised, octagonal stone planter surrounding a cherry tree, a gourd-shaped doorway, ornate filigreed windows, large natural rocks set in place, and various living bamboos.

If these examples seem a bit claustrophobic or confined, it is because their designers tried to shrink the great outdoors, immense landscapes of mountain chains, rivers, and lakes into small, human-scale habitations. This ingenious attempt to miniaturize nature also included the use of mirrors and zigzag paths to make the garden spaces appear larger and longer than they actually were. The gardens are divided or compartmentalized by the clever use of white, gray, or red walls, with borders and shallow pools. Bamboo thickets and trees cast shadows onto walls that are also part of the intended design. The famous "moon doors" and windows in the shape of fans, leaves, vases, a pomegranate fruit, or a stylized flower are common. Objects are framed and outlined, with fanciful depictions of flowers, birds, and mythical animals, such as dragons. Another aspect of miniaturization is the elaborate *p' un' tsoi*, little trees and shrubs grown in ceramic planters, comparable to Japanese containerized bonsai. In China, favorite garden flowers are treasured for their symbolic meanings in art, literature, and society. The peony represents springtime, health, distinction, and passing one's school exams. Flowering plums represent happiness and friendships. In China, the shrubs that we call magnolias are known as jade halls, so they were planted close to buildings.

American gardens have been greatly enriched by ancient and modern Chinese horticulture. The Chinese were the first to import and develop fruit trees (cherries, pears, peaches, and plums) from Persia (now Iran) or other Mediterranean countries. These trees were imported by caravans along the famous Silk Road, extending four thousand miles from China to the Mediterranean, especially during the Han Dynasty (206 BC–AD 220). The Chinese turned these fruit and timber trees, once used to make furniture, into blossoming ornamentals. We have also benefited from the Chinese love of early-flowering native trees and shrubs. This includes their deciduous magnolias and the wintersweet (*Chimonanthus*), which are often in bloom before March 21. The Chinese adored flowering sprigs of wintersweet as hair ornaments, and they were also used to perfume linen cupboards. It's the Chinese who gave the world the moutan, or tree peony, flowering crab apple, daylily, camellia, and daphne as domesticated plants. Do you admire or perhaps grow tea roses? The Chinese grew them because their aroma reminded them of drinking tea. Lastly, would we recognize the exquisite impressionistic paintings of Claude Monet without his lovely Chinese wisterias?

Some of the flowers most revered by the Chinese have never been popular in the West or in Japan. In China, one of the hardy native *Cymbidium* orchids is a symbol of spring, and the plants are still grown by the millions each year in ornamental pots. The Chinese love these orchids for their fragrant flowers (not sweet but with coumarins, chemicals evoking the scent of a freshly mown lawn), and for their undulating leaves (common in classic Chinese paintings). We don't care much for this terrestrial orchid in the West. Its flowers are too small and drab for our tastes. The Chinese are also charmed by the edible persimmon (*Diospyros kaki*) because its dark, gnarled branches and twigs are covered in delicate, velvety, white blossoms each spring. They plant these trees in traditional courtyards. But all we want is their softened, delicious orange fruits in autumn.

Later expeditions to China by Europeans brought more plants the Chinese admired and immortalized in their landscape paintings and poetry but infrequently domesticated. These included the wild rhododendrons, various lilies, primroses, roses, silenes, and carnations that would be used in the West as breeding stock for hybrid blooms. The list goes on and on, but in America the flower poems and tales that we cherish come instead from two great ancient civilizations that developed in the Mediterranean basin.

Gods and Goddesses in the Garden

Roaming the hills of mainland Greece, the Greek isles, or the scrublands of Israel in a year when the rains come, one is awed by the brilliant displays of wildflowers: *Adonis, Anemone, Anthyllis, Cistus, Cyclamen, Iris, Nerium, Papaver, Prunus,* and *Ranunculus*. Many of these plants have bloodred or deep purple flowers visited by pollinating beetles and are the stuff of classic Greek and Roman lore. Several of our favorite garden blooms gave rise to myths in which the hero becomes a flower, or his blood stains a blossom we know and love (e.g., narcissus, peony, hyacinth, Ajax delphinium, windflower).

Classical Greco-Roman mythology comprises a body of myths that has insinuated itself into Western art. This includes the tales found within the Homeric epics (the *Iliad* and the *Odyssey*), along with the written tragedies of Aeschylus, Euripides, and Sophocles. As the Romans adopted and absorbed Greek myths, their poets, such as Ovid, wrote about the gods and goddesses and their earthly encounters with flowers.

The windflower, genus *Anemone*, in the buttercup family, is a common red, pink, blue, and purple garden flower native to Europe and Asia. Windflowers, along with unrelated fragrant, resin-bearing trees gathered for incense, are the subjects of Greek myths such as the one about Myrrha, Aphrodite, and Adonis: The queen of Cyprus claimed that her daughter, Myrrha, was more beautiful than the goddess of love, Aphrodite. The goddess was understandably outraged. She caused Myrrha to lust after her father, King Cinyras. Myrrha drugged her father every night and subsequently became pregnant. The king tried to execute his daughter and chased her across many of the Mediterranean lands. In turn, Aphrodite changed Myrrha into the first myrrh tree (*Commiphora myrrha*), the source of the resin myrrh burned as incense in the Holy Land. King Cinyras attacked the tree with his sword and a ravishing baby boy fell out. Aphrodite claimed the boy and named him Adonis. As a beautiful young man, Adonis became Aphrodite's lover, but was also desired by Persephone the goddess of the underworld and spring growth.

Gored by a wild boar during a hunt, poor Adonis died at a tender age. The love-struck Aphrodite cried over his corpse. Her immortal tears mixed with the blood pouring from his wounds and turned it into flowering crown anemone plants (*Anemone coronaria*), with their red sepals and nearly black stamens. For millennia, Greek women swooned over the legend of the beautiful Adonis. The Adonia were summer festivals celebrated in Greek towns during late July after all the spring wildflowers had dried up in the summer heat. The female celebrants (often courtesans and prostitutes) carried pots of sprouted seeds or cut flowers to the festival, which included loud partying and drinking binges. Later, the dried seedlings and withered blossoms were tossed into the ocean on a spring morning, in remembrance of the sea-born but lovesick Aphrodite, and the myth of returning the dead Adonis to Aphrodite.

Curiously, the men of classical Greece seemed largely uninterested in private pleasure gardens, unlike the later aristocrats of imperial Rome. The beloved Greek myths addressed the origins of agriculture (e.g., Hades and Persephone), but so do the myths of all ancient agrarian societies. Think of the almost universal Garden of Eden story told by Semitic-speaking peoples. But the Greek myths had two unique features adopted by the later Romans: First, the Greeks viewed useful trees (for timber, spices, resins, food, etc.) as feminine, representing the metamorphoses of beautiful females (Phyllis, Myrrha, Daphne, and others) into graceful, woody plants. Second, herbs bearing colorful or fragrant blossoms were more masculine in nature. They represented the transformations of males (usually but not always "pretty boys," including Orchis, Hyacinthus, Narcissus, and Adonis). However, these wildflowers were and still are common weeds appearing in agricultural fields throughout the Mediterranean. In many of the extinct religions of this region, people believed that flowers appeared the spring after a human male was sacrificed. If the flowers had any further use in the culture, it was in perfumes or as adornment for people or sacrificial animals at religious festivals.

The only major deity in the Greek pantheon to own a nice garden was the ever-unpopular goddess Hera, with her tree of golden apples in the Hesperides garden. As for Hades's attempt to garden and beautify the underworld, his Elysian fields weren't exactly pleasant or pretty places. They were envisioned as wastelands choked with one or more species of asphodels (*Asphodelus*, drab relatives of true lilies). In Greece, asphodels were typically associated with fallow and infertile places. Even wild goats don't care to eat them. No, the Roman Empire was the place to visit, or look to, for gardening inspiration and innovations.

Planted in Ash:
The Roman Gardens of Pompeii and Herculaneum

The cataclysmic eruption of Mt. Vesuvius, only five miles from modern Naples, Italy, on August 24 of AD 79 buried the prosperous coastal Roman cities of Pompeii and Herculaneum, killing an estimated sixteen thousand people. Here frozen instantaneously in time are remarkable, although gruesome, casts of bodies in pumice and tufa ash, along with homes, intact art, and possessions. Homes of these wealthy Roman citizens were architectural and cultural marvels. Frescoes and intricately colored tile mosaics on floors and courtyard walls depict elaborate and verdant garden scenes. Delicate ivy (*Hedera*) and stylized grapevines along with other woody climbers were used as decorative elements. Most of the homes of Pompeii and Herculaneum had beautiful gardens. Typically, these mansions had central, open-air courtyards surrounded by Greek peristyles (columns). The gardens also had porticos (covered walkways), with spacious atria (large open spaces) allowing light and air to enter the buildings.

Some houses had a garden nymphaeum, with its fountain and a monument within an artificial grotto consecrated to the water nymphs. This sanctuary was filled with flowering plants, sculptures, stone fountains, balustrades, and fresco paintings that were uncannily three-dimensional. These trompe l'oeil depictions tricked the viewer into believing that two dimensions could become three, giving people the illusion that they could walk into a larger, more sumptuous garden.

Wealthy Romans adored water effects. Their ponds contained aquatic plants including water lilies, reeds, and rushes and were well stocked with colorful fish. Conquering Romans brought both the blue and the white water lilies from Egypt. The surviving paintings and mosaics provide evidence that Romans were fond of oleanders, myrtles, and bay laurels, grown mostly for their ornamental and scented foliage but also for their flowers. Preserved tree branches have been identified as examples of olive, lemon, and apple trees grown inside the atrium of one home. When these trees bloomed in spring, that atrium would have been colorful as well as pleasantly fragrant. Such was the country-villa lifestyle of the Roman elite, wealthy merchants, senators, and emperors.

Ornamental gardening, in ancient cultures, universally began as a pastime of the powerful nobility, or wealthy few, performed on a large scale at first. Imagine the expense of a lavish personal garden inside crowded imperial Rome. The epigrammatist Martial (c. 38–c. 102), of Nero's Rome, complained that his own garden was so small and crowded that his violets couldn't smile, and his figs were frightened to expand. The Roman elite could afford to import beautiful plants or engage in abundant leisure-time pursuits that became our own gardening traditions.

The Romans had quite a taste for the sort of kitschy garden ornaments many of us still fancy today, including balls, obelisks, pyramids, spirals, and those often grotesque little ceramic statues and figurines. Pliny's *Natural History* and Martial gave credit to Roman citizen Cnaeus Matius Calvinus for introducing the first topiary sculptures into Roman gardens. Woody plants typically used for ancient and modern topiary pruning include the European box (*Buxus sempervirens*), bay laurel (*Laurus nobilis*), holly (*Ilex* spp.), myrtles (*Eugenia* or *Myrtus*), common privet (*Ligustrum*), and yews (*Taxus* spp). Pause and give a moment of thanks to Roman citizen Cnaeus as your boat drifts past the hippopotamus, pig, poodle, bear, elephant, and other living topiary sculptures outside Disneyland's beloved "It's a Small World" theme park ride since its opening in 1966. I knew it well, having grown up in Southern California only a few miles from Walt Disney's original Magic Kingdom.

We can draw a simple lesson from these ancient cultures, their appreciation of flowers, and how they gardened. If a culture had agriculture and a polytheistic religion, several of their deities were often associated with local wildflowers. Within each culture a flower became associated with an aspect of agriculture (e.g., narcissus and wild gladiolus), or irrigation water for the crops (e.g., water lily and lotus). Many of these plants moved across the Old World via cultural diffusion. As a wild shrub, the pomegranate grows only in central northern Africa (Libya), yet potted pomegranates and their crimson blossoms in artworks and on porcelain pots are associated with several dynasties in ancient China.

Imperial Rome fell in the fifth century, and gardening for pleasure in Western Europe went into a similar decline until much later in the Middle Ages and later during the Renaissance. The standard reason given by historians of gardening and the history of cultivated flowers is that pleasure gardening and the excessive use of flowers at banquets and weddings were associated with pagan degeneracy of the emperor(s) and the aristocracy. Flowers were only for church altars, or as medicines, and flower culture, such as it was, and flowers retreated inside walled monastery gardens. The people of Western Europe descend from many Roman colonies. We will see how they once again acquired a love of flowers, but first let's cross the Atlantic and witness the rise and fall of a genuine but surprising flower-adoring culture.

Aztec Marigolds

When it comes to the Aztecs, actually the Mexica of the Triple Alliance in central Mexico (c. 1300–1521), we seem to think only of the brutality during the sixteenth century when Spanish conquistadors took the last Aztec emperor, Moctezuma II (Montezuma), prisoner. We also imagine the horrific bloody rituals atop tall step-pyramids such as the Aztec Templo Mayor (Main Temple) in Mexico City. This site, among others, was used for human sacrifices. It's likely that these honored sacrificial victims wore floral garlands. The Aztecs were avid gardeners. Flowers formed a huge part of their culture. They planted and grew flowers in profusion, especially in their capital, Tenochtitlán, the incredible island city in the middle of former Lake Texcoco. That island is now mostly covered over, merely part of the sprawling Mexico City suburbs. Hundreds of years ago the island had urban gardens for commoners along with royal temple gardens constructed by the Aztec nobility. The Aztec culture gave Spanish conquerors garden flowers we now take for granted, many of which later spread into Europe and India.

How do we know that the Aztecs grew flowers? The greater part of

Aztec lyric poetry praised and described true marigolds (*Tagetes* spp.), dahlias (*Dahlia* spp.), tube roses (*Polianthes*), zinnias (*Zinnia*), and other blossoms of the subtropics, mountain pine forests, and deserts within their empire. The Aztecs may also have used bromeliads, cacti, and yuccas in their color-coordinated public and private gardens.

When Hernán Cortés, with his six hundred foot soldiers and fifteen horsemen, invaded Tenochtitlán in mid-August 1521, the Spaniards couldn't believe their eyes. Not only did the Aztec capital have an estimated population of fifteen thousand households, it was a unique garden paradise. The architectural splendor, wide, straight roads, canals, ponds, and bridges were unlike anything in Spain at the time. Even the battle-hardened Cortés was moved to describe the Aztec gardens in the nearby Aztec city of Chalco:

> Gardens are the largest, freshest, and most beautiful that were ever seen. They have a circuit of two leagues [six miles] and through the middle flows a pleasant stream of water. At distances of two bow-shots are buildings surrounded by grounds planted with fruit trees of various kinds, with many shrubs and odorous flowers. Truly the whole place is wonderful for its pleasantness and its extent.

The Aztec historian Ixtlilxóchitl described the garden splendors of King Nezahualcoyotl of the neighboring city-state Texcoco. The king of Ixtapan had a taste for elaborate mazes, outdoor baths, irrigation canals, numerous fountains, square flower beds with marigolds, various trees, and plantings that included over two thousand pines. Many different flowers, especially scented blooms, and trees, both local and those imported from far away, were used in garden design. Moctezuma I decreed the establishment of an extensive botanical garden at Oaxtepec. Entire shrubs and small trees, with their root balls wrapped in mats, were collected, transported, then planted in his royal garden.

Floating Gardens of Mexico City

Created by the Aztecs, and a World Heritage site since 1987, the famous floating gardens of Xochimilco still exist. An extensive system of canals was first created at the former Lago de Texcoco, a natural lake within the Valley of Mexico. Only vestiges of ancient Lake Texcoco exist, as salt marshes, three miles east of present-day Mexico City. When the Aztecs built their capital on an islet near the western edge of Lake Texcoco, they began to farm. The island was small but they ingeniously expanded the area available for growing crops by turning part of the lake into new arable land. Branches from a native juniper tree of the marshes, the *ahuejote*, were cut and tied together forming large rafts onto which lake-bed mud and soil were heaped. The rafts sank and new rafts were constructed atop them. More and more soil rafts, forming artificial islands, were constructed. Vegetable and flower crops were planted on these "floating gardens," known in Spanish as *chinampas*, a unique agricultural technique devised by the pre-Hispanic peoples of the region a thousand years ago. Although many have been lost to urbanization or soccer fields, the remaining *chinampas* are actively cultivated today, filled with ornamental bougainvilleas, cacti, dahlias, and even dwarf bonsai trees. They are one of the most productive and sustainable farmlands anywhere in the world.

From nine massive docks, two hundred small, nonmotorized, wide, flat-bottomed boats called *trajineras* float along the calm waters of the canals. In the past they moved goods, but today they carry thousands of Mexico City weekend visitors and tourists from many countries. Looking like wide-bodied, roofed gondolas, they are whimsically painted with every color imaginable in floral and geometric designs. Historically, they were decorated with arches of living flowers and branches of *ahuejote* juniper trees. Each vessel is equipped with a long wooden table and chairs for eating and drinking. The floating gardens of Xochimilco have a party atmosphere, especially on weekends and holidays when there seem to be more boats than open water. Nevertheless, charm is mixed in with all the commercialism. Here you can buy flowers for your sweetheart from a woman paddling by in a small canoe or be serenaded by floating loud mariachi bands or attempt to be romantic while lazily cruising along the surreal waterways.

The Gardens of Paradise

Drawing upon garden designs first developed in the ancient cities of western Asia (Iran) and Roman influences surviving in North Africa, the Muslims quickly developed their own unique gardening styles. The most important flower in the Persian garden is the rose. The Persians' name for the rose, *gul*, is also their generic word for "flower." Fruit trees became integral and major features in all Islamic gardens, especially orange and other citrus trees imported from India and China. Their blossoms would have added a heady sweetness to the Persian nights. The city of Isfahan became famous for its tulips, while other parts of Persia were known for their crown imperialis, jasmine, narcissi, orange buttercups, stocks, and violets. Persian roses were domesticated and gardened early and were likely derived from the native rose (*Rosa foetida*). Early rose varieties had petals that were orange on one side and yellow on the other, so Iran is the source of all our yellow roses, sent originally by the caliph (ruler) to his allies in Granada, Spain, while it was ruled by the Moors. Hollyhocks, jasmines, lilacs, calendulas, and pomegranates were among the earliest flowers grown in Islamic gardens. Interestingly, elaborate mosaic-like patterns were set in the ground using pebbles or tiles. Artificial plants including trees made of metal and precious stones were also "planted" here. Ponds or pools were central to elaborate Persian garden designs.

North African Islamic gardening reached its peak, not in Morocco, but when the Persian gardening styles returned to Spain under the Moors. The most famous of these Spanish Islamic gardens was the Medina Az-Zahra near Seville. It boasted marble-terraced hillsides and walkways paved with mosaic tiles. Myrtle hedges divided the garden into smaller and smaller rectilinear units. Fountains embellished with gold and precious stones completed the exquisite garden setting. A common feature of these gardens were sunken flower beds and places for trees, but lawns were not in use. Whenever flowers were grown, they were usually contained, growing in large earthenware pots.

For the final great period of Islamic gardening we turn to India and the Moghul gardens. These were spectacular places, usually not less than fifty acres. Ancient Indian gardens often included a central pavilion and a rectangular lake with four irrigation canals, often lined majestically with blue tiles. Many waterfalls and long-roofed pergolas supporting flowering and fruiting vines including grapes are noted in their descriptions. The gardens created by Emperor Babur (of Samarkand) were especially ostentatious and magnificent. In India, although it's not gardening per se, in a later chapter we will encounter floral motifs in marble, along with Diwali festivals and cows wearing colorful garlands of marigold blossoms, part of human devotional and artistic traditions.

The spread of Islam throughout the Fertile Crescent and then into Persia and Turkey provided an introduction to a garden culture that all Muslims could share. This explains the broad diffusion of flowers domesticated in Persia to Turkey (e.g., tulips, jasmine, lilacs, horse chestnuts), throughout Arabian trade routes, east to India, west throughout the Christian Mediterranean, and finally into northern Europe, when Turkey allowed trade with the ship-going infidels.

In a Japanese Garden

Just as Islam stimulated an interest in gardens throughout western Asia, the influence of the Chinese garden reached across to the islands of the Pacific. Asian gardens are indeed different from those created in the West. Pleasure landscapes didn't reach Japan until the sixth century and were strongly influenced by Chinese and Korean cultures. Early Japanese gardens used many flowering shrubs, especially azaleas, peonies, and camellias, favored by the Chinese. The earliest Japanese gardens were bright with flowers, but this was not lasting. The classical Japanese garden that expresses the Japanese love of nature dates from the tenth to twelfth centuries. These artificial landscapes (based on idealized landscape paintings) also offered open-air living spaces. Depending upon time and culture, it was perfectly acceptable, and desirable, to make ornamental gardens without vividly colored flowers. To create such an intimate, walled-in private garden, you don't need colorful, smelly flowers unless you like them.

The oldest symbolic element of early Japanese gardens was the *horai*, a supposed island where tortoises, cranes, and immortals lived. In such gardens only "auspicious" plants, such as pine, bamboo, and plum, were allowed. Decorative rocks were also used in an entirely different way in Japanese compared to Chinese gardens. In abstract or dry landscape gardens, rocks were grouped and often laid on sand, often arranged in "auspicious" numbers, odd groupings of three, five, or seven. Plants were often clustered in these numbers as well. From the 1720s onward Japanese gardens came under a second influence of Chinese landscape paintings. Ironically, European gardens were at the same time falling under the influence of European landscape paintings.

Many Japanese gardens contained water elements; ponds, streams, and waterfalls were often traversed with elegant high-arched wooden or stone bridges. Stepping-stones were dominant themes in garden ponds.

Clipped and exaggerated cone-bearing shrubs and trees dominated these managed landscapes, made to look like the gnarled and twisted wind-sculpted trees on far-off islands. Some flowering trees (e.g., plums and cherries) were used, but remained in the minority. Color mainly came from the various nuanced shades of leaves, especially in autumn, including from the now-famous Japanese maples. Japanese gardens in public botanic gardens in the United States are deceptive and often inauthentic. They combine a number of Japanese landscape styles used and abandoned over several centuries.

European Gardens after the Fall of Rome

The fates of European gardens, garden designs, and styles following the end of the Roman Empire are complicated and not easy to summarize. As in Japan and China, landscape styles and preferences changed a great deal and in varying ways over fifteen hundred years. As in Japan, some garden motifs in Europe never incorporated what we recognize today as "flower beds" or trees with big, fragrant blossoms. Examples of shifts in garden sensibilities included highly formal but stereotyped knot or parterre gardens, found especially in France and England. These plantings consisted of tightly clipped hedges with gravel paths, and usually no flowers at all. These gardens utilized heavily trained shrubs (clipped or wired into formal shapes) of European boxwood (*Buxus sempervirens*). Some ancient Roman gardening tricks (e.g., topiary) carried on in gardens in some countries but grew unfashionable in others.

Trade and commerce between European countries and Muslim neighbors introduced "garden favorites," such as the beloved tulips. New garden darlings included the lilacs and horse chestnuts. Elsewhere, we will discuss the tulip craze in Holland during the mid-seventeenth century. Colonization of the western hemisphere and Asia added many more species, but this trend occurred slowly at first, or in fits and starts. The Tradescant family of London (John Tradescant the Elder [c. 1570s–1638] and his son, the Younger [1608–62]) were notable for collecting and moving plants around the globe. John the Elder was gardener to England's King Charles I. Father and son were the first to grow exotic fruits, including pineapples and nectarines, in Europe and introduced red columbine (*Aquilegia canadensis*) to the gardens at Hampton Court. For a time ornamental flowering plants from North America were highly favored by the English aristocracy and other wealthy gardeners, until it became easier for collectors to plunder China for its plants in the nineteenth century. Limited trade with temperate Asia, including central China, before the 1700s gave Europeans their first true chrysanthemums and the daylilies (*Hemerocallis*). The age of Spanish conquest brought the dahlia, tuberose, nasturtium, and the true marigold to the New World.

Once the industrial revolution began to accelerate in England and Western Europe, new maritime and horticultural technology made it possible for garden novelties to arrive faster and more dependably. Governments and entrepreneurs found it easier to plan expeditions just for collecting exotic plants. From the nineteenth through the earlier decades of the twentieth century, the number of plants available for use in ornamental gardens in Europe increased annually compared to the sporadic and unreliable arrival of dahlias, tulips, and tuberoses in centuries past. Modern horticultural trade and commerce had begun in earnest.

When Europeans entered South America, Africa, and Asia, they came to stay. The age of imperialism fostered trading posts. Seeds, bulbs, and tubers are dormant but durable packets of life and easily shipped. They can survive for months on a sailing ship if kept away from sunlight, seawater, black rats, and cockroaches. The famous mutiny on the *Bounty* occurred, in part, because the breadfruit saplings on board received more freshwater and better care than the crew! Not a plant was lost until the ship's officers and unlucky botanists were set adrift in the Pacific Ocean. By the nineteenth century, some of the most beautiful orchids, bromeliads, and other jewels of tropical forests were transported overseas to European nurseries in protective iron-and-glass Wardian cases, precursors of the modern terrarium.

As in Japan and China, big, ornate, and expensive ornamental gardens in Europe were primarily hobbies of royal families and aristocrats, until they were claimed by captains of industry, bankers, and a rising middle class. The camellias, magnolias, and rhododendrons of temperate Asia were fashionable because they framed that great status symbol, the country estate. Glasshouses stocked with the flowering gems of tropical forests reflected good taste and the ability of the nobility and private citizens to influence horticulture and scientific thought via botanical gardens. A generation of wealthy collectors eagerly shared their orchids, vines, and carnivorous plants with Charles Darwin upon his request.

In America, however, eighteenth- and early-nineteenth-century plea-sure gardens and private parks were more likely to reflect nationalistic, intellectual, and egalitarian themes.

Patriotic Gardens of America

We can learn a great deal about America's passion for gardening, even empire-building and the birth of our nation, by visiting Washington's Mount Vernon, Jefferson's Monticello, and Madison's Montpelier, and even the small farm created by frugal John Adams called Peacefield. Our founding fathers were all avid gardeners and amateur botanists. They used flowering trees and shrubs to beautify their private landscapes. Revolu-tionary and visionary Benjamin Franklin believed that agriculture was the only honest path for any nation to acquire wealth. He placed plants at the heart of the country's struggle to emerge independent and free from British rule. Franklin knew that America, with its natural resources, could become self-sufficient, and to this end he experimented with grains and other crops in his Philadelphia garden. Surprisingly, the creation of the American nation, gardens, agriculture, landscapes, and protection of nature are all intertwined. One symbol of the new nation was the Liberty Tree, an ancient American elm that grew in the Boston town common. From its branches, an effigy of Andrew Oliver, the hated Stamp Act tax collector, was hung in protest by the angry colonists.

During the American War of Independence, General George Wash-ington continued his private affairs and correspondence, which included directing gardeners at work on his majestic Mount Vernon estate border-ing the Potomac River. He directed the planting of diverse and native tree species including stately white pines, tulip poplars, alabaster dogwood, aspen, black gum, maples, honey locust, mountain laurels, sassafras with their yellow blooms, and red cedars. His five-hundred-acre, landscaped property established a national trend and exemplified gardening in this period. It was an *American* garden, where imported British trees were not welcomed. Washington's towering pines and red cedars were a reflection of a defiant, strong, and vigorous young United States of America.

Standing upon the wide "vegetable terrace" of Jefferson's Monticello estate, one notices the sweeping lawns edged by the encroaching forest of hardwoods set against the panoramic vista of the Blue Ridge Mountains. Even the orderly rows of squashes, gourds, and cabbages are somehow majestic and stirring. A late-October visit to Monticello offers the visual splendor of an arboreal ocean of reds, oranges, yellows, and browns from red maples, oaks, hickories and tulip poplars. The orchard comprises orderly rows of fruit trees, including apples, pears, and cherries, and lawns are bordered by ribbons of flowers from native and exotic species. Jefferson, as scientist and reluctant politician, was as adept in his garden plantings as in his stirring founding words in the Declaration of Independence.

Jefferson, Washington, and Madison all purchased plants from John Bartram, a famous eighteenth-century American farmer and well-known plant collector. With the British obsession with gardens, many native American plants were collected and introduced into English landscapes by Bartram's efforts. Over four decades Bartram sent hundreds of large wooden crates overflowing with seeds and plant cuttings to Peter Collinson, a wealthy English merchant. America's Eastern flora transformed European parks. The American trees that flooded British estates benefited from Bartram's plant evangelism. Plants and ideas were exchanged actively across the Atlantic. Englishman Joseph Banks added thousands of plants from Africa, temperate Australia, and the Far East to Britain, and many of those plants arrived in America as part of the cross-Atlantic exchange. In fact, the charmingly traditional look of our oldest Southern gardens, so incomplete without crape myrtles, owes a lot to the acumen of Europeans collecting plants in Asia.

Many American gardening traditions and styles can be traced directly to post–Roman Empire gardens in Western and Mediterranean Europe, especially Italy. After all, they gave us the concept of green mown lawns, fanciful topiary shapes, floral clocks, and other creations. America ultimately inherited French, British, and Dutch-Belgian concepts of garden design, and their formality, while American plant collectors and entrepreneurs (including the father-and-son team of John and William Bartram) exchanged native American flowering plants for European and Asian favorites. Thanks to the Bartrams, Europeans received over two hundred species to grow in their gardens, including mountain laurels (*Kalmia*), the huge bull bay (*Magnolia grandiflora*), and that infinite curiosity the Venus flytrap (*Dionaea muscipula*). In reverse, William Bartram's friendship with the French botanist André Michaux (1746–1802) probably encouraged America's importation of Asian camellias, silk trees (*Albizia julibrissin*), and our long fascination with the crape myrtle (*Lagerstroemia indica*).

Fickle Gardeners

Today, thumbing through the pages of any gardening catalog is a feast, until all that glamorous eye candy in the color photographs starts to blur together. Thousands of flower varieties derived from hundreds of plant species are for sale. Garden catalogs are exercises in one-upmanship as companies vie to produce the next best-of-show winning combination of ruffled petals and unusual shapes and colors. How did we get to where we are now? How did your grandmother's garden of *Cosmos* or carnations (*Dianthus*) turn into extravaganzas of unusual plant breeding and artificial selection? We will explore this in an upcoming chapter.

American gardens of the earliest, prerevolutionary colonists were far simpler in design, hosting relatively few flowers with mostly hardy vegetables, and a few medicinal herbs. By the eighteenth and nineteenth centuries American citizens had become more experimental, even daring, with their garden plots, especially in colonial Willamsburg, New York State, and areas around Boston. In New England, these gardens were similar to the English cottage gardens in which flowering shrubs, such as roses, were mixed with annuals, perennials, and various vegetables. More formal public and larger private gardens were likely to be united around a design theme of rectilinear geometries defined by clipped, formal, low hedges. Flower beds and scattered trees (both European and American species) followed the "French-Italianate" style. Away from the main buildings larger expanses of lawns were interspersed with native American trees producing park styles (think of New York City's expansive Central Park) that we have kept and admired to this very day.

The major trend in American gardening from the seventeenth to twenty-first centuries has been a long and gradual shift away from Roman and European designs. Today, some city fathers still want our public gardens to be more formal than Versailles or Hampton Court. Others wish public spaces to be relaxing, inviting us to linger, in the style of Frederick Law Olmsted (1822–1903), best known for his design of Central Park in Manhattan. American gardens now embrace more naturalistic designs, since most of us can't afford to employ a staff of full-time professional gardeners. We have commercial mowing and pruning companies "for the aged" who can no longer care for their properties, while workaholics and soccer moms are rarely at home or in the garden. To save on water bills, we've created xeriscape rock and cactus gardens. Even so, America remains a country of innovative gardeners and we adhere to various gardening fads. Since World War II we have added color gardens, scented gardens for the visually impaired (with plant identifications in braille), community gardens, container gardens, hanging gardens, herb gardens, roof gardens, victory gardens, fairy gardens, and feng shui gardens. These landscapes demand careful attention to appropriate species and reflect the passions of amateur horticulturists. For the career-oriented with little time for gardening, flowers selected may be limited to those that flourish best in pots or hastily dug flower beds. Most are annuals or tropical plants that will die with the autumn frosts, such as *Impatiens*. They are purchased almost full grown at nurseries and hardware franchises because we seem to lack the time or patience these days to grow our own zinnias and marigolds from seeds. As noted in the beginning of this chapter, tulip and daffodil bulbs are easy to obtain and can be planted on one autumn day if the weather is nice.

Speaking of fads, a somewhat messy natural or wild look is now in vogue. Organic is in for gardens. Some brave souls have even dug up their difficult-to-maintain chemically fueled green lawns and replaced them with enticing low-maintenance flowering meadows (following the lead of the late Dame Miriam Rothschild on her Ashton Wold UK estate). Many gardeners have created diverse and wonderful wildlife gardens for birds, bees, butterflies, and bats. You can have your wildlife garden certified by the National Wildlife Federation and proudly proclaim your nature garden to passersby with official signage. Recently, specialized pollinator gardens have emerged where flower-visiting insects and hummingbirds dine on nectar and pollen, often mating and reproducing in season. Some working couples and partners have now decided to spend some of their after-work leisure hours relaxing in the *Datura*- and jasmine-scented air of their very own "moonlight and fragrance" garden. I want one of these!

CHAPTER 5

Flowers for Eternity

They are love's last gift—bring ye flowers, pale flowers!
—Felicia Hermans

Side view of a backlit cactus (*Echinopsis*) blossom

It's a cold February morning in Orange County, California. My family, and our relatives and friends, gather on a green lawn, in the Garden of Contentment, an older area within the sprawling Rose Hills Memorial Park in Whittier, California, the largest cemetery in the United States. A friend has given the eulogy for my father, Stanley, who has died at age fifty-seven. Our family walks to the open grave hand in hand. My father's sister carries a bouquet of flowers. One by one, we come forward, adding colorful bouquets atop the metal coffin. Floral wreaths rest next to the gravesite on tall stands. Earlier that morning, several hundred friends, family, and relatives paid their final respects during a funeral service in the flower-filled First Congregational Church of Buena Park. Now, our family and a few others remain graveside among the floral tributes before the casket is lowered.

Such earthen burials in cemeteries are repeated about six thousand times each day in the United States and many more times around the world. Much of the florist industry is based on these services and other floral tributes. With their beauty, flowers comfort us; they make us smile and ease our grief. They help us to heal and recover from losses and emotional wounds. This has always been true. Our ancestors used cut flowers as grave offerings since the time spiritual beliefs first stirred in humans. Archaeological excavations of ancient burial sites in Iraq and Israel, along with tombs of Egyptian pharaohs, such as Tutankhamun, provide us with glimpses into the burial customs of these ancient mourners, and flowers for eternity.

Buried with Flowers

Deep within the Zagros Mountains of northern Iraq is the famed Shanidar Cave. Early humans, Neanderthals, lived here seventy thousand years ago and buried their dead. Excavations in the 1950s by a Columbia University archaeological team unearthed ten Neanderthal skeletons buried along with an assortment of stone tools. At least one individual may have been laid upon a bed of stems of joint pine (*Ephedra*, shrubs that make no flowers) and also adorned with bouquets of flowers. Pollen from twenty-eight flowering species was identified from the gravesite soils. Pollen-grain concentrations were higher within the grave than in the surrounding areas of Shanidar Cave. This sensational discovery was widely reported in the media and sparked debate. Did the family group of Neanderthals have ritualized burials? Was this the first evidence of floral grave offerings? Or, as has recently been suggested, was it merely interred pollen brought into the cave by generations of gerbil-like rodents hoarding grasses and wildflowers? For now, the story is unclear.

Not as old, but far more scientifically convincing, is a twelve-millennia-old gravesite inside Raqefet Cave on Israel's Mt. Carmel studied by archaeologists at the University of Haifa. Here, four graves from the Natufian culture (radiocarbon-dated to be 13,700 to 11,700 years old) were lined with flowers at the time of burial. In one grave, an adult male and an adolescent were buried together atop a thick bier of floral offerings. Judaean sage (*Salvia judaica*), along with other unidentified mints (Lamiaceae) and members of the snapdragon family (Plantaginaceae), were used. Interestingly, Judaean sage has been a ritual plant since ancient times. It has commonly followed Mediterranean peoples from cradle to grave, like rosemary (*Rosmarinus officinalis*) and true myrtle (*Myrtus communis*). Myrtle remains entwined and is used with one Jewish holiday, Sukkoth, the Feast of Tabernacles, still celebrated each autumn.

Archaeologist Dr. Dani Nadel spoke with me about the Raqefet Cave ancient graveyard, explaining that the inner grave surfaces were plastered with mud, capturing imprints of the delicate stems and finest floral impressions at the time of inhumation. Based upon the types of local wildflowers used, these may have been spring burials. Perhaps flowers were offered as grave goods not only for their beauty but also for their intense scents, which would have masked the odors of decomposition. Sages, along with mint stems and leaves, are especially fragrant, used to this day in cooking and burned as incense. A visitor to the Mt. Carmel hillside today walks among Judaean sage, a plant as common there now as it likely was millennia ago. The Natufians were possibly the first people to transition from a nomadic hunter-gatherer lifestyle to permanent settlements with agriculture, animal husbandry, and true graveyards.

Honoring the Dead or Appeasing the Gods?

From the earliest times, humans have displayed two interrelated behaviors using flowers. We have buried them with our dead, but we have also adorned statues of deities with garlands or left blooms on sacred altars to propitiate the deities. Why is it that something as ephemeral and delicate as a flower took on this new role in the theologies of so many divergent cultures? How could a flower provide comfort for grieving mourners if we evolved from fruit-eating ancestors? Why not use something else? Shouldn't we be decorating sarcophagi and coffins with fruit, luscious red ripe grapes, apples, or figs?

Perhaps it happened because the blooming of flowers around the world proceeds in a predictable, seasonal pattern. Flowers of the dry season are replaced by flowers of the rainy season in the tropics. In cooler-milder zones, three or four seasons offer a diverse but revolving carousel of buds that open and wilt at appointed times.

Catastrophic destruction by unexpected droughts, wildfires, or floods interrupts annual climate cycles but not forever. Given time, the flowers return. Early humans certainly noticed that when their kin were buried in shallow graves, these sites were later colonized by blooming, opportunistic, short-lived wildflowers ecologists call ruderals. This mode of natural renewal had been noted by most generations of poets, regardless of era. In Shakespeare's *Hamlet*, Laertes offers the then-widespread belief that good flowers spring from the grave of a good person. He hopes that violets will spring from his sister Ophelia's grave, although her death was a suicide. Thus, Mt. Carmel hides more than one ruined necropolis in plain sight. On warm days in January a trained botanist can show cyclamens, red anemones, winter narcissi, and mandrakes poking out between the tips of the half-buried ossuaries.

Bouquets, Mummy Garlands, and Floral Collars

On a far grander scale, death rites and religious worship were intertwined in the Egypt of the pharaohs. Flower arrangements were used in festivals and for special occasions. Most popular were the spike-topped papyrus reeds, and flowers of sacred blue and white water lilies. Bouquets were presented to deceased relatives at the time of burial and on various festive occasions and anniversaries at the necropolis and mortuary temples. Beautifully designed fresh-flower arrangements were also worn as broad neck collars (wide necklaces) by participants at Egyptian funerary rites and their associated feasts. Bouquets were brought to burials, and papyrus stems played an integral part since these abundant, aquatic reeds symbolized the resurrection of the deceased. Bouquets and persea (*Mimusops laurifolia*) branches were found inside King Tutankhamun's multiroomed royal tomb in the Valley of the Kings (ancient Thebes) when it was first opened by Howard Carter in 1922.

Ancient flower collars and dried-but-once-fresh flowers are found on mummies and draped on statues placed within tombs. When nineteen-year-old pharaoh Tutankhamun was buried in 1323 BC, many floral garlands were placed as offerings on his three nested, gilded coffins. A small wreath of olive leaves, blue water-lily petals, and blue cornflowers (*Centaurea*) surrounded the symbol of office, the vulture-and-serpent motif above the king's brow. The floral decorations on Tut's innermost coffins were especially elaborate. Here, layers of wrapped linen were crisscrossed by four bands of long floral garlands. The plants used in the garlands have been identified as olive leaves, cornflower, willow, lotus (*Nelumbo*), and celery leaves. A one-foot-wide floral collar encircled the king's sculpted, solid gold funerary mask. When fresh, before the sarcophagus was sealed, this brilliant floral collar resting on the golden innermost coffin lid must have been a lovely sight. Unlike the previous garlands, this collar contained blue glass beads, lotus petals, more cornflowers, the scarlet berries of deadly nightshade, along with yellow mandrake fruits and the yellow-flowering heads of yellow hawkweeds (*Picris*).

The royal mummy of Rameses II (1290–1224 BC) had thirteen rows of floral garlands, along with single blue flowers of water lilies under the bands sealing the mummy wrappings. This king, along with others, was found in a "mummy cache," likely placed there a century later (c. 1087 BC) by Egyptians to avoid the rampant tomb robbing of that time. The garlands of persea leaves and blue and white lotus on the mummy wrappings of Rameses II might have been placed there reverentially during his hasty reburial.

Northwest from Egypt, on islands of the Aegean, the Minoan peoples traded with the Egyptians, who coveted Minoan saffron (*Crocus sativus*) as a spice and a dye. These people also enjoyed an elaborate vision of death, flowers, and deities, but it seems more cheerful. Amateur botanist and historian Hellmut Baumann has addressed the relics of this civilization, and its Greek invaders. The Cretans, for example, decorated their sarcophagi with motifs depicting the flowering stems of native dragon arums (*Dracunculus vulgaris*) and related members of the philodendron family (Araceae). They also painted the glorious white and wonderfully scented sea daffodils (*Pancratium maritimum*) on these baked clays as it was a favorite of their goddesses. These deities were believed to favor wild lilies, including the white-flowered species we today call the Madonna (*Lilium candidum*), and the Cretans protected the mauve flowers of the saffron crocus. One sculpted goddess wore a crown made of the fat round fruits of opium poppies.

The Minoan Empire came to a violent end around 1570 BC when volcanic eruptions and tsunamis devastated their islands and left the survivors vulnerable to waves of invasion from the Greek mainland. The invaders brought in a new, male-dominated pantheon. The mighty Minoan goddess became Crete's nymph under the name of Britomartis or Dictynna. She was a dutiful daughter of Zeus and a virgin.

Classical Greek religion believed in gods who loved flowers. As they were immortals, their worshippers decorated their temples with "immortal" arrangements of everlasting daisies (*Helichrysum*), as they hold their shiny yellow color and sun shapes when dried. Sacrificial oxen were adorned with flowers of wild carnations (*Dianthus*) and rose campions (*Lychnis*). Greek priests and poets insisted that their gods had sacred plants, and some of these bore beautiful flowers. The first Olympian gods invented floral wreaths at the wedding of Zeus and Hera, weaving together wild-flowers such as primroses, candytuft (*Iberis*), leopard's-bane (*Doronicum*), and mouse-ears (*Cerastium*). Pindar (522–443 BC) wrote odes associating Apollo and Aphrodite with sweetly scented violets of the field.

Flowers followed a Greek woman through the most important rituals of her life. Virgins wore garlands of wild, white-flowered species at their weddings, typically incorporating crocuses, white snowflakes (*Leucojum*), white storax (*Styrax*), and snowdrops (*Galanthus*), according to season. The modern fashion of the pure white bride's bouquet derives from these sweetly scented garlands and wreaths. But the wedding bouquet of classical Greece was more likely to contain garlic and other pungent herbs to drive off jealous wandering spirits! The citizens of ancient Rome picked up many Greek wedding customs but seemed to prefer colorful, scented flowers including violets, wallflowers (*Cheiranthus*), and stocks (*Matthiola*). The Greeks also favored roses (sacred to Aphrodite), but the Romans so expanded the wedding fashions that they may have used the flowers of four or five different *Rosa* species. Wealthier Romans also tried to turn their wedding nuptial chambers into a fertile garden of flowers and greenery.

As a matron, the mature Greek woman celebrated the summer rites (Thesmophoria) sacred to the grain goddess, Demeter. This included sleeping on makeshift beds sprinkled with the blue-purple flowers of the chaste tree (*Vitex*), to keep them faithful to their husbands and to increase their fertility. These flowers were sacred to Demeter, Hera (goddess of marriage), Aphrodite (goddess of love and fertility), and even Asclepius (god of medicine). At a woman's death, a purple iris might be planted on her grave, and funerals in ancient Greece were elaborate rituals lasting several days.

At the moment of death, the soul (Psyche, portrayed as a winged deity or butterfly) was believed to leave the body through the mouth as a puff of wind. By law, the decedent's body was prepared at home (the prothesis), usually by elderly female relatives. The corpse was washed, anointed with fragrant oils, and dressed. Then it was placed on a bed of wooden planks and adorned with a crown of tree branches and flowers. Romans adored their floral crowns but also decorated the funerary couch with many fresh flowers. Once burial was complete, both Greeks and Romans scattered flowers on the grave (violets were popular tributes), and both cultures believed that planting herbs and sweet flowers around the burial site purified the earth. Urns containing the remains of the deceased could also be cleansed using offerings of cut flowers.

A Passion for Lotuses

Even as the peoples of Crete, Greece, and Italy abandoned their old pantheons less than two thousand years ago, flowers continue to play a living role in the cultures and countries embracing the various branches of Hinduism. Indians still celebrate rites wearing garlands of flowers, and they give them away as gifts. Their use of flowers is associated with sexuality, one of the aphorisms of love, for example, in the *Kama Sutra* by Vatsyayana. The ancient Indian text is not just about erotic love and sexual positions; it also contains information on the sixty-four arts, including flowers, especially fashioning flower carriages and artificial flowers, the adorning of idols with rice and flowers, decorating couches or beds with flowers, stringing necklaces, making garlands or wreaths, and the simple pleasures of gardening.

In their worship and portrayals of deities, Hindus are infatuated with flowers. The name of the Hindu worship ritual *puja* is translated as the "flower act." Among Hindus, the Indian lotus flower (*Nelumbo nucifera*) is their foremost symbol of beauty, fertility, and prosperity. According to Hinduism, within everyone resides the spirit of the scared lotus flower. The lotus symbolizes purity, divinity, and eternity, widely used in ceremonies, where it denotes life, especially feminine beauty and renewed youth. In the Bhagavad Gita, a Hindu text, humans are admonished to be like the lotus, holding high above the water, like the flower itself. In hatha yoga, the familiar lotus sitting position is used by practitioners as a way of striving for a higher level of consciousness.

In Hinduism, the lotus also represents beauty and nonattachment. The aquatic plant produces a large, beautiful, pinkish blossom, but it is rooted fast in the mud of a shallow pond or lake. Its stiff leaves rise above the water's surface, neither wetted nor muddy. Hindus view this as an admonition for how we should live our lives, without attachment to our surroundings. Several Hindu deities are likened to the lotus blossom. Krishna is described as the Lotus-Eyed One in reference to his supposed divine beauty. Deities including Brahma, Lakshmi, Vishnu, and Saraswati are also associated with the lotus blossom. The "wooing" of Hindu gods is normally done with adorning clothing, jewels, dances and music, perfumes, betel nuts, coconuts, and other foods, but especially with vermilion dusts and many flowers.

During Holi, the festival of colors during the spring, worshippers paint their faces with brilliant vermilion powders. Flowers are everywhere on display for Holi and Diwali (the festival of lights, celebrated in India and Nepal). Colorful floral displays called *rangoli* are created for indoor or outdoor use by the celebrants. The Diwali holiday marks the victory of good over evil (Lord Rama's victory over the demon-king Ravana). Villagers commonly paint the faces of sacred cattle with vermilion and drape their necks with long floral garlands, using marigolds, and red-purple *makhmali* (flowering heads of long-lasting amaranths) in Nepal. In an interesting form of what may be considered cultural diffusion with flowers, Hindus prefer the fat, hybrid heads of marigolds (*Tagetes*), apparently unaware of their earlier association with bloody human sacrifices performed by Aztec high priests.

In India, *yatra* are the pilgrimage festivals celebrated at Hindu temples. Idols are carried aloft in a special procession on a *palki* (sedan chair). These ceremonial platforms are highly decorated, festooned in colorful live flowers including marigolds and *makhmali*. Cremation is mandatory for most Hindus. In India, after the elaborate cremation ceremonies performed by male family members, the deceased's ashes are gathered and usually scattered on the waters of the sacred Ganges River (especially at Allahabad), or at sea. Mourners often place floating bowls containing the ash remains and flowers in the river. They also scatter flower petals and whole flowers on the waters as part of this ritual.

Buddhism originated in northern India. Although often considered a spiritual path or way of life, rather than a formal religion, its many followers use and admire flowers in their rituals and daily lives. The lotus is often stated to represent the most exalted state of man and is the symbol of knowledge and the Buddha. Legend has it that wherever the Buddha paced to and fro in meditation, lotus flowers sprang up in his footsteps. In most Buddhist art, the lotus flower symbolizes the Buddha and transcendence to a higher state. The lotus is also thought to represent in Buddhism four human virtues: scent, purity, softness, and beauty.

In contrast, some Hindus and Hindu offshoots, such as Jainism, eschew flowers. Orthodox Brahmans and Jains oppose using flowers because, although no blood is spilled, a "sacrifice" is made by cutting the stem of the plant, which kills the flower. Allowances are often made and flowers are used by these groups in worship. However, the very best flowers, as offerings, are those that fall naturally to the ground so their lives were not taken by picking. India's Mahatma Gandhi (1869–1948), made famous by inspiring nonviolent acts of civil disobedience among his followers, avoided the use of floral garlands. Gandhi preferred garlands made of cotton or necklaces of plain sandalwood beads.

Flowers of Bali

The Hindu use of flowers is most vibrant and lavish on the island of Bali, in the Indonesian archipelago. The ancient Sanskrit word *bali* means "tribute" or "gift," especially surrounding temple ceremonies and the use of flowers. Wandering the streets of Ubud, you see minipalettes, three-by-three-inch woven-palm-leaf trays filled with colorful flowers of frangipani (*Plumeria*; a relative of our milkweeds), ylang-ylang (*Cananga odorata*; related to custard apples), and *Impatiens* (the same tropical weeds we grow as summer shade-garden annuals). These offerings are called *banten* in Balinese. Incense tops the vibrant offerings, adding its wisps of fragrant smoke to appease nature spirits, and the numerous gods and demons of Balinese Hinduism.

These miniature offerings in Bali take on many different forms. They always contain flowers, but may include cookies, cigarettes, rice, or money. The offerings are not always contained in the plaited-palm trays. Often, they are merely small piles of colorful flower petals. The items used in the offerings seem to be less important than the act of creating these tributes. Balinese women spend a large part of each day creating and placing these ritualistic offerings along roadways and paths, often perched where you least expect them. The offerings are everywhere, sitting atop walls, planters, and stair steps. Individual flowers and garlands adorn stone statues, such as those of Ganesha. This beloved elephant-headed god of wisdom and art is often depicted holding—you guessed it—a lotus blossom. In Bali, the sweet floral scent of frangipani and ylang-ylang perfumes the air of courtyards, homes, and temples.

Early every morning, before most tourists have risen from their guesthouse beds, the Balinese are out on the streets. They sweep away the previous day's now-wilted floral offerings and wash down the streets and gutters. The offerings are daily devotional gifts, repeated acts of faith, cornerstones of their belief system. The slightly darker side of the practices is that the offerings are meant to appease and disperse demon spirits who might be hanging around one's home or a nearby street corner. These are far more than simple street decorations for foreign tourists, which I'm sure most foreign visitors believe they are.

Many of the country's religious ceremonies are conducted within Hindu temples. *Odalans* are temple ceremonies lasting three or more days. During these observances, the temple walls are covered in colorful golden thread fabrics. Offerings of bright fruits, flowers, and rice cakes are carried balanced on women's heads, then placed around the temples. The Hindu gods are believed to take the essence (*sari*) from these food offerings, which are later brought home and consumed by the worshipping families.

On Bali, flowers play as important a role in death as they do in life. The dead, inside their coffins, are placed inside large, elaborate, gilded sarcophagi made of papier-mâché. These often take the form of bulls or the demonic Bhoma guardian with a fearsome, openmouthed head, staring down at the onlookers. They are impressive works of art accompanied by flowers. The black and gold sarcophagi are highly decorated with real and paper flowers. Floral garlands (chrysanthemums) adorn the necks of the impressive mythical beasts.

During the funeral ceremonies, everyone wears bright costumes, and village women prepare food offerings to be eaten by the mourners during the festivities. The distinctive ringing tones of gamelan music are an integral part of Balinese culture and their funeral traditions. Finally, the ornate funeral pyres with their garlanded animals are set ablaze with added gasoline for good measure. After the flames have done their work, the family separates the ashes and bones of the deceased from the remaining residue. The cremains are tenderly placed inside folded white and yellow cloths along with flowers and buried twelve days later, after a final purification rite, again augmented with flowers.

The "Conversion" of Flowers

When trade brought the lotus to Egypt around 500 BC, it displaced the blue and white water lilies used in worship. Favorite flowers find new religions, and it's a never-ending circle, with Mexican marigolds and frangipani used extensively by Hindus in India and on Bali. Therefore, it should not surprise us that the goddesses of the Mediterranean basin gave their grandest white flower to Christianity, recognizable to most as the white Madonna lily (*Lilium candidum*). In the United States, this is the omnipresent potted Easter lily.

In early Christian liturgy, Mary's tomb was filled with these white lilies after her assumption into heaven. The Madonna lily also figures in Renaissance paintings of the Annunciation. Its white color represents her presumed virginity and immaculate conception. Today, flowers taking on similar Christian symbolism include the lily of the valley, the snowflake, and the snowdrop, once worn by Greek brides. White, the color of purity and innocence, and red, Christ's sacrificial blood, represented by roses, have been emblems of the Virgin Mary. They were also sacred to Venus and Aphrodite in earlier times.

Ironically, the earliest practices of the Christian church largely avoided ceremonial uses of flowers as they were associated with former but often appropriated pagan rites. These restrictions were modified over time, so now Christian services and funerals seem incomplete without flowers. For Catholic services, floral arrangements are usually placed on shelves, the gradines, behind the main altar. Although white flowers are most often used, even red flowers are allowed, along with ferns and other greenery. Often an attempt is made to match flower colors with those of the clerical vestments. In the Catholic Church flowers are used in moderation during Advent but are often "given up" for Lent. Historically, rosary beads used in Catholic prayers were formed from dried and compressed rose petals instead of the wooden, glass, or plastic ones commonly used. In Europe during the Middle Ages and the Renaissance certain flowers were associated with Christian saints and used during the saint's day and other celebrations. Saint Valentine was associated with crocuses or violets. The tradition of giving violets on Saint Valentine's Day was common in the United States, persisting in New York City at least until the early 1960s.

Christianity, though, is both messianic and missionary. As the Spaniards introduced it to our American Southwest and Mesoamerica, the use of flowers in the old religions mixed with the new. Anthropologists studying these hybridized beliefs note that the worshippers often speak of a Flower World, a spiritual place where humans might contact spirits or ancestors through rituals or by ingesting hallucinogenic plants. The belief in a spirit Flower World is common throughout Mexico, other Latin American countries, and the pre-Hispanic southwestern United States. These flower beliefs seem to have been widespread among ancient Amerindians speaking a common language (e.g., Uto-Aztecan). In an earlier chapter we were introduced to Aztec rituals utilizing flowers. Flowers for the Aztecs, especially true marigolds, signified a spiritual-afterlife paradise world, but also universal creation and the blood of human sacrifices. Knowledge of the Flower World was traditionally passed to each succeeding generation in song. We also find exquisite depictions of flowers on Mayan textiles, the pottery of the modern Hopi, and in the ancestral groups of the Mogollon, Hohokam, and Anasazi (ancient Pueblo) cultures of Arizona, New Mexico, and Sonora, Mexico. In their minds, the Huichol people of west-central Mexico "visited" the colorful Flower World in their peyote-cactus pilgrimage ceremonies.

In the northern Mexican villages of the Mayo and Yoeme (Yaqui) tribes, leading up to and during Easter week children throw flowers at dancers dressed as evil spirits, the *fariseos* and *chapayekas*, who symbolically attack the Catholic Church. Flowers, real and paper ones, and colorful confetti are used as adornments. Altars, churches, village buildings, and homes are decorated profusely with colorful paper flowers. The Yoeme concept of flowers (*sewam*) has been treasured in legends and songs for many generations. Today, flowers are associated with the Virgin Mary, and flowers are believed to have miraculously sprung from the spilled blood of Christ at his crucifixion. Prior to their religious conversion, flowers were spiritual blessings, important in the native religious beliefs of the Mayo and Yoeme. I have attended the elaborate Yoeme deer dances of the Pascua Yaqui tribe in my home city of Tucson, Arizona. Flowers are important symbols in these rituals. Masked pascola deer dancers, dressed in white, wear wide belts with jangling deer hooves or brass bullet cartridges. Their ankles are festooned with tenevoim, pebble-filled cocoons of giant silk moths (*Rothschildia cincta*). Their stomping feet sound like alarmed rattlesnakes sounding their warnings. Atop their heads the dancers wear a large real or paper flower, usually red. Yoeme and Mayo funerals are mixtures of Catholicism and traditional cultural beliefs.

For the Yoeme, their world concept is a mix of five worlds; the desert world, a mystical world, the dream world, the night world, and the flower world. Flowers are also viewed as the souls of departed family or tribal members. Sometimes older Yoeme men may greet one another with the phrase *Haisa sewa?* (How is the flower?).

These ancient Aztec-speaking groups not only traded goods north and south but also their religious ideas and beliefs. Thus, we have clues that the Flower World concepts traveled north out of Mexico, to Chaco Canyon in the eleventh century, and to the Hopi mesas in Arizona by the 1400s. In the Mimbres Classic period (1000–1130), mortuary rituals, using symbolic flowers, eased the passage of individuals into the spirit world. Caches from archaeological excavations reveal the presence of painted wooden and leather flowers, likely worn by performers, just as modern katsina (kachina) dancers wear flowers, later left as grave goods. Flower worlds are depicted in fifteenth-century murals inside sacred kivas. Hopi, and other Southwestern, pottery show symbolic representations of flowers. According to Hopi traditions, butterflies are "flying flowers" and in various forms are associated with the underworld, with spring and renewal, and with the direction south. There is strong evidence that modern pueblo and ancient Mesoamerican iconographies are intertwined, historically related via trade routes and intercultural exchanges. Flowers, either real or depicted in art, formed a large part of the myths, legends, and daily life of these Southwestern indigenous cultures.

Christian and native flower cultures merge vibrantly but positively during Mexico's Day of the Dead celebrations. In the final days of October, before the American holiday of All Hallows' Eve (Halloween), Mexicans prepare for their own traditional holiday for the dead, but in a different way from the commercialized trick-or-treating holiday Americans know. As the days grow shorter and the nights grow colder, villages and towns all over Mexico come alive with renewed energy and anticipation for the coming festivities. On November 1 and 2, Mexicanos come together to celebrate Día de los Muertos, their traditional Day of the Dead celebration. Across the country, families honor the memories of deceased loved ones around family burial plots gaily decorated with real and paper flowers, lively paper streamers, glowing candles, and offerings of the decedents' favorite foods.

To appreciate the modern Day of the Dead celebrations, we recall Aztec beliefs. Aztecs didn't fear death, or Mictlantecuhtli, their god of death, as much as they dreaded the uncertainty of their brutally short lives. Mictlantecuhtli would not punish the dead. A dead person's role in heaven was determined not by how he lived, but by how he died. Exalted warriors were believed to fly around the sun in the form of butterflies and hummingbirds, as were women who died in childbirth. Dead infants fed at the milk-giving tree. Everyone else just faded away to Mictlan, like a quiescent dream on their road toward final death and nonexistence. The ferocious Aztec sun god, Huitzilopochtli, demanded the most precious fluid of all, red human blood, spilled in sacrifice, amid garlands of golden marigolds, to slake his never-ending thirst. The beating hearts and blood of human victims were exchanged for abundant crops. Death paid for life in the Aztec world. An Aztec "war of flowers" ensued, tournaments in which neighboring tribes were forced to compete to the death, adding their bodies to the ever-growing demand for sacrificial victims.

Flowers have always played a crucial and significant role in the Mexican Day of the Dead. On All Hallows' Eve, the spirits of dead children return home, but must leave by midday on November 1. Bells ring out all afternoon on this day from churches, announcing the arrival of adults, the "faithful dead," returning to their scattered villages. Candles burn on flower-filled home shrines and altars chock-full of marigolds, other flowers, candy skulls, and family photographs. The sweet fragrance of burning copal incense (from ancient Mayan and Aztec traditions) fills the air inside the homes. Often, trails of scattered marigold petals lead to doorways, meant to show wandering spirits of the dead their way back home. You can also witness many of these same customs on the streets and cemeteries of mountain villages in northern Guatemala. Marigolds are the foremost flower among these ceremonies and are native plants of Mexico. However, in Oaxacan and Cuernavacan markets as elsewhere, celebrants also buy the cloudlike floral sprays of baby's breath (*Gypsophila paniculata*), a domesticated plant that grows wild in its native Russian steppes. Mexicans also use the brilliant flamelike heads of cockscomb (*Celosia*) to decorate their shrines, church altars, and graves. Once a religion includes flowers in its worship or mourning, the original distribution and mythology of an attractive bloom is no barrier to its acceptance among new rites in other distant locations.

The Flowering of Roadside Memorials

Whenever I drive the roadways of Sonora, Mexico, or those in southern Arizona, spots of color vie for my attention. Are they flowers in the desert, even during the winter when all the grasses are withered and brown, when nothing should be blooming? No, these little gardens of grief are roadside memorials, shrines honoring the dead, called *descansos* in Mexico. They mark places where someone died in an automobile crash. The memorials usually have a white cross, and often a saint's figure and a votive candle, but invariably flowers, plastic ones, or fresh flowers refreshed on anniversary dates and holidays. Occasionally, I stop out of curiosity to read their names, or to admire the decorative floral arrangements. I'm reminded of the sidewalk and roadside floral tribute gardens that stretched for miles following the September 6, 1997, funeral of Diana, Princess of Wales. Whether permanent roadside shrines or a single flower left in an open jar, they are omnipresent reminders of the immensely powerful social customs and values of flowers as memorial tributes.

A roadside memorial (*descanso*) in Arizona

Victorian Funeral Customs

In contrast, the use of flowers in contemporary American funerals seems a bit restrained. To understand our relation to flowers and death we need to cross the Atlantic and study our Victorian forebears as they established the funerary customs we still use or prefer to avoid. In particular, before twentieth-century embalming practices took hold in the funeral industry, stately, large wreaths and immense bouquets of flowers composed of strongly fragrant white lilies and hybrids of the so-called Oriental lilies (derived from *Lilium speciosum*) masked the odors of bodily decomposition. Along with burning candles, flowers served the role of air-fresheners.

English Victorian-era funeral processions were grandiose and expensive social events. A prominent English family planned and arranged for a stylish processional costing twenty to fifty British pounds sterling, equivalent to the purchasing power today of about $5,000 (I chose the year 1850). For most of the Victorian era, a pound sterling might buy $100 worth of goods today. The processions were led by foot attendants, pallbearers with batons, a featherman holding tall ostrich plumes, pages, and mutes who dressed in gowns and carried wands. Stylish carriages transported family members, and relatives followed behind. The glass-sided hearse had elaborate black with silver and gold decorations. It was covered with an ornate canopy of black ostrich feathers and pulled by six black Belgian horses, each with its own black-plumed headdress. The ornate, draped coffin inside was clearly visible, and the interior of the hearse was jammed with a wide variety of flowers. Several hundred mourners might attend such a lavish funeral.

After the services, most of the flowers were returned home and became part of elaborate home-parlor memorial shrines. Queen Victoria sent primroses to the funeral of her favorite prime minister, Benjamin Disraeli. Large floral arrangements surrounded photographs of the deceased, and the room was often decorated with one or more stuffed white doves, holding a red rose in their beaks. The British, during Queen Victoria's sixty-three-year reign (1837–1901), were the last society to truly celebrate death with great pomp and circumstance, as had the ancient Egyptians. In the Victorian age, people welcomed the dead, continued to bring their dead, in open coffins, into their parlors and homes (the origin of the modern funeral parlor). In death flowers led the way.

Victorians had their own flower superstitions, gleaned from older traditions in British folklore. For example, if the deceased had lived a good and proper life, then colorful flowers would supposedly grow and bloom on his or her grave. If people had lived otherwise and were deemed evil, then weeds would assuredly grow unattended and bloom profusely above them. If anyone noticed a roselike scent in the home, and no roses were nearby, then someone was about to die. A single snowdrop (*Galanthus*) plant found growing in a garden also foretold a death in the family. It was considered extremely bad luck to mix red and white flowers in a vase, especially inside a hospital, as a death would surely follow. Proper mourning etiquette was essential. Widows grieved for two years and wore solid black clothing with no trim, and bonnets with long, black face veils. No flowers were used. Their veils were shortened during the second year, and white or purple flowers were then permissible as decorative adornments to their plain black bonnets.

The Modern American Way of Death: Flowers and Dying

Today, Victorian practices have evolved further into an immense, nearly $21 billion US funeral industry, whose customs vary widely depending upon ethnic background, religious beliefs, region of the country, and socioeconomic stratum. Some people will not grow or bring scented narcissus (*Narcissus tazetta*) into their homes because their fragrance reminds them of embalming fluid. However, a little-known change in the treatment of the dead—the use of formaldehyde and other embalming fluids to prolong viewing life (the time available for an open-casket ceremony during a funeral or memorial service)—has occurred. Unknown to most, unless you are a mortician or are employed in a modern funeral home, is another surprising use for floral fragrances: dead bodies are being perfumed like real flowers. The new practice is not altogether unlike those of nineteenth-century America, when home parlors were jammed with large and fragrant floral wreaths, of white lilies and other flowers, to mask death's telltale scent. Today, the unmistakable nose- and eye-stinging scent of formalin (aqueous formaldehyde) has changed. New, milder-scented embalming fluids are used, and even the Civil War–era formalin has been modified to assuage modern sensibilities. Now, embalmers typically add strong floral-based scents to their embalming fluids. The sweet fragrance of white lilies has been chemically synthesized and is sold to funeral parlors as an additive for their embalming solutions. Flowers have come to our rescue. To paraphrase the famous marketing phrase of a modern chemical-manufacturing giant, perhaps now we also have "better dying through chemistry."

It's my impression that flowers now used at funerals are less fragrant than previously. Those pale gladioli, now in vogue, have no scent at all. Is it a coincidence that the beautiful, large, white, durable, and waxy white blooms of the nearly odorless calla lily (*Zantedeschia aethiopica*) from southern Africa seem perfect for placing in the hands of a corpse during an open-casket memorial? I don't think so, but it's perhaps ironic that these blooms belong to the same family of arum lilies the Minoans used to decorate their sarcophagi.

While fresh flowers seem such ever-important elements of modern US funerals, their use dwindles as their costs rise. In the United States today, floral arrangements might comprise roughly 10 to 20 percent of the total cost of a modern funeral averaging $8,000. We want and expect to see flowers during our times of grief. Flowers lift our spirits. Even with the recent "in lieu of flowers" practice where friends and family are asked to make cash donations in the memory of the deceased to a favorite charity, flowers and flower-giving have not gone out of fashion. A significant portion of the $34.3 billion (in 2012) florist-industry revenues are spent on cut flowers, potted plants, and wreaths supplied for funerals, memorial services, and placement on graves. The more than twenty-two thousand funeral homes in the United States stage more than 2 million funerals annually, about six thousand each day.

Returning to that February day of my father's funeral, I have vivid memories of honey bees alighting to drink nectar from the sprays of white flowers draping his silver-blue casket. It was a chilly Southern California day with a few cumulus clouds. The sixty-degree morning temperature was barely warm enough to get bees out of their hives, up and flying, in their continual quest for flowers. My eyes watched as those softly buzzing bees visited every blossom, drinking their sweet nectar. At the time, I was a twenty-two-year-old graduate-school student. Throughout my career as an entomologist, I've studied bees (melittology), along with their biology, and floral interactions, the science of pollination ecology. I don't believe the bees were any kind of spiritual omen, but seeing them visiting my father's graveside flowers reminded me of happier boyhood times spent together. The flowers and their bee visitors helped ease my grief on that somber California morning four decades ago.

Now, we leave the rituals of death and dying behind and move to the showiest of them all, flowers (dahlias, roses, lilies, sunflowers, and more) bred for their spectacularly vivid colors and sex appeal. Gardeners enter flower shows hopeful that their prize blooms will win a coveted Best of Show ribbon, along with accolades from their gardening peers. We enter the high-stakes world of technology-dependent, commercial plant breeding—the creation of unnatural blue or brown roses, and black petunias, in the laboratory and field. Gardeners are cautioned that modern flower breeding, especially its newest hybrid creations, may reduce pollinator-attracting floral scents, along with pollen and sweet nectar— essential foods for bees and other pollinating animals. Pollinator gardens may appear bountiful, yet can in reality be unrewarding nutritional deserts. The pomp and circumstance of London's one and only Chelsea Flower Show is revealed with its phantasmagorical artificial environments, new floral introductions, dream merchants, and fanciful exhibits. Step into the verdant exhibit booths. On with the show.

CHAPTER 6

Best of Show

Radial symmetry in an African daisy (*Gerbera* sp.),
imaged with a flatbed scanner

Six of us pushed our way through the crowded metal benches and aisles past hanging bromeliads (plants in the pineapple family) and orchids of every imaginable color, including the tiniest flowers of wild, untamed species. We'd wandered away from the main group of one hundred revelers enjoying beer and wine in the heat of the afternoon. After all, this was a Tucson botanical tradition, the 33rd Annual Summer Solstice Celebration, many of which I'd attended over the years. The invitation boasted that the event would be "a gathering of xerophytes, heliotherms, and other extremophiles." I chuckled at this jargon-rich terminology. Such words are used to describe drought-adapted and sun-loving desert plants, ones living on the edge.

The place for the party was the Old Pueblo, near my home in Tucson. Every year our green-thumb host for this famous party is one and the same, botanist and plant breeder Dr. Mark Dimmitt. Mark's annual solstice parties are famous, almost a Tucson institution. The partygoer mix included owners of native-plant nurseries, die-hard fans of succulents and other bizarre plants, University of Arizona professors and students, Arizona-Sonoran Desert Museum employees, and local artists and musicians. Here the weird-plant faithful gather once a year among Mark's amazing collection. His famous "pot" parties are invariably scheduled on or within a few days of the summer solstice under the blazing Tucson sun. Despite the oppressive temperatures, the attendees have come to reconnect and chat, and most important, to admire his amazing collection of exotic plants, rare succulents such as the Karoo roses, other desert plants, and especially the orchids and bromeliads. The event is almost like an art opening, with everyone admiring flowering plants in the ground and in pots as they would visit an art gallery to view paintings on a wall. I crept through the tangled orchid and bromeliad house making my way toward the back of the overflowing plant menagerie. I continued hunting rare orchid blooms with my digital camera, macro lens, and flash and encountering old friends.

On another visit to Mark Dimmitt's greenhouses, I'd come to learn about plant breeding firsthand. My friend has a greenhouse devoted exclusively to species and varieties of Karoo rose (*Adenium*). These plants came originally from African deserts. They are grown for their bizarre, gnarled, and elephantine forms, and for their spectacularly colorful blossoms that remind people of frangipani (Karoo roses and frangipani belong to the same dogbane family, Apocynaceae). As I walked along the greenhouse isles, I noticed that many plump buds were scantily clothed in thin bridal-veil netting. Since part of his greenhouse is open to the desert, these veiled bags kept out local pollinators hungry for pollen and nectar. The only pollinator allowed inside was the one wearing the floppy sun hat, Dimmitt himself. Carrying a small notebook, plastic vials, strands of red yarn, and a small camel's-hair paintbrush, Mark selected his flowers. Aha, that bud wasn't open yesterday. Mark moved in, gently removing the net bag. He plucked off the fat anthers one by one, storing them in a small glass vial. This flower would become one of his pollen-donor fathers for the hand pollinations he would make.

"Crossing" is the placing of donor pollen from one flower (like sperm from an animal father) onto the female receptive stigma of a different, usually unrelated, mother plant. Like bees on two legs, plant breeders often do their work holding a camel's-hair brush dipped into a vial of freshly collected pollen. Once the sperm in the pollen tube meets the egg, hidden inside the immature seed, the tube releases its sperm to the egg cell, they unite, and the combined chromosomes are shuffled, called crossing over. When they've ripened, the fruits are opened, and their seeds are collected and planted. The mature plants from these crosses are screened for their desirable characteristics, defects, or faults. Further crosses are made to improve, stabilize, or expand upon the desirable phenotypic traits (the plants' appearance), such as altered or intensified floral colors or an increased number of petals.

Mark moved to another *Adenium* and selected a netted beauty. This one had been emasculated in the bud stage. Previously, Mark had forced the bud open and nipped off the pollen-containing anthers. Now, the open flower was a sort of floral eunuch. It could no longer function as a male, but these flowers, like most, are bisexual, and its pistil was ready. Dipping his paintbrush into the vial of oily pollen, he gently swiped the gold-dust-like pollen across the sticky end of the now-receptive female stigma. No fanfare, no cigarette or afterglow; nonetheless, this was plant sex. His surrogate-pollinator role fulfilled, the pollen he'd added would fertilize the immature seeds within the ovary. Mark tagged the cross he'd just made with the name and number of the plants' parents.

If everything went right, a long, skinny fruit would develop. A few years later, he would have planted the seeds from this forced sexual union, grown out the plants to flowering age, and waited. Almost like an expectant father, Mark wanted to know if he'd made the right choices, or how the genes had reshuffled. Only then would Mark be the proud foster parent of a new *Adenium* floral hybrid, perhaps a combination of shape and colors not previously seen, either in nature or any greenhouse. Such is the way of independent plant breeders around the world, ever hopeful that they will create, with understanding and a bit of luck, a brand-new and exciting flower for the global floriculture markets.

Sexual Discovery

Plants are sexual organisms, but they lead sedentary lives and move on a timescale much too slow for us to notice. Furthermore, their pollen grains and the receptive tip of their pistils are best observed under magnification. That's why it took a long time for the scientific world, then gardeners, and eventually everyone else to catch on that plants make sperm (enclosed within pollen grains) that fertilize ovules, much like animal reproduction. Some European botanists, including Englishmen John Ray (1627–1705) and Nehemiah Grew (1641–1712), made observations leading them to believe that plants engaged in sexual reproduction and that pollen was the male agent. A German botanist, Rudolf Jacob Camerarius (1665–1721), conducted the first critical garden experiments on sexuality in flowering plants. A physician and a botanist, he became director of the botanical gardens at Tübingen, Germany. Among other studies, Camerarius observed mulberry trees, castor-oil plants, spinach, maize, and Mercury plants (*Mercurialis*). He discovered that if female mulberries grew at a great distance from the nearest male trees, they bore empty fruits without seeds. Similarly, when he cut off the male flowers, the tassels, of maize (corn), no seeds formed on the "female" cobs. These European scientists were only rediscovering what Asiatic date-palm farmers had known for thousands of years. Obviously, various cultures discovered plant sexuality at different times and stages of their botanical enlightenment.

The earliest plant breeder to use what we would recognize today as scientific methods was a German investigator, Joseph Gottlieb Kölreuter (1733–1806), one of the most important biologists of the eighteenth century. He was the first scientist to hybridize plants and study them systematically. His earliest subjects were tobacco plants (*Nicotiana rustica* and *N. paniculata*). Later, Kölreuter made crosses and produced hybrid plants between different species of carnations (*Dianthus*), four-o'clocks (*Mirabilis*), and mullein (*Verbascum*). He observed these hybrids and noted that the plants were intermediate in form between the two parents in most ways. However, Kölreuter also noted that his hybrids were never quite as fertile as their parents. By backcrossing hybrids to one of their parental species, the next generation looked more like the original, wild progenitor.

Almost everyone knows about Luther Burbank (1849–1926) and his russet Burbank potato, especially ardent fans of McDonald's french fries. Making hand crosses in the manner of traditional plant breeding, Burbank, "the wizard of horticulture," created dozens of new varieties of fruits and vegetables, along with the much-beloved Shasta daisy and ninety-one other types of ornamental plants. Similarly, today many plant breeders are working to modify agricultural crops and ornamental plants at universities and government and private horticultural laboratories around the world.

Sinful Hybrids (Rated X)

The hybridizing work of Kölreuter was taken up by a number of scientists and amateurs in the nineteenth century, such as Burbank. Some competed for prizes, bringing their best crosses to affairs known as florists' feasts, while others shared their breeding records and data with Charles Darwin. Throughout the twentieth century professional scientists determined that naturally occurring hybridization between closely related wild species was surprisingly common. In nature, hybrids typically do not evolve into new species, but hybrids do survive for years and years as living gene banks for one or both parental species. When a bee transfers pollen between a parent species and its hybrid, this backcrossing allows new genes to filter into the parent population. If this occurs many times over several generations, this may trigger the evolution of a new plant species. This process, known as introgression, may be responsible for the origins of many of our American species of sunflowers (*Helianthus*), Louisiana irises, prickly pears (*Opuntia*), and beardtongues (*Penstemon*).

Likewise, hybrids occurred within European and Chinese gardens for centuries whenever people collected and grew a range of wildflowers, bushes, and even trees. After pollinating bees "married" these different species, gardeners and orchardists kept their seeds for later propagation or conserved the seedlings that arose spontaneously in cultivated flower beds. This brought about some of our first garden daffodils (*Narcissus*), polyanthus (*Primula*), and soulangeana magnolias (*Magnolia*). Many garden hybrids are so old that no records exist about who first made or grew them, or where. During the eighteenth and nineteenth centuries horticulturists made hybrids between wild species, only to be astonished that they were merely re-creating ancient garden-flower favorites. Botanists who classify plants had to do something about the scientific names they'd given to these old mongrels.

If you see a plant tag in a garden shop in which the genus and species are interrupted by a lowercase *x* (meaning "times" or "crossed with"), you know it's an old garden hybrid posing as a true species. That blue-purple salvia you like so much is *Salvia* x *superba* because it is the result of *S. nemorosa* crossed (hybridized) with *S. sylvestris*. The common garden gladiolus is *Gladiolus* x *gandavensis*. A single gladiolus flower carries gene combinations from at least four distinct wild species. A fifth species is involved if your gladiolus flower has contrasting spots or blotches on its lower petals. Plant pedigrees can be as complicated as tracking down your own family ancestry and genealogy.

Curiously, hybrid plant origins were something horticulturists often tried to conceal in the not-so-good-old days. In parts of Western Europe and America, hybrid plants were often regarded as ungodly, or certainly at least unnatural and to be avoided. Prideful man was not permitted to ape his Creator by producing a new kind of living thing. Even Shakespeare was no fan of hybrid plants. His charming heroine Perdita (in *The Winter's Tale*) points out the beauty of spring-blooming flowers to her friends until one asks her about cultivated, "pied" (harlequin) carnations. She will simply not have them. They are nature's bastards! This sounds ridiculous today, but even Luther Burbank told a story about how a minister, posing as Burbank's friend, denounced him from the pulpit for flouting God's laws by creating hybrids. It seems that Burbank's Shasta daisy, proudly grown in American gardens for more than a century, is not so innocent a bloom despite its many, pure-white "chaste" petals.

Voted "Most Popular and Likely to Succeed"

Flower lovers around the world have their favorite blooms. It all depends on whether the buyer wants his prized flowers displayed in a vase or grown in a pot or an outdoor flower bed. Floral preferences vary widely between countries, cultures, and different historical periods. When it comes to bouquets, roses, especially red roses, are clear winners in the United States. The USDA's Economic Research Service records and tabulates flowers sold for the florist industry. Not surprisingly, roses, grown mostly in California, beat out carnations (at number two), chrysanthemums (number three), and the parrot feathers (*Alstroemeria*) (in fourth place). Although parrot feathers are comparatively recent arrivals, derived from wildflowers native to temperate South America, they are valued for their long vase life. That may be the reason why the shorter-lived tulips, as cut blooms, are now in fifth place, followed by gerbera daisies (*Gerbera*). True lilies (*Lilium*), glads (*Gladiolus*), irises (*Iris*), and baby's breath (*Gypsophila*) follow in turn. Fads, pricing, and a flower's introduction to mainstream horticulture have all contributed to changes in rankings and popularity over the decades.

Roses are also most popular in the United Kingdom, but there lilies come next, followed by the sweetly scented freesias (*Freesia*), derived from wild bulbs native to southern Africa. Next, the British favor tulips, followed by sweet peas, various orchids, carnations, sunflowers, and crown anemones. If we travel to Japan, we find floral arrangements incorporating moss pinks (Shibazakura, moss *Phlox*) among European favorites such as tulips, roses, and lavender. Japanese parks showcase the traditional sakura cherry (*Prunus serrulata*). The Japanese enjoy their centuries-old pastime of flower viewing and picnicking (called *hanami*) under blooming cherry trees. Spring cherry blossoms are the most popular, but the people of Japan know that every season brings blossoms worthy of admiration. In China, though, plum blossoms are even more popular than flowering cherry trees. Chinese gardens reveal a deep traditional admiration for their peonies, chrysanthemums, native *Cymbidium* orchids, China rose (*Rosa chinensis*), camellias, azaleas, lotuses, and the fragrant olive (*Osmanthus*). During their New Year's spring festival the water-fairy flower makes its appearance as a forced bulb in artistic ceramic planters, but she is nothing but a hybrid narcissus imported ages ago from Mediterranean lands.

Orchid fanatics often express different passions in different countries. Americans still clamor for hybrids based on crossing cattleyas to laelias to brassias and their allies, giving us variations on the ultimate high school prom corsage. The Brits are more likely to culture sprays of those big, tropical, multiflowered terrestrial cymbidiums. And down under, Australian tastes appear to be shifting from cymbidiums to the native tropical-Asian *Dendrobium* orchids.

When it comes to gardening at home, Americans are more likely to plant their garden beds using flowering plants that differ somewhat from the favorites of the cut-flower trade. We do, however, preserve our loyalties for the rose. Rosebushes remain top sellers at nurseries, although suburbanites invariably find them challenging to grow and keep healthy. The second most popular garden flowers are, ironically, the annual and almost unkillable zinnias (*Zinnia*). Lilac bushes (*Syringa*) are in third place, followed by tulips, and finally there is a wide choice among irises. This list varies in different parts of our country since we have so many different plant-hardiness zones along with regional preferences for flowers. For example, commercial growers in Florida spend most of their time propagating annual bedding plants such as *Impatiens*, *Petunia*, *Geranium* (from cuttings), *Geranium* (from seeds), marigold (*Tagetes*), and various hybrids sold as pansies (*Viola* x *wittrockiana*). Our current top five bestselling

American perennials are daylilies (*Hemerocallis*), followed by coneflowers (*Echinacea*), black-eyed Susans (*Rudbeckia fulgida*), plantain lilies (*Hosta*), *Salvia*, and purple coral bells (*Heuchera micrantha*). However, plantain lilies are grown more often for their brilliantly colored leaves than for their equally conspicuous white or pink blooms. Hostas are among our few garden plants that thrive in deeply shaded areas, unless you are keen on nonflowering ferns as part of your garden greenery.

The World's Costliest Extravagant Blooms

A secretive and global network of eccentric plant collectors, fanciers of rare orchids, cycads, bonsai, cacti and other succulents, carnivorous plants, and large-specimen plants, exists largely out of view. In some cases, plants may have been illegally collected and imported. Wealthy Asian, European, and US collectors sometimes fall into this world of obsessive plant collecting. Recent books, including *The Orchid Thief, The Scent of Scandal,* or *Orchid Fever*, detail the surreal world of uncommon flowering plants, and the often extravagant prices that some will pay to possess these rare beauties. With the recent global economic downturn, the public may have less discretionary money to buy flowers or rare specimen plants, let alone afford the expense and high maintenance of building or caring for even a small private greenhouse or solarium. Recently, many orchid-growing nurseries have gone out of business from lack of support from middle-class orchid hobbyists, or from competition from orchids sold for ridiculously low prices in supermarkets and hardware stores. Yet, a few ultrawealthy, fanatical collectors still fulfill their desires for unfamiliar blooms at any price.

If you live or have lived in rural areas of the United States or abroad, wildflowers have generally been available free for the picking. Flowers have always been inexpensive gifts for rural cottagers and small farmers. Older English friends of mine remember how they were encouraged to pick wayside cowslips (*Primula*), along with violets and lady's-smocks (*Cardamine*), in the early spring. Bouquets of these were presented to relatives in nearby towns and cities. Until recently, similar flower gathering has happened on this side of the big pond. Schoolchildren and lovers have always gathered up wildflowers as gifts. Of course, plucking any wildflowers, or seed heads, in state and national parks is taboo. Conservation laws in the United Kingdom and the United States have wisely stopped individuals and a few commercial interests from gathering up scarce wildflowers, thereby protecting common and rare species alike.

Until recently, flowers have mostly been luxurious and expensive commodities for city dwellers because of their short life spans, rarity, tenderness, and difficulty of being shipped long distances or held more than a few days in transit. Not prized as edible commodities, flowers nevertheless create unique beauty and add value in our natural and living environments, providing enjoyment for everyone. In past centuries, cultivating flowers to cut or growing bedding plants for gardening or decorating home or public-building interiors was prohibitively expensive except for wealthy merchants or royal families.

In seventeenth-century Holland (peaking in the spring of 1636), bulbs of the rarest tulip varieties such as the Viceroy or Semper Augustus (only twelve bulbs were known in 1624) sold for as a much as 4,150 guilders at a time when even the most skilled artisan was fortunate to earn 300 guilders per year. During this famous tulipmania, one rare flame-tulip bulb could sell for as much as a fancy canal house. The skyrocketing prices were for bulbs while they bloomed in pots. Buyers likely believed it was a grand investment because tulip bulbs, with proper care, multiply by making daughter bulbs (offsets). Or perhaps the purchaser thought he could raise a new generation from seeds.

The rare flame tulips (see the dust-jacket art of this book) were actually plants infected with a virus that produced the broken-effect, streaking colors in the pigment cells within their petals. However, since each virus caused different colors in the flower, the buyer lived under the delusion that he or she had purchased a one-of-a-kind plant and cornered its market.

Tulip flowers were among the most highly prized status symbols in Dutch society. Successful Dutch bulb traders might earn as much as sixty-thousand florins in one month, the astonishing equivalent of $61,700 in today's currency. One could never have enough of the prized blooms. Wealthy Dutch citizens placed cleverly concealed mirrors in their gardens to increase their apparent riches. Today, the members of the Wakefield and North of England Tulip Society are dedicated to preserving and exhibiting the rare broken-feather or flame-type tulips like those from 1630s Holland.

Almost no flowers today can match the excessive prices paid for fancy tulips in mid-seventeenth-century Holland before the tulip speculation bubble finally burst in the winter of 1636–37. For discriminating buyers, however, today's global market offers some pricey flowers. Horticulture and floriculture can indeed be expensive hobbies. Fortunately tulip bulbs no longer command astronomical prices as they are easily mass-produced. Even the most sought-after bulbs rarely cost more than a dollar apiece. Many print or online bulb catalogs sell tulips for only forty to fifty cents each. They are even cheaper when you buy them in twenty-, fifty-, or hundred-bulb lots as most gardeners do. Today, the most expensive bulbs belong to other genera and species.

A small tuber of a Japanese rice-cake flower (*Arisaema sikokianum*) sells for as much as $40. It's an aroidlike plant similar to the jack-in-the-pulpit. Members of this genus are now fashionable since they prefer shady areas and have striking patterns on their hooded floral spathes. A single bulb of the giant Himalayan lily (*Cardiocrinum giganteum*) will cost $20 each, and you are buying a four- or five-year-old bulb. Why? It simply takes that long for the bulb to store up enough energy to bloom. They flower and then promptly die. You can keep their seeds and start again, but it's another six-to-seven-year wait for a flowering stem to appear.

Cut blooms can be just as expensive to buy, and they wither and die in a short time. Visiting any gourmet market or high-end florist shop reveals high-priced, but not exorbitantly so, cut-flower stems. King proteas, originally from South Africa, are now grown in Hawaii or Australia commercially and sell for about $10 per stem. Stargazer or Siberian lilies ($8 each), torch gingers ($8), bird-of-paradise (*Strelitzia*, at a modest $4), anthuriums ($6), and tall heliconias (banana relatives, up to $15 apiece) have high prices. These are, however, mere "throwaway" blossoms compared to a few recent notables.

Currently, the top contenders for the world's priciest plants, not surprisingly, are orchids, especially when they're sold at auction. A modern hybrid, the Shenzhen Nongke, is a *Cymbidium* variety (terrestrial orchids originally from montane-to-low, tropical Asia), but it sold at auction in 2005 for a staggering 160,000 British pounds sterling ($262,112) to a single Japanese bidder. Amazingly, this green, purple, and fringed orchid flower doesn't look all that glamorous. Rare, wild orchids also command top prices. On the slopes of the tallest mountain on the island of Borneo, Mt. Kinabalu, in the Malaysian state of Sabah, lives Rothschild's slipper orchid (*Paphiopedilum rothschildianum*), an endangered species now found only on a few mountain acres. This slow-growing species takes up to fifteen years before flowering. When it has been produced and infrequently offered for sale, individual plants have sold for as much as $5,000. *Phragmipedium kovachii* is another tropical slipper native to South America. It was smuggled into the United States not in compliance with international CITES (Convention on International Trade in Endangered Species) regulations. It created many scandals, leading to both prosecution and embarrassment for the Marie Selby Botanical Gardens in Sarasota, Florida. When it first came to the United States around 2002, it sold for between $5,000 and $10,000 per plant. Following mass propagation, the showy plants now sell for a more modest $350 each.

Japanese collectors love one of their rarest native species, the furan (rich and noble) orchid (*Neofinetia falcata*). These handsome, small, white orchids were favored by shoguns and samurai in the past. Their delicate blooms have a six-inch-long nectar spur and are pollinated by long-tongued moths at night. Today, small *Neofinetia* plants from a California producer sell for as much as $250. Just a few years ago, however, several of these orchids were sold by a producer in Japan for $250,000 per plant. One of the buyers of this rare orchid, at his death and according to his last wishes, was buried along with his pricey orchid. Today, with tissue-culture propagation, most of these rare orchids are still extravagant for the average orchid hobbyist but don't sell for outrageous amounts.

If you're an independent orchid breeder and exhibit your prize specimens at national or international plant shows, and your specimen is judged best of show, that can put real money in your pocket. This is especially true if your orchid wins a First Class Certificate or Award of Merit, one of the few, coveted annual awards from the American Orchid Society. In fact, you can almost take it to the bank. Suddenly, your $50 orchid is a national social media star, perhaps even world famous, and clamored after by many eager buyers. People everywhere are tweeting about it. Now, it might fetch $5,000, instead of mere pocket change.

Live Long and Prosper: Life after Cutting

Vase life is the term the cut-flower industry uses to describe how long cut flowers, or foliage, retain their healthy appearance in a vase after they're sold. Plant breeders are always on the lookout for flowers with longer vase lives. A slow and lingering death is preferred, and highly profitable. I admire and enjoy parrot feathers (*Alstroemeria*) along with various orchids because they often remain fresh more than a week following floral decapitation. Most orchid flowers are built to last anyway. They wear a thick, waxy cuticle to retard evaporation and are reinforced with many woody veins providing water and internal support.

However, other commercial cut flowers must be primed before shipment. This includes dunking them in buckets or spraying them with harsh preservative chemicals, especially roses exported from South America. These cut flowers are then stored in low-temperature warehouses with controlled atmospheres, narrowly limiting humidity, oxygen, and carbon dioxide levels. The main benefit of controlled-atmosphere storage is the active suppression of the plant's ripening and death hormone, ethylene gas. Amazingly, the roses you bought for your sweetheart or mother on Valentine's Day may have been picked in Ecuador or Colombia way back in December, then held, chilled, for as long as two or three months in controlled-atmosphere warehouses until they're purchased, then shipped, just before February 14. Few customers ever guess that their Valentine's Day red roses are the Methuselahs of the cut-flower world.

During harvesting, trimming, packaging, and transportation, cut flowers are subjected to many physical abuses. All the jostling, bouncing, wrapping, and being stuffed into tight cartons create large and small abrasions and breaks in their tissues. These plant wounds produce and release the colorless, odorless ethylene (C_2H_4) molecule we met earlier.

If you put a rock-hard, unripe pear inside a paper bag with a ripe apple, the pear will ripen faster. That's because apples are champion producers of ethylene, sending the gas out through special pores on their peels. Apples are also the reason any good florist will frown and shake his or her head inside many supermarkets. Invariably, the market's produce department proudly displays their cut flowers next to the fruit bins, then wonders why the flowers don't last as long as they did before. The role of ethylene gas as a fruit-ripening hormone has been known since 1935, and the gas can be generated by burning organic fuels, including kerosene. Ripening by burning fuel was a tradition in some ancient cultures. Supposedly, ancient Egyptians gassed their figs, while the Chinese burned incense in closed rooms to enhance the ripening of pea pods.

With flowers, it's a bit different. Ethylene is the chemical trigger that signals the flower to change from maiden to matron. It's time for Cinderella to shed her delicate petals and become a fat pumpkin, or another fruit. The fertilization of an ovary by pollen tubes containing sperm is a potent trigger stimulating ethylene production by the parent plant. Once the flower is exposed to ethylene, it aborts its petals and the tips of the sexual organs shrivel. The surviving ovary expands as the parent plant gives it more water, and ripening seeds within make the young fruit bulge. Think of a rose flower and those wide, succulent rose hips that develop after the pretty petals shrivel.

Now that the complete genomes of popular flowers, such as petunias, have been elucidated, plant breeders have begun to use their genomic maps to attack formerly intractable problems, such as ethylene sensitivity. In effect, this is a trick to make petunias unaware they've just had sex by making them less sensitive, or totally insensitive, to ethylene. Early genetic-modification experiments have resulted in petunia flowers that hold their petals four or even ten times longer. So far, it has been easier for producers and packers to use ethylene-blocking chemical sprays, or to include "ethylene-scrubbing" packets with the flowers they ship. Perhaps in the future, imaginative breeders will give us ethylene-immune blossoms that don't require drenching in toxic chemicals before being air-shipped to buyers in the United States and elsewhere.

Breeding for Longer Vase Life

Flower breeders are always trying to improve their existing cultivars and new varieties for the marketplace. The top priorities now include changing genes so our flowers are showier (more intense colors and more petals), have greater disease resistance, and produce flowers that live far longer after being cut to better survive harvesting and shipping before they reach a florist shop. But the chemical, temperature, and atmosphere tricks discussed previously are not enough to produce a durable flower. Yes, grandmother had her own techniques for making roses in bowls last longer, but not everyone today recuts flower stems, changes water, or dissolves an aspirin or plant food in the water as he or she should. Please refer to appendix 3 for what you should be doing.

Plant breeders try to select for longer-lasting blooms, seemingly impossible when considering something as ephemeral as flowers. As usual, some tropical orchids live longest as cut flowers in a vase. The flower of a moth orchid (*Phalaenopsis* spp.) may live for a couple of weeks in a vase or five to eight months if left as an unpollinated flower on a potted plant. Other orchids such as hybrid cymbidiums, with their tough, almost woody stems, may persist for weeks in vases of clean water. Under natural conditions, orchids and roses may produce dozens or more unique scent molecules in the same flower. Fragrance, unfortunately, is something that breeders don't try to preserve and is often lost quickly through genetic modification because most flowers must go through several biochemical pathways to make only one fragrance molecule. Thus we have the lovely but unscented Leonidas roses.

A Visit to the Los Angeles Flower Market

Just after dawn, I found that the flower market was already abuzz, not with pollinators, but wholesale flower vendors, prospective buyers, and curious, flower-struck, wandering individuals, gawkers like myself and my partner, Kay, there to smell the roses, and hoping to get a great deal on a bouquet or entire bucket of magnificent freshly cut blooms. None of us went away disappointed, or without a few new acquisitions.

Taking time to introduce myself and speaking with several of the vendors gave me a sense of the place, its long history, and what the flower workers thought of their jobs, working day after day surrounded by all this natural beauty, and, as it occurred to me later, what it takes to be successful as a merchant of floral sexual organs.

Surprisingly, the market didn't smell like flowers; it was different, with an overriding "green" aroma emanating from leaves and the juicy surfaces of cut stems. Sure, there were floral overtones, but they all blended together into something generic or artificial. If I wanted to inhale the fragrance of one kind of flower, I needed to pick up a bouquet and bring it to my face. I stood in a sea of blooms on the day of our visit, including bestsellers such as the moth orchids, purple lilacs, hydrangeas, roses, regular and fancy parrot tulips, blue thistle, the newly popular miniature calla lilies, old favorites such as the Stargazer lily, and its new incarnation, the Starfighter. Vendors talked with potential customers, pointing out the just-arrived-and-displayed blooms, breaking into smiles as they picked up a single bloom or arrangement to show it off and close a sale. Other small-business owners and their assistants chattered away incessantly on their cell phones, making sure that purchased flowers were delivered on time to customers in Los Angeles, or farther away, in Orange or San Diego Counties.

Although the shop owners change frequently, and many now sell vases and pots in addition to cut flowers and live plants, the old-timers have worked in the flower market for ten or twenty years. They work and socialize together, many attended local Los Angeles schools together, and they help one another during some workdays lasting up to twelve hours. On certain days the market opens at midnight, the public is allowed in around 8:00 a.m., and by noon everything is over, except for putting delicate blooms, such as the roses, back into their cooler rooms. One worker I spoke to, Garcia, had worked at the market since 1995 and had learned all the flower names and the business from his uncle. He performs the daily routines of unboxing the flower shipments, which arrive twice weekly, recutting the stems, and placing them in buckets of fresh water out on the concrete floor of the vending area. Garcia, like many others, also plucks off the bright orange or rusty-colored anthers of Stargazers and other lilies, thereby emasculating them. Customers complain that their oily pollen stains fancy tablecloths and their clothing. Personally, I'm against floral mutilation, or emasculation, in any form. I want my anthers!

Flowers come to the Los Angeles Flower Market from all over the world. Long-stemmed roses come from Ecuador (the best), but also from Colombia and, recently, from Dutch-funded flower farms in Kenya. *Dendrobium* orchids make their way from Thailand and Singapore. Blooms exported from growers in Mexico come to the market after their brief inspection stopovers at the Miami or LAX Airports, or from California, such as from the many farms within a hundred-mile radius of this place now growing moth orchids. Mexico is also a major exporter of cut flowers, many of them nontropicals.

Established by Armenian immigrants and still located at its original 754 Wall Street address in downtown Los Angeles, the Original Los Angeles Flower Market and American Florists' Exchange has been a landmark of this area, and major contributor to its economy, since 1921. More than fifty independent floral vendors pack the crowded fifty-thousand-square-foot warehouses making up this flower market. Not just a haunt of wholesale merchants wanting to buy the freshest and most diverse flowers for their shops, the market is also open daily to the public for retail sales. This is the best place in Los Angeles to get bargains on flowers, whether you are a wholesaler or an individual buyer just wanting the freshest blooms for your dining-room table or a loved one.

Marteen, a worker employed by a tropicals shop owner (flowers and leaves arriving twice weekly from Costa Rica and Hawaii), mentioned the seasonal trends, of anthuriums, gingers, and heliconias used in Southern California luaus, or the heart-shaped spathes of brilliant red anthuriums on Valentine's Day, or the ever-popular potted moth orchids as Mother's Day gifts. Here were Hawaiian ti plants (*Cordyline fruticosa*), philodendrons, and heliconias, along with many orchids. Previously, Marteen had worked in a nearby restaurant, but he joined the market eighteen years ago, never regretting his vocational choice. He winks at me. These days he's not as excited about the flowers as he once was. He compares working with flowers to wearing the same-color clothes day after day, but then confides that he still enjoys bringing cut flowers home for his wife and family, at least now and then.

Breeding Flowers for Modern Gardens

We've explored how hybrids sometimes happen between plants in nature and, historically, how plant breeders have hybridized flowers producing some of our favorite and showiest garden blooms. Many new breeding efforts are aimed at producing better and new types of bedding plants. These plants (chrysanthemums, marigolds, pansies, petunias) are annuals or tender perennials specifically planted for massed spring and summer colors in the garden. Growing them in colder regions always means they will die with autumn's first freezing temperatures.

Much of modern plant breeding remains the same as practiced in the early days of plant pioneers such as George Washington Carver (c. 1864–1943) and Luther Burbank. Parental plants are selected for desirable characteristics (colors, disease, or insect resistance; yield and nutrition if they are crop plants) and then hand-crossed to produce new variants among the resulting progeny.

In contrast, when a plant breeder produces a new variety, it takes additional years to build a supply of seeds or plantlets to have enough to send out for about three years of "trialing." During this period, the trialing company is contracted to grow and evaluate the new plant cultivar under a variety of different climatic conditions. Typically, the plants are grown at five or six geographically and climatically distinct locations, and the plants' responses to different regimes (e.g., muddy soils, hot summers, early freezes, etc.) are carefully recorded. If a new plant looks promising, the original grower/company will only then begin mass propagation for commercial release and marketing. Three years of trialing can cost $40,000. When the propagation, release, and marketing are added in, the developing company will have spent more than $100,000 getting its new flower to market. Bringing a new annual plant to market is the fastest, at only four or five years. Perennials may take six to ten years, and shrubs, the longest, often more than ten years to enter the marketplace.

Ornamental-Plant Breeding Today

Modern plant breeding has gone high-tech with the use of gene guns, irradiation, embryo rescue, and other intricate methods. Commercial plant breeders can use a gene gun to blast DNA into unsuspecting cells in tissue culture. Extracted DNA from a host plant (or animal!) is coated onto microscopic gold particles. These gene-coated particles are shot into egg cells, a few of which absorb and adopt the foreign DNA. This is a rapid way of introducing diverse DNA into target chromosomes within cells. Gene-gun blasting is, however, expensive and tedious, used only by the largest companies, especially for breeding new crop-plant varieties. Gene blasting is much more profitable for developing and selling new agricultural crop plants, with their huge and lucrative markets, than for bedding plants, with much smaller markets and research budgets.

Since the early-twentieth century, "mutation breeding" has routinely used combinations of radiation and/or mutagenic chemicals to generate mutations or "freaks" in older cultivars. Plants are commonly subjected to either X-rays or gamma rays. Techniques to produce these mutagenic plants or seeds were first developed in the 1920s and are still widely used to produce new crop plants (about 75 percent) and ornamental flowering plants (about 25 percent). Chrysanthemums are an example of a flower crop whose breeders have extensively used irradiation for many decades to produce new flowers. Mutagenic plants are less well documented or publicly announced (or leaked) compared to the widespread transgenic processes leading to the creation of genetically modified organisms (GMOs) used in our food supply.

Molecular genetics now affords plant breeders unique insights into their breeding programs. Mapping plant genomes, or the use of DNA fingerprinting, has been used to identify genetic materials and kinships among plants. Now, breeders can understand true genetic affinities (relatedness) and not be fooled by flowers that are ecological look-alikes. Thus, modern flower breeders are attempting crosses between species that they would never have tried in the past.

An exciting new technique called embryo rescue is being used to preserve unlikely crosses that would otherwise die in the seed. Plant breeders frequently make crosses that never become mature fruit or contain viable seeds because the recipient/mother plant aborts the offspring. Instead, the usually doomed embryos are surgically removed from the failing seeds and grown on sterile media inside culture flasks. This captures a lot of genetic diversity, and the new progeny live long enough for evaluation as promising new flowers for the garden. Additionally, breeders often engender sterility, creating a floral mule. As the sterile plants can't make seeds, they are tricked into continuous flowering (called throwing, by the industry) all summer long. With their flowering season now extended unnaturally, nothing could be better for the prospective breeders and buyers. An example of sterility in modern breeding programs is the trailing snapdragon Summer Wave (*Torenia*), from Proven Winners LLC in Florida.

Genes in a Bottle Unleashed?

Beginning in Europe, then spreading to America and around the world, a public largely ignorant of plant-breeding techniques, and declining in overall scientific literacy, has been frightened by otherwise well-meaning environmentalist organizations concerning our food supply. Today, processed-food companies are clamoring to rid their foods, and their labels, of the evils of GMOs, prodded by public debates, street demonstrations, and violent outcries. A current estimate puts the percentage of our processed foods containing one or more GMO ingredients at a staggering 70 to 80 percent, largely due to the American monoculture corn and soybean crops. Thus, there is cause for concern.

As a pollination ecologist and evolutionary biologist, I don't favor moving genes between largely unrelated organisms, for example from one phylum to another (e.g., freeze-resistant fish genes into Flavr Savr tomatoes, or bacterial plasmid genomes into flowering plants). The latter, however, has happened naturally many times during the evolutionary history of the angiosperms since their origin about 130 million years ago. There is something undesirable about playing God with natural selection, or playing Dr. Victor Frankenstein, modeled after Mary Shelley's fictional character, with our food-producing organisms. This is especially true if they can escape from cultivation or domestication (very likely) and release their aberrant genomes upon the natural world. That is my biggest fear. Mandated isolation distances between evaluation test plots of crop-plant varieties are typically much less than honey bees and other pollinators normally fly, setting a dangerous precedent. Several genes from GMO crops have already found their way into their closest weedy crop-plant relatives (as in some wild radishes and sunflowers).

It is uncertain whether GMO crops produce inherently unsafe "Frankenfoods" for humans, our livestock, other food animals, or our pets. I suppose we'll find out soon enough. Ironically, the current abject horror that many people feel toward the use of new methods (GMOs and gene guns), and not-so-new (e.g., hybrid flower crosses, mutational breeding) historical techniques to alter plant genomes, is much the same as previous religious opposition and utter disgust about creating and using man-made hybridized garden flowers once expressed to Luther Burbank by his minister.

The Little Black Flower

"Black" flowers are mysterious, foreboding, but also somehow elegant. They seem to spring from another time, or a dreamlike fairy-tale world. According to florist-company marketing mavens, black flowers are supposed to symbolize power, elegance, mystery, and farewell. The romantic message of a black flower is dour, perhaps used hastily or cruelly by someone breaking off a relationship. The floral marketers and public relations experts, however, seem to think a single black blossom, along with a tasteful gift, is a powerful romantic gesture with just a hint of mystery. Does the person still love me? In Victorian and Edwardian times in England, black flowers were eagerly sought out or created artificially using black velvet, lace, or crepe paper.

Examples of nearly black blooms are restricted in nature to the bat flower (*Tacca*) and some of the Mediterranean and near-Asian irises. During the twentieth century, hybridizers gave us a black dahlia, the dark calla lily, Queen of the Night tulip, Black Magic hollyhock (*Alcea*), and most recently the Black Velvet petunia. The Bowles' Black pansy is derived from a combination of much older hybrids between the alpine viola (*Viola cornuta*) and the heartsease (*Viola tricolor*). Both of these wild pansies produce melanistic forms in which two petals are so intensely purple that they appear black, with three additional petals with sooty tips. Plant breeders exploited and exaggerated this color form until the flower was all-black with a yellow center.

I spoke with ornamental-flower breeder Jianping Ren about how she created Black Velvet, the world's first black petunia, in 2006, for Ball Horticulture Company and Ball Colegrave, the UK horticultural giant. This flower came into existence using traditional hybridizing methods, crosses and genetic recombination, not sleight-of-hand genetic alchemy, or inserting genes from a totally unrelated organism. In 2003, Jianping noticed an unusual green petunia among one of her breeding plants, apparently a natural mutant. Green had never revealed itself among the ranks of commercial petunias. She decided to play with the greenish flowers a bit to see what additional or unusual colors might arise.

Jianping used the green mutant to produce generations of petunias with "dirty colors," not the expected bright and saturated floral hues. Soon, she had something unusual, a luscious velvety-black flower, a first in petunia breeding. Including the traditional crossbreeding, and two years of trialing at different locales and under different growing conditions, it took Jianping and her colleagues four years to develop their black petunia for commercial release to growers in 2010. It has been available for consumers since 2011. Black Velvet has had excellent sales and gardener approval in both the United Kingdom and the United States. With the first release of plants in Britain, during 2011, individual plants were selling for the handsome price of three pounds sterling. The marketing tagline for the new petunias was "Black goes with anything!" How can anyone argue with basic black and haute couture fashion? The little black flower meets the little black dress. I'm thinking that black-clad Goth gardeners are already familiar with this annual bedding plant. Jianping, however, does not expect this "niche flower" to ever replace the popular white, pink, red, and blue hues of the always top-selling garden-shop petunias.

No wildflowers are truly black. They are all a bit of an optical illusion. Floral petals have no inklike black pigments. There are only "optic black" flowers, including the Bowles' Black pansy and the Black Velvet petunia and similar cultivars. We see these flowers as black because they have a double petal skin with purple pigments in the uppermost layer and blue pigments in the one below. When sunlight interacts with these layers, our eyes and brains are fooled into thinking they are black, the very absence of color. It's just another trick played on us by sunlight interacting with objects.

Natural selection has produced wildflowers with nearly black floral parts or pollen, typically with darkened floral centers or petals displaying a black web or a starlike pattern. The most spectacular of these are the so-called black irises, found from Israel north into Turkey and Central Asia. Other wildflowers with dark bull's-eye patterns, or black somewhere, include opium poppies, orange buttercups, red anemones, and the red Adonis flowers of the Middle East. In South Africa, flowers with dark, almost black, spots are found in the iris, daisy, hyacinth, and amaryllis families. The dark blotches, most often advertised discreetly at the petal bases, are contrasting color signals especially attractive to certain pollinating insects. When broken by two white dots, the dark patches are called beetle marks. In southern Africa, specialized scarabs called monkey beetles use the beetle marks to find their way to iris and amaryllis blooms. For the black irises, the jet-colored blotches are believed to mimic sleeping holes used by male bees as dormitories that they vacate the following morning.

Quest for the Holy Grail: The World's First True Blue Rose

Vibrant blue roses have been portrayed in world literature since at least the twelfth century. These fanciful flowers are symbols of unrequited love, or a quest for the impossible to those who seek it. The blue rose is only for those willing to risk everything in the endeavor. The book *Kitab al-Felahah*, written in Arabic, has tantalizing references to azure roses found only in the Orient, but alas they were clever fakes. Astute growers or merchants inserted a blue dye between the bark and the roots of otherwise normal white or cream-colored roses. After a few weeks they had their blue roses, and presumably duped buyers willing to pay premium prices.

In reality, blue roses simply do not exist as wildflowers. They are more unicorn than flower, a mythic garden vision. Plants in the genus *Rosa* are genetically handicapped. None of the one hundred or more kinds of wild roses has the right genes to produce the blue pigments. In fact, blue flowers are not all that common in nature, and most won't adapt to garden life. For blue hues, we should be grateful to the delphiniums, forget-me-nots, geraniums, bellflowers (*Campanula*), and morning glories (*Convolvulus*) willing to bloom in our yards.

You can, however, buy blue roses, of a sort, in almost any market or florist shop. What's going on here? Turns out that it's easy to dye floral petals blue or other colors. You can do it yourself at home by dissolving water-soluble dyes (e.g., food coloring) in a bucket of water and letting the cut flowers do the rest by drawing up those pigments through water-conducting tissues in their severed stems. Voilà! We now have blue roses, or blue or green or pink carnations. Even worse, many flower vendors spray paint their flowers to create the various colors, including blue ones. Glitterati blooms—ones artificially enhanced with glue, glitter, and faked colors—are here, apparently to stay. Online, there are YouTube flower-painting tutorials, and special aerosol paints are sold in craft stores to help enterprising plant artists get what evolution denies. Sorry, but I draw the line here at this blatant artificiality on the stem. I may, however, be in the flower-buying minority, because these fake creations are popular, selling in huge numbers and in many countries.

Suntory Holdings Ltd. is a global behemoth in the alcoholic-beverage and food industry, seemingly driven by its motto *Yatte minahare* ("Go for it!" in Japanese). Adding to its portfolio of more than two hundred subsidiary companies, Suntory's chairman of the board, Nobutada Saji, made a strategic purchase of Florigene, an Australian biotechnology company in 2003. Among plant breeders, it was rumored that the multimillion-dollar deal might have a hidden agenda. Billionaire Saji is an ardent flower lover and dearly wanted the GMO blue rose that Florigene had been secretly developing since the 1990s. Florigene was rumored to have spent A$45 million developing the flower. If so, Saji would have prominently displayed the world's first man-made blue roses in Suntory's corporate offices in Osaka, Japan. We can only imagine the lavish reception party that would have accompanied their glorious corporate debut. After various twists and turns, the new acquisition morphed into Suntory Flowers Ltd.

In the Florigene laboratories, molecular engineers used genetic engineering to rearrange the genetic blueprint for rose-petal pigments. The complex research took thirteen years. They began with a white rose and needed three more steps in an elaborate process. First, the researchers borrowed the delphinidin gene from a pansy and put it into an heirloom purplish rose, Cardinal de Richelieu. The now genetically enhanced rosebush produced a rose the rich color of burgundy wine. A molecular technique called RNA interference was then used to hold back the rest of the color production by blocking a specific protein. This procedure allowed only the new blue color to show through within the petals. The first announcement of the blue rose, called Applause, was made in 2004.

Unfortunately their RNA gambit didn't go entirely as planned. Some of the original reddish rose color remained in the petals. Rose petal cells are more acidic than pansy petal cells, and acid turns blue pigments red (think of litmus-test papers). The much-anticipated blue rose from Suntory is more of a lavender or pale mauve than a true sky blue, at least to my eye. Released into Asian and European markets, Applause roses sold for staggering prices, up to $35 per stem in Japan during 2010. Messing with preexisting genes to add novel colors to flowers isn't as easy or straightforward as floriculture scientists had once hoped. Only with traditional plant breeding or more insightful genetic engineering to make the rose petals less acidic might the gene shufflers at last have their true blue commercial rose. Whether the flower-buying public will steer clear of GMO flowers has yet to be determined. Perhaps Suntory's blue rose will become the poster child for genetically engineered blossoms.

Gardeners and Pollinators Beware!

We have been modifying the way flowers look and last for centuries, even though some techniques for increasing mutation frequencies are relatively new. A question we often fail to ask, though, is how good (i.e., nutritionally rewarding) are these new flowers for bees, butterflies, sphinx moths, and hummingbirds?

A nationwide citizen science project was conducted in England to determine which garden flowers were most visited by bumble bees. Under the direction of M. Fussell and Sally Corbet, schoolchildren observed more than thirty thousand bees on common garden-flower varieties in the United Kingdom. In this clever project, bumble bees were "asked" to choose among wild types and modified garden cultivars. Coming out as a clear favorite was the little shrub rockspray (*Cotoneaster horizontalis*). Branches on this bush were alive with buzzing bees that could be heard from some distance away. Other bumble bee favorites included red clovers (*Trifolium pratense*), an excellent source of nectar for long-tongued bees. These same bees often avoided flowers that upon closer examination lacked rewards. For example, they avoided a pretty doubled variety of trefoil (*Lotus corniculatus*), whose yellow blooms no longer secreted nectar. "Doubled" flowers often lack nectar as the production of extra petals stops development of nectar glands. Doubling also reduces the number of pollen-making stamens. Thus, the "bee bread" in such flowers is reduced or more difficult for bees to collect.

You can't tell at first glance whether the flowers bought at your neighborhood nursery will attract and reward pollinating animals. Floral scents are routinely diminished or altogether absent in many popular floral varieties. Scent is often the first thing lost when breeders create longer-lasting cut flowers. Fragrance molecules are metabolically expensive to produce. A flower with no or limited scent lasts longer on the plant or in a vase.

If you want your garden beds to attract the winged jewels we call hummingbirds, butterflies, and other insects, you need to choose appropriate seeds and seedlings. You can search online (e.g., the Pollinator Partnership or the Xerces Society) or at local native plant nurseries for the very best, pollinator rewarding, flowering plants that can be easily grown in your region. Many of the best plants to use are locally adapted native wildflowers.

May the Best Illusion Win

A botanical flower spectacle beyond all others takes place in London every spring. It's difficult to call it a flower show or utter its name in the same breath with any major flower exhibition anywhere. Simply called the Chelsea, its fame spread long ago around the globe and is rekindled each year when attendees scramble to buy tickets. Gardeners and florists daydream about it in the days prior to the show's opening. They fantasize about walking amid the extravagant displays of fragrant, colorful blooms, foliage, and more.

An entire book could be devoted to the pageantry, traditions, history, and spectacle that are the Chelsea. These aren't just potted plants on parade, ones with blue ribbons that you can find almost anywhere else. The show is pure spectacle and surrealistic eye candy. Assembled here are world-class specimen plants and floral displays with more than a bit of behind-the-scenes trickery. Some of the plants have been forced into flowering early for the show via temperature control, proper lighting, and timing—watered with plenty of money. The hundreds of exhibitors are more dream merchants than vendors. I can't think of another national or international flower show where the competition is so keen, and where awards are given for imaginary landscapes, botanical dreamscapes of every description. The Chelsea is all about grand illusion. Even human royalty arrive to delight in the extravagances of their flowers.

The Chelsea began in 1862 as the Great Spring Show, held by the Royal Horticultural Society (RHS) at its garden in Kensington, which today is an affluent and densely populated district of west London. In 1888, the RHS moved the Chelsea show to the heart of London at the Temple Gardens, whose recorded history dates to 1307, the time of the Knights Templar. The roses for which the Temple Gardens have always been famous are mentioned in Shakespeare's *Henry VI: Part I*. The Chelsea Flower Show is arguably the largest and most important flower show in the world. All the major plant-breeding companies are represented, displaying their latest creations. Here, the world's rarest and most expensive flowers are first introduced to the public.

The show is held for five days in May. Since 1905, it has been held on the grounds of the Royal Hospital Chelsea in London. Today, the show is attended by more than 160,000 visitors, only limited by its relatively small, eleven-acre exhibition site. The show is covered intensely on television by the British Broadcasting Corporation, and at least a few members of the British royal family routinely attend its gala preview and open the gala event. New flowering-plant varieties are showcased and launched. The show is very much like a haute couture, Parisian spring fashion show premiering the latest clothing from famous designers. Here, ruffled blooms are the showstoppers, instead of starved, leggy female models in exclusive designer gowns.

Historically, important and startlingly beautiful flowers have been introduced at the Chelsea Flower Show. I'm thinking of the 2006 introduction of the amazing camellia-like Juliet rose by legendary UK plant breeder David Austin, which took the horticultural world by storm. This abundantly petaled, pale rose was fifteen years in the making at an estimated cost of $4.72 million.

The Chelsea dream-makers are at work every year trying to best one another for bragging rights and awards, and to best their previous already-extravagant displays. It's always a surprise and a delight to experience what they create. Illusions and dreamy imaginary landscapes are created from scratch, botanical worlds and floralscapes that you will never experience anywhere else. A prime example was the ostentatious and lavish "Ace of Diamonds" garden-landscape exhibit created (by David Domoney) for the 2010 Chelsea show, more costly than all the other Chelsea exhibits combined during its more than hundred-year history. It not only featured plants named after jewelry, but rare jewelry inspired by plants. Included within this fanciful environment was a daisy-shaped custom ring created for the show, set with a rare $5 million blue diamond, along with other smaller diamonds loaned by a Bond Street financier. Nearby, several large security men stood watching the crowds, giving this pricey garden the feel of a nightclub doorway on Ipswich High Street in the preclosing, early-morning hours. The garden filled six thousand square feet and was valued at more than $31 million. Plenty of green spent on flowers and their elegant bejeweled temporary home.

CHAPTER 7

Arriving by Jumbo Jet

The jutting lips (petals)
of a hybrid orchid (*Cattleya* sp.)

Flowers grown halfway around the globe can be yours, shipped to your doorstep with next-day service in most countries. The virtual image on your computer screen today becomes your reality tomorrow when your flowers arrive. This is globalization in action with a huge international impact. Time and space have been altered in a way nature never planned.

Millions of flowers move across continents every day as freight aboard aircraft and inside eighteen-wheeled semitrailer trucks. In a year, billions of flowers are quickly moved from country to country, from growing regions to auctions, packers, and distributors, then on to their final retail destinations. Most of the fascinating journeys of these cut blooms go on out of view of the public, a little-told story in modern global commerce.

Not long ago, Americans visited local family-owned florist shops, making all of their purchases in person, chatting with shop owners or knowledgeable clerks about flowers available that season, or which ones were the freshest. Historically, the majority of cut flowers Americans purchased were grown on US soils on flower farms or inside greenhouses, especially ones in the San Francisco Bay region, coastal valleys of California, and parts of Florida. Today, customers still visit florist shops, but their purchases seem quaint in the rush to order flowers online for fast delivery or as impulse purchases at the supermarket or big-box stores such as Lowe's or Home Depot. Now, the single-stemmed cut flowers that each of us buys are largely grown and shipped to us from overseas, from growers and packers in Latin American countries. In what seems to be the cultural mantra for American shoppers, not only do we want our flowers right away, but they'd better be fresh, must look absolutely fantastic, and be available at ever-lower prices.

Flower-Growing Moves toward the Equator

Large-scale producers, or affluent hobbyists, grow flowers under glass or plastic films in greenhouses because their plants, especially "tropicals," thrive under these warm and humid conditions as if they were still growing on their native soils in tropical forests. Greenhouse production of cut flowers (spring bedding plants, annuals such as petunias and marigolds, are mostly raised in US greenhouses) is an expensive commercial option, not for the faint of heart. Whenever possible, it costs less to grow bedding plants or cut flowers outdoors using traditional row-crop agricultural methods. The largest growers of cut flowers were once located in California's coastal and central valleys, and scattered along the Pacific Rim as far north as coastal Oregon and Washington. Today, large farms for cut flowers continue in California, but they are remnants of a once-great American agribusiness. Like so many other US industries, our cut-flower farms have also moved offshore. The domestic flower industry could not compete with more favorable corporate tax rates and cheap labor. Flower-growing for cut-stem markets moved toward the steamy and hot equator. Here are nutrient-rich volcanic soils, a favorable year-round climate, and laborers willing to work under harsh conditions and at wages unacceptable to most US citizens.

Among Latin American cut-flower-growing countries, Colombia leads the way, followed by Ecuador and Costa Rica. Colombian-grown flowers dominate US markets, with roughly a 70 percent market share, over $1 billion in stems sold each year. Amazingly, this billion-dollar business sprang from a 1967 botany term paper written by Colorado State University graduate student David Cheever. In his study, entitled "Bogotá, Colombia as a Cut-Flower Exporter for World Markets," Cheever extolled the virtues of a former-lake-bed savanna, near the small city of Facatativá, close to Bogotá at eight thousand seven hundred feet above sea level, and 320 miles north of the equator. In his business plan, the rich soils, equitable climate, and nearly consistent twelve hours of daylight year-round were perfect for growing a crop that everyone wanted 365 days a year: cut flowers on long, straight stems. At higher elevations in the tropical Andes, the moist and cooler climate mimics conditions favored by domesticated plants descended from temperate species. Exporting roses to other countries would probably be more profitable for farmers in this mountainous region than growing and selling apples, pears, and strawberries in the hot valleys below.

In 1969, while his friends were likely partying at Woodstock, Cheever and three partners together invested $100,000 in a new business, launching their flower-producing dream start-up company, Floramerica. They used assembly-line production methods and modern shipping-by-air methods to bring their ultraperishable products to US and other markets. Floramerica started by growing carnations in greenhouses on that savanna near Bogotá's El Dorado International Airport, with a short three-hour flight north to Miami. The Californian cut-bloom industry would never be the same again. In 1991, the US government suspended import duties on Colombian flowers, hoping to limit coca-shrub farming and the cocaine trade in violence-ravaged Colombia by creating decent-paying jobs outside the pervasive drug cartels. The results were quick and decisive for Colombia, but essentially wrecked US floral-stem production on California farms and for other regional US growers.

Thus began an economic revolution in Colombia, one fueled by beauty, not addictive illegal drugs. In 1971, growers of cut flowers in the United States produced 1.2 billion blooms (carnations, chrysanthemums, and roses), while the country imported a mere 100 million cut flowers. By 2003, the floral-stems balance had reversed. That year, the United States grew a scant 200 million cut stems, while it imported a staggering 2 billion, all the desirable favorites. Flowers had become a global commodity not unlike DVD players, flat-screen televisons, or tablet computers.

Today, visiting any of the cut-flower producers in Colombia, Ecuador, or Costa Rica is an eye-opener if you are accustomed to a patch of flowers growing in your home garden. This is indeed big business in blooms. Ecuadorian flower farms near Quito are typical of the large-scale South American flower growers. You see ramshackle greenhouses with clear-plastic films stretched and stapled tightly across wooden frames, but high-tech flower factories are inside. Rows of workers, usually women and girls, stand along opposite sides of slowly moving conveyor belts. If roses are being packed, the workers first remove the thorns using chain-mail gloves or special tools. Diseased, blemished, or torn leaves are removed along with substandard flowers. Stems are trimmed to standard lengths, and the stalks once again placed on the moving belt for the next worker along the line. Eventually, the floral bouquets are dunked, usually by men, into foul-smelling metal, fifty-five-gallon drums of fungicide, then shaken off or hung briefly to drain. The "tank mixes" may include a veritable soup of harsh chemicals, including floral preservatives. These are clearly not organic flower operations. In the recent past workers used substandard respirators or no protective gear while handling the now-toxic flowers, but conditions are gradually improving for the workers.

For the women who do most of the trimming, sorting, and packing of the cut blooms, these labor-intensive jobs lead to debilitating repetitive-stress injuries along with exposure to dangerous agricultural chemicals. Many of these chemicals are now banned for use in the United States or used under limited conditions and with adequate protective equipment. Greenhouse and field conditions on the South American flower farms are getting better. Many of the producers now provide fully protective clothing and respirators, along with health benefits and on-site recreational facilities or child-care services. Still, the work is harsh for the largely underpaid flower workers, not substantially different from the backbreaking routines that migrant workers experience while harvesting and boxing vegetables in the Imperial Valley in Southern California.

Once wrapped and packed into their boxes for shipping, the Ecuadorian cut roses and other blooms are briefly moved into cold rooms. From there, the flowers are loaded into refrigerated trucks and driven to the nearest airport. There, workers stack the thousands of flower boxes onto wooden pallets that are then shrink-wrapped and loaded by forklifts into the cargo holds of waiting jumbo jets. The flowers are the only passengers inside these stripped-down aircraft on their brief journey to Miami International Airport. It will, however, be several days before the thirsty flowers will again have water.

Arriving by Jumbo Jet

The tarmac at Miami International Airport is a busy place for passenger aircraft with their belly cargo, in addition to the frantic activity of the dedicated air-freight haulers. More than a hundred international air carriers, including the major Latin American airlines, have made Miami their main or only port of call. The cargo division is far from the gates and terminals filled with scurrying passengers. Cut flowers arrive inside aircraft with covered windows and no visible corporate logos. The planes have only two pilots, a flight engineer, no flight attendants, and maybe a coffeepot, with no seats or amenities for passengers, since there aren't any. Here, the cargo pays. Every day, more than a dozen aircraft may arrive, every one jammed full of fresh flowers. Around Valentine's Day, that number can increase to a frenetic fifty daily flights from South American airports.

The big cargo aircraft begin landing around four o'clock in the morning. Once the cut flowers are unloaded from inside their contoured aluminum containers, the ULDs ("unit load devices," each holding about 160 cubic feet of cargo), they are whisked to refrigerated coolers inside massive transit sheds, for unpacking, sorting, processing, and final inspections, prior to the next phase of their journey to markets and waiting flower lovers.

The inspectors at the Miami airport are Department of Homeland Security employees, and they are all-business, with few smiles. The inspectors shake out sample bouquets onto white backgrounds. If even one dead insect falls out or a fungal spot is found on a flower or leaf, the entire shipment can be rejected (tossed into a Dumpster or similarly disposed of) or ordered fumigated, expensive costs all borne by the original owner and shipper. Because these cut flowers are not intended for human consumption, they are not tested for illegal pesticide residues. The inspectors also examine the sampled boxes for contraband (they are automatically X-rayed). This doesn't happen much anymore, but in the past even romantic Valentine's Day red-rose stems were once hollowed out to conceal cocaine or other illegal drugs. Such commerce will always find a way.

By the early morning, many of the flower trucks are already speeding along Florida highways, especially north on Interstate 95, past its intersection with I-10, then continuing along the Eastern Seaboard to New York City's flower district, and other populous Eastern-city destinations.

Americans buy about 4 billion cut stems a year, amounting to 10 million flowers every day. About 88 percent of the several billion cut flowers imported to the United States arrive by air at the Miami airport en route to their final destinations. Additional air-cargo shipments of fresh flowers are handled at Los Angeles, Boston, Chicago, and New York airports, but not nearly as many as at the flower hub that is Miami. In the first two weeks of February an extra 12 to 15 million roses pass through the Miami airport every day.

The number of globe-trotting blooms making up the modern cut-flower trade is staggering to consider. Globally, about 15 billion cut flowers make their way from growers to sellers every year, shipped by air or by trucking lines and independent haulers. By 2003, cut flowers and floriculture had grown to become a multibillion dollar industry worldwide, growing by about 6 percent annually.

Lusting for Spring Blooms

It is important to distinguish between the domestic and foreign cut-bloom industry (largely roses), and the seasonal potted and bedding-plant commercial trade. Some US bedding plants travel here from Europe, through Holland, but the majority are grown in the United States by the largest wholesale nurseries. People, especially those living on the East Coast, delight in buying potted hybrids, especially primroses, hyacinths, cyclamens, tulips, and daffodils, early in the season, almost before the ground has thawed. These spring beauties help to relieve the common psychological malaise of "winter sickness," with everyone hoping for sunshine and warmer weather, a time to plant. Many of these inexpensive potted plants are annuals such as pansies, tufted violas, petunias, and verbenas. They are sold as throwaways and are headed for the Dumpster after they bloom or die from improper care. Also, no florist sells begonias or cyclamens as cut flowers. Their lives are too short and they fall apart when handled. Apparently, turnabout is fair play, since Europeans now buy potted native American plants, especially our cacti, but these American/Mexican succulents began their lives in Israeli kibbutzim before being exported to Europe.

Meanwhile, messages bombard us by Internet, television, radio, newsprint ads, and end-counter displays in our local nursery or garden center, encouraging us to buy small potted shrubs with buds and blooms in advance of their actual blooming season. These potted beauties are forced into blooming in greenhouses or warm outdoor locations, then shipped to nurseries and hardware stores. Why? Spring gardeners are eager for anything flowering at the onset of spring. Favored plants seem to be late-winter pots of forced bulbs, forsythias, lilacs, and azaleas already in advanced bloom. Today, who has the time or patience to wait for Mother Nature? This same "florific" anticipation occurs again in late summer when we can't resist budding and blooming pots of "autumn" chrysanthemums from various purveyors.

Nurseries get in on this advance-bloom psychology as well. Go to any dedicated nursery, or hardware-store-chain nursery-sales area, in the spring. Take note of what is for sale, and what is blooming. Here are rhododendrons, azaleas, forsythias (in the Midwest and Eastern US), lilacs, and many others. These plants are in glorious full bloom a full month before their buds should have expanded into flowers. This isn't early blooming caused by global warming; it's a fact of plant-industry marketing ploys, planting the seeds of hope and desire in our minds.

The Dutch Connection:
Bidding for the World's Blooms

Dutch businessmen and women are consummate flower traders and dealers. Just as in the seventeenth-century tulipmania, when the fervent desire for fancy tulips seized wealthy speculators in a bubble market, today the world turns to Dutch auctioneers for buying and selling their prized blooms. The Dutch are the world's leading flower exporters. Europeans are more familiar with the Dutch flower business than Americans—since only about 5 percent (roughly 200 million) of US flowers pass through Holland—due to the unique business practices and traditions of the Dutch auction houses. There isn't an easy way to know the provenance of cut blooms sold at your favorite market.

In Europe, the Middle East, and Asia, the majority of cut flowers and bulbs first pass through Amsterdam's Schiphol Airport. From the airport, they enter the massive Dutch auction and computerized bidding system before resuming travel to their final destinations in many countries. Flowers sold in the Dutch auctions may have come from as far away as Colombia, Ecuador, Costa Rica, Ethiopia, and several European countries, along with Israel, Kenya, South Africa, or Zimbabwe. Flowers can spend up to a week transported through various warehouses, airports, and often the Dutch auction houses, before reaching their final destinations, looking almost as fresh as the day they were harvested somewhere far away. Looking at why this happens, and its history, makes for a fascinating story, even if you aren't a fan of plant auctions.

The Aalsmeer flower auctions, close to the Schiphol Airport, are now world famous but had simpler beginnings. They were started in 1911 by a group of Dutch bulb and flower growers meeting in a café. They came up with the idea of holding an auction they called Bloemenlust as a way to gain more control over the prices they got for their flowers and how they were sold. Many auctions followed, but by 1968 the largest became known as Bloemenveiling Aalsmeer. By 2008, the Aalsmeer flower auction had merged with the auctions of Naaldwijk and Rijnsburg and became Flora-Holland. Not only a major auction center, Aalsmeer also serves as a sort of regional distribution center, where flowers get rerouted by air to destinations around the world.

The immense FloraHolland building in Aalsmeer encompasses a staggering 10,750,000 square feet and is the largest single building, by its footprint, in the world. Its proximity to the Schiphol Airport, only eight miles away, makes it an ideal location for the daily auctioning of many of the world's blooms. The facility whirs with frantic activity, starting before dawn, nearly every day of the year. Truckloads of flowers unloaded at Schiphol begin arriving as early as midnight, and bidding starts before dawn. The nearby city of Aalsmeer, with a population of only twenty thousand, provides a workforce up to twelve thousand to move, buy, and sell all the flowers in the FloraHolland complex. Around 21 million flowers change hands here daily. The selling volume increases by 20 percent or more around Valentine's Day and Mother's Day.

Alstroemerias, carnations, roses, gerbera daisies, lilacs, freesias, chrysanthemums, and tulips are the major types of cut flowers on the auction block at Aalsmeer. Houseplants are sold here, too, including 9 million ivy plants and 13 million fig trees (*Ficus*). Pots of forced flower bulbs, ferns, cyclamens, begonias, and other decorative greenery for the florist trade are bought and sold, along with annuals, and bedding plants including petunias and pansies. In the FloraHolland building, hundreds of carts are loaded with flowers and stored in giant refrigerated rooms. Soon after their arrival, the flowers are graded by inspectors, getting around thirty inspections, and finally ending up graded A1 (the highest-quality blooms), A2, or B, the lowest-grade blossoms.

The cavernous building is noisy, alive with activity, as hundreds of workers shout out to one another while trying to avoid collisions amid the squeaks, creaks, and bangs that the rolling-cart trains make. Some workers stand while driving their sexy orange-and-black scooters that look a bit like Segway vehicles. Seated drivers steer electric vehicles pulling small trains of a dozen or more linked aluminum cars, each one a mobile rack holding one to seven layers of colorful potted plants or cut blooms. It seems chaotic as the flower trains make their way into and out of bidding halls scattered throughout the complex. Tourists walk, talk, and stop overhead on a network of metal catwalks, taking in the frenzied action on the warehouse floor. More than three hundred thousand international tourists visit the Aalsmeer flower auctions every year.

The five immense auction halls have tiered seating. More than a thousand wholesalers, mostly men, bid on trainloads of brilliant flowers as they move slowly by on the auction floor below, with about sixty thousand transactions daily. Everything seems to happen nonstop, as carts, people, and flowers are kept moving. Auction workers pick up a plant or bouquet at random, holding it aloft for all to see. This is called a Dutch auction, and unlike American auctions, where bidding starts low and ends high with the winning bid, in the Dutch system the auction price starts high and quickly works its way down.

A pair of huge, circular electronic wall clocks stare down upon the bidders like giant orbs. LED numerals on the clocks display the lot number, asking price, and information about the kind and quality of the flowers being offered for sale. Lots for each kind of flower appear only on one clock. The auctioneer starts the clock, and the digital lights sweep around the clockface (marked in euros, not seconds). The winning bid, actually the first bid registered, is reached long before the clock time expires. The first fast-fingered buyer to press his or her buy button has the winning bid. Dozens of transactions can be handled in under a minute. Bidders have only a few seconds to view, judge, and decide whether to buy before the flowers are moved out of the auction room and soon shipped to their new owners, often half a world away. This is an amazingly efficient way to see, move, and sell all those millions of flowers and plants every day.

Why all those flowers need to make a personal appearance on the bidding blocks near Amsterdam for Dutch auctioneers seems a bit mysterious, perhaps inexplicable to the rest of us. There are huge costs, and an immense jet-fuel carbon footprint, in transporting more than 5 billion flowers annually in and out of Holland during their quick but long-distance, jet-assisted journeys around the world. Why subject ultra-perishable fresh-cut flowers, of all things, to the added time and expense of getting them to and from Aalsmeer? Why waste the extra day or more of precious floral vase life that this complex process takes? It all seems absurd. No global television, automobile, beefsteak, or brussels sprouts auctions are taking place in Los Angeles, Hong Kong, Beijing, or Manhattan. I don't have an easy answer. Perhaps it is just a venerable and proud Dutch tradition.

200 Million Red Roses!

It's February 14, Saint Valentine's Day, once again. If you're a married man, or in a committed relationship, you better have planned ahead for your holiday purchases. Your reserved bouquet is waiting to be picked up at the local florist. If your iPhone calendar-app reminder was set for February 14, instead of the twelfth or thirteenth, you may be in deep trouble. No red roses may be available in any store. A card and a box of chocolates won't get you out of that! Mothers and grandmothers seem to be more forgiving than flower-slighted spouses or lovers.

The biggest flower-giving day in the United States is Valentine's Day (Mother's Day is a distant second). A staggering 224 million roses were grown, mostly in South America, for Valentine's Day in 2013. Almost all of these were long-stemmed, red-rose varieties. About 110 million roses are sold in the United States on Valentine's Day each year, with men making up about 75 percent of the buyers. Since red roses signify passionate love, about 43 percent of all freshly cut roses sold on Valentine's Day are red varieties. Another 29 percent of the Valentine's Day flowers are roses, but colors other than red. Women also buy flowers on this day, for their daughters, mothers, and grandmothers. Some women buy and have roses sent to themselves. Sales of Valentine's Day flowers are greatest if the holiday falls during the week, and dismal if it falls on a weekend. About $1.7 billion were spent by US consumers on Valentine's Day flowers in 2011. Although California produces 60 percent of the roses grown in the United State each year, the majority of long-stemmed Valentine's Day roses are imported from Central and South America. US purchases amount to more than 1 billion roses every year from overseas sources, mainly Colombia.

As we've seen, roses have symbolized many things over time and in various cultures. During the dynastic War of the Roses (1455–85) for the throne of England, a white rose was associated with the House of York, while a red rose stood for the rival House of Lancaster. Roses were sacred to the Roman goddess Venus, and she represented beauty, love, pleasure, and garden fertility.

Green Flowers

Our flower-buying tastes and habits were different in the past and they keep changing today. The demand for organically grown flowers is increasing, and this has led to more growers becoming certified as organic producers. US customers now want to know if they are buying safe, organic products, especially as regards flowers imported from other countries, whose pesticide regulations may be lax or nonexistent. A significant problem for certifying organic blooms has been that the bouquet you bought at Trader Joe's, or any other market, surely contains mixed blooms, perhaps organic flowers from California growers, along with flowers of unknown origins, or chemical treatments, from South American producers. Typically, there has been no easy way to follow the blooms from individual growers after they hit the tarmac in Miami, then make their way through the convoluted chains of distributors, resellers, and bouquet stuffers. The homeland origins of the flowers, and how they may have been farmed, or chemically treated postharvest, are somewhat mysterious and unknown to the average flower buyer.

So-called green-label flowers are one way that consumers can be more confident when making their purchases. With labels, consumers can learn about how their flowers were grown, if they were chemically sprayed, and perhaps about the seller's concern for social and environmental justice, including if the workers were equitably paid and labored under safe conditions. Many countries have created their own certification programs, especially European ones since the mid-1990s. The Dutch program known as Milieu Programma Sierteelt (MPS) certifies growers in Africa, Asia, Europe, Latin American, and the United States. Around forty-five hundred growers are members of this program, with roughly 85 percent of flowers sold in Aalsmeer now rated by MPS officials. Switzerland has its own certification agency, the Max Havelaar Foundation, and in the United Kingdom the watchdog organic-certification organization is the Fairtrade Foundation.

The United States has come around somewhat late to implementing flower certification. Things started to change in 2001 when Gerald Prolman entered the market with his Organic Bouquet brand of green-label flowers sold online. Working with SCS (Scientific Certification Systems), a group eventually developed a national ecofriendly flower-certification procedure and identification label: Veriflora. The certification by Veriflora is a big deal now, with key, large industry players including Delaware Valley Wholesale Florist (one of the top US wholesalers) and Sierra Flowers (in Canada) using certifications.

Even the South American producers have moved ahead with certification programs. Nevado Ecuador now has a line of organic roses, with the added bonus that they have the elusive fragrance you expect roses to have. The marketing campaign by Nevado Ecuador includes the slogan "Roses with a conscience," setting them apart from roses from other growers. Thus, it has become easier to recognize and buy organically produced blooms at food co-ops, certain florists, and even some retail markets. No doubt flowers certified as organic will increase in visibility and market share in the coming years, especially since Veriflora and Organic Bouquet have pioneered the way. Consumers, at least some, now expect to find organic blooms as a buying alternative, just as with produce in your local supermarket.

The Future of Flower-Growing

It's difficult to predict what technological or marketing surprises may be in store for US flower buyers, or flower lovers around the world. Today, you can order fresh flowers online at Amazon.com and from other suppliers and have them delivered in as few as one or two days. My guess is that by about 2018, within sixty minutes of completing your online order with Amazon Prime, a drone aircraft—a speedy, agile, little octocopter—might just land on your front sidewalk, deliver a small bouquet of flowers, or a boxed corsage plus chocolates, then speed away. What your dog might think of this, I have no idea.

Other flower producers in different regions around the globe, especially Africa, are also entering the market, and that will change the dynamics of how and where we get our flowers. Farmers in Yunnan, China, are developing cut-flower farms and are exploring global markets for exports. In Dubai, a new plant and flower auction, the Dubai Flower Centre (DFC), opened its doors in 2005, focused on the rising demand for luxury flowers in the Middle East. If the tax-free Gulf emirate becomes a floriculture logistics air hub, it might just prove to be a thorn in the side of the Dutch.

Since the DFC opened ten years ago, what has happened? Not surprisingly, with local oil revenues, this extensive luxury-flower market and distribution center has unfurled like the petals of its costly blooms. The Dubai flower market's auctions are different from their cold, stark forebears in gray, overcast Holland. Dubai has become a global city, a business and cultural center of the Middle East, as well as a famous playground for celebrities and the ultrawealthy.

The DFC is located on the grounds of the Dubai International Airport. Over 130 airlines make daily stops here, connecting to at least 220 cities around the world. The Dubai flower brokers are emulating the Dutch, but also innovating and reinventing the flower business in their own way. Here you will find one-stop shopping for local and international buyers, for traders, producers, and exporters. The DFC advertises itself as a transshipment center for "cool chain processes" that safeguard the quality of freshly cut flowers. This is achieved via the highest technology, with strict temperatures and atmospheric controls from the time flowers are unloaded. There are few if any breaks in the supply chain that might negatively affect flower vase life. Here also are controlled-atmosphere storage facilities for fruits and vegetables, prior to their distribution and sale.

The center excels in consolidating shipments and repackaging, along with the value-added services of bouquet-making. Eventually, the facility will be fully automated with flower-sorting robotics and quick turnover in and out of the center. Its initial capacity to handle 150,000 tons of flowers annually (along with perishable fruits, vegetables, and foilage) may eventually exceed 300,000 tons (compared to Schiphol's 736,608 tons). Ultimately, this center could serve the needs of over 2 billion flower-buying customers.

Consider for a moment that underneath the seats and flooring of your next international flight, commercial floral shipments may be additional passengers en route to Dubai, Holland, Miami, or another destination. Cut flowers have truly become items of globalized commerce, now removed from nature and their countries of origin, but playing ever-important roles in our daily lives.

PART III

~

FOODS, FLAVORS, SCENTS

Rocky Mountain columbines (*Aquilegia caerulea*) near Aspen, Colorado

CHAPTER 8

Eating Flowers

Queen-of-the-night cactus bud
(*Peniocereus greggii*) opening
after sunset

A chef wields culinary forceps, arranging blue and yellow, delicate Johnny-jump-up flowers, along with brilliant orange nasturtium petals, on each plain white plate, sticking them to an encircling line of spiced béchamel sauce. Rose petals and nasturtium blossoms are also sprinkled into the arugula and mesclun (baby greens) salad. Shimmering from within the ice cubes in water glasses are delicate blue and white, starlike borage blossoms (*Borago officinalis*). The herbed butter on the table was made with the diced flowering heads of purple chives and the tiny, blue petals from chicory flowers. The cocktails were garnished with colorful blossoms of snapdragon and hibiscus. Innovators of modern cuisine are having fun using flowers as garnishes to add or complement flavors, arranging and decorating foods to enhance their aesthetic appeal.

In this century, cooking with flowers is making a comeback in Western cuisines. Flowers began showing up in upscale grocery stores and trendy restaurants in the first years of the twenty-first century. Unfortunately, some people remain unsure about what is an edible flower and what's not. This is just as true for home gardeners and chefs as for restaurant patrons ready to dine. Which posy is edible and which is an appealing garnish for our eyes only?

Some American states have enacted laws regarding the use of fresh flowers in restaurants. If the flowers are displayed in a vase on your table, they are for decorative purposes only. Please don't eat the daises. If anything floral shows up on your plate, logically it should be edible. But, ask first. Home gardeners also wonder what they can safely eat. Are the contents of our home flower beds ever toxic? Flowers sprayed with insecticides or plants fed a fertilizer containing systemic insecticides should also be a concern of potential gourmets. You need to know the prior care and culture of your flowering plants received before you snip them for the table as edible additions.

Flowers impart a range of tastes not commonly found in other ingredients. They are not true spices (except for saffron and cloves) nor major food items, but make up a unique category. The flavors of edible flowers range widely, from insipid to sweet, spicy, and piquant. Most can be eaten raw, but some blooms must be carefully cleaned and their bitter parts discarded, while others require cooking. Most dramatically, they add beauty to our foods and dining tables.

In the most remote times of early humans and our hominid ancestors, we can envision them stooping in a meadow or alongside a stream to pick and enjoy the sweetness of flowers. Along with the nectar of flowers, and honey stored by true honey bees and their social-bee relatives, these were the first natural sweetening substances known to humanity.

Why Eat Flowers Anyway?

Typically, modern eaters do not consume large quantities of flowers during a single meal unless they are flower buds. In contrast, fully open or blooming flowers are far more difficult to gather in large quantities and aren't very nutritious or satisfying. No, flowers are usually relegated to only the visual delights of a colorful garnish, and many stare at them on their plates wondering if they can be eaten or only admired.

Perhaps this uncertainty is the fault of modern chefs, or the lack of widely available educational materials about edible blooms. Nevertheless, edible flowers contain small amounts of tasty nutrients including sugars, proteins, amino acids, lipids, antioxidants, and various pigments. Served by themselves as "flower confetti" or in syrups or sauces, or added to salads, main hot and cold dishes, drinks, or desserts, they color our food palettes and enliven our gustatory repertoire. Even flowers of the same species can taste different depending on their growing conditions and provenance. Terroir (the influence of the geography, soils, and climate of a certain place interacting with the genetics of edible plants and animals) not only applies to wines, olive oils, and cheeses, but also to the delicately flavored flower petals used in culinary arts.

In the guise of vegetables, Americans and Europeans routinely eat many different cooked flower buds and their budding stems. Whenever you eat broccoli, cauliflower, capers, or artichokes, you are eating the unfurled flowers or flowering heads of familiar crop plants. It's all a matter of selective breeding. Grow *Brassica oleracea* for succulent leaves and you get a cabbage. Breed it for fleshy, brainlike flower stems, and you get a cauliflower. Likewise, the seeds of *Brassica rapa* give us canola oil, while varieties bred for flower buds are sold as rapini.

Thistles and Roman Capers

When citizens of imperial Rome and other ancient Roman cities sat down to shared meals, some of them included flowers and flower parts. Famously, Romans feasted on the boiled or roasted artichoke or cardoon (*Cynara scolymus*) as part of their distinctive Mediterranean cuisine. The edible and choice artichoke is the large, tightly packed flowering head of a large plant resembling a thistle. This distinctively spiny garden plant was selected then domesticated from a colonizer of fallow fields first eaten by donkeys. Early Greeks on Sicily ate the young leaves and the unopened flower heads, cultivating them as early as the ninth century AD.

Wild artichoke plants were selected over millennia for their supersize buds (actually a compound structure, the capitulum: a flower stem consisting of hundreds of massed tubular flowers). These thistles came to Greco-Roman cuisine, then to our tables as the prized but curious vegetable we enjoy today. The fibrous "choke" portion (the white pappus surrounding the immature seeds) is removed, leaving the tender artichoke hearts and attached stems. These are the beloved artichoke hearts and protective bracts we eat in salads or grilled over hot coals, canned, and marinated, or slathered with delicious sauces. Sometimes they are served as a separate course or added as a prized component of an antipasto plate. Not all Romans approved of eating artichokes. The natural-history writer Pliny the Elder (23–79) called artichokes monstrosities of nature.

The buds of a prickly shrub or vine have been used since antiquity to add nuances to our salads and cooked foods. Native to the Mediterranean basin and eastward, the caper (*Capparis spinosa*) is highly prized for its unopened flower buds once they are marinated or salted. Caper berries are the harvested and pickled fruits of the same plant. Domesticated from wild caper ancestors at least three thousand years ago by the Romans, they are a dominant condiment, adored by gourmands everywhere. We should also admire their beautiful white, purple, and tubular flowers, but most never open, the victims of foodies.

Flavored Waters and Desserts

Flavoring beverages and sweets with floral fragrances fell out of fashion in most European cookery over the past few centuries. It wasn't always that way, though, especially in England. The good wives in the age of Queen Elizabeth I made a syrup of violet flowers to flavor cordials, and they also knew when to add cowslips (*Primula veris*) to flavor imported wines. When their husbands visited inns and taverns, carnations (*Dianthus*) were thrown into various drinks because the petals had such pleasantly spicy fragrances. Accordingly, several carnations were known as clove pinks and sops in wine.

In contrast, many desserts concocted from Turkey southwest through the Middle East and northern Africa would remain incomplete without rose water or orange-blossom water. Today, both flower waters are in such high demand they are sold commercially in shops but are usually diluted to half strength. So are boxes of the world-famous confection—Turkish delight. The pink ones are flavored with rose water. Egyptian-born food writer Claudia Roden continues to write nostalgically of flower-flavored recipes. She remembers her aunt Latifa, who made her own flower waters in a copper still. Roden writes fondly of the perfect dessert *dondurma kai-mak*. The best versions of this frozen custard were prepared with buffalo milk, the starchy flour of wild orchid tubers (*Orchis*), and flavored with rose water and crystallized resin from the mastic tree (*Pistacia lentiscus*).

Cooking with Flowers:
Main Courses, Desserts, and Beverages

Progressive chefs, including Alice Waters, executive chef and owner of the Chez Panisse restaurant in Berkeley, California, know how to use flowers in their recipes. They have been growing special edible-flower gardens for many years, and Waters offers her restaurant patrons delicious and amazing floral works of art for their gustatory pleasure. This seems novel until we realize that other cultures use fresh flowers in a wide variety of sweet or savory dishes.

Vietnamese cooks use banana flowers in a number of main dishes and salads. In several Mexican states, pumpkin and squash blossoms are sold

Marigold blossoms and petals garnishing a plate of sushi

in local vegetable markets. They are chopped up and added at the last minute to vegetable soups to give both color and the sweetness of their nectars. In America, these same blossoms are more likely to be dipped in batter and fried as thin fritters or stuffed with fancy mixtures of soft cheeses, chives, and paprika. However, Mexican and American chefs use only male flowers, as the females are left to fruit. I've given you my own recipe for stuffed squash blossoms in appendix 2. The flowers of true day-lilies (*Hemerocallis*) are an important ingredient in some Chinese soups and are known as golden needles. They can also be steamed or sautéed as buds or flowers. When the largest buds are dropped into chicken broth and allowed to poach quickly, they taste a bit like a melding of onions and asparagus.

A current trend in American cooking is the use of the aforementioned flower confetti. Petals and whole flowers of pansies, nasturtiums, Johnny-jump-ups, and chive blooms are tossed with a range of greens to add color and flavor to salads. Fresh flowers of borage are more likely to be served with sliced cucumbers or frozen inside ice cubes.

Candied Blooms

On the dessert cart at a trendy restaurant, you may find flowers in lavender ice cream or floral shortbreads and various pastries. Sometimes they are sprinkled as edible confetti across sweet desserts. Flowers can be candied to produce elegant creations as edible garnish or dessert toppings. Pansies, Johnny-jump-ups, and borage flowers are excellent choices for candied flowers, made with vodka, egg whites, and powdered sugar.

Candied European sweet violets (*Viola odorata*) were once popular treats in German-style candy shops in the United States, especially in Brooklyn, New York. Today, in Vienna, they are still used to flavor and decorate desserts with white frosting based on meringues and whipped cream. These delicate sugared flowers look almost too pretty to eat. Colorful edible flowers can be diced or added whole to your favorite ice creams, fruit sorbets, or gelati. Various edible flowers can be added whole or minced to honeys to make flower honey, flower syrup, or floral jellies, floral sugar, or flower candies.

Flowers find their way into cold beverages and can be especially refreshing, such as hibiscus, rose, or chrysanthemum petals in iced tea, lemonades, or other iced beverages. Many edible blooms and petals are just as good flavor enhancers or accents in your favorite alcoholic drinks.

Edible Flowers: Top Ten Favorites

Although cooks or aspiring chefs have dozens or hundreds of edible flowers to select from, I've taken the guesswork out of choosing by summarizing the top choices of notable flower chefs, and my own, below. This annotated list has just about everyone's top ten favorite edible flowers. Please join in the fun by making the foods you eat, and their colorful presentations works of art on the canvas of a broad plate or serving dish. Let them eat marigolds!

1. **Calendula or pot marigold** (*Calendula officinalis*), daisy family (Asteraceae). Has a slightly bitter flavor and was historically used as one of several substitutes for true saffron. Can be used in rice dishes, potatoes, or cakes. Use with caution as large quantities may affect women's menstrual cycles, and the flower should not be consumed by pregnant or nursing women.
2. **Chives** (*Allium schoenoprasum*), lily family (Liliaceae). Have an onion-like flavor, but are not overpowering. Can be used in gazpacho, potatoes, salads, and many other savory dishes. We are talking about purple chive flowers, not their familiar green stems. The flowering stalks are usually not for sale in supermarkets, but they are easy to start from seed and flower annually even when they are grown in large pots.
3. **Daylily** (*Hemerocallis* spp.), grass-tree family (Xanthorrhoeaceae). Daylily flowers or buds yield a sweet floral or vegetal "green" flavor and are much favored in Chinese cuisine (see above under "Cooking with Flowers"). Dried, these flowers are used in sweet and sour Chinese hot soups. They can be used in pancakes, flower butter, and shrimp, chicken, and pork dishes. Be careful if you eat daylily tubers, since they can cause diuretic or laxative reactions in some people.
4. **Mint** (*Mentha* spp.), mint family (Lamiaceae). Has the minty-fresh flavor everyone is familiar with. The various mints include apple mint, orange mint, peppermint, and spearmint. Used in tabbouleh, mint sauces, garnishing drinks, in cakes and ice creams. Mint flowers are delicate additions to your cooking. Since you won't find these along

with familiar mint leaves in stores, you may have to grow your own for
the table.

5. **Nasturtium** (*Tropaeolum majus*), nasturtium family (Tropaeolaceae).
Nasturtium petals impart a spicy-peppery flavor to dishes. The curious
round leaves are also edible. They can also be used in flower vinegars
and vinaigrette salad dressings, as well as sauces such as beurre blanc.
Experiment with them in Italian cooking along with tomatoes, cheese,
and pastas. The gorgeous bright orange, scarlet, or yellow petals make
fantastic garnishes to many foods.

6. **Pansy** (hybrids of *Viola tricolor* and the horned violet *V. cornuta*), violet family (Violaceae). The name of this favorite garden bloom comes
from the French word *pensée*, meaning "thought" or "thinking of you."
The countenance-like blooms are thought to represent someone's face
in deep contemplation. Experiment with these facelike flowers in your
kitchen. They are perfect tasty additions in pasta or potato salads, and
dark syrups. An imaginative chef in St. Louis (Barry Marcus) has
used large, dark pansy varieties to look up at diners from inside large,
rounded ravioli! They are a perfect adornment that add zesty colors
and interest to many dishes.

7. **Rose** (*Rosa* spp.), rose family (Rosaceae). Rose petals, with their
engaging, sweet scent, make exquisite sauces. Rose petals can also
be added to julienned vegetables and used in salads and vinaigrettes.
Don't forget them in desserts, as colorful, fragrant, and tasty additions
to sherbet. Roses, and their loose petals, make wonderful sprinkled
trousseau additions to meals as garnishes and on-table decorations.
Some believe that the tastiest roses to use are species including the
Japanese rose (*Rosa rugosa*), Damask rose (*Rosa* x *damascena*), or
apothecary rose (*Rosa gallica*). The hybrid known as the cabbage rose
(*Rosa* x *centifolia*) is grown extensively in Eastern Europe to make rose
water and rose-petal jam.

8. **Sage** (*Salvia officinalis*), mint family (Lamiaceae). For centuries sages
have been thought to have powerful curative and healing properties.
It is not surprising that they have found their way into the cuisines of
diverse cultures. Try mixing sage flowers into soups, salads, and savory
dishes, including those with mushrooms and fish. Again, these are the
delicate sage flowers, not the familiar and easily obtained leaves of the
same plant. The stems of some varieties are bitter, so it may be best to
pick off the flowers first.

9. **Signet marigold** (*Tagetes signata*), daisy family (Asteraceae). This true marigold, native to New Mexico through Mexico to Argentina, has the best flavor of any marigolds, like a spicy version of tarragon. Marigolds can be harmful if eaten in large amounts; please exercise caution by eating them only occasionally and in moderation. Marigold petals are wonderful in marigold butter, deviled eggs, and in potato salad. Try them also with quiches, pastas, and sweet desserts including fruit muffins.

10. **Squash blossoms** (*Cucurbita pepo* var.), squash and gourd family (Cucurbitaceae). These colorful yellow-orange blossoms add a delicious floral and vegetal flavor to other ingredients. This is an excellent culling method for preventing too many large tough zucchini in your home garden. Simply pick off and cook the female zucchini or squash blossoms (look for the pickle-shaped ovary at the base of the blossoms) for the table. Squash blossoms go great with peppers and corn, Mexican masa-flour tamales, or Italian pasta dishes.

Other edible blooms should not be missed, with the cautionary advice to make positive identifications and to know without doubt that they haven't been sprayed or otherwise tainted with chemicals. These favorites include the lovely, delicate blue and white blooms of borage (*Borago officinalis*), although some diners complain of the prickly hairs on the flowers. In addition, some books suggest that overeating these flowers may cause liver ailments. In season, there are always Asian chrysanthemums (*Chrysanthemum* x *morifolium*, or *Dendranthema grandiflorum*); dandelions (*Taraxacum officinale*) from a nonsprayed lawn; red hibiscus (*Hibiscus rosa-sinensis*); the essence of a night-fragrance garden, night-blooming jasmine flowers (*Jasminum sambac*); the petite, smiling faces of Johnny-jump-up; the tiny, blue flowers of garden rosemary (*Rosmarinus officinalis*); and sweet violets.

Choice edible blooms also include anise hyssop, basil, bee balm, and chamomile. Try the flowers of carnations, dill and fennel, elderberry, honeysuckle, lavender (it's not just for soaps and potpourri bundles), marjoram, mustard, sweet orange, garden pea, pineapple guava (with amazingly delicious sweet petals), pineapple sage, red clover (watch out for lawn-care chemical treatments), scented geranium, sunflower, thyme, and tuberous begonia. Some people suggest eating the white petals of yucca flowers of the Southwestern states. However, from tropical Mexico south through Central America, people grow giant yucca (*Yucca elephantipes*). It is used as a living fence, but when it buds and blooms, the flowers are pickled in vinegar to be served on stuffed, grilled tortillas known as *panchitas* or *papusas*. Probably the best, and easiest, way to safely sample edible flowers is to try prepackaged assortments of edible blooms from your favorite market.

Flowers to Avoid: Don't Eat These!

We can't talk about eating flowers fresh out of your garden without mentioning some important caveats, the do's and don'ts of eating the daisies. Certain blooms can sicken or outright poison you or invoke pollen or food allergies in sensitive individuals. While some flowers can be eaten in their entirety, others need to be dissected, carefully prepared for the table, to be at their best. The most toxic flowers include anemones, buttercups, calla lily, clematis, daffodils (including jonquils), delphiniums, four-o'clocks, hyacinths, hydrangeas, irises, lantanas, lily of the valley, lobelias, the true marsh marigolds, milkweeds, morning glories, nightshades, oleanders, periwinkles, privets, all rhododendrons (including azaleas), spring adonis, spurges, trumpet flowers (*Solandra*), and wisterias. Even sweet peas (*Lathyrus*) cannot be trusted. Their "sweetness" refers to their floral scent, not to their often-nasty cellular components.

This is far from a complete list of poisonous flowers to be avoided. Before eating any flower not mentioned in the top ten edible favorites, you should refer to the excellent books by authors Cathy Barash and Rosalind Creasy for a complete list of edible flowers, and how to prepare them. As with any "wild-crafting" (mushroom hunting or foraging for wild greens, berries, other fruits and seeds) you need to educate yourself before you go off, wicker basket in hand, to the woods or the familiar and seemingly safe confines of your own flower or vegetable gardens. The most important rule of all is—if you can't positively identify a flower to genus and species, *never* eat it. It is important to learn and use the proper scientific names of the plants, and their flowers, you intend to eat. Also, remember that the toxicity of a plant may change as it ages. Plant molecules are just like medicines. Their physiological effects on human beings vary widely with the health, age, weight, and gender of the consumer.

Research the flowers you are considering for the table with authoritative books on the subject, not just a few minutes spent web-surfing. The genus and species (for example—the signet marigold, *Tagetes signata*) will distinguish this edible species from look-alike bitter species, or in rare cases confusion with truly poisonous blossoms. Use genus and species names to look up reliable information on the plant in question. This is the reason scientists always use scientific names. Most Greek and Latin words are unfamiliar to many people; but they are universally understood, a lingua franca among scientists, naturalists, and gardeners. Learn to speak their language. Avoid common names because they are too variable and totally unreliable for proper plant identifications.

Preparing Flowers

Soak flowers for five or ten minutes in a bowl of cold or iced water. Shake and dunk the blossoms in the water. This will dislodge any soil particles or insects hiding within. Drain your flowers in a colander or in a salad spinner to remove the excess water. Separate flowers from their stems. A few flowers that can be eaten in their entirety include clover, Japanese honeysuckle (*Lonicera japonica*), Johnny-jump-ups, runner beans (*Phaseolus coccineus*), and violets. For most flowers, you should use only the flower petals. For roses, it is important to remove the whitish petal bases, since they are usually bitter tasting. This is also true for the flowers of chrysanthemums, carnations, English daisies (*Bellis perennis*), and marigolds.

If not used immediately, edible flowers can be preserved for the table by drying (using a commercial food dehydrator), by candying (see "Candied Blooms" above), or by adding to vinegars. Syrups are prepared by quickly and gently boiling whole flowers in water and refined sugar. The solution can be filtered through a common kitchen strainer, and the cooked blossoms are then discarded. Popular books on edible flowers, including the two already mentioned, have instructions and recipes for preserving and preparing flowers for the table in many interesting and delicious ways.

Follow These Simple Rules to Safely Find, Prepare, and Consume Flowers

1. Eat a flower only when you have positively identified it to species and know its scientific name and confirm that it is not poisonous. Don't be

fooled by garden look-alikes or similar common names for different plants.

2. Do not consume flowers purchased from florists, garden shops, or supermarkets when they are sold as whole plants. You do not know the history of these blooms, and they may contain internal insecticides (systemics) or might be coated with dangerous chemicals.

3. Do not eat blossoms from plants growing along roadsides. They often contain heavy metals, such as lead, and other pollutants absorbed from automobile and diesel-truck exhaust.

4. Simply because you are served flowers in a restaurant, any restaurant, doesn't guarantee their edibility. Ask your restaurant server, or the chef, if you are in doubt about eating any flowers placed on your serving plate or table. Don't risk an upset stomach or worse.

Flowers in Hot Water: Floral Teas

Flowers and flower petals make it into some of the world's most beloved hot beverages and tonics. Hidden inside tea bags, or as floating fragments, flowers are in plenty of hot water these days. Herbal teas commonly include whole flowers or petals as their essential ingredients. A longtime favorite in England and America is chamomile tea, an herbal tea made from the tough but fragrant blooms of chamomile (*Matricaria chamomilla*). This tea is favored by those who relish its calming or sleep-inducing effects. You should be careful not to overindulge, as chamomile in large doses can produce uterine contractions and miscarriages. Chamomile is far more potent as a flavoring in Manzanilla. This after-dinner cordial tastes a bit like apples (*manzanilla* means "little apple" in Spanish) and is mentioned in the first act of the opera *Carmen*. Also, if you are allergic to ragweed you should avoid chamomile, due to cross-reactivity. The lovely red or pink petals of hibiscus (*Hibiscus* spp.) are ingredients in Red Zinger from Celestial Seasonings teas, as well as in the herbal teas of other purveyors. Other popular hot drinks derived from flowers include jasmine, rose-petal, and lavender teas.

Green, black, and white teas from China, India, and Japan started out as handpicked new shoots of the tea bush (*Camellia sinensis*). Therefore, the tea in a tea bag is leaf-derived, not floral. However, the Chinese are fond of teas that appear to "bloom" in hot water. They are bundles of dried tea leaves surrounding dried flowers. When infused, the bundle "flowers" expand like an opening blossom. Dried flowers used in these tea bundles include chrysanthemum, globe amaranth, jasmine, daylily, hibiscus, and fragrant olive (*Osmanthus*). Flowering teas are especially common in the Yunnan Province of China. At least thirty-six kinds of flowers are used in them.

Flowers Spice Up Our Lives: Saffron and Cloves

Ounce for ounce as costly as pure gold, the crimson, dried threads of saffron crocus (*Crocus sativus*) from Southwest Asia have been prized throughout history as a seasoning, dye, fragrance, and medicine. Saffron, as a spice, was domesticated and first cultivated in Crete, at least thirty-five hundred years ago. In antiquity, saffron probably originated from the wildflower *Crocus cartwrightianus*. The true saffron crocus has a large, mauve-colored flower and long, exaggerated pistil "arms," but produces only a few fertile pollen grains. The little bulb reproduces by generating baby bulbs, so the saffron crop is uniform wherever it is grown. A restored Minoan fresco (dating from 1600 to 1500 BC, or perhaps older) in a ruin on the Aegean island of Santorini shows two young girls and possibly a trained monkey gathering the crimson pistils in a field of saffron crocuses, under the watchful eye of a seated mother goddess. These frescoes may have depicted the collection and use of saffron largely as a therapeutic drug and as a yellow dye.

In a well-known Hellenic legend about saffron, the handsome mortal Crocus falls in love with the beautiful nymph Smilax. His amorous advances are rebuffed by Smilax, and the Olympian gods transformed Crocus into the saffron plant. To this day, the saffron crocus, especially its radiant red-orange pistil arms, are symbols of an undying idyllic but unrequited love.

Botany explains why saffron is among history's costliest and most treasured substances. Each saffron flower makes only three pistil branches, and that is the sole source of the spice and the dye. The individual flower rarely lives longer than a day. The pistils make up only a tiny fraction of the entire flower, and they lose most of their weight upon drying.

As in ancient times, the pistils are picked individually between thumb and forefinger in backbreaking stooped labor. Usually, only one to five blooms open daily on each plant. The production of just one ounce of saffron requires the harvesting of 14,000 styles from 4,667 flowers. A pound of dried saffron requires a staggering 74,666 flowers. Most of the world's saffron is produced in Iran, India, Spain, and Greece.

The aroma and flavor of saffron are like nothing else. Saffron has an acrid taste, with a somewhat haylike fragrance, and underlying metallic notes. The love of the saffron flavor in cooking spans millennia, and several continents. In modern foods, chefs and home cooks use saffron, albeit sparingly because of its cost, in their favorite recipes. Whether powdered or as the familiar threads, saffron is used to color and flavor risotto and other rice dishes. It is an essential spice to create flavorful bouillabaisse or Spanish paella dishes.

Stuck into the rounded surface of delicious baked holiday hams are other flowers that have been used as a spice through the ages. This spice comes from the unopened, dried flower buds of a tropical tree (*Syzygium aromaticum*) in the myrtle family (Myrtaceae). Native to Indonesia's Maluku Islands, clove is a familiar household spice throughout the world, lending its unique flavoring to meats, marinades, curries, and some desserts. It is especially popular in the cuisines of Africa, Asia, and the Middle East. Cloves flavor the smoke of local cigarettes (*kretek*) popular in Indonesia and Malaysia.

From Flower Nectar to Bees to Us: Honey

Floral nectar is either the primary or secondary reason that animals visit flowers. Photons in sunlight strike the tightly stacked grana within chloroplasts, the green microscopic units inside the leaves of plants. Through a complex photosynthetic biochemistry, sugars are made from carbon dioxide in the air, and water in the leaves, when light strikes chlorophyll molecules. A portion of these sweet sugars are moved from the leaves into a flower's nectaries, often in crevices hidden at the bases of flowers, between the petals. The sugars manufactured are usually the "big three," the double molecules of sucrose (one part glucose and one of fructose), and the single molecules of glucose and fructose. These molecules are transferred to nectar glands from leaves via special interconnecting tubes known as the phloem.

Bees and other pollinating insects seek out the sweet nectar from flowers. Mostly, it is used as a metabolic intermediary to power their flapping wings, carrying them aloft. Bees drink the nectar, sucking and lapping, then carry it home to their nests within honey stomachs. Back at the nest, the bees stand motionless while regurgitating the dilute nectar onto their tongues (proboscides). As it is spit out and reswallowed, back and forth hundreds of times, the nectar is gradually concentrated into honey as the excess water is driven off. (I never claimed honey-making was pretty.) Honey bees also add an enzyme, invertase, that breaks down compound sugars into simpler ones and prevents your jar of honey from turning into a crystalline mass. The honey is finished and ready for the bees to store in their honeycombs when it reaches 80 percent sugar and 20 percent water. In wildflowers and garden blooms, nectar concentrates are usually 20–50 percent dissolved sugars.

Honey comes from various races of the Western honey bee, including the Italian race, which are the dominant bees kept by US and European beekeepers. Having evolved in the Asian tropics but spreading into the temperate regions of Africa, Europe, and Asia, the eleven species of true honey bees (*Apis*) have become hoarders, stockpiling the sweet stuff as insurance against long, cold winters. Colonies need to store and use several hundred pounds of honey in capped combs, the bees' pantry, in areas such as the northeastern United States, regions with intense winters.

Solitary, ground, and twig-nesting native bees consume nectar for themselves, as flight fuel, but also mix nectar with pollen to feed their grublike larvae. Only honey bees and the stingless bees (*Melipona* and its relatives; the meliponines), all of tropical origins, store honey in double-sided honeycombs, or grapelike, waxen storage pots in the case of *Melipona* and allied genera. In the mountainous regions of North America and Asia (especially China), the charismatic black-and-yellow-striped, fuzzy bees known as bumble bees (*Bombus* spp.) also store honey in their underground nests. These social bees make grape-size, waxen honey pots. However, unless you are a hungry skunk or other small animal, the few teaspoons of honey you might get by digging up a bumble bee nest would not be worth the stings.

Beekeepers extract honey from the combs of Western honey bees kept in Langstroth hives with their handy removable frames. Hot electric knives slice through the wax cappings, and the frames are placed upright side by side in a metal centrifuge. Spun at high speeds, the viscous, amber-colored honey is thrown out of the wax cells, hitting the side walls of the centrifuge and trickling down into a reservoir below. Raw or organic honey is not processed further, except sometimes by filtering it through cheesecloth prior to bottling. Most commercial honeys sold in supermarkets have been pasteurized. After being heated to 161 degrees Fahrenheit for a time, the honey is pumped hot through a filter using diatomaceous earth before being bottled. For a real treat, try raw floral honeys, which are much tastier than the heated and/or blended honeys most people are used to eating.

For the best that honey has to offer, look for small wooden boxes or plastic rounds that hold natural comb honey. Beekeepers placed these inside hives and the bees filled them up. This is the most natural, unprocessed, and flavorful honey you can experience. Comb or chunk honey is great as a gift to family and friends, ones who don't know the pleasure of this culinary delight, straight from the flowers to the bees to us.

Inside flowers, in the thin tissues that secrete nectar, much is happening. These aren't simple sugar factories. Trace amounts of rarer sugars other than the big three (sucrose, fructose, glucose), along with amino acids, proteins, glycosides, and phenolic compounds, are added. Some of these nonsugar molecules give nectars, and subsequently the honeys made from them, their characteristic tastes and other properties. Some bitter honeys fluoresce yellow, green, or blue under an ultraviolet light, such as almond honey. The bitter phenolic chemicals are a flower's way of keeping ants from stealing all the sweet stuff without pollinating. Crawling on flowers and buds, ants are usually nectar robbers and not efficient pollinators, unlike bees and other hairy-bodied insects.

The Many Kinds of Floral Honeys

Floral nectar is not honey water, and honey made by bees is not sugar syrup. If you want a cheap, flavorless sweetener, buy cane or beet sugar. For the best experience, that of the honey-loving connoisseur, don't settle for anything less than real honey, especially unprocessed or comb chunk honey. We love honeys not only for their sweetness, but their delicate and unique flavors and aromas. Like wine or beer, no two honeys are alike. This is because the nectaries secrete a unique blend of sugars and other flavor components. Most important for its flavor, nectar pools inside a blossom, resting against the flower's diaphanous petals, waiting for a pollinator ship to dock, absorbing their delicate floral scents. This is why each honey has a unique flavor, its terroir.

Walking down a supermarket aisle, you will likely find a half dozen different kinds of honey. Most of these come from the largest commercial honey producers, the big trade-organization collectives such as Sioux Honey Association (SueBee honey), which began in 1921. Consumers seem to prefer light-colored honeys, like those from clover blossoms, instead of the darker amber ones that many beekeepers such as myself prefer. Clover honey is a standard, dependable, if somewhat bland example. Sure, it has the characteristic honey flavor, but for me it lacks any special or delectable floral character. You might also find "wildflower" honey at your market, which could be a mix of nectars from almost any of wildflowers from different regions. The United States has few regulations for identifying and labeling the floral sources of honeys. Caveat emptor! Still, you can reliably find flavorful gems such as orange-blossom or tupelo honey (from tupelo or black-gum trees, the genus *Nyssa*). Tupelo is an especially favored honey because it doesn't crystallize and harden in the jar during storage.

For a bit of fun, go to a specialty shop, or online, and sample some unifloral honeys. These are honeys made from only one type of nectar. Organize a honey-tasting party for your family and friends. See if they like the deep rich brown and molasses-like flavor of wild buckwheat (*Fagopyrum esculentum*) honey, or the greenish honeydew honey (bees collect exudates from feeding aphids or scale insects) from fir trees in the Black Forest of Germany. Or try some of my favorites from down under, including Tasmanian leatherwood (*Eucryphia lucida*; sublime!) or pōhutukawa (*Metrosideros excelsa*) honey.

The Best Honey in the World

If you are traveling to the southern Mexican states of Yucatán or Quintana Roo (including the cities of Mérida, Cancún, or Chetumal) in the Yucatán Peninsula, be alert for what might just be the best-tasting and most flavorful honey in the world. Several honey bee–size native bees from the low, tropical forests of this region collect floral nectars from canopy trees and distill them into runny, but exquisite-tasting honey. My favorite comes from the sacred or "lady bee" (*xunan cab* in the Mayan language; scientifically, *Melipona beecheii*) bees, which have been kept in log hives (*jobones*) by Mayan beekeepers and farmers of this region for three millennia. Visitors to the popular archaeological sites of Cobá and Tulum can see representations of the Mayan bee or descending god (Ah Mucen Cab) holding grapelike wax and resin clusters, the honey pots.

You may have the best luck finding genuine stingless-bee honey in Mérida, or driving into the Mundo Mayan lands, and Mayan cities such as Felipe Carrillo Puerto, about a two hours' drive north of Chetumal, near the Belize border. Since each bee colony produces but one or two quarts of golden honey each year, prices are high, and beware of counterfeits (you may be buying honey from Africanized honey bees). Unfortunately, for now, you will have to travel there in person to try this fabulous bee ambrosia, since federal agricultural regulations forbid its importation into the United States.

Flower Pollen: The Perfect Food for Bees, and People?

Another gift from the world's flowers that you may not have thought about is pollen. The oily dust staining your fingers after touching the large, orange anthers of an Easter lily are its pollen grains. They are a superlative food for bees and a few other pollinating animals. The grains contain all of the protein, essential amino acids, lipids, minerals, vitamins, and the sugars that bees need to rear their young from egg to adulthood. Pollen is like beefsteak or soybeans are to us, while floral nectar and honey are the energy-rich sugars that these insect fliers need to power their foraging trips in search of more flowers.

Fresh pollen differs in nutritional content according to the flower's mode of pollination. Flowers pollinated by bees are rich in amino acid and oil. Unfortunately, it's hard for humans to collect enough pollen in daisies or petunias to have enough for a meal. Yes, you can put a wiremesh pollen trap behind a hive's entrance and knock pollen pellets off bee legs, but you might also be eating a few bee hairs and bee lice. This is the natural pollen product sold in health-food stores.

Wind-pollinated flowers release clouds of pollen often containing starch granules, but who wants to climb a tree or knock grains out of thousands of grass heads? One plant does provide lots of pollen, for a few days in spring, that's easy to harvest providing you don't mind wet feet. Cattails (*Typha*) are found in temperate, freshwater sites all over the world. While some North American tribes may have harvested cattail pollen, the Maori of New Zealand are the ones known as pollen-pastry cooks. As late as the 1880s they were still collecting *pungapunga* (cattail) pollen by the bucket, mixing it with water, and baking it into cakes. The botanist William Colenso (1811–99) ate some and found its taste reminiscent of gingerbread.

While you can easily buy honey bee–collected pollen pellets online, or from your local health-food store, pollen is an expensive and, to my thinking, far from ideal human food. People simply aren't bees; we didn't evolve guts with enzymes for handling and digesting tough pollen grains. Since honey bees often collect pollen from wind-pollinated allergenic plants including grasses, eating pollen can be risky if you are a pollen-sensitive individual. If you suffer from hay fever, after your most recent encounter with the airborne pollen ragweed, mulberry, or olive trees, you may think of it as a scourge rather than as a gift. But you would be wrong because the cereal grains—domesticated grasses including wheat, barley, oats, millet, rice, and corn—keep the world's 7.2 billion people from starvation. Roughly 35 percent of our global agricultural diet comes from animal-pollinated fruits and vegetables.

We've traced around the world the casual and fine art of eating certain flowers, how they flavor our meals, add spice and excitement to our palates, and create divinely scented flower waters (rose and orange waters), honeys, and sweet condiments. Now, it is time to boldly go into purely aromatic delights, to understand why roses and other flowers delight our noses, and to understand the secrets of perfumery.

CHAPTER 9

A Little Dab behind the Ear

Ruffled petals of an orchid bloom (*Cattleya* sp.)

Almost everything in nature has a scent, and perhaps you've wondered why flowers have the fragrances they do. The world of flowers is alive with charismatic, often familiar, yet strangely alluring odors. We should think of floral scents as "private communication channels" between flowers and certain animals. Imagine you are a bee trying to find one kind of bloom among dozens of similarly colored ones in the same meadow. Individualized scents aid flowers in attracting, and keeping, their most faithful pollinators. This promotes cross-pollination and the next generation of seeds.

Humans are also attracted to floral fragrances, but for different reasons. Our hominid ancestors noticed fragrant flowers and may have perfumed themselves and their dwellings with them. Then, there is that expensive substance we call perfume. Before the tenth century, skilled Arab chemists had learned to distill fragrances from fresh flowers, thereby creating the perfume known as rose water. In Egypt, enfleurage, the trapping of scents using animal fat, may be quite ancient. The word *perfume* has been with Western civilization for thousands of years. It may not mean what you think. The word *perfume* is derived from the Latin *per fumare*, which means to "pass through smoke." This suggests that the earliest perfumes around the Mediterranean were actually forms of incense. However, most incense is made from fragrant plant resins. When a plant takes terpene molecules and links them together, they become a sticky but fragrant resin that dries upon exposure to air, giving us myrrh and frankincense, from *Commiphora* and *Boswellia* trees respectively.

The blossoms of *Catasetum* or *Stanhopea* orchids smell like cloves or Vicks VapoRub. Truly, we've stolen some of nature's finest advertising, the scents released into the air by flowers. Now, we use those floral essences to lure and seduce our own potential mates by changing how our bodies smell, forsaking our own bawdy odors. We also use floral scents to alter how our homes and other environments smell. A multibillion-dollar global industry has developed around making and selling human perfumes and colognes, along with myriad other scented modern products used daily, right under our noses. Scent sells.

Wake Up and Smell the Perfume

Nearly all animals rely upon their sense of smell to navigate and interpret the world around them, with the exception of most birds. Olfaction is also one of the most basic and primitive ways animals interact with each other and navigate within their preferred environments. Insects are especially attuned to the fragrant landscape of flowers, plants, and other animals. Their specialized olfactory abilities have been finely honed by natural selection for more than 400 million years. Some of the most primitive flowering-plant species are strongly scented, leading us to conclude that among the very first flowers (like *Archaefructus*) of 125 million years ago, floral scent likely played an important role in communications between the first flowering plants, their earliest pollinators, and enemies.

Few flowers are truly scentless. This is true whether we think of a native wildflower growing in a remote location or a favorite garden rose. Most flowers release fragrance molecules from their petals or other floral structures. These "volatiles" have low molecular weights, so they disperse rapidly from a flower's skin at moderate temperatures. These molecules linger above and around all blossoms until carried away by the breeze. They make up the "headspace" above a flower, the characteristic scent of that species. When these scent molecules are released, they become mixed into currents of air, the way smoke rises and is then turbulently dispersed from a chimney. When fragrance molecules leave the surface of a flower, bees and other insects use them to find the flower, aided by vision, memory, and learning. These animals have a lot to memorize as the scent of a flower is often composed of dozens of distinct molecules. For example, for thousands of years women in tropical Asian countries have worn the fresh flowers of the joy perfume tree (*Magnolia champaca*) to add an alluring aroma to their hair. This medium-size, yellow flower emits no less than fifty-two different molecules.

Back in the 1960s chemistry professors Calaway Dodson and Harold "Hal" Hills first studied the chemistry of orchid fragrances after discovering that males of many species of metallic orchid bees (euglossines) scraped orchid petals to collect their scents and then turned them into their own sexual attractants. Floral fragrances have been isolated and analyzed from both rare and common flowers in almost every habitat. Biochemists and floral biologists have cataloged more than one thousand seven hundred volatile compounds from almost a thousand plant species in a hundred families of flowering plants. Some flowers produce only one or two kinds of scent molecules. The flower of another species may have up to two dozen fragrance components. Plant species that are no more closely related than we are to goldfish may employ the exact same molecules but in different concentrations. Sometimes the blending is so similar that a damask rose in your garden can smell just like a blue sun orchid (*Thelymitra macrophylla*) in Australia.

Floral scents have much in common with birdsongs, as noted by evolutionary biologist and flower chemist Robert Raguso. Both are highly evolved signals, and both are difficult to understand without advanced technology and expertise. Not until 1958, however, was the sound spectrograph (sonogram) invented. Then, for the first time, ornithologists could visualize birdcalls, understanding how they were organized into frequency patterns with passing time. Likewise, in 1966, Dodson and Hills used gas chromatographs and mass spectrometers to understand, visualize, and identify orchid floral scents.

Plants, and their blooms, are chemists par excellence. Flowering plants have had a long, at least 130 million years of evolutionary history, experimenting diversely, adapting, and modifying their fragrance chemistries. Human efforts pale by comparison with what flowering plants have done for millions of years. We are comparative newcomers to this scented game.

There is a fun way to play chemist, to find out if your favorite blossom has a scent, and what kind of fragrance it releases to the world. Go into a garden or any natural area and select one or more flowers you want to investigate. Perhaps it is an old favorite, or heirloom variety, or something entirely new. Bring the flowers home in a plastic bag inside a chest cooler. Select a small, thoroughly washed and dried glass jar with a tight-fitting lid. Place just one type of flower in the jar. Set your jar in a warm, sunny place such as a windowsill and come back in an hour or two.

Carefully open the lid and sniff. Inhale deeply, without guilt. Can you smell anything? If you've selected a blossom with even the faintest scent, you should be able to smell it now, since the fragrance molecules have concentrated inside the jar. You are an experiential chemist, doing headspace analysis using your nose and brain as chemical laboratory instruments! Try the jar with different flowers, especially ones you believe are unscented. Use leaves or stems from the same plant. Do they smell the same or different? Try crushing a leaf. This is a simple yet powerful way to become a citizen scientist, a chemical ecologist exploring the sensual and aromatic world of flowers. Let other family members sniff the jar to determine if their reactions are the same as yours. Again, smell the flower within the odor chamber, writing down the names of familiar things your flower reminds you of. Does it smell like cloves or wintergreen mints or almond or vanilla extract? Think about how you swirled, smelled, tasted, and compared different wines at your last wine tasting. Interestingly, many of the same things can be done with flowers and a few old jam jars. Why not host your own sniffing party over the season when your garden flowers are in peak bloom? You can always include honey and wine tasting to your event.

From the Putrid to the Sublime

As nature's foremost chemists (along with insects), flowers make, store, and dispense a scented universe of diverse chemicals, using simple to complex biochemical pathways. The exact details aren't important to our story. What matters is an appreciation for how unrelated kinds of flowers lure their pollinators, often narrowly focused animal specialists, enticing them to feed, drink, and gather nest-building materials or mate, rest, or sleep within their scented floral embrace. We'll look at a few examples of the many potential fragrant stories that could be told.

Some flowers smell bad, downright awful, to us. Because these blooms don't show up in Valentine's or Mother's Day bouquets, we don't usually think of them, but they are an important part of nature. You may have a potted starfish plant (*Stapelia* spp.) growing on your kitchen-window ledge. When it finally blooms, you begin searching earnestly for the putrefying mouse corpse under the cupboards or behind the refrigerator as mentioned previously. Or, perhaps you are familiar with blooming skunk cabbage (*Symplocarpus foetidus*) worming its way up through a spring snowfall. As in man-made perfumes, concentration matters. The daffodils in our gardens we think of as sweet-smelling, but bring a bunch indoors and suddenly they are not nearly so pleasant. Indole, one of the chemicals in their fragrance, is a common floral volatile. It smells somewhat fecal and repulsive to most people at higher concentrations. However, when greatly diluted, indole is perceived as floral and nice. It finds its way into many perfumes.

You may recall my travel account of the giant carrion flower of Borneo (*Rafflesia arnoldii*). All of these blooms have characteristic scents, tuned to attract blowflies or dung beetles. Normally, you find these flies dining and laying their eggs on mammalian feces or the bodies of dead mammals and birds or rotting fish along a shoreline. These specialist flowers have tapped into the smell of death to attract pollinating flies, using chemical mimicry and deceit. The female flies show up, duped into laying their eggs on the faux meat, then carry away pollen to the next foul-smelling blossom.

Flowers pollinated by bats usually do not smell much nicer. The pollination literature is being kind when the aroma of bat flowers is described as "fermented, fruity, or garlicky." In fact, bat-pollinated flowers such as those of kapok trees, some wild bananas, and others often release sulfur-containing molecules reminiscent of rotting eggs and rancid butter. In Arizona and northern Mexico, some giant *Agave* (century plants) have flowers that smell like yummy coconut, while the saguaro has creamy-white blooms that remind me of the scent of a ripe honeydew melon. Both agaves and saguaros are visited by bats at night, and bees early the following morning.

We humans enjoy the natural perfumes of flowers pollinated by bees or night moths and even some pollen-eating beetles. As mammals, shouldn't we like the odors of bat-pollinated blossoms? Swiss biochemist Roman Kaiser compared the sweet natural scents preferred by people. He concluded that we like those flowers that can be grouped into four basic categories. We have already described the spicy scents made by tropical American orchids and some wild European carnations. They smell like incense because they contain the same molecules that link together to form resins. Kaiser then added the rosy scent from many pink and purple flowers, such as old breeds of roses, cyclamens, and sweet peas. Curiously, they are based on the breakdown of hidden yellow pigments giving us phenyl ethyl alcohols (more on this sweet note later) and their cousins, geraniol and linalool.

Kaiser's white-flower form, indicative of jasmine, honeysuckle, and orange blossoms, is similar to the rosy-scent form but activated by the loss of light, as the sun sets and temperatures fall. Finally, in the fourth category are the rich and complicated ionones (*io* or *ion* is an old Greek word for "scented violets"). Flowers make them as their beta-carotene molecules degrade and link up with aromatic alcohols. Examples of this floral-scent class include the previously mentioned joy perfume tree, the freesias, the aptly named fragrant olive (*Osmanthus*), and the amazing brown boronia flower (*Boronia megastigma*) of Western Australia.

Our Scented World

By the middle of the nineteenth century, chemists had learned that nature is its own copycat. The components of pure rose oil were identical to molecules found in other plants and plant products. Linalool, found in flowers, is also known from cinnamon sticks and muscatel wine. Geraniol, also found in roses, is released when you bruise the stems of lemongrass. Since that innocent era of biochemical exploration, industrial chemists have created a multitude of commercial products containing man-made duplicates of natural molecules to lure us into liking and buying them.

Today, a global multibillion-dollar industry develops new fragrance molecules, blends them into products, and aggressively markets them. Many companies are dedicated solely to the production and wholesale of commercial fragrances that go into essentially everything we use, whether or not we are consciously aware of their presence. Unless you shop carefully for unscented products, you cannot easily escape scented detergents, hand soaps, shampoos, shower gels, hair gels, aftershaves, baby wipes, hand lotions and creams, air fresheners, facial and bathroom tissues, paper towels, furniture polishes, cleaning solutions, candles, incenses, and myriad others.

A modern supermarket or pharmacy sells hundreds of packaged products containing eugenol, limonene, menthol, and all the aforementioned molecules. Many of these synthetic add-on fragrances in products are floral or at least meant to mimic the pleasant fragrances of garden favorites.

Manufacturers purposely add a generic "outdoor fresh" or floral-like scent to their laundry detergents, fabric softeners, and soaps. I'm not sure if the "fresh" component is due to just one compound or many. Perhaps they are adding oil of wintergreen (methyl salicylate) to some of their creations. I wonder if we couldn't do without four-ply, scented bathroom tissue printed in a floral motif? Intense marketing advertisements blast at us across all media channels suggesting that we cannot live without these products. Industry chemists, psychologists, and numerous test panels all aid in new-product formulations and customer-appeal decisions, the subtle but powerful olfactory nuances that play a major role in our product selection and buying decisions. Perfuming a bathroom or kitchen is one thing, but changing the scent of the human body has a far older, more glorious, and sexier history.

Perfumes in the Ancient World

Incense, especially frankincense and myrrh, was ranked with gold and jewels among the most precious of all possessions. When burned, incense provided a way to communicate with various deities via the smoke rising to the heavens. In the Middle East, the ancient Assyrians perfumed their long and ornately coiffed beards. Perhaps apocryphally, King Sardanapalus, a sybarite of the seventh century BC, reputedly said that his ultimate pleasure would be to die lying amid his wives and his perfumes. From the profane to the sacred, we have the Song of Songs from the Bible, in which a man's bearded cheeks "are like a bed of spices yielding perfume." The female figure in this poem is described as "a lily among thorns," and it is said of her, "Pleasing is the fragrance of your perfume." This is the only biblical passage to mention saffron and the sweet rush (*Acorus calamus*).

The Greeks grew flowers specifically for the scent trade. The Roman Empire expanded on the earlier Grecian practice, and upper-class Romans wore perfume-scented togas and shoes with scented soles. Roman baths were sometimes perfumed using precious rose water. Roman emperors also bathed in rose wine. At banquets, servants or slaves sprinkled fragrant rose petals on dinner guests from upper galleries, so plentiful in one case that they reputedly suffocated a guest. Romans, so unfettered by moral rectitude, lavished rich perfumes on themselves, often with different scents for various parts of the body. Elite Roman women had a group of slaves (the *ornatrices*) who were in charge of their daily toilettes, and for massaging and applying their precious unguents and other perfumes. Pliny criticized such extravagance as wasteful. He also observed that after a time the perfumes could only delight others but not the wearer. Today, we know this effect as nose fatigue, and modern perfumes gradually become less noticeable to those wearing them. This is why it's best to try only three or four new perfumes during the same perfume counter visit. It's no surprise then that the Romans gave us the earliest form of attar, the fragrant essential oil distilled from petals of roses. They made it by allowing fresh rose petals to dry upon a screen placed over a pail of lard. The pork fat was now contaminated with the rose scent molecules, which could easily be applied to the skin.

The first records of a culture using true perfumes are from the Persian civilization in what is now modern Iran and Iraq. By AD 810, the ruling caliphs of Baghdad were accepting thirty thousand precious bottles of rose water as part of their annual tribute from the Persian empire. The Persians also commissioned perfumes that became famous across the ancient world. The hero of perfumery was an ethnic Persian known as Ali Ibn Sina (980–1037), or Avicenna, as he was known in the West. One of the great Muslim intellectuals, he was known for his writings on many subjects, including medicine, and this led to his profound interest in concentrating scents from flowers and other substances. The modern production of distilled perfumes starts with this man.

Ancient Egypt: Flowers for Perfumes, Unguents, and Cosmetics

Other ancient kingdoms added much to our lore and literature of perfumes, but Egypt under the pharaohs was a truly scented civilization. They were unusually creative in scent manufacture for a culture that bloomed and collapsed before the first iron or bronze distillation stills were invented. By land and sea, fragrance-trade routes converged on Egypt. Ancient Egyptians were the first to place an emphasis on personal beauty, adornment, and sumptuous fragrances. Theirs was a citizenry of refinement, luxury, and excess. Fragrance routes led to Egypt from the Mycenaean civilizations on Crete and Cypress. Egypt was once the perfumer to the Mediterranean basin. They exploited the natural scents of lilies, irises, roses, and blue water lilies. The Egyptians also used fragrant unguents for their hair, and other cosmetics including the world's first eyeliner and makeup.

Today an older generation looks wistfully at the stylish ways that the houses of Arden and Rubenstein packaged their products, but the ancient Egyptians understood that artistic containers were preferred for their best cosmetics and perfumes. Egyptian fragrances must have had an aura of exclusiveness, rarity, and often divine use. Scented products were often stored in alabaster jars or fine blue and polychrome glass bottles. A common genre of Egyptian scent containers has whimsically shaped, half-naked girls swimming or floating. In front of them, they push floating animals, often ducks, which are the actual unguent storage boxes. Some alabaster unguent boxes depict young women playing musical instruments in floral settings. Egypt was a finishing house for processing scented wood, roots, leaves, and flowers into the most luxurious and coveted fragrances and beauty products of the ancient world.

Egyptian wall paintings from tombs and temples and bas-reliefs depict flowers known to be fragrant. Paramount among these is the blue water lily (*Nymphaea caerulea*). The artworks show women and men holding these flowers or their petals to their noses, enjoying the rich smells. Others show how women of the court wore flowers on their heads, often combined with other fragrant leaves and fruits.

Only a few true floral-based perfumes were commonly used by the ancient Egyptians. Rhodinon, or rose perfume, was a popular favorite. It was made from olive oil, rose petals, crocus blossoms, camel grass, sweet flag, honey, wine, and salt. Rhodinon may have been dyed red with alkanet. A surviving recipe for lily perfume called for two thousand lily (*Lilium candidum*) blossoms, eight pounds of "balanos," almost five pounds of sweet-flag (*Acorus* spp.) blossoms, myrrh, and fragrant wine, along with cardamon, saffron crocus, cinnamon, honey, and salt. A perfume known as "the Egyptian" contained cinnamon, myrrh, and sweetened wine. It was aged for up to eight years and sold in perfume shops in Athens during the fourth century BC. Iris perfume, made from a base oil and orrisroot, was known in the classic world, described by Theophrastus and Pliny. Kept in alabaster containers, cool and out of the sun, iris perfume would last for six to twenty years!

The task of an Egyptian, or any, perfumer, is to make these naturally ephemeral scents, especially those from fresh flowers, last as a product that can be applied to one's body, clothing, hair, or the statue of a god or goddess in a temple. The Egyptians had a unique way of trapping scents. Temple and tomb paintings depict elegant Egyptian ladies wearing something strange on their heads. These are unguent cones, made largely of animal fat, *ainu*, to hold floral scents and other scented products. The fat melted slowly as the women dined at lavish banquets or attended court, scenting and shining their hair and faces. Surviving recipes call for the fat of oxen, geese, or pigs, with one part of melted animal fat mixed with two parts of chopped scented-plant parts including the flowers of sweet marjoram (*Origanum majorana*) and the bright yellow blossoms of a number of stiff-branched, erect shrubs in the pea family (*Cytisus, Genista, Calicotome*) we now call brooms.

The last active pharaoh of Egypt was Cleopatra (Cleopatra VII Philopator, who ruled from 51 to 30 BC), a member of the Ptolemaic dynasty. A great beauty, Cleopatra was reputed to be a mistress of luxury and extravagance. Cleopatra is rumored to have used four hundred denars' worth (about $800 today) of scented unguents each day solely to perfume and soften her hands and arms. She used perfumes to seduce both Julius Caesar and Marc Antony. At her first meeting with Marc Antony, on the Nile, she commanded that the purple sails of her royal barge be soaked in perfume, so the two could relax, bathed in the luxury of its scent. Ah, love.

The Rise of Flower-Based Perfumes

Nothing can compare with the sensory experience of walking through blooming fields, acres of lavender, jasmine, or roses, at harvest time. I recently visited the Red Rock Lavender farm in Arizona during their annual open-house celebrations, when their fields had turned to purple and bees foraged among the blooms. Yes, lavender is grown for its scented flowers and leaves, and scent distillers prefer stems cut when the flowers are in full bloom to add additional floral molecules absent from the vegetation. Perfumes have aptly been called "the breath of flowers" by Cathy Newman, a perfume-book author. Getting scents into a bottle involves a bit of magic, luck, skill, and the ability to learn from one's predecessors. It takes specialized knowledge, just the right terroir, and good farming practices to raise a crop of flowers, the first step in getting ingredients inside a fancy bottle of perfume.

Like recognizable, individual estate-bottled cabernet sauvignons from a favorite Napa Valley vineyard and vintage, or coffees or cheeses from special locations, flowers grown in different countries or regions often smell different. Lavender farmers in France proclaim that they can distinguish lavender oils from one another even when their originating stems bloomed only a few miles apart. We all know that crops grown for favorite foods originated in many different parts of the world. Chocolate, for example, came from a small tree in southern Mexico and farther south, but African countries now produce most of the world's cocoa beans. Likewise, the favorite flowers used by the perfume industries grow a long way from their homeland forests and meadows.

The ylang-ylang flower (*Cananga odorata*) comes from orchards in the Comoros Islands of the Indian Ocean, but the species is native to the Philippines. Roses, grown for their petal oils, from Turkey, Morocco, and Bulgaria are based on bushes native to warmer parts of Western Europe. The mimosa perfumes of France started as fluffy, yellow blossoms in Provence, France, but are nothing more than acacia species from Africa and Australia.

This area of Provence from Grasse to Cannes has been famous for its fields and orchards of perfume flowers for centuries. Francophile tourists continue to come and fantasize about the meadows of perfume. Grasse celebrated its sixty-fifth jasmine festival in 2014 during the first weekend in August. The French insist that Spanish navigators introduced this night-blooming wonder to Provence in 1560. This may be an illusion. Sadly, little jasmine is grown in France now. Many of the flower fields have moved to other countries, mostly places with cheaper labor, including Bulgaria, Morocco, Turkey, and India.

Many legends surround the development of the perfume industry at Grasse, including a number about the much-despised queen Catherine de Médicis (1519–89). She brought high styles of dress, cuisine, and cosmetics to a relatively barbaric France. She patronized the artisans of Grasse for their perfumed leather gloves. (It's also said that she had the linings of those gloves poisoned and gave them as gifts to her enemies.) The perfume flowers of Grasse increased in diversity with the great age of European exploration. Unlike the British, French explorers preferred to bring live plants or viable seeds back with them. Australian acacias made their debuts at the home of the Empress Josephine before their virtues as perfume flowers brought them to Grasse.

A visit to the rose-growing area near Grasse reveals roses grown for their fragrance molecules. Here you find the pale pink *rose de mai*, the rose of May (*Rosa gallica* var. *centifolia*), grown for its highly fragrant petals. Harvesting the blooms by hand, a worker could pick (before the labor moved to Bulgaria) about twenty-one hundred blooms in an hour. The harvesting is done early in the morning, when the blooms are the most fragrant. By 10:00 a.m., the flowers begin to wilt and the harvest ends for the day. It takes 1,763 pounds of rose petals to make a mere 2.2 pounds of concentrated *rose de mai* absolute. The Bulgarian absolute, considered one of the world's best, sells for about $2,150 a pound. Most of the French rose absolutes are purchased by Chanel and only used in their finest perfumes. Such natural rose scents are used as main ingredients in three-fourths of the world's prestige perfumes (e.g., Chanel No. 5, Eternity, Joy, L'Air du Temps, and Trésor).

Commercial jasmine (*Jasminum grandiflorum*) culture may have declined in Grasse, but it is alive and vigorous near the village of Virapandi, India. There, women and girls harvest jasmine flowers individually into wicker baskets carried under their arms. They arrive at the fields by 5:30 a.m. and pick nonstop until 9:30 a.m. By that time, the window of maximum scent production is over. The flowers are night bloomers, adapted as sirens for their moth pollinators. By midmorning, the flowers have lost most of their delicate aroma.

Growing, picking, and distilling flowers into absolutes is costly. Moroccan rose absolute costs $600 per pound. Sweet jasmine (*Jasminum humile*) from Italy and Egyptian jasmine sell for $500 per pound. The remaining jasmine fields in Grasse possess true snob appeal, and their distilled oils sell for an astounding $12,000 per pound. It is used sparingly, and only in the world's most valuable perfumes. The damask rose (*Rosa x damascena*) petals from the fields in the Gouna Valley in southern Morocco provide $1 million to a poor region. The flowers are all harvested during one month of the short growing season and then processed immediately into rose absolute.

Wherever flowers are picked, further processing awaits. Typically, bags or baskets of blooms are carried to cool sorting sheds and processing centers. Women laboriously pluck all the petals from the flowers. Gathered together into giant piles, often weighing a ton or more, the petals are scooped up and immediately distilled or treated with solvents. They are turned into the precious concentrates, the floral absolutes that will be sold by the company owners to the largest perfume houses in Europe and the United States, the only buyers who can afford such expensive raw ingredients.

How Floral Scents Are Extracted

The three main methods to get scent molecules out of flower petals are steam distillation, solvent extraction, and, as was first practiced by the Romans, enfleurage. Early Arabic chemists discovered how to distill rose petals and make rose water. They found that if fresh roses were plunged into boiling water, the blooms would release their aromatic essential oils into the steam. The steam was then trapped in coiled metal tubes, which were cooled. The rose volatiles condensed and floated to the surface of the rose water that remained below. Around the tenth century, this imaginative floral-distillation process made its way to Spain. The Spanish, along with other Arabic nations, produced rose perfume and used the rose distillates to flavor many of their foods. Today, steam distillation is still a common way that flowers are stripped of their precious scents. The extraction equipment has changed greatly in the intervening centuries, but the underlying process is basically the same as in ancient times. Today, flowers of some rose varieties and lavender are commonly processed using steam distillation. For a few flowers such as jasmine and mimosa, steam distillation is too harsh, and the scents of these blooms are extracted with solvents.

Solvent extraction, using organic solvents such as hexane, is somewhat gentler than distillation, with its high temperatures and potential for chemical degradation. For extraction, flower petals are layered on top of perforated metal plates. Then, the flower-laden plates are lowered into a vat of hexane and gently heated. All the essential oils, surface waxes, and pigments are extracted from the petals. Next, the mixture goes into a pot still, and the concentrated floral essence becomes the final product, called a concrete, which is dissolved in high-proof alcohol and filtered. This purified "breath of flowers" is known in the perfume industry as the floral absolute. The absolute is heavier and thicker than an essential oil.

The gentlest method of all, enfleurage, is no longer used commercially for collecting and concentrating the scents of flowers. The Roman method of making attar of roses was crude but highly effective, and later generations of Europeans similarly took individual flowers, such as jasmine, and laboriously embedded each petal onto glass plates coated with animal fats.

Later, the floral-enriched fats were extracted using organic solvents, and the enfleurage product collected. This sounds complex, but is basically the same thing that happens when you put an uncovered stick of butter next to something smelly, such as onions or garlic, in your home refrigerator. The fatty butter absorbs these odors, and you throw the butter out. You can, however, also impart pleasant floral scents to butter by mixing it with fragrant roses, other petals, or lavender, for your dining pleasure. Scientists use an extremely gentle scent extraction method called headspace collection to sample unknown odors from living flowers still attached to their plants.

The Music of Perfumes

Commercial perfumers are more like musical composers, ones commissioned by symphony orchestras, than chemists, or perhaps cooks who prepare scented meals for the senses. We can consider fine perfumes like a three-part fugue by Beethoven, Bach, or other baroque composers. Perfumes are likened to a musical metaphor as having three notes (which produce a chord)—three characteristic scents—based on temperature and their volatility. The idea of scented "notes" is largely used in marketing, for describing the attributes of fine perfumes to us, their intended customers. Perfumes, however, are highly individualistic, and their chemical blends react differently depending upon the skin chemistry and the temperature of the wearer.

Modern perfumers consider any perfume to have a top note (or head), a middle or "heart" note, and a base note. The three notes are usually represented diagrammatically as a fragrance pyramid, one with a broad base, a tapering midsection, and a pointed tip. Our fragrance-awareness clock begins ticking immediately after a perfume is applied to human skin. The numerous chemicals within begin to evaporate, drifting away in the air. Only now can they be perceived by the wearer and others as a recognizable perfume.

Perfumery uses as many as two thousand distinctive notes, although many variations are on familiar themes, including rose notes (such as those from Bulgarian, Moroccan, French, or Turkish roses), citrus notes, and exotic, dark, resinous notes such as frankincense (also known as olibanum). We also adore the woody notes of cedar, juniper, pine, or sandalwood. From the garden, we extract bracing herbal notes, including basil and lavender. Consider the downright unpleasant notes of ammonia and decay, skunky ones, or the animal sex pheromones such as musk, which we have adopted for our own sexual purposes. All these find their way into today's perfumes, toilet waters, and colognes, and ultimately onto your skin.

Perfumes can be amazingly rich and complex, and today an average perfume contains from sixty to a hundred chemical ingredients. Some contain around three hundred constituents, while Estée Lauder's perfume Beautiful likely holds the world perfumery record for complexity with around seven hundred!

The top notes of a perfume are the ones we notice first, those that command our immediate attention. They are the lightest, the lowest-molecular-weight chemicals within the mixture. These compounds evaporate first and are used up the fastest, typically lasting only five to thirty minutes following application. These give us our first impression of a perfume, and first impressions in perfumery matter a great deal. Customers usually decide instantly whether they like a perfume or not upon first whiff of the distinctive and powerful top notes. Often these top notes are described by perfumers as having assertive, sharp, or fresh aromas. The scents of gingerroot and citrus rinds are commonly used as top notes by perfumers.

Once the fresh and lighter top notes have nearly evaporated, we begin to take notice of the heart of the perfume, the middle notes. They are due to the heavier molecules, ones more reluctant to launch into the air around the perfume wearer. Perfumers often refer to the middle notes as being more rounded or mellow. They reveal themselves ten to thirty minutes, even one hour, after you first apply a perfume. Chemicals that smell like roses or lavender are most commonly used as middle notes by today's perfumers.

Finally, the bulk of the perfume reveals itself often an hour or more after it hits the skin. Middle notes mix and cavort with base notes. Together, they are the main and most long-lived fragrance theme, the olfactory essence of any fine perfume. The base and middle notes are onstage together. These compounds are part of the "fixative" of the perfume. Perfume fixatives are oils, alcohol, or extravagantly expensive ingredients such as ambergris used in only the world's most expensive fragrances. Fixatives help to hold back the lighter top and middle notes of any fragrance. In any perfume, they are the largest, heaviest, and stickiest of the chemicals used. Most often, the base notes are animalistic in nature, rich and complex scents. They may even be somewhat unpleasant and are termed skunky or sexual, like real and synthetic musks. Often, the musk notes are easily perceived on the skin a day or more after the perfume was originally applied. These base notes have staying power.

If we examine a much-beloved perfume, we can understand how the different olfactory notes combine to complete their harmonius scented performance. Coco Mademoiselle by Chanel was released in 2001 with an onslaught of advertising messages aimed at women in their twenties. This fragrance has lots of citrus notes and smells great. Its top notes are bergamot, orange, and grapefruit. A bit later, you perceive the heart notes of jasmine, lychee, and rose. Finally, when your Coco Mademoiselle begins to dry down, the strong base notes kick in. Here are the rich and deep notes of bourbon vanilla, Indonesian patchouli, Haitian vetiver (*Chrysopogon zizanioides*), and white musk. To some "perfumeophiles" this is liquid sex in a bottle, having more than the usual reputed aphrodisiacal or attractant qualities of many famous perfumes.

Perfumers, Industry Noses, and the Scent Organ

Most of the largest perfume and fragrance houses have several highly paid, uniquely talented individuals at the heart of their business. These are the "noses," the master perfumers, who make everything happen. These individuals are responsible for evaluating new compounds that their company may have synthesized de novo in the laboratory and patented, or created using the slower and more laborious scent-bar mixology of sniffing and sniffing and blending, trying to create the next new designer perfume to edge out the competition. Perfume design is complex and daunting because of the tens of thousands of odorant molecules available.

You can't easily go to perfume school, for there aren't many around. One is the famous Institut Supérieur International du Parfum in Versailles, founded in 1970 by perfumer Jean-Paul Guerlain. To become a perfumer, not unlike a sommelier, is difficult and challenging. Even if you have the nose for it, it can easily take ten or fifteen years of work to truly excel in the field. Learning to distinguish the various scents singly and in blends is all part of the training, and the perfume business. Fine fragrance perfumers are an elite craft guild, members of the secretive, high-stakes fashion industry. It may cost a million dollars to bring a new fragrance, a single molecule, to market.

Some perfumers have worn their new perfume creations prerelease in taxicabs or while lingering at a shopping-center cosmetics and fragrance counter. What will be the reaction of the men and women who smell the new fragrance? Usually surveys and professional paid sniffers also contribute to the decisions in developing new perfumes. Other perfumers live with their new scents day and night, while others dream or previsualize them, proceeding as if they were conducting a symphony orchestra, directing and bringing in the right molecules for just the right part, and timing, of the performance. They constantly readjust their perfumes, like blending whiskeys or fine wines. Perfumery is a high art.

One feature idiosyncratic to the profession is the scent organ. Not a human nose, the traditional scent organ is a special tiered and curved wooden desk with many small niches. A perfumer sits in the middle, at the console of the organ, surrounded by hundreds of bottles and small vials of scent. They dip long, narrow, pointed strips of inert white filter paper into the vials of pure fragrances. They set them on wooden rails or in fan-shaped arrays in small holders to wait for their dry-down changes. They sniff each one immediately and take careful notes. They begin adding top, middle, and base notes into a first blend, a working draft of sorts. They wick up the blend, sniff, and let it rest. Rapidly, the top notes float off, followed by huskier molecules during the next hour or so. They keep sniffing their paper strips at intervals, thinking and recording their observations. They sniff again at the end of the day, and again early the next morning.

Creating a new perfume can take a day, many months, or even years. In the past, it was common to take three to seven years to perfect any new perfume. Famous perfumer Edmond Roudnitska, who died in 1996 at age ninety-one, created only seventeen perfumes in his seven-decade career. Today, a "rushed" perfume for a famous client might be created in as few as eight weeks.

A perhaps apocryphal myth surrounds the 1921 creation of Chanel No. 5 perfume (imbued with jasmine, rose, sandalwood, and vanilla) for fashion designer Coco Chanel. She reputedly picked number five in a series of test perfumes as a lucky number (perhaps an association with *Cistus*, a five-petaled rose, from her teen years at Aubazine, a convent orphanage), and from her lifelong fascination with mysticism. Chanel was also known to love the smell of soaps and fresh scents and kept herself scrupulously clean. Previous perfumes used citrus notes to achieve this freshness, but they did not last on the skin. Did an unknown Chanel assistant make a serendipitous mistake by adding a higher dose of aldehydes, themselves not used in earlier perfumes, or was it a conscious act by master perfumer Ernst Beaux? Perhaps we'll never know.

Famous and Classic Perfumes

Every year a hundred or more new perfumes are launched commercially with great fanfare by European and American companies to the buying public. Adding to this buyer sensory overload, the older perfumes are "still in print," and there are lots of them. Like fashionable clothes, perfumes come and go, in and out of style. A few champions have staying power, such as Chanel No. 5, and amazingly Jicky, from Guerlain, which has been in continuous production since 1889. The majority of perfumes, however,

Decorative modern perfume bottles

have a shorter half-life, given our short attention spans and fickle allegiances to our favorite brands. If you are shopping for a new perfume for you or your partner, study the mesmerizing and humorous accounts in *Perfumes: the A–Z Guide* by Luca Turin and Tania Sanchez, who describe with wit and charm a mere one thousand eight hundred of the world's most alluring scents.

The classic and highly successful perfumes for women include Angel, Après l'Ondée, Black, Bois de Violette, Boucheron, Homage, Mitsuoko, Rive Gauche, and the classic older perfume Shalimar. Among the best masculine scents are Azzaro pour Homme, Eau de Guerlain, New York, Pour Monsieur, and Timbuktu. Of course, it's fun to sometimes mix things up. After all, there is nothing wrong with men wearing feminine-branded scents, and vice versa. Go ahead, live dangerously, get out of your perfume comfort zone.

Perfumes have evolved since the days they contained only natural substances. Today, most fine perfumes contain more than 90 percent synthetic chemicals, which makes economic sense when considering the extreme cost of some of raw materials. Orrisroot has sold for as much as $13,605 per pound. With the synthesis of coumarin in 1868, perfumery changed in a monumental way and never looked back. Vanillin, heliotropin, ionones (the smell of violets), and others soon followed. Synthetic chemicals leveled the playing field for perfume companies by adding rich scents that were easy to manufacture and far less expensive than purely natural ingredients. Citral, a common lemon-scented ingredient, can be had for only $12 for twenty-four pounds. Natural sandalwood oil still smells the best, but starting in 1935, a number of synthetic sandalwood scents (santalol and Javanol) hit the market. Similarly, the Himalayan musk deer and the civet cat, both endangered mammals, are no longer threatened in their homelands, at least not by the perfume industry. Numerous synthetic animal musks (musk Baur, musk ketone) followed, some, strangely enough, like musk Baur, the results of research on the high explosive TNT.

I've wondered why perfumers haven't created fragrances that smell exactly like one type of flower, say a rose or lily of the valley. I'd buy them! Or why, when I smelled Queen of the Night, a commercial perfume, it was nothing like the actual floral scent of my beloved queen-of-the-night cactus (*Peniocereus greggii*), which unfurls its straplike petals but a few nights each year. I suppose that a "soliflores" (single-compound-dominated perfume blend) would be boring to most and wouldn't have the same slow-release effects of the blended, abstract but sumptuous olfactory creations that we enjoy today.

Indeed, the rich combination of scents in modern perfumes play upon the synergistic mysteries of chemistry, the behavioral associations of memory, and the beauty of the human body—a coded, nonverbal language we all understand in our own way. But flowers also have been used as part of another secret language, and we will explore that next.

PART IV

FLOWERS IN LITERATURE, ART, AND MYTH

Looking close, floral parts of gerbera daisy
(*Gerbera* sp.)

CHAPTER 10

The Secret Language of Flowers

The complex form of the blue passionflower
(*Passiflora caerulea*)

In 1890, in the early morning in a fashionable London suburb, a courier has just knocked, left something, then quickly departed. A young woman answers the door, but finds nobody there. She looks down to the doorstep and retrieves a small floral bouquet. She brings it to her face, smiling broadly while appreciating the scent of sweet violets, carnations, and daffodils. What could they mean? The woman's expression becomes concerned. Is the bouquet a message from her best friend, the sister of a handsome young man not well liked by her overly protective parents? Is her friend acting as a go-between helping to arrange a secret rendezvous with the young man later that evening? All these things, and more, are written into the bouquet, in a formalized and secretive language of the flowers, if she can only deduce their true meaning. She brings the flowers to her room and consults her treasured book by the Reverend Hilderic Friend (1852–1940), *Flowers and Flower Lore* (1884). Let's see—violets were included, so that could mean modesty, virtue, or possibly affection by her admirer.

Historically, flowers have been admired and used decoratively, adding their scents and beauty to our lives. But nineteenth-century women, especially those living in France and England, were caught up in a formalized culture of flowers, often painting elaborate floral scenes. Some claimed that the symbolic meanings given to flowers were an unstated universal language to be studied and used. This diversion originated in Asia and was introduced to England, France, and other countries via the published letters of Lady Mary Wortley Montagu (1689–1762) of England. Her ladyship was a personal friend and confidant of the satirical poet Alexander Pope, with whom she corresponded from Turkey from 1716 to 1718. She told of a mysterious language among the people of Istanbul utilizing flowers that was about gallantry and courtly love.

A "Turkish love letter" required no ink or paper. It consisted of a small purse containing several objects. Each represented a different word or phrase, so the purse might contain a pearl mixed with cloves, a tulip, a piece of soap, coal, and a straw.

Articles, pamphlets, and entire books on the symbolic language of flowers first appeared in Paris and other French cities around the end of the Napoleonic Wars (1803–15). In literature, a prominent culture of flowers included elaborate flower poetry, such as love poems written by Charles-Louis Mollevant in 1844. He considered flowers to be charming couriers, *le courrier charmant*, used by shy young ladies, a way for them to secretly communicate with friends or lovers, thereby evading detection by their inquisitive parents.

The most important event that codified the language of flowers was the publication of a Parisian book in 1819 by Madame Charlotte de Latour, a pseudonym. Most scholars agree that the author's real name was Louise Cortambert (1775–1853), the wife of geographer Eugène Cortambert. The Latour book, *Le Langage des fleurs*, listed flowers by their seasons, and meanings that single blooms or a mixed bouquet would convey between friends or lovers. For example, orange-colored flowers signified hope, while marigolds indicated despair, sunflowers represented constancy, and roses indicated beauty. A rosebud whose stem had its thorns and leaves intact signified "I fear, but I am in hope." A rose with its thorns removed might convey the idea of "love at first sight." Certainly, this was a complex and nonintuitive way to communicate one's feelings.

Latour's book was extremely popular in France and other European countries, yet regarded as somewhat risqué, perhaps because flower-messaging could be used to facilitate romantic encounters. Nevertheless, her readership was broad, and the book was reprinted many times. Other writers during this period were also infatuated with the idea of communicating symbolically using flowers. In his *Le Nouveau Langage des fleurs* (of 1898), Sirius de Massilie combined an examination of floral colors and their scents to produce a catalog of floral meanings. In his classification, white flowers conveyed purity, orange-colored blooms signified virginity, red flowers meant ardent love, green flowers expressed hope, yellow ones meant marriage, and violets were appropriate for widows. Roses of various hues had around twenty-one different meanings.

Jean Ignace Isidore Gérard (1803–47) was a famous Parisian cartoonist usually writing under the pseudonym J. J. Grandville. His greatest work, *Les Fleurs Animées* (1847), is an imaginative and delightful mix of satirical and poetic verses accompanied by colorful illustrations of flowers that morph into human beings. The careers and personalities of women, as anthropomorphized flowers, are indicated by the colorful flowers they wear as hats, dresses, or ornaments. In one, "Chardon," we see a woman as a prickly thistle standing her ground while confronted by a donkey in formal attire.

The Flowers Personified: antiquarian image of a thistle flower by Parisian cartoonist J. J. Grandville from his *Les Fleurs Animées* (1847)

The Latour language-of-flowers book finally hit American shores in 1834, in New York City, under the title *The Language of Flowers, or Alphabet of Floral Emblems*. Additional books on the subject by Albert Jacquemart (1808–75) and many others followed soon after, and each had its own devoted following of readers and admirers. The introduction of inexpensive color printing (lithography) in popular books of this period helped promote and spread information about flowers, and how they could be used for covert communication.

The symbolic meanings of flowers in different cultures have not remained consistent throughout history. We don't find inviolate or universal meanings, as suggested in the 1800s through the many editions of Latour's book. Today, similar highly popular books and short accounts of floral symbolism and hidden meanings are still being published in France, England, and the United States.

Although the historical symbolic meanings of many different flowers have simply been lost or changed, a few have remained intact to this day, as follows:

Aster (*Aster*). Thought to represent daintiness and love.

Azalea (*Rhododendron*). Said to symbolize temperance, passion, and womanhood (in China), along with fragility and taking care of oneself.

Baby's breath (*Gypsophila*). Reputed to indicate purity of heart, innocence (they're white), and Christian religious ideas, including the breath of the Holy Spirit.

Begonia (*Begonia*). Believed to indicate a fanciful nature, or a cautionary note, telling someone to beware.

Calla lily (*Zantedeschia aethiopica*). Said to represent magnificent beauty. Certainly, they were symbols in paintings by artists such as Diego Rivera and Georgia O'Keeffe.

Camellia (*Camellia*). Suggests admiration, perfection, are a gift meant to bring good luck to a man, and also represent gratitude and noble reasoning.

Carnation (*Dianthus caryophyllus*). Said to represent fascination, impulsiveness, capriciousness, joy, devoted love, along with disdain or refusal (if white carnations are used). Green carnations were sometimes worn by homosexual males.

Chrysanthemum (*Chrysanthemum*). Especially in China, they denote abundance, cheerfulness, a hope for wealth, optimism, truth (white mums), hope, rest, and friendship, and lasting love (red mums).

Gardenia (*Gardenia*). Suggested to mean secret love, purity, and refinement.

Iris (*Iris*). These usually purple and yellow-throated blooms indicate faith, wisdom, cherished friendships, hope, valor, promise in love, wisdom. That's a lot to ask of one flower.

Lilac (*Sryinga vulgaris*). Indicates beauty, pride, youthful innocence, and youthfulness itself.

Marigold (*Tagetes*). Symbolizes grief, despair, and sorrow.

Orchids (*Cattleya, Cymbidium, Laelia,* etc.). Said to inspire love, beauty, refinement, having many children, thoughtfulness, and maturity.

Rose (*Rosa*). Symbolizes many things, but love is usually mentioned above all other connotations. Roses are also used to indicate remembrance, passion (red roses), purity (white roses), happiness (pink roses), infidelity (yellow roses), and unconscious beauty. I wonder what green and blue roses are telling us.

Tulip (*Tulipa*). Represents fame and perfect love. Red tulips mean "believe me" and are a declaration of love; variegated tulips mean "you have beautiful eyes"; and yellow tulips, "there is sunshine in your smile." Cream-colored tulips say "I'll love you forever."

Violet (*Viola odorata*). Indicates modesty, but for some, a blue violet means "I'll always be true." A white violet means "let's take a chance on happiness."

Zinnia (*Zinnia*). Meant to symbolize thoughts of absent friends, long-lasting affection, constancy, goodness, and daily remembrances of loved ones.

Flowers as Living Tributes

We can agree that the nineteenth-century's largely European language of flowers, no matter how charming, is almost defunct. In times past, though, presentations of flowers as wreaths, garlands, and chaplets had far more lasting and significant meanings.

In Greek and Roman times, laurel wreaths were given to champion athletes, including winning gladiators in Rome's Colosseum, or to political leaders and victorious army generals. Floral garlands on religious statues were widely used to honor Roman deities. We've discussed the floral garlanding of animals, statues, and altars as part of Hindu and other religious ceremonies. In ancient Rome, garlands of roses were worn by banquet guests, floors were littered with roses, and they were often dribbled down from balconies, by servants or slaves, onto guests at banquets and other festive occasions. Real or painted roses on the ceilings of meeting rooms were reminders for participants to speak the truth. This is the origin of the term *sub rosa*, "under the rose," to speak in confidence and secretly.

The ancient Olympic games were first celebrated in 776 BC, and for a millennium thereafter, in Olympia, Greece. These competitions had but one winner, the Olympionic. A judge placed a palm leaf in the winner's hands while as many as forty-five thousand spectators cheered and threw flowers. An olive branch, the victory crown, was also placed on the head of the winner, who was given special status and advantages for the rest of his life in his home city or town. In Simonides's ode to Astylos of Croton, a fifth-century Greek Olympic athlete, the poet proclaimed, "Who of men today has been adorned with so many petals and myrtles and crowns of rose thanks to his victory in the Games?"

In today's winter and summer Olympics, we follow similar ancient traditions when medalists, or women's Wimbledon winners, are given a bouquet of roses, along with a medal on a colorful neck ribbon, for their victories.

Today, all over the world, we use flowers as measures of recognition and tribute to worthy individuals. We present bouquets of various kinds of flowers, wreaths, or garlands as greetings to visitors (e.g., leis of fragrant *Plumeria* blooms to tourists upon disembarking by airplane in the Hawaiian Islands), and as tributes to musicians, actors, singers, other entertainers, and to visiting dignitaries and politicians at many public events. The most commonly used tributes or rewards for musical, theatrical, or athletic performances are bouquets of long-stemmed, red roses.

Among the world's scientific, literary, and peacekeeping elite are the Nobel laureates. Each year about seventeen thousand carnations, chrysanthemums, tulips, and roses, along with apples and evergreen plants, are transported to Stockholm, Sweden, from the Italian city of San Remo, where Alfred Nobel (the prize's founder) died on December 10, 1896. These magnificent floral displays decorate the Blue Hall of the Stockholm City Concert Hall, where the Nobel Peace Prizes are awarded each December 10.

Wearing Your Words—Flowers as Personal Signs

Corsages worn on wrists or pinned to the bodice of a gown, along with boutonnieres for men's lapels or buttonholes, are another form of signaling between humans. These floral emblems also denote social rank, status, and roles at various events and ceremonies.

The word *corsage* is confusing and misunderstood. It actually refers to the bodice portion of a dress, two halves laced together over the chest. The word comes from the term *bouquet de corsage* or *bouquet de bodice* and refers to a bouquet of flowers, a flower bud, or bow worn on the corsage between the breasts. Today, the word means a grouping of flowers worn on the breast, waist, or wrist.

Boutonnière is the French word for "buttonhole" and also refers to the decorative flower placed in the buttonhole of a man's suit coat or tuxedo. The term and practice originated in the 1700s in France and England. The boutonniere was devised to ward off diseases, possibly evil spirits and ameliorate bad body odors. Men of the period often wore a boutonniere blossom daily. Over the years, men's boutonnieres became reserved for formal and special events including weddings and proms. Today, they are used simply to tie together the look of a couple or to accent a man's formal ensemble.

Corsages and boutonnieres are especially common at dances, weddings, and funerals in Europe and the United States. Corsages are a small floral arrangement, or single flower, attached to a pin, and the corsage is typically worn on the left side of the chest. Nowadays, this type of corsage is less popular with women since it may interfere with the style of their gown or weigh down a strapless dress. The boutonniere is more popular with men and usually pinned to the left lapel of a sports jacket or formal suit coat. The flowers of choice for urban, male boutonnieres are white or red carnations. The carnation had one rural competitor. Americans know this flower as the bachelor's button, but the British and Germans know it as the bluebottle or the cornflower (*Centaurea cyanus*). If a country boy wore one, it meant that he was madly in love. However, if the flower faded too quickly, it was an omen that the object of his desire did not truly care for him.

In present times, speakers at conferences, judges, or officials at various events and meetings often wear corsages or boutonnieres as symbols of their authority, stature, or functionary role. Similarly, speakers or officials at conferences wear corsages or colorful ribbons setting them apart yet inviting recognition and interactions with other attendees.

Floral Gifts as Cultural Messages

Since antiquity, flowers have been given by individuals to family members, friends, or lovers as cherished gifts. Pronounced cultural differences exist for the flowers used and which ones might offend the recipient. For example, it is inappropriate to give white flowers as a gift in modern China since they are mostly used at funerals.

Nonetheless, flowers are one of the safest bets for a gift that will be appreciated. This is true for almost every culture (except those of the Islamic faith, where flowers are not given as romantic gifts between men and women). Rites of passage (birthdays, anniversaries, graduations, retirement parties, weddings, funerals, and various religious ceremonies) are all good opportunities to give flowers. For business travelers and corporate gift-giving, flowers are often a preferred and appreciated gift.

Flower gifting is prominent in China (especially to teachers). Peonies are the most popular flowers to give, along with chrysanthemums, and are often given at wedding ceremonies. Roses, lilies, and carnations are the most widely used blooms for funerals and expressing sympathy. These tightly compressed blooms express cycles of birth, life, death, and rebirth. Red is a lucky color for the Chinese, and they often give red blooms. In Russia, a single flower or a bouquet of flowers is often given as a birthday gift. Russians like to give flowers in odd numbers for joyful occasions. They give yellow flowers only to people who are sick or at funerals to express sympathy. On Women's Day in Russia, red roses are given, along with spring flowers such as tulips, hyacinths, and goldenrod.

European countries have a strong culture of flower giving, especially England, France, Germany, and Switzerland. In England, guests visiting someone's home often bring flowers, but not white lilies, for they signify death. As in the United States, red roses are typically reserved for romantic gifts. Germans consider red roses a bit too sentimental, or only for romance. Giving carnations, chrysanthemums, or lilies should be avoided because these symbolize mourning. France has similar traditions. In Europe, giving odd numbers of flowers seems to be an old tradition still in practice today. Giving thirteen flowers, however, is avoided, as this is considered unlucky. In Mexico, Colombia, Italy, and other countries where All Saints' Day is celebrated, marigolds are used, but not given as gifts because they symbolize death and mourning.

Giving flowers in Africa has become especially popular in recent decades in larger cities and in Kenya and South Africa. The flowers given not only include roses and other perennial favorites, but hardy natives including proteas from the areas supporting flowers of the Cape region of southernmost Africa. Flowers, including the king protea (*Protea cynaroides*), are exchanged extensively during the Christmas holidays in South Africa. In Egypt, flower giving is mostly confined to weddings and funerals. And Muslims typically do not give flowers, especially among the most devoutly traditional sects, such as the Sunni.

In America, flower giving happens for almost any reason and for most of the ceremonies and occasions noted above. Poinsettias and Christmas cactus (*Schlumbergera*) are commonly given at Christmas, Madonna lilies at Easter, and roses and mixed bouquets for many other occasions.

What happens in countries in the southern hemisphere where the seasons are reversed? In Australia, Valentine's Day is held in the dead of summer, but roses remain the appropriate bouquet. However, May is an autumn month in the southern hemisphere, so Mother's Day means white chrysanthemums. When Australians celebrate their Remembrance Day and Anzac Day, out come the plastic, red poppies.

Poppies appear on lapels, which may also be adorned with sprigs of the herb rosemary after Shakespeare's famous line "rosemary for remembrance." John McCrae penned the famous poem "In Flanders Fields" based on his observation that the red corn poppies (*Papaver rhoeas*) had colonized war graves. By about 1920, essentially all English-speaking countries had adopted this flower to celebrate Veterans Day to remember those fallen in war. This flower had a completely different meaning in Greco-Roman art. Brilliant red corn poppies invade fields of wheat and barley and were associated with the spring return of Persephone to her mother, the grain goddess, Demeter. The recent use of this poppy to honor war dead has now displaced the ancient and long-held belief that the flower heralded the resurrection of a goddess from the land of the dead.

Flowers as National or State Emblems

Can a lowly flower come to represent an entire country, or state? Yes, it can, and the association is old and has its roots in royalty and in many heraldic coats of arms across numerous countries and lands.

Sovereign nations have often selected a particular flower to represent them based on a rich folklore or religious beliefs coupled with the heraldry of old ruling families. The national flower of Malaysia is the bunga raya, the Chinese hibiscus (*Hibiscus rosa-sinensis*), while the lotus (*Nelumbo nucifera*) is the national flower of India, and the fleur-de-lis emblem, derived from the iris, represents France. German-speaking peoples adopted the lowly cornflower or bachelor's button. Queen Louise of Prussia (1776–1810) fled Berlin with her children to escape Napoléon's army. She hid them in a field of blue cornflowers and kept them from crying by weaving garlands of the blossoms. A century later the cornflower became a favorite of Kaiser Wilhelm, and the cornflower has never quite lost its reputation as a flower of the First World War.

A National Flower for America?

A flower meant to represent an entire nation can present a problem. Its roots suck up a lot of unpleasant history about royal prejudices, religious biases, and military adventures. Perhaps that's one reason America took so long to select a national flower. In 1986, President Ronald Reagan signed legislation to make the rose (any rose would do) the floral emblem of the United States. The push for a national flower began decades earlier thanks to Republican senator Everett Dirksen (1896–1969), who favored the marigold that originated in Mexico. By the time Reagan signed the flower bill into law, our national flower became the Peace rose, not one of our many native, wild species. The Peace rose is a European hybrid! Think about it. A "frenchified" garden pleaser became our national flower two hundred years after we adopted the bald eagle as our national bird. No wonder literary critic Lewis Mumford once remarked, "Our national flower is the concrete cloverleaf."

The search for a flower to represent each American state started in the 1890s, but there has never been much concern for our resplendent and diverse native flora or botanical accuracy. Maine made the cone of the white pine (*Pinus strobus*) its state flower in 1895, but a pinecone isn't a flower. Vermont, possibly in deference to its dairy industry, voted for the red clover (*Trifolium pratense*) in 1894, with its nutritious leaves and flowers for cows. Alaska waited until 2004 to legitimize the common forget-me-not (*Myosotis alpestris*).

Some US states have been a bit schizophrenic about whether to choose native wildflowers or imported but popular garden flowers from faraway lands. Alabama has been represented by the Asian camellia (*Camellia japonica*) since 1959 before promoting their native oak-leaf hydrangea (*Hydrangea quercifolia*) to state wildflower in 1999. Sometimes the logic runs backward. Tennessee stuck with its native flora and voted for the maypop (*Passiflora incarnata*), one of the few passionflowers native to temperate America, in 1919, but then brought in garden irises in 1933. Things are even worse in Pennsylvania. Its citizens voted for the lovely mountain laurel in 1933, but then added the Eurasian crown vetch (*Securigera varia*) as their conservation flower in 1982, since it prevents soil erosion. Today in the state it is regarded as an invasive weed.

My home state of Arizona, which moved from territory to statehood in 1912, chose in 1931 to make the former territorial flower, the creamy-white flower of the spiny, columnar cactus the saguaro (*Carnegiea gigantea*), its state bloom. I like that choice. If you are curious about your own state, my website (www.stephenbuchmann.com) gives a listing of all the state flowers in the United States.

Bluebonnets Not Billboards

One state flower rises above its role in a popularity contest. The great state of Texas wisely chose the bluebonnet (*Lupinus texensis*), a spiked, brilliant blue legume known as a lupine, for its state flower in 1901. During the spring, it can cover thousands of acres across the hill counties, especially around Austin, beautifying the landscapes around the Lady Bird Johnson Wildflower Center.

The irrepressible, dynamic former first lady "Lady Bird" Johnson (1912–2007) popularized this little Texas plant. She used it as a wonderful example of how to beautify America during the presidency (1963–69) of her husband, Lyndon Johnson. She believed that American highways and roads deserved the ornamentation, colors, and beauty of native wild-flowers, not ugly billboards. The choice of bluebonnets to seed the road-sides of new and upgraded highways was brilliant. The flowers grow close to the ground and don't impair a driver's roadside vision; prefer fast drain-age, luxuriating in gravel and broken stones by the side of the road; and don't need fertilizer. Bluebonnets also provide nectar and pollen for many bees while their leaves are food for caterpillars of hairstreak butterflies. This wildflower requires little care as it's a winter annual, sprouting and greening the landscape during wet, cold months, then flowering, seeding, and dying in spring. Texas is one of the few states that actively seeds its highways with its state flower, along with other native Texas blooms.

From the mysterious florigraphic bouquet left on a doorstep in nineteenth-century London to an online order of red roses for delivery to one's wife or husband, flowers continue to be silent yet potent couriers delivering our feelings and cultural traditions to one another. In the next two chapters, we explore the meanings of flowers in various forms of artistic expression, from Shakespeare to the lavish still-life paintings of Dutch masters to the postmodern art world, exemplified in works by O'Keeffe and Warhol. Flowers live not only in gardens and roadsides and the wild, but in our imaginations in literature and art as well.

CHAPTER 11

Flowers on the Page

Arizona's state flower, the bat- and bee-pollinated
saguaro blossom (*Carnegiea gigantea*)

Regardless of time or place, all literate cultures have used flowers as the
subjects for poetic imagery of people and their environments. Some story-
tellers and poets enjoy flowers as they are, while others use them as metaphors for the brevity of pleasure, beauty, and life itself. Yet flowers are
immortal; gardens grow in poems about love and death.

A full recounting of the flower in literature would require thousands
of pages, so instead, a sampling—or my selected bouquet if you will—will
have to do. The oldest preserved writing, from ancient Sumer, as cuneiform marks gouged into clay tablets, are records of daily business transactions. An exception is the Sumerian *Epic of Gilgamesh* (predating 2000
BC), the earliest known surviving literary work. This tale recounts King
Gilgamesh's attempt to find the plant of immortality at the bottom of
a freshwater ocean. The lyrics describe the specimen as a boxthornlike
plant bearing flowers that give a wonderful fragrance. Gilgamesh finds
and picks the flower, but loses the prize to a hungry vegetarian snake.

The Western tradition of rich and diverse flower poetry does not flow
from this early masterpiece. But what about the Bible? As Christianity

spread throughout Europe, those famous "lilies of the field" lines inspired generations of authors, right? While scripture is a wonderful place to learn about the economics of plants (crops versus weeds), in the earliest days of the Middle East, biblical verses about flowers are rare. In 1952, Harold and Alma Moldenke published *Plants of the Bible* to explain and reinterpret its many plant references, of which the vast majority were about seeds, leaves, resins, and wood. Relatively few mention flowers, and the species are not well identified in most translations. Even today, Israeli botanist Amots Dafni is exploring the Bible, extracting similar botanical and elusive floral inferences. Examples of biblical verses mentioning flowers are:

"I am the rose of Sharon, The lily of the valleys. Like a lily among the thorns, So is my darling among the maidens."

Song of Solomon 2:1–2

"Like a flower he comes forth and withers. He also flees like a shadow and does not remain."

Job 14:2

"As for man, his days are like grass; As a flower of the field, so he flourishes.

Psalms 103:15

"The wilderness and the solitary place shall be glad for them; and the desert shall rejoice and blossom as the rose."

Isaiah 35:1.

"My beloved has gone down to his garden, To the beds of balsam, To pasture his flock in the gardens And gather lilies. I am my beloved's and my beloved is mine, He who pastures his flock among the lilies."

Song of Solomon 6:2–3

These quotes reveal that scripture sets the recurring theme of flowers, but specific references to lilies and roses probably represent deliberate mistranslations. Why? Because the genus *Rosa* is not native to that part of the world. The Moldenkes thought that these were in fact references to the gaudy flowers of rockroses (*Cistus*, not in the rose family) or even rose of Sharon (*Hibiscus syriacus*), both shrubs of waste places and abandoned fields. *Lilies* can refer to all sorts of spring wildflowers that arise from bulbs or tubers, including hyacinths, cyclamens, red buttercups, daffodils, and jonquils. In fact, members of the genus *Lilium* are relatively uncommon in that part of the world today. When Hebrew and Aramaic words are carefully examined, some modern Israeli scholars suggest that the "lilies" in Matthew and again in Luke 12:27–28, surpassing the glory of King Solomon, were really the ubiquitous, hardy, and vivid blossoms of spring anemones (*Anemone coronaria*). Most are red, but some populations mix crimson flowers with blue, purple, and cream. All have the same, striking centers of clusters of nearly black stamens.

Certain linguists insist that there is an ancient tradition in the Bible of naming cities after flowers. The metropolis of Shushan may take its name from an anemone or chamomile, while Tirzah (another name for Jerusalem) could refer to an autumn or winter crocus. Nevertheless, floral references in the Bible are infrequent. If we want to find the origin of flower-based poetry in Western civilization, we need to stay in the Mediterranean, but travel north of the Holy Lands.

That's Why We Call It an Anthology

A word is hiding in plain sight to take us to that first garden of poetry. Since seventeenth-century English, we have called organized collections of short stories, poems, plays, and other works of creative prose and poetry *anthologies*. Why? The reason has its roots in ancient Greece. The Greeks had a word, ἀνθολογία, which meant a collection of flowers, a direct reference to one of the earliest Greek anthologies, *The Garland*. Its compiler, Meleager of Gadara, was a first-century BC poet. *The Garland* is a collection of poems by Meleager and other poets, and its introduction compares each of the anthologized Greek poets to different flowers. Before *anthology* entered the English language in the seventeenth century, earlier writers referred to *miscellanies* to describe collected short literary works. In medieval Europe, where Latin was the lingua franca, a book of compiled excerpts from other writings was better known as a florilegium.

And who was the poet who ultimately made flower analogies tradition in the Greco-Roman world? One sees references to flowers in the works of Sappho of Lesbos, Cynaethus of Chios, and Pamphos of Attica, but the man or men we know as Homer from the eighth or ninth century BC still receives credit as the fount of floral poetry for early Western civilization. Consider his hymn to the grain goddess, Demeter, hinting at the rape and abduction of her daughter, Persephone, by Hades, when she picked the first narcissus, probably one of the flowers we know as jonquils (from *Homeric Hymns*, III):

> Apart from Demeter, lady of the golden sword and glorious fruits, she was playing with the deep-bosomed daughters of Oceanus and gathering flowers over a soft meadow, roses and crocuses and beautiful violets, irises also and hyacinths and the narcissus, which Earth made to grow at the will of Zeus and to please the Host of Many, to be a snare for the bloomlike girl—a marvelous [*sic*], radiant flower. It was a thing of awe whether for deathless gods or mortal men to see: from its root grew a hundred blooms and it smelled most sweetly, so that all wide heaven above and the whole earth and the sea's salt swell laughed for joy. And the girl was amazed and reached out with both hands to take the lovely toy.

Ultimately, most of the references to flowers in the Greco-Roman world go back to the stories sung by Homer and his contemporaries. In the *Iliad*, Gorgythion, one of Hector's half brothers and his charioteer, dies of an arrow wound, and his demise is compared to a drooping poppy-seed head heavy with dew. Hera plots the Greek victory by distracting Zeus upon Mount Ida. As the two deities copulate, the earth sends up fresh flowers of clovers, crocuses, and hyacinths. In the *Odyssey*, Odysseus carries a plant called moly to resist the enchantments of Circe. It has a white flower and black roots and may have been wild garlic or perhaps a cyclamen.

In Ovid's Garden

Who could resist such adventurous tales? Certainly not the Roman poet Publius Ovidius Naso (43 BC–AD 18), better known as Ovid. His fifteen-book mythological narrative, *The Metamorphoses*, contains twelve thousand verses reinterpreting hundreds of myths derived from Greek, Etruscan, and Latin traditions. This and other works by Ovid had strong and lasting effects on Western literature and art long after Rome fell. Here, for example, is Ovid's commentary on flowers that emerged purportedly from the death of two handsome men (Ovid, *Fasti* 5, 193ff, translation by A. J. Boyle, in *Roman Poetry C1st B.C. to C1st A.D.*):

> As soon as the dewy frost is cast from the leaves and sunbeams warm the dappled blossom, the Horae [Seasons] assemble, hitch up their coloured dresses and collect these gifts of mine in light tubs. Suddenly the Charites [the Graces] burst in, and weave chaplets and crowns to entwine the hair of gods. I first scattered new seed across countless nations; earth was formerly a single colour. I first made a flower from Therapnean blood [Hyakinthos, the hyacinth], and its petal still inscribes the lament. You, too, narcissus, have a name in tended gardens, unhappy in your undivided self. Why mention Crocus, Attis or Cinyras' son, from whose wounds I made a tribute soar?

All Princess Dryope wanted was to pick a flower to please her infant son, but Ovid relates her shock and horror in Book IX of *The Metamorphoses* (as translated by A. D. Melville):

> . . . when I saw drops
> Of blood drip from the blossoms and the boughs
> Shiver in horror. For this shrub, you see
> (Too late the peasants told us), was a nymph
> Lotis who fled Priapus' lechery And found changed features there
>   but kept her name.

Dryope tries to pray her way out of the situation but is transformed into a tree. Her son, Amphissos, grows up in her shade and warns all never to pick flowers, but "fancy every bush a goddess in disguise" (*Metamorphoses*, Book II, 846–75).

Flowers of Purgatory

Rome fell but Latin lived on as the language of the educated elite as the empire had established colonies throughout much of Western Europe, allowing the Romance languages to evolve. Italian Durante degli Alighieri, usually simply referred to as Dante (1265–1321), is recognized as the major Italian poet from the Middle Ages, and his greatest work is the *Divine Comedy*. We don't expect to see flowers in hell but Dante and his guide, the soul of the Roman poet Virgil, leave the underworld and emerge into a terrestrial paradise leading to purgatory. Here Dante beholds an innocent and virginal woman, known later as Matelda, and he compares her to Ovid's goddess Proserpina (Persephone) and to Venus (Aphrodite). She is outdoors picking wildflowers. More flowers fall from the heavens, and the soul of Beatrice, Dante's great unrequited love interest, steps out of the cloud of blossoms. Alas, Virgil vanishes as he lacks a saved soul and can't progress farther.

Beatrice remains unobtainable and rejects Dante's earthly sentiments. She says, "'Why does my face so entrance you that you do not turn to the lovely Garden that flowers below the rays of Christ? There is the Rose, in which the Divine Word made itself flesh: there are the Lilies within whose perfume the good way is taken.' And I, who was eager for her wisdom, surrendered again to the struggle of my weak vision" (translation by A. S. Kline).

The rose is one of the most omnipresent and powerful symbols in all literature, in addition to being one of the most complex for us to understand, especially across the mists of time. Seemingly, for Dante, the rose is no less than his solution to the riddle of the universe. In the final cantos of the "Paradiso," finally purged of sin and perfected, he is permitted a mystic vision of eternal glory. The poet first perceives a huge white rose on whose petals rest many saints. Finally, Dante lifts his eyes to the sun, then a primary symbol of God, shining down upon the rose. The symbols of the sun and the rose are inseparable during this period.

Blossoming Sonnets

By the time of the Italian Renaissance from the fourteenth to sixteenth centuries, flowers return again with renewed emphasis and impact on literature, where they come to represent both sacred and profane issues. For those of us who speak English as our first language, the great poet of posies is always William Shakespeare (1564–1616). By reading his diverse works, we come away with a personalized yet broad glimpse of the English countryside, with its wildflowers, cottage gardens, and hedgerow floras. Shakespeare would have been familiar with the splendid formal gardens of the great houses of Warwickshire, as well as the more famous public ones sloping down to the bank of the river Thames in London.

As a poet, Shakespeare was indebted to surviving verses in Latin for narrative, myth, and metaphor. Consider his long poem "Venus and Adonis" as an Englishman tipping his cap to Ovid. As usual, Adonis is killed by the boar he hunts, and his gore will become a flower as the love-struck goddess looks on:

> By this, the boy that by her side lay kill'd
> Was melted like a vapour from her sight,
> And in his blood that on the ground lay spill'd,
> A purple flower sprung up, chequer'd with white,
> Resembling well his pale cheeks and the blood
> Which in round drops upon their whiteness stood.

Is it possible that Shakespeare never saw a red, living *Anemone coronaria*, commonly found throughout the Mediterranean? In fact, he influences future generations of poets in his sonnets and plays by mixing the *Anemone* species favored in Greece and Italy with those native to his chillier British homelands. Here's one of his most famous passages from *A Midsummer Night's Dream* (2.1.255–60), with a few botanical and geographical asides:

> I know a bank where the wild thyme [domesticated *Thymus*; Mediterranean] blows,
> Where oxlips [*Primula elatior*] and the nodding violet [wild *Viola* species throughout Europe, including England] grows,

Quite over-canopied with luscious woodbine [*Lonicera periclyme-*
    num; throughout Europe, including England].
With sweet musk roses [domesticated *Rosa moschata*; west-
    ern Himalayas] and with eglantine [wild *Rosa rubiginosa*;
    throughout Europe, including England]:
There sleeps Titania sometime of the night,
Lull'd in these flowers with dances and delight.

Shakespeare's Oberon sends the hobgoblin Puck to the west to find the
flower "love-in-idleness." That's one of the many common names English
cottagers gave to their wild and garden pansies (*Viola tricolor*).

Perdita may live in Bohemia in *The Winter's Tale*, but she seems overly
fond of the spring wildflowers found alongside English lanes and their
adjacent hedgerows. She names daffodils and primroses but insists, "The
fairest flowers o' the season are our carnations." Was she referring to the
native cheddar pink (likely *Dianthus gratianopolitanus*)? The cheddar pink
is now domesticated and cultivated all over the world, but the English
depleted their native populations over the centuries, and wild plants now
only cling to higher cliffs and ledges of limestone in remote areas.

As a final Elizabethan example, in agreement with our earlier dis-
cussion of Greek and Roman burial beliefs and customs, here is one of
the most famous Shakespearean quotes, from a scene in act 5 of *Hamlet*
(5.1.237–43). We find Hamlet and Queen Gertrude expressing the common belief (in this case, for Hamlet's beloved Ophelia) that violets would
spring forth and grow on her grave, the grave of a truly good person:

Lay her i' the earth:
And from her fair and unpolluted flesh
May violets spring! I tell thee, churlish priest,
A ministering angel shall my sister be,
When thou liest howling.
HAMLET: What, the fair Ophelia!
QUEEN GERTRUDE: Sweets to the sweet: farewell!
(Scattering flowers).

The Daffodil Challenges the Rose

Shakespeare wasn't the only Elizabethan poet to usher in native plants and marry them to once-favored Greco-Roman species. However, once Shakespeare departed, new trends of anthophily developed in English verse. Editor Sarah Maguire notes in her anthology, *Flora Poetica: The Chatto Book of Botanical Verse* (2001), that most poems in English that include flower imagery do not stick to a single plant species or even a genus, with the exception of poems about roses. The poems in her collection do leave you with the impression that solitary odes to lilacs, lilies, and legumes become respectable and desirable as Shakespeare's literary children and grandchildren multiply. We gradually see a shift in those flowers favored and extolled by writers and poets alike.

For example, poems including daffodils (most likely the English native, *Narcissus pseudonarcissus*) begin with British poet laureate Robert Herrick (1591–1674), especially with his love poems. Herrick retains, once again, the metaphor of fast-fading beauty: "Faire Daffadills, we weep to see / You haste away so soone [*sic*]."

These traditions were kept alive by many others, and the romantic poet William Wordsworth (1770–1850) leads the narcissophiles in the opening stanza of his notable poem "Daffodils":

I wandered lonely as a cloud
That floats on high o'er vales and hills,
When all at once I saw a crowd,
A host, of golden daffodils;
Beside the lake, beneath the trees,
Fluttering and dancing in the breeze.

English Gardens in Poems

Let's not forget that the British not only admire gardens but are often inveterate gardeners, in ink, at least. In John Milton (1608–74), we have an English poet, polemicist, and man of letters. He wrote of a chaste water nymph, Sabrina, knitting together the sinuous stems of water lilies. His poem "Lycidas" (1637) is a brief pastoral elegy. It was hailed in his life as

Milton's best poem, and some consider it the greatest lyrical poem in all the English language. An excerpt:

> Bring the rathe Primrose that forsaken dies.
> The tufted Crow-toe, and pale Jasmine,
> The white Pink, and the Pansie freakt with jeat [*sic*],
> The glowing Violet.
> The Musk-rose, and the well attir'd Woodbine,
> With Cowslips wan that hang the pensive hed,
> And every flower that sad embroidery wears:
> Bid Amaranthus all his beauty shed,
> And Daffadillies fill their cups with tears,
> To strew the Laureat Herse where Lycid lies.

In the works of Alfred Tennyson (1809–92) we see many nature poems describing flowers amid the lives of his characters and natural landscapes. Like Milton, he had a thing about water lilies and what they represented. Tennyson imagined his Lady of Shalott under a spell of solitude forced to gaze into a mirror in her castle on a lonely island. "Half sick of shadow" she breaks the spell, but it's fatal. Before she dies "she saw the water-lily bloom." One of Tennyson's best-known poems is "Maud." The setting is a garden where the author waits for his beloved, Maud. Even the garden flowers discuss their love for her and impatience to see her:

> There has fallen a splendid tear
> From the passion-flower at the gate.
> She is coming, my dove, my dear;
> She is coming, my life, my fate.
> The red rose cries, "She is near, she is near";
> And the white rose weeps, "She is late";
> The larkspur listens, "I hear, I hear";
> And the lily whispers, "I wait."

Ah, but be careful when you allow the flowers to speak!

Grimm Blossoms

The Reverend Charles Dodgson (aka Lewis Carroll, 1832–98) was a contemporary of Lord Tennyson's. Once Alice takes her fateful first step through the looking glass, she finds a pleasant garden where the flowers talk, as well, but have only the least regard for her. Instead, they await the arrival of the Red Queen, and their conversation imitates the taxonomy of the blossoms in the poem "Maud" with one big exception. When Martin Gardner (1914–2010) annotated the Alice books in 1960, he noted that Carroll decided to change the tearful passionflower into a tart, a talking tiger lily. Carroll learned that the passionflower was a potent symbol of the Passion of Christ, and as an Anglican deacon, he wasn't about to poke fun at it.

While the nineteenth century showed the blossoming of flowers in English fairy tales, it wasn't restricted to England, and much of it derives from earlier French authors and German folktales. The Countess d'Aulnoy (1650–1705) wrote of Felicia and her pot of pinks (carnations). That flowerpot is enchanted and turns into a fairy prince who will marry Felicia. Meanwhile, in Grimms' version of "Little Red Riding Hood" (1812), the wolf delays the little girl's arrival at her grandmother's house by telling her to gather up pretty woodland flowers.

The Brothers Grimm also revised (1812) the much-earlier Charles Perrault story (1697) of the beauty sleeping in the wood ("La Belle au bois dormant"). Some of the translations of the Grimm tale named the princess Rosamond. After she touches the spindle and falls asleep, thorny branches cover the castle until a prince appears a century later searching for "this beautiful Briar Rose." The thorny branches kill knights who arrive too soon, but they burst into bloom the moment the curse ends, allowing the prince to safely pass. Some of the other enchanted flowers in the Grimm tales are not benign at all. When a maiden gathers a dozen lilies for her twelve brothers, they are transformed into ravens.

Hans Christian Andersen (1805–75) was a prolific writer, playwright, novelist, and poet. Flowers appear in some of his children's stories and do strange and unexpected things. A childless woman plants a seed in a pot. It grows into a flower resembling a tulip, and Thumbelina emerges when its petals unfurl. When a swallow carries the tiny girl to the warm southlands, she meets and marries a fairy prince whose people live inside flowers. Why do the flowers in "Little Ida's Flowers" hang their heads the day after they are picked? After all, they aren't wilted. Instead, they're exhausted after spending all night dancing at the flowers' ball. Once the elf of "The Rose Elf" leaves his rose, he becomes witness, judge, and executioner of a man who has killed his sister's lover. His head is buried inside a potted jasmine, but the elf rouses the jasmine spirits to kill the murderer with their poisonous spears. This is a children's story?

Similar stories stimulated a charming tradition in children's literature from the late nineteenth century through the early 1960s. A new generation of author/illustrators humanized common garden and wildflowers, and often depicted them as anthropomorphic flower people or flower fairies. Sometimes these characters must deal with equally humanized and caricatured insects.

The master of this genre was the socialist artist and poet Walter Crane (1845–1915), who produced at least three books of flower people. *Flora's Feast: A Masque of Flowers* (1889) is the most often reprinted. We follow a march of England's garden and woodland flowers from early spring until winter including "Great Peonies in crimson pride, and budding ones in green that hide." Later in the season, "Wide Oxeyes in the meads that gaze on scarlet poppy-heads a-blaze."

Some regard Cicely Mary Barker (1895–1973) as the English queen of floral fantasy for the nursery set. Her first book on the topic, *Flower Fairies of the Spring*, was published in 1923, followed by seven more volumes, all of which attracted a huge popular following. Her illustrations dressed each sprite (depicted as a child) in the petals and sepals of a flower, and this picture was accompanied by a poem about the appropriate plant species in nature or planted in gardens.

Continuing in the flower-fairies and garden-flowers tradition, we have American author Elizabeth Gordon (1866–1922), whose flower-people books reflect the uses of plants and their natural histories. Often, she gives her readers scientific names of the plants, while "flower persons" dance with a pollinator, as in the following:

Wild Columbine (*Aquilegia canadensis*)
"I keep my sweets," said Columbine,
"For Humming Bird, a friend of mine;
He comes at sun-down every night,
And is so grateful and polite.

Walt Whitman (1819–92) gave us wonderful imagery of garden lilac blooms in his poem "When Lilacs Last in the Dooryard Bloom'd." The poem is about the untimely death of beloved president Abraham Lincoln, affectionately symbolized in the poem as the "great star early droop'd," and it became one of the most famous eulogies in American history. A few lines from Whitman's lengthy, praise-filled poem follow:

When lilacs last in the dooryard bloom'd,
And the great star early droop'd in the western sky in the night,
I mourn'd, and yet shall mourn with ever-returning spring.

Ever-returning spring, trinity sure to me you bring,
Lilac blooming perennial and drooping star in the west,
And thought of him I love.

The poet most responsible for promoting a modern aesthetic is American Ezra Pound (1885–1972). He used floral imagery in his 1913 imagist poem "In a Station of the Metro," talking about "the apparition of these faces in the crowd; Petals on a wet, black bough." Pound seems to be describing the faces in a crowded New York subway station, and the "wet, black bough" is likely the background subway walls or the pressing crowd. By calling the faces in the crowd petals, their fragile beauty in the metaphor also captures the beauty of the human individual.

The Australian author, cartoonist, and illustrator May Gibbs (1877–1969) produced a trio of books with a delightfully different twist about the adventures of the gumnut brothers Snugglepot and Cuddlepie, usually accompanied by Little Ragged Blossom. The characters are only a few inches high and have stamens for hair (no eucalyptus flowers have petals), and their bush land is run like a city. Flowers of other Australian plants are animated as well, but the greatest enemies of the gumnut babies are the "big bad banksiamen," based upon the fruits of *Banksia serrata*.

In the twentieth century, a husband-and-wife poetic team, American Sylvia Plath (1932–63) and the British Ted Hughes (1930–98), separately write of daffodils. Plath's "Among the Narcissi" describes the daffodil's petals as "vivid as bandages" and unites them with the figure of a man in a blue pea jacket recuperating from a lung ailment.

Ted Hughes was appointed Britain's poet laureate in 1984. Hughes, considered a nature poet, was described as one of the twentieth centu-ry's best poets writing in the English language. Plath and Hughes were married from 1956 to 1963. Following her death by suicide, Ted Hughes penned a poem called "Daffodils" about their life, and poignant family memories with their children, the opening lines of which are:

> Remember how we picked the daffodils?
> Nobody else remembers, but I remember.
> Your daughter came with her armfuls, eager and happy,
> Helping the harvest. She has forgotten.

Pulitzer Prize–winning and US poet laureate Louise Glück (b. 1943) has written several engaging poems about flowers, death, and lifelong memories including "The Wild Iris" and especially "Nostos," whose open-ing lines are:

> There was an apple tree in the yard—
> this would have been
> forty years ago—behind,
> only meadows. Drifts
> of crocus in the damp grass.

Thus ends thousands of years of flower poetry and lively stories from across Western Europe and America. Half a world away, the Asian tradi-tion, though, often reflects a different sensibility, philosophy, and appreci-ation of different flowering plants among their flower cultures.

The Asian Tradition

Certainly, flower-infused literature in Asia is as old or older than in West-ern cultures. But unlike the prose and poetry of the West, where flowers are largely about ephemeral life, lust, and love, poetry from ancient China and Japan is mainly concerned with themes of symbolic beauty, land-scapes, and love.

Unlike in most cultures, the earliest literary forms in China were not narratives, but beautiful lyric poetry. Chinese poems of earlier centuries focused on patterns of daily rural life, often with unstated hidden emotions and meanings that these poets knew their readers would understand. English translations of Chinese lyric poems are challenging to interpret and often imprecise. Love is a common theme of these poems, along with nature (flowers) and politics. The earliest collection of lyric poems is the *Book of Songs*, from about 600 BC. The Han, Tang, and Song Dynasties produced exquisite lyrical poems from their most renowned poets, especially Li Po, Tu Fu, and Su Shi.

Chinese poet Li Po (701–762) wrote of a professional courtesan who has fallen in love with an absent man. Conjugal affection is symbolized by his mentioning mandarin ducks, and a dancing girl might gain a man's attention via a sidelong glance. The yin mist, flower petals, damp silk, and the white moon are all symbols understood at the time as emblems of her tears:

Misted the flowers weep as light dies
Moon of white silk sleeplessly cries.
Stilled—Phoenix wings.
Touched—Mandarin strings.

Chinese poet, calligrapher, and gastronome Su Shi (1037–1101) was a major influence of the Song Dynasty in China. Su Shi writes about falling date-flowers and flowering crab-apple trees in the following two short poems, often poorly translated. The date-flowers in this poem are more likely to belong to a persimmon (*Diospyros lotus*), known as the Chinese date plum. The berries are tasty, but the Chinese appreciate it as a magnificent courtyard tree because its twigs and older boughs become covered in fleecy, tiny, white blossoms in spring. It's as if the old wood on the tree is wearing a crust of snow. The same species grows as far west as the Middle East and probably appears in some classic poetry as well. Here is one poem by Su Shi:

Date-flowers fall in showers on my hooded head,
At both ends of the village wheels are spinning thread,
A straw-cloaked man sells cucumber beneath a willow tree.
Wine-drowsy when the road is long, I yawn for bed;

The widespread printing of books, using ink on paper, first began in the Tang Dynasty (618–907). The earliest Chinese inks, like modern ink sticks, are themselves highly decorated and often embossed with elaborate floral motifs. Ink, called *mo*, is used in Chinese calligraphy. It was developed around 256 BC using carbon black (soot) and fish glue, which was later replaced with pine-tree resin. The *Diamond Sutra*, a Buddhist text, was printed in 868 and is likely the oldest known printed book, using block-printing methods. Flower poetry spread widely in villages across ancient China with the adoption of block-printing methods and of aesthetically pleasing, handmade mulberry paper, called *kozo* (from the bark of the paper mulberry tree).

In Japan, the *waka* poem is one of the most ancient and beloved forms in all of Japanese literature. *Waka* have thirty-one syllables, arranged in five lines of five, seven, five, seven, and seven syllables. A flower poem by the famous Heian-period female poet, one of Kinto's thirty-six immortals of poetry, Ono no Komachi (825–900), follows:

> The flowers withered,
> Their color faded away,
> While meaninglessly
> I spent my days in the world
> And the long rains were falling.

Beautiful, short Japanese poems have been used to express feelings for centuries, often written to celebrate special occasions. Many Americans are familiar with and may have tried writing another form of Japanese poetry: haiku. Like the first three lines of any *waka*, they follow a syllable count of five, seven, and five. Haiku reached their greatest height of expression in seventeenth-century Japan, but are still extremely popular today. Authentic early examples of Japanese haiku appear in the writings of Sōgi (1421–1502), but Matsuo Bashō (1644–94) is considered by many Japanese as their finest haiku poet. Although haiku are internationally fashionable, even among young children, authentic haiku have concerned themselves with wit or rhetoric, gimmicks, or pretense. The best haiku are deceptively difficult to write. Three examples of early poems by haiku master Matsuo Bashō are:

> Come on let us see
> all the real flowers of this
> sorrowful world

After the dream
how real
this iris!

Cherry blossoms?
in parts like these the grass
always bloom as well

The early-tenth-century *Kokin Wakashū* ("collection of Japanese poetry ancient and modern") was the first of twenty-one poetry anthologies compiled by imperial decree, under the rule of Emperor Uda (867–931). This extensive collection of 1,111 *waka* was compiled from 915 to 920. Their topics range widely, including the natural world of spring-blooming flowers, autumn seasons, love, mourning, death, travel, and other concerns.

Poet Ariwara no Narihira (825–80) is considered one of the six so-called immortal poets of ancient Japan. Narihira was mentioned in the preface to the *Kokin Wakashū*, which include thirty of his poems, such as:

If cherry blossoms
One day ceased to exist
In this world of ours,
Perhaps our hearts in spring
May know some tranquillity.

Supposedly, in this introspective poem, cherry blossoms are metaphors for Narihira's amorous affairs. Another classic Japanese *waka* poet, also included in the *Kokin Wakashū*, is Wani Kishi, a legendary scholar who came to Japan from Korea around the later third century. One of his flower poems is:

Nanywa Bay, now the flower
blooms, but for winter. Here
comes spring, now the flower
blooms.

A Summer of Roses

You don't have to move to Italy to read or hear lyrics (librettos) sung about flowers. New York music-publishing houses and songwriters dominated the popular-music industry in the late-nineteenth and early-twentieth centuries. Song lyrics from now-popular classics emerged in a small area, between Fifth and Sixth Avenues, in Manhattan. This area is now part of Manhattan's NoMad neighborhood, and part of the Flower District, where flowers are bought and sold. Later, this area came to be known as Tin Pan Alley, supposedly because a *New York Herald* article about the sounds of out-of-tune pianos being struck like tin pans banged in an alleyway. The colorful nickname stuck and generally came to refer to everything about the US music industry. From musical comedies and songs born in Tin Pan Alley, to the extensive use of flowers and their symbolism in operas including Puccini's *Madama Butterfly*, to modern popular—including rock-and-roll—songs, many lyrics rely upon the magic of flowers to move their audiences.

I have found at least ninety modern American and British songs that describe flowers in their titles and lyrics. Roses are a dominant song element, whether as plastic, wild, red, tattooed ones from Tokyo, or those found in everyday rose gardens. Other common garden blooms finding their way into contemporary songs include amaryllis, apple and cherry blossoms, buttercups, columbines, daisies, edelweiss, hyacinth, lilies, lotus, magnolias, marigolds, morning glories, orchids, sunflowers, and tulips.

One of the oldest modern flower songs is certainly "My Wild Irish Rose" (1899) by Chauncey Olcott (1858–1932). Olcott's wife, Margaret, visited Ireland, his mother's homeland, in 1898, where a young boy gave her a flower. She asked him what kind of flower it was and he replied, "A wild Irish rose." She saved the pressed flower in an album. Later, when Chauncey needed a title for his latest song, she remembered the pressed flower. Some of the lyrics of "My Wild Irish Rose" are:

If you'll listen, I'll sing you a sweet little song,
Of a flower . . . that's now drooped and dead,
'Twas given to me . . . by a girl that I know,
And I call her my wild Irish Rose.

Many examples could be given of contemporary musicians singing about flowers, or having lyrics mentioning flowers in their songs. Who could forget the classic Beatles song lyrics from the *Sgt. Pepper's Lonely Hearts Club Band* album with their "cellophane flowers of yellow and green," or "on a bed of roses" from the song by Jon Bon Jovi. Another popular song weaving flowers into love, pain, and other human emotions is "Desert Rose," sung by Sting. The opening lyrics are:

I dream of gardens in the desert sand . . .
Her shadows play in the shape of man's desire
This desert rose

The dark-themed but wildy popular countrylike rock ballad "Dead Flowers," written by Mick Jagger and Keith Richards, is track number nine on the Rolling Stones album *Sticky Fingers*. The song includes these now-classic Stones lyrics:

And you can send me dead flowers every morning
Send me dead flowers by the mail
Send me dead flowers to my wedding
And I won't forget to put roses on your grave. . . .

Or finally, leaving roses aside, we have the popular song "Sugar Magnolia," from 1970, written by Robert Hunter and Bob Weir and sung by the Grateful Dead, with these opening lyrics:

Sugar magnolia, blossoms blooming, heads all empty and I don't
    care,
Saw my baby down by the river, knew she'd have to come up soon
    for air. . . .
She's got everything delightful, she's got everything I need.

Roses and magnolias end our sentimental journey, one that began millennia ago with a mythical Sumerian flower blooming at the bottom of a sea, and now we turn to an equally rich tapestry and canvas of flowers depicted in the world's fine and decorative arts, where we explore the meaning of flowers in art.

CHAPTER 12

Flower Power:
The Meaning of Flowers in Art

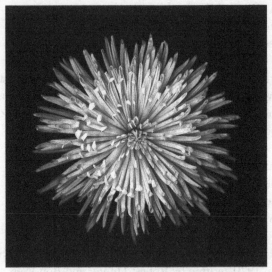

Streamerlike petals in a mum (*Chrysanthemum* sp.)

Almost everyone appreciates the myriad forms and inherent beauty of flowers. We don't know who in ancient times first depicted flowers before historical written records or art was made that survived to the present. Cave paintings along with incised petroglyphs created by many cultures do not generally include recognizable depictions of flowers. In rock art around the world, we usually find geometric shapes, along with the fierce, large game animals that provided food, hides, sinews, and bone tools for these hunter-gatherers. These animal-inspired cave paintings are some of the first and finest artistic expressions demonstrating our ancestral appreciation of the natural world. Widespread symbolic depictions of flowers by artists came much later.

The Oldest Depictions of Flowers in Art

For the oldest depictions of flowers, we return to the ancient Egyptian culture and its stone monuments along the Nile, where garden scenes appear in numerous frescoes and stone bas-reliefs in homes and temples as early as 2600 BC. Water-lily flowers are often portrayed, with people enjoying the sweet scent of their blooms, as in the often-reproduced image *Nakht and His Wife Taui Admiring a Blue Water Lily*.

Flowers played important roles in myths and legends of the Greeks and the Minoans. Flowers were important components of the fabled mosaic-tile murals created by Minoans in Crete and much later by the Romans, such as those found in the homes and gardens buried in the coastal cities of Pompeii and Herculaneum. A few Minoan murals have survived. The beautiful *Springtime Fresco* of Akrotiri (1500 BC) from the Aegean island of Santorini reveals the Minoan fascination with flowers native to their archipelago.

From 550 to 800, as the Roman Empire collapsed, floral art images began to vanish from Europe. Early Christians looked upon flowers, and floral art, with suspicion. They viewed flowers as symbols of the dead and dying, and also of nearby decadent pagan cultures, and had little to do with them. But at the time Charlemagne was crowned Holy Roman Emperor in 800, he had seen flowers in Muslim gardens during the Crusades in Moorish Spain, and it was a time for a resurgence in floral arts.

In Far Eastern Asia, traditional Chinese gardens date to the Han Dynasty nearly two thousand years ago. Chinese gardening was closely allied to Chinese landscape paintings on mulberry paper, of which many surviving examples can be found in museums and private collections. These paintings often portray flowering plants, including bamboo, fruit trees including loquats, lotus blooms and leaves, and also conifers such as pines. They are sometimes known as bird-and-flower paintings. Landscape painting was regarded as the highest form of Chinese painting and generally still is by most scholars. Japanese artists also had an early start, depicting the flowers (e.g., lotus, azaleas, cherry blossoms) of early *shinden-zukuri* gardens, from at least the Heian period from 785 to 1184.

Flowers were drawn and recopied frequently in the books of plant-based medicines we know as herbals. Flowers were also used as symbols by

Christians. For example, Christ's wounds on the cross were symbolized by the five petals of a wild rose, and passionflowers (*Passiflora* spp.) had similar religious symbolism. Flowers were lavishly illuminated and brilliantly colored in the borders of the pages of medieval manuscripts, regardless of topic. They also appear in early paintings as wildflowers among the rocks, as in the *Adoration in the Forest* by Fra' Filippo Lippi from 1459.

A Renaissance of Flowers in Art

After the invention of vision-extending instruments, scientific tools such as the telescope and microscope, people could and did look at the world of nature, including flowers, in minute detail, and in different ways than ever before. Leonardo da Vinci (1452–1519) described, sketched, and painted numerous Italian wildflowers, especially those near the hamlet of Anchiano, in the small town of Vinci. The German painter Albrecht Dürer (1471–1528) painted flowers with meticulous care, including his *Violets* (1503). These were essentially floral portraits, as if the flowers he painted were people. Mainly, the depiction of flowers in Renaissance high art contained both sacred and profane pictorial messages. Thus, the Archangel Gabriel offers a white lily to the Blessed Virgin Mary, symbolizing her purity. We also find huge paintings derived from earlier stories in Roman myths showing Venus surrounded by flowers and her various immortal and human lovers.

Flower Painting and Dutch Still Lifes

The Dutch East India Company held a two-hundred-year monopoly in the spice trade that made Holland a rich country, especially from the 1600s to 1700s. The spice and sugar trades gave the country's new ruling class of bankers and merchants unprecedented but often temporary wealth. Much of this money enabled private sponsorships of the visual arts, literature, and science, often including collections of seashells, posed taxidermic animals, exotic insects, and other natural-history curios and unusual artifacts. These nouveaux riches remained in touch with everyday life, and the commissioning and buying of paintings was extremely important to them.

During the seventeenth century in the Netherlands, flowers were the next big thing, a mania and passion resonating across all levels of Dutch society. The great Dutch bulb industry began in the early 1600s with importation of species, flower mutants, and hybrids from the Ottoman Empire. As these unusual large flowers were acquired and admired, their representation in flower paintings achieved unprecedented popularity in Holland. Earlier artists sponsored by the Roman Catholic Church now found themselves without Church patronage as the Reformation kicked up its heels and the Calvinist Church took hold in Holland. Enterprising freelance artists got to work, studying and painting flowers of all types, but especially the new darlings of the garden, tulips, crown imperials, red ranunculus, Mediterranean narcissi, and peonies.

The Dutch took the painting of flowers to an almost clinical level; their floral depictions are virtually photo-realistic. Most of the flowers in Dutch paintings of this period had religious symbolism—lilies for purity, and sunflowers interpreted as conforming to God's world. Floral still lifes were especially popular in Antwerp, with artists including Pieter Brueghel the Elder and Younger. Most famous for his floral paintings was the influential Jan van Huysum (1682–1749), whose paintings, for example *Bouquet of Flowers in an Urn* and *Vase with Flowers*, both had a popular aesthetic appeal and also served decorative functions.

Exemplars of fine Dutch floral painters include Ambrosias Bosschaert the Elder (1573–1621), Balthasar van der Ast (1593–1657), and Jacob Vosmaer (1584–1641). Many paintings, such as Vosmaer's elegant but dark *A Vase of Flowers*, combined blossoms from many countries in a single vase, in one grand flowering visual feast. For wealthy Dutch merchants, and royal art collectors such as Emperor Rudolf II in Prague, the floral oil paintings were a significant part of life and their interests. These wealthy collectors also owned showy flower gardens containing rare plants that often cost more than commissioning original floral art.

Amazingly, tulips, omnipresent today, were then prohibitively costly. Hiring a famous Dutch artist of the period to paint a floral still life was less expensive than owning even a single tulip grown in a pot. A flower painting would everlastingly capture the beauty and essence of an unobtainable possession, a prized rare living flower. The dates of these paintings convey the eras in which certain ornamental species from Asia and North America entered northern-European horticulture. A painting of a vase attributed to Gillis van Coninxloo II (1544–1607) overflows with marigolds from Mexico, while a second painting by Hendrick de Fromantiou (1633–94) has another Mexican marigold, but that flower is joined by a tropical passionflower (*Passiflora foetida*).

What's Wrong with This Picture?

The best still lifes were exacting portrayals yet mere illusions of real flowers. Look carefully at a selection of Dutch floral still-life paintings. I imagine that any modern florist (or artist) would be envious of these immense and spectacular floral arrangements. They seem to defy gravity. It's doubtful if a single additional flowering stem could be crammed anywhere into their vases. Not only that, but does the choice of the flowers by the Dutch artists seem a bit strange to you? They should. Yes, some paintings stick to themes in specific seasons, such as the flowers of early spring or autumn. The majority of Dutch paintings from this period, though, mix species from many lands and from all seasons. They bloom together although they were painted in an era without greenhouses or overnight florist delivery services. Take, for example, the lovely arrangement by Jan Davidsz. de Heem (1606–84) in which a floral arrangement competes with tempting platters of fruit. The ripe cherries and currants of summer share their table with the English daisy (*Bellis perennis*), hybrid primrose, and pansy of spring.

In *A Bouquet of Flowers in a Crystal Vase* (1662), an oil on canvas by Nicolaes van Veerendael (1640–91), a shiny glass vase is jammed to overflowing with intricately rendered blossoms (fancy tulips, peonies, carnations, iris, a marigold, hibiscus, and others). Typically, the still lifes are arranged with harmonious colors, in a convincing illusion of three-dimensionality, with flowers centrally placed and symmetrical. The background of this painting, along with most Dutch still lifes, is extremely dark, almost black, forcing the viewer's attention to the front and center, focusing on the exuberantly displayed flowers. A sulfur butterfly rests daintily on a peony in the lower left-hand corner of the Veerendael composition. Several small insects are usually included in the paintings of this genre: ants, caterpillars, or beetles crawling over the greenery, or on the supporting table. Fanciful, colorful butterflies flit, or sometimes a fat bumble bee flies in the air around these Flemish bouquets.

One of the most powerful depictions of a flower from any period of history is the engaging *Self-Portrait with Sunflower* by Flemish baroque artist Anthony van Dyck (1599–1641). This painting exuberantly shows the artist in an elegant reddish silk shirt pointing to a magnificent sunflower. The sunflower (*Helianthus annuus*), loved both for its massive flowering head (with up to two thousand individual florets) and edible seeds, is North American in origin and was originally grown by New World civilizations and tribes. By the time Van Dyck immortalized a flowering stem in oil, this species had been grown in Europe for little more than a century.

The Dutch still lifes focused on good and pleasant things, flowers and foods, that are ephemeral. Their message is one of unique but transient beauty. The flowers will soon wilt and die along with everything else depicted in these paintings.

The Pre-Raphaelites

Colorful flowers abound in Pre-Raphaelite art. Many European painters gave us detailed studies of women and flowers. They were obsessed with the subject, depicting over and over young women and flowers, especially yellow flowers. You virtually can't find a Pre-Raphaelite canvas in which lovely young ladies, wearing fanciful medieval costumes, aren't looking at, picking, smelling, or in various ways posing with flowers: lilies, roses, mayflower buds, forget-me-nots, yellow irises, and even foxgloves. Paintings by Élisabeth Sonrel (1874–1953) are especially delicate and intensely floral. They are photo-realistic but engaging, combining Pre-Raphaelite intensity and a French symbolist painting style. These artists, such as John Waterhouse, draped women in beautiful gowns and elegant floral garlands. In dreamy scenes, young maidens and muses look wistfully into the distance with hopeful expressions. Other notable artists of this genre include Eleanor Brickdale (*Natural Magic*), Emma Harrison (*A Dream of Fair Women*), Lizzie Siddal, Sir Frank Dicksee (*The Sensitive Plant*), Arthur Hughes (*Ophelia*), and Sir John Millais (*Ophelia*).

Ponder, for example, the famous *Hylas and the Nymphs* (1896) by John William Waterhouse (1849–1917). It's a memorable scene from the story of Jason and the Argonauts. Hylas wants to gather water from a pool, but the nymphs find him so beautiful that they drag him under the water. As they are water nymphs, naiads, their pond supports a healthy population of white water lilies (*Nymphaea*). But look carefully at the yellow flowers in their hair. Those are yellow pond lilies (*Nuphar*), native to North America! The Victorians enjoyed yellow pond lilies in their goldfish ponds.

Flowers and Modernism

By the twentieth century, with the rise of Modernism, realistic still lifes had become unfashionable. Édouard Manet (1832–83), the father of Modernism, painted flowers, but used them as secondary elements in his canvases. In his *Olympia* (1863), a female nude is attended by her maid holding a bouquet of flowers. Late in life, Manet created simple pastel flowers (e.g., *Moss Roses in a Vase*, 1882). His loose and free brushstrokes bear no resemblance to the exquisitely detailed flowers in the Dutch still-life paintings.

Claude Monet (1840–1926) emerged as the leading artist in outdoor impressionism. Nearly everyone who appreciates fine art enjoys viewing his diverse impressionistic paintings, whether they are haystacks, bridges, bowlers, or flower studies and painting series. He favored garden and landscape scenes most of all, and like other impressionists of the time, he applied color in tiny dabs of pure paint, unmixed, and without using blending strokes. The flowers in Monet's paintings are not realistic but "impressions" of color, grand painterliness, and decorative elements. In his *Wild Poppies* (1873), his flowers are simple, short brushstrokes instead of realistic blooms, splotches of bright red set against a green background. In 1883, Monet settled near the village of Giverny, about fifty miles from Paris. His lavish gardens allowed him to paint en plein air amid the sunshine, peony bushes, and buzzing bees. Here, he created his famous water garden with abundant water lilies, great clumps of irises, and lush flowering stems of *Wisteria*. In his later paintings, the flowers become less important than the abstracted masses of colors. Monet seems to have painted flowers not for their own sake, or symbolically, but as an exploration of his continued growth in art.

Interestingly, Monet suffered from blurred vision due to cataracts during most of his later career. As his visual acuity diminished, his color perceptions also shifted to yellowish hues. His palettes changed dramatically from the dreamy pastel hues of his earlier works to the much darker reds and browns, muddied tones, used in the last years of his life. Perhaps Monet's dreamy surrealistic landscapes were the direct result of his blurred vision. Eventually, he underwent cataract surgeries in 1923, two years before his death at eighty-six. Artist Edgar Degas (1834–1917) also suffered from chronic visual problems that are reflected in his works.

In contrast, Odilon Redon (1840–1916) imposed a personalized style on the flowers in his paintings. They appear to be floating in air, as in *Day*, painted in 1910. In *Ophelia among the Flowers* (about 1905–8), they are not depicted as they flowered in nature. In this period of later Modernism, there seems to be no reference to the visible world as the paintings gradually become abstract art. Over time, floral themes were generally eliminated from these and other Modernist compositions.

American artist Georgia O'Keeffe (1887–1986) was also influenced by the abstract art movement. O'Keeffe's stark linear quality, with thin, clear colors, and bold compositions, produced her signature abstract designs. However, when she wasn't painting vast Southwestern landscapes, O'Keeffe focused on enlarged, intimate features of flowers, their folds and crevices, as well as their sexual parts. Critics and scholars of O'Keeffe talk about the cycles of life, birth, death, and decay symbolized in her work. Others interpret her vibrant flowers as sensuous symbols of overt human sexuality and actually compare them with a woman's genitals. This aspect of her work is still debated among professional and armchair art critics. O'Keeffe herself denied the sexual interpretations of her flower paintings. Perhaps the last word should belong to O'Keeffe, who is reputed to have said, "If you don't understand it, too bad."

Nevertheless, by the mid-twentieth century, painting flowers had little to do with mainstream modern art. Now, flowers were simply not subjects that professional artists chose to paint.

Pop Goes the Flower

Postmodernism is a term applied to American art of the 1960s meant to encompass the post–World War II era and has become a descriptive term for the many fluctuations and modifications in modern society and culture. This is the artistic movement that rejected everything grand, along with universal stories and paradigms of religions, philosophy, gender, and capitalism that have defined culture in the past. In this postmodern world, flowers as something worthy of artistic rendition have been rediscovered and rehabilitated.

Andy Warhol (1928–87) painted *Do It Yourself Flowers* in 1962. Part of the work was created using a commercial, hobbyist paint-by-numbers kit. In his work, flowers were irreverently used in kitsch, mass-produced prints. In a 1964 exhibition titled *Flowers*, his images were silk-screened prints of flowers with added paint. Here we see flowers stripped of all their sensuality, along with much of their realism and beauty.

Now, consider flowers by artist Janet Fish (b. 1938) from this same period. They are engaging and beautiful, painted in a more realistic style. In her *Daffodils and Spring Trees* (1988), daffodils are placed against a background landscape. Her flowers are skillfully painted, filled with light, vibrant colors and interesting small details. In a way, paintings by Fish parallel the earlier Dutch still lifes.

Artist Ben Schonzeit (b. 1942) also created beautiful flower paintings. His *Floral with Self-Portrait* (1988) is an especially representative example of his work. Here, the flowers are once again sensuous, painted with great attention to realistic detail in an almost photo-realistic style. Schonzeit created traditional still-life images of a vase with flowers on a table. He often painted them as a pastiche, with a backdrop theme of borrowed Degas or Picasso images in tones of black, white, and gray, with his bright flowers in the foreground.

Baby boomers will remember how flowers were repeatedly used as common motifs in the pop art and the peace-culture art of the 1960s. They decorated thousands of Volkswagen minibuses, all sorts of hippie buses, and posters perhaps best appreciated under black lights or under the influence of various mind-altering botanicals. Most of these images could not be identified in a standard field guide to the local flora. Despite the kitschy overuse of blossoms not found in nature, they represented a noble sentiment of the era—"make love, not war." Indeed, this was flower power at its best and most potent.

Flowers in Historical Fine Art Photography

As painters lost their interest in flowers for their own sake, they were embraced by the new art of photography. Although the pioneer photographers of the nineteenth century primarily focused their creative attention on portraiture and grand landscapes, when they did turn their lenses to fresh flowers, it was long before color film. Today, we forget about these photographic pioneers as millions of people around the world now take snapshots of their favorite blooms, then post, tweet, share and "like" them with Facebook friends millions of times every day. This photographic equalization has essentially destroyed the ability of most professional photographers to earn a living wage. Today, digital blossoms exist by the billions, ready for illegal reproduction or sharing, are highly undervalued and sold from myriad online sources.

It is uncertain who was the first photographer to capture the image of a flower. Certainly, some famous photographers have produced classic black-and-white (panchromatic film) images of flowers in nature or in the studio. Ansel Adams (1902–84) shot roses on driftwood, along with trilliums and other wildflowers when his large, eight-by-ten-inch view camera wasn't pointed in the direction of a prominent landscape in Yosemite or the California High Sierra. The great Edward Weston (1886–1958) and Brett Weston (1911–93), no relation, also created elegant black-and-white floral images. Edward Weston enjoyed photographing the delicate petals of *Magnolia* blooms, along with *Paphiopedilum* orchids, cactus flowers, and lilies. His flowers are equally as sensuous as the curves of his erotic bell peppers, seashells, and human nudes, such as those of his model, muse, and lover, Charis Wilson. Two of Edward Weston's photographs, a nude (1925) and a shell (1927) are among the most expensive black-and-white silver gelatin print photographs ever sold, as of 2013.

San Francisco–based artist Imogen Cunningham (1883–1976) was another powerful innovator and pioneer in still-life flower photography. Cunningham's night-blooming cactus explodes starlike against a jet-black background, or witness her unopened magnolia bud or several magnolia flowers (especially her close-up of magnolia pistils entitled *Tower of Jewels* [1925]). Then there's her version of calla lilies, the famous *Two Callas* (1929). In Europe, German Karl Blossfeldt (1864–1932) is widely known and appreciated for his influential book *Unformen der Kunst* (1928), containing exquisite close-up photographic studies of flower buds, ferns, and leaves.

The erotic quality of flower images returns again in the photographs of Robert Mapplethorpe (1946–89). With the possible exception of Brett Weston, Mapplethorpe emulated the exquisite sensuous vegetable (peppers, etc.) and flower studies of Edward Weston like no other photographer. Mapplethorpe's flower photographs display sensuality and sexuality, emphasizing the phallic quality of some species. *Calla Lily* (1988), for example, captures the lush folds and surface texture of the stiff, waxy bract (a colorful modified leaf) that enfolds the phallic cob of flowers known as a spadix. Who said botany isn't sexy?

Mapplethorpe makes comparisons and fully understood that flowers are the genitalia of flowering plants. *Poppy* was one of his few color flower photographs. When first exhibited, it was perceived as erotic. That Mapplethorpe's flowers are perceived as overtly sexual is likely because, in gallery exhibitions, they were often displayed alongside his panchromatic photographs of explicit homoerotic images. Perhaps someday his flower art will be judged solely on its merits, the appraisal not biased by the cultural controversies that developed during the late 1980s, when his life was claimed by AIDS.

We also remember *Flower Power*, a Pulitzer Prize–winning historic photograph taken in 1967 by photographer Bernie Boston for the now defunct *Washington Star* newspaper. We've all seen this powerful photograph of a young Vietnam War protester placing carnations, by their stems, inside the barrel of the rifle of an equally young National Guardsman confronting him only a few feet away. Fortunately, the outcome was peaceful.

Flowers in Modern Fine Art Photography, and Flatbed Scanning

It isn't possible to name, or review, all of the living photographers creating evocative floral portraits. Dominique Bollinger (b. 1950), a French photographer now living in Italy, creates exquisite black-and-white flower photographs. Those from 1996 to 2011 are extremely sensuous and soft, with tender, sweeping curls and spirals, and usually a soft focus. His photographs of lilies, roses, magnolias, fuchsias, orchids, and camellias are all cropped in a manner that evokes Weston's style. He's produced two books of his works, including *Fleurs* in 2012.

Arizona photographer Robert Rice has produced a rich body of floral photographic work. His full-color, brilliant images of irises, roses, and peonies, along with many other blooms in alluring combinations of studio lights and background reflectors, fairly glow. Rice studied under Ansel Adams in the 1970s, and many of his photographs have a similar look to that of his mentor. Like Rice, working in brilliant color, is J. Scott Peck of

Berthoud, Colorado. Peck's blooms have an exceedingly luminous quality, based on intricate studio lighting techniques. Some of his favorite subjects are irises, hibiscuses, and the popular Stargazer lily. Carol Henry has also produced large color images of various flowers. Flower photographs have been created by David Johndrow, using selective focus and digital sepia-toning of his subjects, while Tony Mendoza creates flowers shot from below outdoors, and from other interesting camera angles.

One of my favorite flower photographers shoots without a camera. Robert Creamer, of Maryland, is a scanographer not a photographer. Creamer uses the flat glass plate of a high-resolution graphical-arts flatbed Epson digital scanner as his camera and lens. The scanner performs as if it were a wide-field microscope, with high magnifications and narrow depth of field views that are impossible to achieve with even the best cameras. Creamer arranges living, dying, and completely dried blooms of roses, peonies, chrysanthemums, and other flowers on his scanner. Like Creamer, and Alfred University moth artist Joseph Scheer, I've been smitten by the lure of the scanners, placing my own flowers, fossils, leaves and insects upon their wide glass eyes. A few fine artists are now discovering the unique lighting and look of flatbed scans for making exquisite fine art floral prints. Flatbed optical scanners are no longer only for copying your receipts at tax time.

Flowers in Commerce:
Coins, Paper Currency, and Postage Stamps

Because flowers have been revered and admired since antiquity, it should not be surprising that flowers are depicted on the sides of ancient and modern coins minted in bronze, silver, and gold, from several countries. Coins minted in Rhodes, the Carian Islands, show either Rhodos, the goddess of the island of Rhodes, or Helios, while on the reverse face of the coins are blossoms, usually rosebuds. Yehud silver coins (c. fourth century BC) minted in Jerusalem depicted flowers, animals, and people. Madonna-lily flowers were commonly used on these ancient coins. Silver coins from Cyrene (modern Libya) of the sixth to fifth century BC show symbolized images of silphium stalks (likely an extinct species of *Ferula*), fruits, and seeds. Some ancient Chinese coins were shaped like plum blossoms with five petals.

A few modern coins depict flowers, including the gold-and-silver, two-euro coin minted by Finland. This coin shows cloudberry flowers (*Rubus chamaemorus*) and berries designed by Raimo Heino. Austrian shilling coins often depicted edelweiss flowers. Coinage from Hong Kong has depictions of hibiscus and other blooms. The *mugunghwa* rose (likely the biblical rose of Sharon) is the national flower of Korea and has appeared on its ten-won coins. Stylized pomegranate flowers grace some modern Iraqi coins.

Flowers also embellish the paper currency of many countries. Jasmine flowers figure on the Indonesian thousand-rupiah note of 1959, and orchids are depicted on banknotes from Singapore. Flowers have been used to decorate banknotes from Belarus, Guinea, Romania, and many other countries. In 1967, the Australian government issued a colorful purple $5 banknote depicting the great English botanist Sir Joseph Banks (1743–1820) and the flowers he collected while part of Captain Cook's exploration of the part of the coast of Australia now known as Botany Bay.

Colorful flowers routinely adorn the postage stamps of many countries, and these paper-and-glue artistic creations are eagerly anticipated, used by the public and collected by amateur philatelists and stamp dealers. Especially beautiful floral designs can be seen on the postage stamps of countries in diverse regions including Australia, Brazil, Egypt, Germany, Italy, New Zealand, Switzerland, the United States, and many others.

The Art of Arranging Flowers

The arranging of groups of colorful flowers into garlands, collars, hair ornaments, corsages, and large formal bouquets has been a human pastime for millennia. Flowers were formed into decorative clusters and ornamentation by the Egyptian, Chinese, Japanese, Roman, Greek, and Byzantine cultures. Over four millennia ago (2500 BC) ancient Egyptians created vast numbers of floral arrangements; pharaohs commissioned literally millions of formal bouquets as temple offerings to their many deities. Giant composite bouquets, three or four feet tall, were created by florist guilds. Wall paintings showed how women of the court wore extensive flower arrangements in their hair. Floral displays were also often used as part of funerary offerings and rituals.

Flower arrangement in Japan became the most subtle of arts and is known formally as ikebana, derived from the Japanese words *ikeru* ("to keep alive, arrange") and *bana* ("flower"). Thus, ikebana is essentially the art of giving life to flowers, or arranging flowers, stems, and leaves, especially when done in a minimalist way. Nature and the human spirit come together in this formalized Asian art. Most ikebana is based on a triangular form, usually scalene. Small twigs usually outline the triangle.

The origins of ikebana are lost to antiquity, but it may have come to Japan with Buddhism in the sixth century as part of rituals of offering flowers on an altar or to the spirits of dead family members. Certainly, ikebana dates back at least five hundred years to the time of the Shiun-ji (Purple Cloud) temple in Kyoto. An early priest of this temple was a master at skillfully arranging and displaying flowers. After that time, other Ikenobo priests became associated with the art of these floral arrangements. By the fifteenth century, ikebana was a well-defined art form with formalized instructions and rules. At least four major styles of ikebana—Rikka, Nageire, Seika, and Jiyuka—exist.

By the twentieth century, ikebana commonly took on expressions of modernism and a free style, with Moribana (standing style) and Nageire (slanting style) predominating. Often stems, leaves, and flowering stems are held upright in a shallow ceramic or wooden bowl of shallow water. Decorative rocks can be added to the arrangements. Ikebana art is shown on Japanese television and taught in schools to foster the appreciation of natural beauty.

Flower arrangements in ancient China occurred by the Han Dynasty (207 BC–AD 221). Followers of Buddhism, Taoism, and Confucianism all placed cut flowers (especially the peony, tiger lily, orchid, and pomegranate) on their temple altars. This veneration of flowers seeped into their paintings, carvings, and embroidered textiles. Floral paintings are seen on plates, silk fabric, scrolls, screens, and vases of these and later periods in China.

European Floral Arrangements

The modern trend in flower arrangements in Europe dates from about AD 1000 and is almost always associated with church ceremonies. During the Middle Ages (476–1400), monks grew extensive gardens containing a mixture of medicinal herbs and decorative flowers. We see decorative flowers in their altarpieces, illuminated manuscripts, and paintings. During the Renaissance (1400–1600), we find the burgeoning of large and impressive floral arrangements, especially set in finely crafted marble, Venetian-glass, and even bronze vases. Foliage was woven with flowers into garlands used to decorate walls, vaulted ceilings, and wall niches. Petals were placed in baskets or strewn on floors or streets, adding their color and scents.

During the early baroque period (1600–1775) floral creations were largely symmetrical and oval, with crescents and S-curves gaining widespread popularity. The Dutch and Flemish preferred well-proportioned, large bouquets. By the Napoleonic era, flower arrangements favored strongly contrasting colors placed in simple lines or triangles displayed in urns. From France to England, the Georgian period (1714–60) preferred oriental designs based on trade with Turkey and the Far East. This popularized some of the most fragrant species as the English believed that their scents cleansed the air. Elite women of Georgian England carried (or wore) floral nosegays so that people meeting them would smell (and see) something nice. Nosegays also perfumed the wearers as they made their way through a malodorous city. Later, tussie-mussies (late eighteenth and most of the nineteenth century) were minature floral arrangements worn decoratively on clothing.

By Victorian times (1837–1901), great heaps of flowers were packed

An antique floral corsage (a tussie-mussie)

tightly into vases and other containers, often in asymmetrical arrays. Popular flowers in arrangements included white Madonna lilies, blue cornflowers, and French calendulas, along with irises, jasmine, narcissi, and pinks (carnations). As the red and black spots on pansies often resemble little human faces, they enjoyed sentimental appeal with many Victorians. Most American styles of flower arrangements from our colonial period through the early-twentieth century merely copied French, English, and Italian styles.

Illuminated Manuscripts

Aside from the depiction of flowers by the ancient Egyptians, Greeks, Romans, and Minoans on works of fine art (frescoes, bas-reliefs, and mosaics), some of the earliest and finest renderings of flowers are in handwritten and illuminated (illustrated) medieval manuscripts in Europe, produced from AD 400 until the early-sixteenth century. Many illuminated manuscripts were concerned with religious themes and were often gilded with foil.

The "illumination" of these manuscripts refers to additions of decorative elements, including marginalia, tiny but intricate illustrations, and those on alphabetical letters. Fanciful geometric illustrations and plant and floral motifs were common in manuscript borders, and some had symbolic meanings. Some of the intended readers of these manuscripts were illiterate, and the flowers and their symbolism moved the story along and helped communicate the message. The types of flowers depicted in these manuscripts are the ones we might expect: lilies and roses, acanthus, anemones, and violets, but also such lesser known flowers as cranesbill (*Geranium maculatum*), dianthus, wallflowers, and even *Cannabis*.

Tapestries and Rugs

Decorative tapestries reached their zenith in the fourteenth and fifteenth centuries, in Germany, Switzerland, and France, and in the seventeenth century in Flanders and Brussels. Flowers, including roses and peonies, were frequent decorative elements. One famous medieval tapestry, *The Unicorn in Captivity* (Netherlands, c. 1500) shows a penned unicorn surrounded by many plants and flowers, in the late-medieval tradition of using fields of millefleurs (thousands of flowers).

Floral designs and geometric flower-inspired patterns on antique rugs were almost universal elements used by carpet weavers in many cultures, but especially those in China, Egypt, India, Israel, Persia, Spain, Turkey, and Ukraine. Floral elements needn't be diminutive or dainty decorative elements. They can be bold features that dictate the placement of neighboring elements within the rug. Some depict bouquets, while others use flowers in garlands, medallions, or exquisitely repeating and interesting patterns.

Rugs from Ukraine and the Caucasus Mountains regions used flowers woven in an abstract and stylized fashion. Rugs from pre-twentieth-century France used lush painterly blooms, with exquisite shading and hyperrealistic details. In antique rugs from China, we find lotus blossoms used symbolically, along with ornate chrysanthemum blossoms as decorative signatures used in myriad ways. In the early-twentieth century, Chinese art deco rugs, featuring floral motifs, were created by American artist Walter Nichols (1885–1960). Persian and Indian weavers were fond of transforming flowers into stylistic "Shah Abbasi palmettes" (a symmetrical palmette having two floral sprays on top), and also used rosettes and other secondary botanical features. Persian city carpets were created in naturalistic styles. These famous city carpets (e.g., Kerman rugs) were almost always woven incorporating floral motifs. Indian Agra rugs also bear rosettes against multicolored backgrounds.

Ceramics and Porcelain

One of the earliest depictions of flowers on ceramics is a tulip motif on a clay pot excavated from the Minoan ruins of Knossos on the island of Crete. Pottery finds in a cave sanctuary at Kamares on Mt. Ida in 1890 revealed a cache of remarkable fine clay pots called Kamares ware vessels. They have abundant floral designs of rosettes and spirals. Nature themes abound with marine life and highly stylized depictions of palm trees, crocuses, and lilies. Late Minoan pottery often takes on a floristic style along with abundant leaf forms and designs.

Floral motifs have been used on Chinese ceramics, especially fine porcelain, since at least the Tang Dynasty (618–907). Bowls created in the shape of upturned flower petals are also Chinese favorites. The famous blue-and-white porcelain-ware produced in China was fully developed by the fourteenth century and is often decorated with flowers. Chinese pictorial designs, including flying birds, fanciful dragons, lotuses, and rose flowers began appearing in the thirteenth century.

Colorful Ottoman ceramics were produced beginning in the second half of the fifteenth century in Turkey, near the town of Iznik. These magnificent blue, red, and green bowls, dishes, bottles, carafes, jars, and other items featuring floral motifs were used in the kitchens of the Ottoman court. Although Iznik ceramic patterns were influenced by medieval European herbals, the most common motifs were flowers from the Turkish countryside gardens: carnations, hyacinths, roses, and tulips, with the slender pointed tulips being the most prized and frequently used.

Exquisite porcelains from England often feature highly realistic and beautiful flowers. Especially fine examples of soup tureens emblazoned with tulips and other flowers are the work of William Billingsley (1758–1828) at the Derby porcelain factory from about 1792 to 1813. Existing examples of Derby porcelain can be found in the Victoria and Albert Museum. Among the sixty thousand decorative patterns found on Limoges porcelain created by Haviland & Company since the 1890s are various floral motifs, especially pale pink roses. Extremely popular and bestselling floral patterns are also found on Wedgwood bone china, produced in England. Wedgwood Kutani Crane plates have a strong Chinese influence, including blue cranes and numerous flowers. Other patterns include floral sprays on the dinner-plate rims. Wedgwood's Charmwood pattern (1951–87) has arrays of brightly colored flowers and greenery, along with bees and colorful butterflies.

Scanned, Then Printed in 3-D

New ways to capture floral shapes and create art include scanning and printing their forms (using laser scanners and 3-D printers). By drying flowers in silica gel, then using a computed-tomography scanner, it is possible to capture the fine details of small flowers and then create bronze sculptures. As with other natural objects I have scanned, I'm now taking my flower scans and preparing the files for 3-D printing. Thus starts the long process of creating molds for lost-wax casting and finally casting in bronze. As mentioned in University of Arizona professor Alan Weisman's 2007 book, *The World without Us*, bronze sculptures will last far longer than most other human art forms or buildings. My cast bronze flowers should be around for a while. In "The Flower and the Scientist," chapter 13, we'll learn of other uses in biological research for the life-size versions of 3-D flowers created on a 3-D printer in hard plastic.

Art in Glass

Tucked away in Cambridge, Massachusetts, within the venerable Harvard Museum of Natural History are the world-famous Blaschka glass flowers. Nearly a quarter million visitors every year make a pilgrimage to Harvard's redbrick Natural History Museum, but most come to gaze in disbelief at the jaw-dropping glass creations. Indeed, these artificial flowers are one of the most popular tourist attractions in the entire Boston area.

Officially known as the Ware Collection of Blaschka Glass Models of Plants, the glass flowers began as a scientific and educational art commission by Professor George Goodale (1839–1923), who was the first director of Harvard's Botanical Museum. Goodale wanted a collection of highly accurate botanical models he could use as instructional aids in his classes, presumably during the harsh Cambridge winters when he couldn't obtain fresh leaves, flowers, and fruits outdoors. Goodale commissioned a Czech father and son, Leopold and Rudolf Blaschka (1822–95, 1857–1939), from Hosterwitz, near Dresden, Germany. As a testament to their skill and stamina, the two shipped numerous fragile glass flower-teaching models to Goodale at Harvard for fifty years (1887 to 1936).

In all, the Blaschkas made 847 life-size flower models (of 780 species in 164 flowering-plant families) by hand in delicate glass. Additionally, they created 4,300 smaller glass models of botanical details including enlarged plant parts, cross sections of flowers, and other anatomical sections. The glass flowers also depict pollination relationships with animals. In 1997, a visiting botanist, David Schnell, was amazed to find that the glass flower of the carnivorous plant we call a butterwort (*Pinguicula*) also held a diminuitive glass bee. At the time, the floral biology of *Pinguicula* was unknown, yet here in the collection were all the unsuspected pollinatory details wrought in glass a century earlier.

In their lifetimes, the Blaschkas were rumored to have invented a secret glass-working process that had made all the magic possible. It is far more likely, however, that they were astute naturalists and talented observers in the fine German tradition and deft master artisans. Today, no other glass craftsmen have been able to master the realistic duplication of flowers in silicon dioxide. It appears that the Blaschkas took their best techniques to the grave, but today's glass artists continue to serve both the science of flowers and botanical education in many magnificent ways.

Byzantine craftsmen developed the intricate and colorful glass we recognize today as Venetian glass, especially from glassmakers on the island of Murano. Better-known styles include millefiori glass, a style that includes many thin layers folded over and over. The word *millefiori* is derived from *mille* ("thousand") and *fiori* ("flowers").

The Rise of the Florilegium

An elephant was in the room, and I was gently fondling it. Actually, it was an oversize elephant folio, a magnificent and famous book on flowers printed in 1799. On a research trip to St. Louis's Missouri Botanical Garden, I ventured to their botanical library. The main collection, with its two hundred thousand volumes, is one of the best scholarly resources on plants anywhere in the world. I rose from a plush leather chair in the opulent dark-oak-paneled rare-book reading room and approached the massive center table. "They must really trust me," I thought to myself, and wondered where were the white gloves, release forms, and the strict instructions I'd been given at other antiquarian book libraries. Left alone, with no overseers, I was free to sample the botanical wisdom and beautiful floral art of the ages.

Before me was arguably the most famous work of botanical scientific illustration of all time, the unique *The Temple of Flora* by Englishman Robert John Thornton (1768–1837). The book is massive, twenty-two by eighteen by two inches thick, and a hefty twenty-one pounds. Few original bound and complete copies exist today. Most have been ripped apart for their thirty-five colored plates—rich eye-candy combinations of aquatint, line etching, mezzotint, line, and stippled engravings. Individual color plates can sell at auction for $8,000. A complete copy of *The Temple of Flora*, especially one with an interesting association (i.e., owned and signed by someone famous), might sell for as much as $250,000.

Slowly and carefully turning its yellowed pages of exquisite images, I saw the famous "Night Blooming Cereus," set against dark woods, a clock tower in ruins, and a brooding sky, like a poster child for eighteenth-century European romanticism and paintings. My personal favorite is the bright and cheery plate simply labeled "Tulips." Seven magnificent stems topped with flame-streaked Dutch tulips are thrust against a cloudy sky, verdant landscape, and coastline. Here is a potent visual symbol of the tulipmania that aroused passions in the Netherlands of the 1630s. Each time I've been in the presence of this book, it moves me to again consider the amazing roles that flowers have played throughout human history.

Robert Thornton was trained and practiced as a physician. Thornton devoted all his earnings and time pursuing botany and producing his monumental book as a tribute to Linnaeus, the father of modern taxonomy. Thornton engaged the most gifted flower artists of the day to craft the luscious oversize lithographic plates. He tried but largely failed to enlist wealthy patrons to subscribe to the edition and then absorbed the costs personally, eventually bankrupting himself and his family when sales of the *Temple* were much less than he anticipated.

The Temple of Flora is properly known as a florilegium, and such books were popular with the wealthy and privileged from the second half of the

Tulips illustrated in Thornton's
The Temple of Flora (1799)

eighteenth century through the early-twentieth century. Meant as works of science, they are often huge folios for two overlapping reasons. First, in an age before photography, a large folio allowed viewers to see the actual size of illustrated plant. Second, the depictions often contained a second insert that magnified the individual organs within a flower. This takes us through the scientific period (from 1735 through 1860) when plants were identified primarily using Linnaeus's method of counting and comparing the number of organs inside a flower. He was only interested in male stamens and female pistils for his plant classification system. His followers added such characteristics as the number of sepals, petals, and how seeds were attached to the ovary walls. To show such fine characters, artists illustrated the greatly enlarged floral parts.

Some florilegia were based exclusively on living-plant collections acquired by powerful people. One of the best if not the greatest among florilegia artists was the Frenchman Pierre-Joseph Redouté (1759–1840). This artist happily drew and colored the flowers owned by members of the French aristocracy, with their sponsorship. When many former patrons lost their heads to Madame La Guillotine, Redouté switched to the ever-expanding gardens of Empress Josephine.

The all-importance of the Linnaean method meant artists and scientists had to work together to describe and illustrate new species of plants. In this age before photography, botanical artists accompanied scientists on expeditions that often turned into long and dangerous voyages. These men were adept at drawing and coloring illustrations of flowers based on fast-wilting specimens or recently pressed and dried materials. The illustration of a flower often outlived its illustrator by centuries as some artists never returned from these early voyages.

Consider the loss of Sydney Parkinson (1745–71). He accompanied Sir Joseph Banks on Captain Cook's 1768 voyage around the world through the southern hemisphere, but poor Sydney died of dysentery off the coast of Java. His great florilegium features the flowers of southern Africa, tropical Asia, and some of the first illustrations of the winter-blooming flora of Australia. They were not published until 1988.

Ferdinand Bauer (1760–1826) was revered by the scientific community of his day. The body of his work was used extensively to understand and illustrate the intimate internal anatomy of flowers and other plant organs. He was known for his florilegium of the plants of Greece, but his real fame came from his trip to Australia under Captain Matthew

Flinders in the early 1800s. By the time he returned from Australia, he had amassed eleven cases of fifteen hundred illustrations of Australian plants. His depictions of eucalyptus flowers with crimson stamens and his masterful drawing of the giant Gymea lily (*Doryanthes excelsa*) and the scarlet banksia *(Banksia coccinea)* are still reproduced on posters, postcards, and calendars across Australia.

Some purists arrogantly consider "mere" botanical scientific illustration to be a craft rather than true fine art. Thankfully, these feelings are changing, and this earlier divide between "high" and "low" art is fading away. Any artist who drafts living or preserved plant specimens using graphite or ink, watercolors or other pigments, or creates engravings or scratchboard art is considered a scientific illustrator. These artists' exacting work is more than beautiful since their photo-realistic renderings also capture scientifically accurate details. I've enjoyed commissioning the exquisite botanical illustrations of fellow Tucsonan, artist Paul Mirocha, for my books and scientific articles. At various times botanical illustrations have shocked and challenged our view of how we see and interpret the natural world around us. The next chapter will show that living flowers, and insights from their careful study, have changed science and also enriched our lives.

PART V

FLOWERS IN THE SERVICE
OF SCIENCE AND MEDICINE

Cutaway view of a chrysanthemum
(*Chrysanthemum* sp.)

CHAPTER 13

The Flower and the Scientist

Ready for buzzing: side view of silverleaf
nightshade (*Solanum elaeagnifolium*)

Flowers live forever in poems, paintings, photographs, and other works of art. But they would appear too fragile and short-lived to be of much use in a laboratory compared to fruit flies, bees, or little white mice. Yet flowers studied as part of scientific investigations have forever changed the way we view our world.

Flowers and Shifting Continents

Let's return to those daring expeditions of the eighteenth and nineteenth centuries, with the botanists and their illustrators collecting and drawing specimens found along the coasts of southern Africa and Australia. These men obviously had daring and productive adventures discovering and collecting new specimens for European museums. But what did they accomplish? All students and followers of that indomitable Swedish explorer-scientist Carl Linnaeus, plant collectors and botanical artists alike, followed his Linnaean method, identifying and cataloging specimens based on the number of sexual organs in each flower. The botanists also noted additional peculiarities such as petal shape, sepal numbers, the presence or absence of nectar glands, and the way that baby seeds (ovules) attached themselves to ovary walls. Such floral features, Linnaeus noted, were far more conservative, less varied, and more dependable than leaf, stem, and bark characteristics.

Over just a few decades, the botanists receiving those dried plant specimens and illustrations came to two unexpected findings. First, most of the plants collected in the southern hemisphere were distinct from those encountered and classified north of the equator. It was as if two creators had been at work. When cataloging the plants of the southern hemisphere, curators needed to publish new scientific names including those for genera and species. Furthermore, the newly discovered species were often placed in entirely new plant families and orders.

The second revelation was of the geographies of these new plant families. In particular, there was the weird family known as the Proteaceae (the macadamia nut family). Using the Linnaean method, botanists easily recognized these plants because their flowers resembled stylized hairpins, elephant heads, miniature long-barreled guns, witches' faces with pouched mouths, or little swans with curved necks. Their flowers came in many colors and were often united in massive flowering branches resembling clubs, cobs, or tiaras. The very name Proteaceae was used to remind readers that the Greek god Proteus assumed many forms. Today, the familiar living or dried flowering branches of banksias, waratahs (*Telopea*), and proteas (*Protea*) command high prices in your local florist shop.

We now know that species in the family Proteaceae are native to every continent and large island in the southern hemisphere. But how did they get there? Imagining connections between now sunken "land bridges" or stepping-stone islands between Africa and South America seemed unlikely. Nor do the seeds of plants of this family, as a rule, float or survive long in seawater. The most logical theory had to wait until the early-twentieth century.

Alfred Wegener (1880–1930) wasn't much of a botanist, but was respected as a great polar meteorologist and an early geophysicist. He theorized that the modern distribution of banksias in Australia versus proteas in South Africa was likely due to the long-term gradual effects of continental drift. Continents were not fixed in one place for all of geological history, according to Wegener. Like thick ice floes on a river, they collided, grinded, and bumped into one another and/or rafted apart over long periods. Many scientists vehemently despised Wegener during his life for his radical ideas, but today a new generation of geophysicists have demonstrated that plate tectonics, and moving continents, are an ancient and modern fact of our planet's geological history.

In your international travels, you may have noticed that wildflowers are not uniformly distributed around the world. Certain kinds of flowers, even entire plant families, are found only on one continent but not others. Flowering plants have contributed to the field of biogeography, in which plant geographers study the natural distributions of plants as they exist now, where they originated, and how they moved in the past, including their slow but inexorable passage on the continents, riding along atop the raftlike tectonic plates.

Nehemiah Grew Plays Cupid

Before the 1680s, the words *plant sexuality* formed an oxymoron. As noted earlier, the ancient Babylonians knew how to hand-pollinate date palms to produce fruit crops, even if they didn't understand the intimate details. Their techniques persist to this day, although some date orchards now employ a pollen "cannon" to blast pollen grains onto female flowers. Otherwise, most people presumed that flowers turned into fruits spontaneously, the same way that tadpoles turned into frogs. After the invention of magnifying lenses and microscopes, such beliefs faded away, thanks to the work of London physician Nehemiah Grew and his associates. His book *The Anatomy of Plants* was published to wide acclaim in 1682.

Grew is remembered for his discovery that the stamens in flowers are the "male organs" of seed plants and their pollen grains are equivalent to the sperm produced by animals. His observations were largely mechanistic as he deciphered how plants functioned, much as one would examine a clock or a similar device. His research stimulated the young science of reproductive botany carried on by Marcello Malpighi (1628–94) and Christian K. Sprengel (1750–1816).

Imagine how this botanical understanding would come to change agriculture and horticulture over the centuries. If you did not like the crops you traditionally grew, *you could make new ones* by crossing existing varieties. All you needed was a hand lens and some feathers or a toothpick to transfer pollen from one blossom to another. You no longer needed to wait for an infrequent mutation to appear. You had the option of seeing what would happen if you crossed two different species in the same garden. Many of the garden flowers that we love and grow today began as hybrids between different species. What were these first crosses? They included the soulangeana magnolias, polyanthus primroses, almost all of our tulips, and thousands of hybrid rosebushes. Not everyone approved. Pious people insisted that godless scientists were defying the laws of creation by making plants without the blessings of their deity.

Pea Blossoms and a Monk

Blasphemous or not, the science of genetics originated from crossing flowers for a scientific purpose. It all began in an Austrian monastery garden more than 160 years ago. In St. Thomas's Abbey, a monastery in Brno, Austria-Hungary (now the Czech Republic), an Augustinian monk made careful observations and predictions while crossing flowers of the common garden pea (*Pisum sativum*).

Gregor Johann Mendel (1822–84) is recognized as the father of modern genetics, the inheritance of physical traits from parents to offspring in plants and animals. Between 1856 and 1863, Mendel expanded the monastery's five-acre garden. His abbot didn't want the friars working on sexual reproduction in animals, so Mendel and his assistants switched to plants, less controversial experimental subjects. During this time, Mendel crossed around twenty-eight thousand pea plants. Mendel's crosses over many pea generations tracked the inheritance of seven physical traits including plant height, pod shape and color, seed shape and color, along with flower position on the stem, and flower colors of white and violet. He noted how these physical traits varied naturally among his pea plants, but wanted to know what happened in the next and succeeding generations.

An example of one of Mendel's simple experiments follows. Like the flowers of most plants, pea flowers are bisexual. Male and female organs are found together in the same blossom. Therefore the flower of a garden pea usually pollinates itself shortly after the petals open. Mendel interrupted this self-pollination by collecting pollen from one parent (the donor or father pea blossom) and rubbing it on the receptive pistil of a flower on a second pea vine (the seed mother). He marked these crosses with short pieces of identifying yarn. If this cross resulted in a pea pod, he let it mature and dry. He counted the peas and noted their color, yellow or green, and if they were wrinkled or smooth. He planted them to find out which traits they had as mature plants.

Mendel took pollen from a violet flower and dabbed it onto a white flower. He gathered and sowed the seeds from this cross. One hundred percent of the offspring plants, the first filial (F1) generation, had violet flowers. Somehow, the white-colored flowers were suppressed. Gardeners, and scientists of the day, believed in "blending inheritance," that the flowers of the next generation should have been mauve or pink, the intermediate color between the parents, or that the progeny should have shown a ratio of 50 percent violet flowers and 50 percent white flowers. This clearly never happened with Mendel's peas.

Mendel allowed the next generation (F2) to self-pollinate. That yielded 705 violet-flowered plants and 224 with white flowers, a ratio of 3.15 of violet to white. One in every four pea plants had purebred recessive traits (white); two of four were hybrid (purple); and one of four had dominant traits (purple again). He concluded that the pea-plant traits were either expressed (visible traits) or latent (hidden but still there). The dominant traits (for example, flowers with purple petals) were inherited, but did not change when different plants were crossed. On the other hand, the recessive traits (for example, white petals) became latent, but reappeared in the second generation.

From his numerous crosses and fastidious record-keeping, Mendel made two generalizations relating to the curious 3:1 ratio that he repeatedly found. This observation became his Law of Segregation (of alleles), and the Law of Independent Assortment. College biology students recognize both of them today as Mendel's Laws of Inheritance.

Where would our knowledge of genetics be without the use of plants to provide answers (in the form of seeds) within one or two growing seasons? (Remember that the use of short-lived fruit flies to study inheritance didn't begin until the twentieth century.) Mendel's story of one gene controlling one plant character (e.g., flower color) was not the end of the story, as we know now from the work of German botanist Carl Correns (1864–1933) and his four-o'clocks, giving genetics its concept of incomplete gene dominance.

Charles Darwin was a contemporary of Mendel's but appeared to be unaware of the monk's groundbreaking but obscure publications. Nevertheless, he shared Mendel's interest in the flowers of annual, domesticated plants, but Darwin's research went further. He was plainly fascinated by variation of floral forms throughout what Victorians called the Vegetable Kingdom. The blossoms of hundreds of species passed under Darwin's microscope. When he couldn't grow a flower, he set off to find wild plants around his countryside home. Who could have predicted that the native orchids and primroses of an English countryside would provide hard evidence for Darwin's evolutionary theories?

Darwin's Trip down the Garden Path

It's time to retire our warm and fuzzy views of Darwin contemplating a chimpanzee (or the chimp contemplating Darwin, which appeared in mocking newspaper illustrations of the time) and his nostalgia for the giant tortoises and the finches of the Galápagos Islands. These charismatic vertebrates certainly played roles in his science-changing theories, but we must emphasize that over forty years of his adult life were spent in and around his country estate in Kent (now one of London's southernmost suburbs). Following the publication of *On the Origin of Species* in 1859, Darwin wrote a series of books based on home-based research that bolstered his new theories. Seven of those books were plant studies, and three of them dealt almost exclusively with the form, function, and breeding of flowers.

Plants illustrate important concepts in *On the Origin of Species*. When Darwin referred to "the struggle for existence," he based his research on his own garden plots and woodlots, not on large exotic birds or beasts. He found that if you crowd too many seeds into the same garden plot, most of the sprouting plants die or fail to mature and flower. Today, we call this "survival of the fittest," and plant ecologists are still studying the effects of overcrowding. Darwin had a far different vision of what flowers could teach us compared to Linnaeus. Darwin used floral sexual characters to identify species, but unlike Linnaeus he was convinced that flower forms had specific functions encouraging a plant's survival. More important, in a Darwinian universe, floral architecture changed over time as environmental conditions and pollinators came and went.

Why was the first book that Darwin published after *On the Origin of Species* all about orchid flowers? While this book has an exhaustively long title—*On the Various Contrivances by Which British and Foreign Orchids Are Fertilised by Insects and on the Good Effects of Intercrossing* (1862)—that title does describe the contents within the book. Darwin begins his analyses on a half dozen wild orchid species growing a short distance from his home. After these flowers, he turns to the tropical blooms in his greenhouse. It doesn't matter whether he's dissecting the flower of a long purple (*Orchis mascula*) collected from the local woodland or a large *Cattleya* from Mexico. All the flowers reveal much the same story, and Darwin provides valuable lessons in floral biomechanics. All those strange organs that are fused together in orchid flowers have a unique way of sending and receiving their pollen on the bodies of visiting insects. Pollen grains are jam-packed into ovoids, shrink-wrapped, then attached to sticky bases that become glued to the back or tongue of a visiting bee or butterfly. The fancy doodads in orchid flowers may look special, but all of them are actually derived from standard petals, stamens, and pistils.

Evolution in orchids represents Darwin's concept of "modification by descent." With natural selection determining which flower will set the most seeds, the orchids we know today wear various contrivances that must have been absent in their ancestors. The flower forms that we see in our greenhouses, prom corsages, and wedding bouquets promote cross-pollination, which was a radical idea for Darwin's readers. As orchid collections became a Victorian fad in the nineteenth century, people presumed that the weird flowers must all self-pollinate in the wild because, in all orchids, male and female organs fuse together. No, Darwin says. When orchid organs unite within the same flower, they promote outbreeding, not inbreeding (selfing).

By 1876, Darwin hammers home the lessons of 1862 with *The Effects of Cross and Self Fertilisation in the Vegetable Kingdom*. Now he's gone down the garden path, or his beloved Sandwalk, his thinking path at Down House, and is concentrating on annual plants, just like Mendel before him, but Darwin is experimenting on dozens of short-lived vegetables and bedding flowers. The Victorians preferred annuals to perennials as they could be quickly massed into colorful patterns in their gardens. When the petunias and marigolds died, the beds were turned over for new seeds or plants. It was a time when bedding plants were being developed from all over the world. Darwin hand-crosses or self-pollinates California poppies (*Escholtzia*), mignonettes (*Reseda*), sweet peas (*Lathyrus*), ragged robins (*Clarkia*), nasturtiums (*Tropaeolum*), pheasant's eyes (*Adonis*), pinks (*Dianthus*), pocketbook flowers (*Calceolaria*), etc., and waits for their seeds.

Do these plants always make the same number of seeds based on cross- or self-pollination? No, you tend to obtain more seeds after cross-pollination. Do the offspring of self- and cross-pollinations show equal rates of survival in overcrowded beds? No, the seedlings grown from cross-pollinated seeds tend to be fitter. Once again, this was a radical notion in Darwin's day, when breeds of cattle, pigs, dogs, pigeons, and poultry were standardized by crossing parents and offspring. It was also a time in which families maintained their wealth by encouraging marriages between first cousins. For much of the nineteenth century an English-woman lost all her property, and right to inherit, as soon as she married. Darwin was well aware of the genetic dangers of inbreeding, in all animals, including people. (Even so, he married his first cousin Emma Wedgwood, of Wedgwood porcelain fame, and together they had ten children, none with birth defects, and seven of whom survived to adulthood.)

Darwin quickly followed the second book with a third based on yet another walk in the woods. *The Different Forms of Flowers on Plants of the Same Species* (1877) begins with the mating habits of primroses and cowslips (*Primula* spp.). This leads us to the two or three reproductive forms found in each population of bluets (*Hedyotis*), lungworts (*Pulmonaria*), loosestrife (*Lythrum*), flax (*Linum*), and buckwheat (*Fagopyrum*). Once again, the pressures of natural selection appear to favor plants that make flowers that avoid self-pollination and retain forms that permit only cross-pollination. Ah, could this also help answer why the majority of animals on this planet have only two genders?

Of course, not all research on flowers has been so universal and earth-shattering. As in most scientific studies, the biological study of flowers increases our knowledge in small but useful increments. And sometimes it has been very practical, helping us to increase the yields of useful plant-derived products.

Flowers, Not Cars, in the Wind Tunnel

When we explored floral pollination in an earlier chapter, the subject of wind-pollinated flowering plants was largely neglected. But such plants and their flowers are important, even if somewhat green and not as showy as most other flowers. About 10–20 percent of the flowering plants in any habitat cast their reproductive fates to the breezes by broadcasting ridiculously large numbers of pollen grains into the air. Further, the wind-pollinated cereal and grain crops (e.g., rice, wheat, millet, rye, barley, and corn) feed the world, providing essential carbohydrate calories that keep just over 7 billion people from gnawing starvation. Wind-pollinated flowers are fascinatingly complex, far more interesting than you might at first realize.

Jojoba (*Simmondsia chinensis*) is a nondescript, native–Sonoran Desert plant that blooms in early February. You may have first met this plant while taking a shower. Most people know the word *jojoba* as a shampoo ingredient. Jojoba fruits, uniquely, contain a liquid wax identical to sperm-whale oil, with its unique properties. (But no whales died to give you nice clean hair.)

Like some of the plants Darwin studied, jojoba is dioecious. There are equal numbers of boy bushes (pollen makers) or girl bushes (oilseed makers). Neither sex bothers to make petals, and breezes, not bees or hummingbirds, move pollen from male to female flowers.

The reproductive biology of this lowly shampoo plant is every bit as exciting as any whodunit. I'd known about the pioneering biomechanical studies of researcher Karl Niklas of Cornell University. I was also familiar with fossil plants from the Carboniferous period that Niklas modeled, along with his ideas about how these ancient plants sieved pollen from the air like a modern snow fence. I telephoned Karl. To my delight, he would look at jojoba, and we collaborated on these studies. I collected fresh female jojoba flowers and pollen. A few days later, the green flowers were "flown" in a wind tunnel in Karl's laboratory. A stroboscopic light flashed four hundred times a second while a movie camera filmed the action. Smooth-flowing, nonturbulent air passed across the flower. Unlike most aerodynamicists Karl didn't use smoke in his wind tunnel to track flow lines (you've seen car commercials with smoke passing over the hood of a luxury sports car). Instead, Karl used a tiny, custom bubble generator. One-millimeter-diameter, helium-filled soap bubbles were released upstream of our female jojoba blossom. We jiggled a wire holding jojoba pollen, and thousands of pollen grains floated toward the female flower.

A few days later, the film had been made into eight-by-ten-inch prints. We couldn't believe our eyes. The shiny, miniature soap bubbles faithfully tracked the smooth airflow, then beautifully demonstrated when the flow broke up into turbulence as it hit, then passed by, the leaves, stem, and flower farther downwind. The rabbit-ear leaf arrangement caused something unexpected to happen: the airstream abruptly shifted ninety degrees toward the flower. The leaves directed a shower of pollen at the female flower. When the leaves were removed, the directional pollen shower was lost. Watching our movie clips revealed how pollen grains had multiple chances to impact the styles. We observed pollen-containing air swirling in tight eddies, called von Kármán vortices, over the tridentlike styles for almost a minute. This "clever" wind-pollinated flower had improved its lottery-like odds of being pollinated. Due to slowly accumulated changes in its floral and leaf morphology during its evolutionary history, the pollen grains remained aloft in the vicinity of its sexual parts, enhancing pollen capture. Never again would I think of wind-pollinated flowers as uninteresting. Nature, it seems, always has surprises for the prepared observer.

Through their long evolutionary histories, wild plants such as jojoba, and the grasses we know as cereal crops, have developed strategies to loft their pollen into the breezes so that some of it, although a tiny fraction, makes its way to female flowers, with their sticky stigmas, waiting downstream.

Capturing and Identifying Floral Scents

I was careful not to rip the delicate turkey oven-roasting bag on the spines of the cactus, since it would ruin our experiment. What was I doing roaming the Sonoran Desert with a plastic oven bag? The plastic (food-grade, heat-resistant nylon) in these bags is perfect—relatively inert, so it won't outgas contaminants that would have confounded our fragrance studies. I was in a remote Arizona-desert cactus patch to collect sweetly aromatic floral scent molecules. In the distance was my prize.

A few individual plants of queen-of-the-night cactus (*Peniocereus greggii*) sent their camouflaged, thin, gray stems up the branches of creosote bushes and ironwood trees. You have to know where to find them because you aren't likely to spot these cryptic cacti otherwise. When in bloom they're spectacular and unmistakable. Rumored to bloom for only one night each year, individual plants actually bloom for several nights during the intense desert heat of May and June. *Peniocereus* is almost a mythical plant among cactus and succulent lovers. I tugged the oven bag over an enlarged bud, one that I believed was going to open in about two hours, then close early the next morning. I adjusted the bag around its stem and attached some flexible, plastic tubing. My partner in scent, Dr. Robert Raguso of Cornell University, did the same thing at another cactus bearing equally promising buds. We connected battery-powered air pumps to the tubes attached to the oven bags. This volatile-trapping technique has been worked out by Rob and other chemists. Outdoor air is drawn through the oven bag over the delicate *Peniocereus* blooms releasing their delicate fragrance molecules. The floral-scented air is drawn across chemically activated material inside short glass tubes, "odor traps," where the molecules get stuck. Later, we wash the cactus smell from the traps with organic solvents and freeze the samples until we are ready to identify the odorant molecules using a gas chromatograph/mass spectrometer.

Only a mile or so away, along a desert wash, close to agricultural fields just across the Mexican border, were flowering clumps of sacred datura (*Datura wrightii*). Unlike the "queen," the *Datura* plants bloom for months, often producing fifty or more big, trumpet-shaped flowers per plant. They are the nectar sources for hawk moths, and the leafy food for their big, green caterpillars. The large hawk moths (*Manduca sexta* and *M. quinquemaculata*) are the familiar tomato hornworms despised by most gardeners. Unfortunately, its usually "squish on sight" for these marvelous animals. The adult moths are equally spectacular, flying miles every night in search of the nectar deep within the creamy-white blossoms. As we watched, the husky moths hovered and unrolled their slender, eight-inch-long tongues, probing the blooms. Others, including the smaller white-lined sphinx (*Hyles lineata*) were forced to land, crawling inside to reach the nectar with their much shorter tongues.

We were here to find out if true chemical mimicry existed between the queen-of-the-night cactus flowers and the sacred-datura trumpets. Both plants bear large, white, nectar-rich desert flowers pollinated by the same kinds of moths. They looked alike, seemingly mimics of one another, so shouldn't they also smell alike? We were going to find out. A few weeks later, back in his Cornell University laboratory, Rob took one of the queen's glass scent traps from his deep freeze and let it come to room temperature. With a few tablespoons' worth of hexane solvent he washed the scent molecules into a laboratory vial. He did the same for traps containing *Datura* scent. Under a stream of nitrogen gas, he concentrated their scent molecules. Using a glass syringe, Rob injected the scent-laden solvent into a scientific oven called a gas chromatograph (GC). Inside, the injected fragrance molecules move along a coiled-glass capillary column, with which they interact. The oven starts at room temperature and is programmed to continually rise and then hold at a high temperature. The lightest molecules, such as hexane, come tumbling out the end of the capillary coil first and hit the gas chromatograph detector, then the heavier fragrance molecules follow in order of increasing size and reactivity.

On a computer screen we could see the separated chemicals as needle-like peaks appearing on the GC trace. After being detected in the gas chromatograph oven, some molecules from each peak are diverted into an instrument call the mass spectrometer. Inside, the molecules are torn apart, and their resulting ions are revealed. Using a gas chromatograph coupled to a mass spectrometer, chemists routinely identify unknown chemical compounds, including pesticide residues on vegetables or priority pollutants in water samples. In all, we saw only eight distinct peaks (chemicals) in *Peniocereus*, but more than a dozen for sacred datura. Surprisingly to us, but likely not to the moths, the queen and the *Datura* scents were not chemical clones. The dominant scent chemicals we found in *Datura* were complex blends of terpenoid, benzenoid, aliphatic, and nitrogen-containing compounds, while *Peniocereus* had only benzene-containing compounds, eight of which were also present in *Datura*. Perhaps a bit of scent mimicry was taking place. To my largely untrained nose, *Peniocereus* smells faintly like wintergreen, and indeed, one of its chemicals, methyl salicylate, is also present in oil of wintergreen, or wintergreen breath mints. Stranger yet, we tested another Sonoran *Peniocereus* cactus (*P. striatus*) and enigmatically found it to be scentless, a rarity for any flower. It likely attracts its moth pollinators solely by the shape and white color of its flowers on moonlit nights.

Raguso has tested many of these scent compounds individually and in combinations on *Manduca* moths flying inside laboratory wind tunnels and in field tests. Using scientific experimentation, we collected, identified, and finally bioassayed (field-tested with living animals) the scent molecules released onto the breezes by the blooming desert trumpets. Moths flew in to inspect our scented artificial blooms.

How Bees See Flowers

In the first chapter we learned that bees see much differently from humans. The ultraviolet (UV) wavelengths that burn our skin at the beach are the same region of the spectrum that some flowers use as a "secret" communication channel with their pollinators. If we could see like a bee, we'd experience flowers as they do. We would be shocked, perhaps terrified, by how different the world of flowers and plants looks to bees. Bees are more myopic than we are, since they have only five thousand four hundred ommatidial cells (special cells that enable bees to see) per compound eye, compared to the 120 million rods and cones lining human retinas. Not surprisingly, bees have difficulty discerning fine details. Think of our own ability to detect the separation of closely spaced parallel lines on a printed page. This is the so-called minimum visual angle. For a worker honey bee, this angle is one or two degrees, while in a human eye, the visual resolution is a fine 0.01 degrees, making our eyes about sixty times better than a bee's in resolving power. However, bees' eyes still function extremely well for them. Why? Bees are small and tend to be close to the flowers and other natural objects that they must see for their survival (e.g., nest mates, predators at the hive).

Using a camera and a special UV filter, we can come closer to experiencing how bees see flowers during their foraging visits. With the right film or digital camera and UV-passing filter, you can experience how some UV-marked flowers might appear to hungry bees. A flower photographed in UV was presented in chapter 1.

Time-lapse (TL) photography is used to make apparent the imperceptibly slow movements of petals and other structures unfurling from tight buds into open flowers. Think of the amazing sequences of red roses in the film *American Beauty*, which were created by TL master Louie Schwartzberg of BlackLight Films in Los Angeles. The opening of a rose or other blooms in thirty seconds of faster-than-life playback is magical. Audiences never tire of seeing the majesty and beauty of flowers revealed by this photographic marvel. I've used DSLR cameras outdoors and in makeshift indoor studios to record the opening and closing of saguaro and the queen-of-the-night flowers. Although it's a fascinating technique used by artists and scientists alike, the subject is too broad to discuss here in greater detail.

Floral Manipulations Trick Bees?

In my first scientific paper, with Dr. Claris E. Jones, published while a sophomore at California State University, Fullerton, we described how modified flowers could control the behavior of free-flying wild bees. In this set of experiments, our Organization for Tropical Studies work group located a legume (*Caesalpinia eriostachys*) in full bloom, to test our ideas. The small tree was growing at the Guanacaste field station, an old cattle ranch in the northwest province of Costa Rica. It was the dry season, of February–March, and the neighboring *Tabebuia* trees were giant masses of yellow or pink blossoms. Our little *Caesalpinia* wasn't as impressive but was abuzz with clouds of noisy, native bees. Groups of digger bees (e.g., *Centris* and *Gaesischia*) whizzed past our heads to and from the nectar-rich flowers. We planned to see if we could trick the bees, altering their behavior, by messing with their little, yellow flowers. That was one of our problem-solving exercises during the eight-week field course.

By using our large, heavy, but portable Sony television camera and magnetic tape unit, we already knew some of the flower's secrets. As a "caesalpinaceous legume" (a subfamily in the pea family), our flowers had four side petals and a fat, uppermost one called the banner petal. Like all banners, this one was for advertising, a miniature billboard, a floral sign-post, if you will, for bees. It was a uniform canary yellow with squiggly, red lines at its base. These lines are guides that show the bees where to probe to find the hidden, sweet nectar, the correct place to drink.

Under the UV gaze of the now-antique black-and-white television camera, we saw the small, yellow blooms as the bees did. The side petals looked bright white, indicating their intense UV-light reflection. The bees saw the lateral petals as a mixture of reflected yellow wavelengths plus UV. Physiologists call this color "bees' purple," even if we don't know exactly how it looks since humans are UV blind. The slender stamens tipped with their plump, orange anthers, along with the upright banner petal, were the same color. However, they appeared black to our panchromatic video camera. Black, the absence of color, indicates that the dark parts of our flowers strongly absorbed the incident UV rays. Further, they reflected only the yellow wavelengths of light, which is how the bees saw them.

We got to work dissecting flowers and modifying others, figuring out what we might test. One of our experiments involved gluing a yellow side petal over the banner with a bit of Elmer's glue. The incoming bees seemed confused. They landed but had a difficult time finding the hidden nectar. We also twisted the flowers to one side, so the UV-absorbing banner was now horizontal. To our surprise, the bees turned and landed sideways, then probed for nectar. We also turned flowers completely upside down. Scientists can be mischievous at times. The bees weren't fooled by our manipulations, instead they executed a quick barrel roll maneuver in midair just before they landed. Upside down on the flowers, they quickly drank the nectar below the banner petal.

Later, we learned that similar floral manipulations were conducted decades earlier by plant ecological pioneers Frederic Clements and Frances Long on alpine flowers near the Carnegie Alpine Laboratory on the slopes of Pikes Peak in the Colorado Rockies. Clements later conducted research at the University of Arizona Desert Laboratory on Tumamoc Hill in Tucson. Gently pestering bees in the name of science seems to have a long and respected history.

Artificial Flowers and Trained Bumble Bees

One eastern-US bumble bee species, *Bombus impatiens*, has almost become the white-mouse or laboratory-rat analog for insect behaviorists across the United States. *Bombus impatiens* occurs naturally east of the Mississippi River, but has been cultured by the millions, then transported to pollinate commercial greenhouse tomato and pepper crops. You can pick up the telephone and order one or more bee colonies. For about $80 you'll get a small starter colony (a queen and her twenty or thirty daughters) handily delivered to your university laboratory by FedEx. Getting bees doesn't get any easier. Much is now known about this bumble bee since researchers have studied and published accounts of its behavior for the past decade. You still must care for your indoor bees, like pollinator pets, giving them pollen and sugar syrup, and providing them with real flowers and places to fly.

Our team of insect behaviorists, pollination biologists, and neurobiologists (at the University of Arizona, and the University of Nevada at Reno; Drs. Dan Papaj, Anne Leonard, Wulfila Gronenberg, and I) decided to test some of the tenets of bumble bee learning and their memory abilities. We especially wanted to learn how bumble bees make their decisions about whether to forage for nectar or for pollen on a given trip, and if they switch their preferences on successive days, or as the colony workforce grows. We were determined to construct artificial, robotic flowers, and to fly, train, and behaviorally test the bees in our respective Tucson and Reno laboratories.

University of Arizona doctoral candidate Avery Russell and I watched closely as the pale-yellow-and-black worker *Bombus impatiens* walked through the clear plastic tunnel leading out of the colony where she had emerged as an adult about a week earlier. She approached the Y-tube junction and turned left. A little farther along the corridor, she entered a wooden and plastic chamber that held *Solanum* flowers with their stamens poking through a central opening. These flowers had artificial petals made of either bright yellow or blue paper, supposedly colors preferred by bumble bees in tests by other researchers. On the way out of her nest, the worker bee walked under a sensor. A tiny, harmless two-by-two-millimeter radio-frequency identification device (an RFID chip) containing a miniature circuit and antenna was previously glued to her back, as was on many of her techno-bee nest mates.

Passing under the radio-frequency sensor, her eight-digit, unique ID code (let's call her bee 54) rang out; the signal was sent to a nearby laptop computer. I watched as her number appeared in the spreadsheet. At least we now knew the whereabouts of bee 54. During her time in the foraging arena, her visits to the blue versus yellow faux flowers would be recorded by a video camera. On her return trip to the nest, laden with a full honey stomach of sugar water, her foraging time would be recorded by the trusty RFID system, just as if she were a human factory worker punching an old-fashioned time clock. Bees have a finely tuned visual system and are capable of rapidly learning associations of floral shape, colors, scents, surface textures, and possibly even electric fields left behind as footprints by previous bee visitors. Our group is using 3-D scans of living flowers, including *Solanum*, to fabricate plastic, exact-scale models of these blooms for presentation to our bumble bees this time in Reno by Anne and her grad student Jake Francis and post doc Felicity Muth. Our artificial flowers will be more realistic, while odorless and uniformly colored, for our further investigations of bee learning.

Work with bumble bees and floral colors has been conducted since the early 1900s, but most scientists have focused on nectar rather than pollen. We are interested in whether workers become nectar or pollen specialists and especially the neglected aspects of pollen collection. In the experiment above, we determined that bumble bees did learn to recognize our yellow and blue artificial flowers while pollen foraging. We have also used RFIDs as laboratory time clocks for bees, exploring questions about bumble bee fidelity to certain flowers and colors, and for recording the comings and goings of free-flying bumble bees outdoors. Our bees remembered these rewarding color associations in the short term, but they didn't remember them once back in the colony even a day later. Hmm, perhaps the bumble bees were dreaming of real flowers, ones brimming with nectar, not our crude, construction-paper, make-believe flowers.

A female bumble bee (*Bombus impatiens*) sonicates pollen from the anthers of a deadly nightshade blossom (*Solanum tridynamum*) in the laboratory

The Telltale Flower:
Pollen and Crime-Scene Forensics

Forensic botany uses leaves, fibers, wood, but especially pollen grains to help solve violent crimes or to settle legal disputes. In recent years, it has been widely accepted by the courts in other countries and to a lesser extent in the United States. Laboratories with resident pollen identification experts (palynologists) are using pollen, along with other plant evidence including DNA samples, to help solve mysteries. Botanical sleuthing has been featured in some of the immensely popular US television shows including *CSI*, *Law & Order*, and *Cold Case*. Pollen grains are composed of a natural biopolymer and are highly resistant to decay. Pollen can even be retrieved from inside solid rocks millions of years old. These microscopic, dustlike particles easily find their way into clothing, hair, nasal passages, under fingernails, and into stomachs of those murdered or the perpetrators. DNA can be extracted from pollen for yet more precise determinations. Pollen grains can remain unnoticed, bearing silent witness to events, long after fingerprints, DNA, and other equally perishable evidence have faded away.

In Christchurch, New Zealand, in 1997, a young woman was pulled into an alleyway and raped. Shaken by the traumatic attack, she was still able to describe her assailant to the police. Shortly thereafter, a possible suspect matching her description was taken into custody. The male suspect admitted being in the area but claimed he had stopped to help her, suggesting that this was why she remembered his face. No DNA trace evidence was recovered, but the police noticed dirt stains on his clothing. He claimed this was from his working on his car. Nevertheless, the police wisely took his clothing as evidence and sent the soiled fabric to the palynology laboratory of the New Zealand government's Geological Survey.

The alleyway where the rape took place was lined on one side by a row of flowering shrubs of wormwood (*Artemisia arborescens*), a plant native to the Mediterranean region and infrequently planted as an ornamental in New Zealand. Some of the plants appeared as if they had been broken or flattened during a struggle. A lot of pollen was mixed in with the soil particles on the suspect's clothing, and 77 percent of it was *Artemisia* pollen. Investigators combed the area near the suspect's home and other areas but couldn't find any *Artemisia* plants except at the crime scene itself. The pollen evidence was presented by an expert botanical witness at the suspect's trial, and he was convicted, receiving an eight-year prison sentence.

How Do We Smell Flowers: Molecular Fit or Resonance?

We think that fragrance and memories are linked because smells plug directly into the primitive part of our mammalian brains known as the limbic system. Part of human memories and emotions also reside in this area of the brain. Natural scents may consist of one molecule, or usually many kinds. Sniff a garden rose and thirty or more different chemical compounds, including dominant ones such as geraniol and geranyl acetate, are pulled into your nose. These fragrant molecules enter the warm and humid channels inside our nasal sinuses and become trapped. Here, neuronal processes occur that nearly instantaneously produce the sensations of smells in our brains. We easily distinguish between flower aromas and other scents. Within our noses, a pair of dime-size, mucus-covered patches are packed with millions of odor-sensing cells. These cells have minute, hairlike structures carrying receptor sites. Here, the scent molecules temporarily bind, causing electrical impulses to race to the brain, which registers them as familiar scents. Ah, the scent of a rose, a sweet violet, or the unforgettably powerful scent of a Stargazer lily; we recognize them all. Amazingly, after a century of research by olfaction scientists, we still don't understand the exact details about how the scent molecules produce their signals, what happens after they bind to their receptor sites—what actually goes on behind the scenes on bee antennae or inside our noses.

Currently we have two competing and dissimilar theories for how olfaction works in our noses at the molecular level. The oldest, traditional model is the stereochemical theory of olfaction (called odotope). Scent molecules are thought to bind in a lock-and-key fashion. Their unique, 3-D molecular shapes fit into receptor sites on the olfactory sensory cells. The sense cells are turned on and register this particular sent in electrical signals sent to the olfactory-bulb region of the brain. Instantly we recognize the scent of a rose! This theory is the one accepted today by most scientists. The details, however, are unclear. Truly, we don't fully understand what happens in the olfactory sense cells at the deepest levels.

A newer (first proposed by Malcolm Dyson in 1928) theory for how scents are detected and recognized is being championed with new data and insights by perfumer and biophysicist Luca Turin. This opposing theory of olfaction is called the vibrational theory of smell. Proponents such as Turin believe that individual scent molecules resonate at a particular frequency that is different from that of other scent molecules. The vibrational frequency switches on the correct receptor. A customized molecular-shape fit alone may not explain how we smell things. The vibration of the scent molecules produces the signal to the olfactory-bulb region of the brain, causing the recognition of a single scent, or blends of scented molecules. Other quantum-level biological effects may ultimately help explain some conundrums in photosynthesis, or vision, and magnetic-field reception in migrating animals. The atomic-level vibration of scent molecules varies widely from molecule to molecule among odorants. We can think of their resonant vibrations as almost like a musician striking a tuning fork while the corresponding receptive sensory cells fire in synchrony with those specific vibrations.

Can Bee Studies Provide Clues to How We Smell Flowers?

Exciting recent work using fruit flies and honey bees may help to confirm the resonance theory of olfaction, at least in these odor-specialist insects. I was fortunate to collaborate in an experimental test of the resonance theory of olfaction using honey bees in the University of Arizona laboratory of Dr. Wulfila Gronenberg and his students. Luca Turin sent us samples of highly purified aromatic compounds. Turin had replaced some of the hydrogen atoms in these fragrant molecules with deuterium atoms. This would make the chemicals behave the same in chemical reactions but produce unique quantum vibrations. They would have exactly the same molecular shape but exhibit different vibrations. If, therefore, worker-bee olfaction operates by shape recognition, then our honey bees should not be able to tell the normal chemicals from their deuterated cousins. If, instead, the bees' sense of smell is based on recognition by their underlying molecular vibrations, they *would* be able to tell the chemicals apart in our laboratory assays.

We used a feeding bioassay called the proboscis extension response (or PER): bees will stick out their tongues (the proboscis) when their feelers (antennae) touch nectar in a flower, or sugar water in the laboratory. Each bee circles and is brought close to a tube delivering one scent at a chosen concentration together with sugar water. The bee will then stick out her tongue and be rewarded with a drop of sugar water. Upon repeated trials (simultaneous paired presentation of odor and sugar reward) the bees learn to associate the odor with the reward and will then extend their tongue to the odor alone. I like to joke with my behavioral colleagues that the bees are sticking their tongues out at us. We tested all of Luca's normal molecules (i.e., those containing hydrogen atoms) and their deuterated substitutes. After only a few trials, and at statistically significant levels, the bees differentiated between the paired test substances. They hadn't been fooled. We assume that they were discriminating between the odorants based on differences in their molecular resonance. This is only the second molecular shape-versus-vibration test using insects, after earlier tests with fruit flies. Previous results with human guinea pigs weren't as conclusive. Therefore, we don't yet know the complete answer to this fascinating question of how humans, or bees, smell flowers, which is all part of the intrigue and fun of doing original scientific research. It's my hope that this chapter has provided not only a historical perspective of studies by famous scientists (e.g., Mendel, Darwin), but also a personalized glimpse into some of my own flower and bee research over several decades. I'm sure that many more exciting discoveries with flowers, and flower-loving animals, lie ahead for both scientists, citizen scientists, and inquisitive individuals everywhere.

CHAPTER 14

Good for What Ails Us:
Healing Our Bodies and Minds

Alpine Colorado lupine
(*Lupinus argenteus*)

A temple priest in ancient Egypt prepares an infusion of precious saffron fibers, the dried and twisted stigmas of *Crocus sativus*, as a bitter-tasting medicine for stomach and intestinal ailments, or applied as a poultice. Cleopatra had saffron added to her bathwater and ate saffron in the hopes that it would make her romantic encounters with men even more pleasurable. Women in China prepare floral teas of chrysanthemum and sweet osmanthus blooms with green tea leaves, during the mid-autumn festival in southern China. The intensely apricot-flavored hot tea is thought to improve the complexion and also treat cancers and diabetes. A mother in India applies a bandage rich in honey, herbs, and dried flowers to a cut on her son's leg, knowing that it will heal faster. A US gardener enjoys the sunshine and gentle summer breezes of her garden among the carnations and dahlias. She bends to harvest a cup of chamomile flowers to make an herbal-tea sleep aid. People from different cultures and times have always used traditional knowledge about flowers to promote their health and happiness.

Biophilia: Our Love of, and Dependence upon, the Natural World

Humans evolved on the African continent. We survived by gathering and hunting food, locating water, and finding shelter. We respond strongly to elements of the savanna environments in which our earliest ancestors lived. This seems to be at least partially why we enjoy our parks and open spaces. These natural elements signaled the likelihood of finding food and water. Wildflowers may have predicted that edible fruits would soon follow. Blooming flowers signal a time of plenty and seasons of abundance. Flowers are a key element in human survival.

Humans have an inborn affinity for nature that goes beyond the tangible benefits we derive from the microbes, plants, and animals of the biomes in which we live. The idea that nature in the form of landscapes, plants, and animals is good for our well-being is old and can be traced to Charles Darwin or earlier. This idea was called biophilia by psychologist Erich Fromm and was studied by Harvard ant biologist Edward O. Wilson and Stephen Kellert. In 1984, Wilson published *Biophilia*, which was followed by another book, *The Biophilia Hypothesis*, edited by Kellert and Wilson, in 1995. Their biophilia hypothesis is that humans have a universal desire to be in natural settings.

This tendency is at least partially genetically determined. Kellert and Wilson concern themselves with natural physical environments, and plants, rather than animals. The notion of a love of nature, biophilia, makes sense because throughout our evolutionary history it has aided our survival. Biophilic affinities can be diminished, or lost, when natural areas, or our access to them, are reduced or eliminated. Biophilic tendencies have perhaps advanced our cultural evolution. The biophilia hypothesis also embraces flowers. Our love of flowers may be learned as well as being part of our deep ancestral genetic heritage.

Humans and the flowers of the garden have an even closer and mutually dependent relationship than we have ever imagined. Just as dangerous wolves were our camp followers waiting for food scraps and were eventually tamed—domesticated into the hundreds of familiar and friendly dog breeds we keep as pets and working dogs today—we can think of garden plants with their flowers as "companion plants" for people. Long ago, we began tending flowering plants. Unlike the hundred or so species of plants that were domesticated as major agricultural crop plants, those feeding the world's 7 billion people, the garden blooms and other flowers offer us nothing in return. Or do they? Garden flowers, potted plants, and cut flowers improve our moods and raise our spirits. Perhaps there has been rapid coevolution between us and the flowers over the last ten millennia, a mutualistic dance in which both partners benefited, still evolving but transforming one another. Flowers always make us smile.

Flowers: Healing Our Bodies

The dried, crimson threads of saffron have been used since antiquity as a flavoring for foods and beverages, and in dyes and medicines. Rumored to be an aphrodisiac, saffron was a favorite ingredient in love potions used by Egyptian pharaohs. The ancient Egyptians did not grow saffron but imported it from Crete. Since Greco-Roman times, fragrant saffron has been steeped in alcohol to produce medicines reputed to reduce fevers, cramps, enlarged livers, or to calm the nerves.

Pressed from the buds of clove trees, cloves are rich in the chemical eugenol. This molecule is used as a fragrant ingredient in potpourri bundles or as a component in perfumes. It is also a powerful antibiotic and painkiller for toothaches. Cloves are also widely used in traditional Chinese and Indian medicines.

Flower-based teas are reputed to have medicinal benefits. Previously, we encountered the dried flowers of chrysanthemum, jasmine, daylily, hibiscus, and fragrant olive (*Osmanthus fragrans*) as "flower bundles" used in Chinese teas. Chrysanthemum tea is popular in southern China. Flower teas are used to treat chest pain (angina), high blood pressure, type

2 diabetes, fevers, colds, and headaches. In traditional Chinese medicine, osmanthus tea is reputed to improve the skin.

The West also has a tradition of flower remedies, but it is not as strong. Chamomile (*Matricaria chamomilla*) was used in Europe, and the practice spread to the western hemisphere after Columbus. Chamomile tea is made from the dried heads of the flower's small, white and yellow blossoms (cousins of daisies and sunflowers). Chamomile is used for calming anxiety, for settling the stomach, and as a mild sedative taken at bedtime. In Spanish-speaking countries it is prized as an additive in cordials and liqueurs.

Flowering heads of pot or African marigold flowers (*Calendula officinalis*) have been prescribed to treat skin infections. The flowers and leaves seem to have astringent properties. African marigold appears to have an estrogen-like effect and has been used to lessen the pain and/or regulate bleeding during menstruation. If you are considering experimenting with these garden favorites, never confuse them with the Mexican marigolds (*Tagetes lucida*), which do not have the same properties. Numerous flowers have made the jump from food additives or teas to traditional medicinal treatments.

Perhaps you were thinking, "What about the medicinal effects of poppy flowers and opium?" Technically, the rubbery exudate harvested to produce opium and other alkaloid drugs comes later than the flowers, from the seed capsules (fruits) that develop from the ovaries of red opium poppy flowers (*Papaver somniferum*). Their medicinal use as painkillers predates written history. Along with the illegal drug heroin, other narcotic, pain-relieving drugs (e.g., morphine, codeine) are isolated from poppy fruits.

Advice from Historical Herbalists

People have turned to plants, their stems, leaves, fruits, and seeds, for millennia as part of their healing pharmacopoeias for numerous ailments. They have also turned to flowers for their intrinsic healing properties. Along with traditional wisdom about medicinal plants transmitted orally by elders and shamanic healers, there is a rich tradition of information in herbals. Herbals are examples of incunabula (the first books created on printing presses after Gutenberg). A commonly heard complaint is that herbals were poorly illustrated books created by copycat monks. This is untrue for herbals produced during the Renaissance. Herbalists had to collect the plants themselves, so the herbals contained carefully executed woodcuts, often colored by hand, making it easier for plant collectors and healers to recognize them. Herbals were the forerunners of natural-history and botanical field guides illustrated with gorgeous paintings or color photographic plates.

In 1629, John Parkinson writes in his *A Garden of Pleasant Flowers*, for lilies, that "the water of the flowers distilled, is of excellent virtue for women in travel of childe bearing, to procure an earie delivery." About primroses he says, "The juice of the flowers is commended to cleanse the spots or marks of the face, whereof some Gentlewomen have found good experience." In 1633, John Gerard (in *The Herbal, or General History of Plants*) proclaims for rose water, "The juice of these roses, especially of Damask, doth move to the stoole, and maketh the belly soluble. . . . This syrup doth moisten and coole, and therefore it alayeth the extremities of heat in hot burning fevers." In his *Botanicum Officinale* (1722), herbalist Joseph Miller states of pinks or carnations (*Dianthus*), "These flowers are cordial, cephalic, and of use in all diseases of the Head and Nerves, as well as in all Kind of Fevers, and of the malignnant Distempers, in Faintings and Palpitations of the Heart." We could go on, with additional unsettling quotes, but you have the idea.

In Elizabeth Blackwell's *A Curious Herbal* (1737), she mentions violet flowers as "one of the four cordial flowers: and esteemed cooling, moistning, and laxative, good in Affections of the Breast and Lungs, helping Coughs and Pleuretic Pains." For primrose, she writes, "The Flowers are commended as good against disorders arising from Phlegmatic Humours," while for foxglove (*Digitalis purpurea*) she says, "The late Doctor Hulze commends y Ointment made of Flowers and May Butter, for Srophulous Ulceres which run much, dressing them with the ointment. And purging two or three Times a Week with proper purges." Foxglove is a genus of about twenty species. It has been used historically and recently for extracts such as digoxin, used to treat irregular heartbeats in human patients. For wild or briar rose (*Rosa canina*) Blackwell writes, "The Flowers of this Rose are thought more restringent than the Garden [rose]: Some look upon them as a specific for y Excess of y Catamenia." *Catamenia* is an old word for "menses."

Healing with Honey

Although technically not produced by flowers, honey is the concentrated, sweet floral nectar that is further processed by certain bees. Honeys have been used since antiquity especially for healing wounds, applied to cuts, scrapes, and burns. The Egyptian Ebers Papyrus (1550 BC) details 147 uses of honey as a medicine. These included treating burns and sores and wounds, along with surgical incisions, including male circumcision. Aristotle wrote about honey as a potent salve for wounds around 350 BC. The Maya of the Yucatán Peninsula keep colonies of stingless bees (e.g., *Melipona beecheii*, *M. yucatanica*, and *Trigona* spp.) in hollow logs for their honey and wax. These get my vote as the tastiest and most intensely floral honeys I've ever experienced. The Maya also used these native-bee honeys as treatments for cataracts and easing difficult childbirths.

All honeys have genuine healing and medicinal properties, but their therapeutic properties may vary by as much as a hundred fold. Bacteria shrivel up and die due to honey's high sugar content (80 percent sugar, 20 percent water) compared to pure water. Honeys provide additional antimicrobial effects due to their low pH and peroxide content.

Honey bees (*Apis mellifera*) add enzymes during the transformation of nectar into honey. The enzyme glucose oxidase is found in all honeys and splits the sugar glucose into water and hydrogen peroxide, the powerful antiseptic you know from your medicine cabinet. Honey is useful for the treatment of puncture wounds and for second- and third-degree burns. Burn wards in some hospitals are beginning to use honeys to prevent sterile dressings from sticking to wounds and to promote faster healing with less scarring.

Manuka honey from New Zealand is prized for its healing properties. Sterile bandages are impregnated with manuka honey, which comes from the nectar of the white blossoms of the manuka or tea-tree (*Leptospermum scoparium*). Manuka bushes, which belong to the eucalyptus family (Myrtaceae), grow throughout New Zealand and southeastern Australia. European honey bees visit the flowers for nectar and make the highly viscous manuka honey, which has a strong flavor, an acquired taste. I prefer it as a medicine rather than spread across my breakfast toast.

The antibacterial component of manuka honey is likely due to methylglyoxal, along with other unknown molecules. Manuka honeys have been rated for their antibacterial activity via the UMF (Unique Manuka Factor), with a score of 10 considered the highest. In vitro studies of methylglyoxal indicate that it can be an effective against MRSA (methicillin-resistant *Staphylococcus aureus*) bacteria. In 2008, a Cochrane Review (from cochrane .org, a high-ranking database for evidence-based medicine) found that manuka honey may improve healing of superficial burns when compared to sterile plain gauze dressings. Dr. Peter Molan, a researcher at the University of Waikato in New Zealand, has studied the medicinal properties of this honey for decades. Because of the high price of manuka honey, it is now counterfeited globally. Some brands are honey other than manuka, or manuka honey diluted with sugar syrup.

The healing power of flowers has advanced wound care. Contrary to the traditional wisdom of open-to-the-air wound care, moist and occlusive environments were found to be more conducive to healing. Honeys of many types, along with pure sugar, were tested by several companies as additives to these advanced wound-care dressings. Malignant wounds are routinely present in 5–10 percent of all cancer patients. At least one study showed the same efficacy for traditional silver-coated bandages and honey-coated bandages. Wound care, especially of foot ulcers, can be critical for diabetic patients, where limb amputations are likely. Derma Sciences Inc., a pharmaceutical company focused on wound care, manufactures Medihoney therapeutic products, including manuka-honey-infused sterile bandages.

Healing Views of Nature Outdoors: Hospitals

In hospitals throughout the ages, flowers or products derived from flowers have been used to treat people suffering from various maladies. Now it appears that hospitalized patients heal faster and with fewer complications if their rooms look out upon trees and lawns, or if they have cut flowers in their rooms. Just giving someone flowers, or inhaling their sweet aromas, makes us smile and promotes elevated moods, positive thoughts, and eases social encounters. Certain memories can be triggered by scents, thus floral scents or perfumes can often help us recall people, places, and events. The belief that plants are beneficial for medical patients is at least one thousand years old. In Europe, during the Middle Ages, monks in monasteries built beautiful gardens to soothe and comfort the ill. Similarly, American and European hospitals of the 1800s frequently used gardens as architectural elements for healing patients. Florence Nightingale (1820–1910), the social reformer and founder of modern nursing, may have introduced this concept of healing plants during her nightly rounds.

Modern US hospitals have largely abandoned outdoor greenery since pay parking lots are more lucrative. Roger Ulrich was one of the first to experimentally document the health benefits of being outside, or simply viewing nature through a window. In his study "View through a Window May Influence Recovery from Surgery," published in 1984, Ulrich analyzed hospital patients following a surgical procedure. Some patients in a Pennsylvania hospital had windows that looked upon trees and lawns, while others saw featureless brick walls. Patients whose rooms looked upon an anthropogenic version of nature had shorter postoperative hospital stays, complained less to their nurses, and required fewer moderate or strong medications for pain. Flowers are often the primary gifts given to hospital patients, and for good reasons.

Some American hospitals have heeded this message. In St. Louis, the eight thousand square feet of the Olsen family rooftop garden occupies much of the eighth floor of their Children's Hospital. It features flower beds, fountains, ponds, and benches. This special area offers a place for children to heal and for worried parents to seek comfort, companionship, and an opportunity to reflect.

Floral Scents: For Pollinators and Us

Inhalation of floral volatiles has been shown to decrease sympathetic neural activity in adults, often lowering their blood pressure. Inhaling the fragrance of a rose, caused a 40 percent decrease in relative sympathetic activity (the so-called fight-or-flight response), and a 30 percent decrease in adrenaline production, by human subjects. Flowers unknowingly excite or calm us with their fragrances. Or maybe they do know. Now that we grow and breed flowers by the billions, perhaps they have begun to turn their scented charms upon us, as a newly evolved part of their complex strategies for reproduction and survival.

It has been suggested that flowers may emit mood-altering chemicals similar to anxiolytics, which are antipanic or antianxiety psychoactive agents. These could imitate the commonly prescribed drug diazepam. If so, floral biologists haven't identified them in their analyses. Since the intended receivers of floral volatiles are pollinators, not humans, it's interesting to speculate if flowers are trying to sedate, calm, or slow down their pollen taxis, as has been suggested for narcotic-acting alkaloids in *Datura* nectar and their presumed affects on moth visitors. Perhaps calmed (drugged) insects at flowers are more likely to linger and thereby transfer additional pollen to the next flowers as they forage.

Can Floral Scents Alter Human Moods?

Can the scent of a flower be therapeutic? Humans apparently secrete chemicals into the air when they are happy, fearful, angry, or anxious. These molecules are released by our epidermal glands. They channel our emotions and affect nearby individuals. Indoor air can be considered happy, fearful, or angry based on semiochemicals left behind by emotional residents. It is believed that people who sniff these leftover chemical messengers respond subconsciously to these messages. A few studies have been conducted in this fascinating new area of human behavioral responses. Perhaps large fragrance companies are at this very moment conducting research on how to affect our moods and desires by managing our indoor air so as to enhance their bottom lines. At least one Japanese company enriched the air in its corporate offices with stimulating botanical scents. They used citrus in the morning, followed by cedar and cypress fragrances later in the day, to reduce worker stress levels. The chemically augmented air was claimed to increase worker productivity and corporate profits. For now, I think I'll use bouquets of fresh flowers set out on my dining-room table.

Odors in the environment, such as those from plants and their flowers, can influence our moods and health. A reduction in human stress hormones was noticed by researchers when subjects were exposed to citrus odors, and to essential oils made from fragrant roses. Some people during massage treatments or aromatherapy experience a calming effect when exposed to flower scents.

In a psychological study by Rutgers researcher Jeannette Haviland-Jones, subjects were exposed to low concentrations of odors experienced subliminally so that the subjects would not be able to consciously recognize a particular odor. The subliminal odors included Chanel No. 5 perfume, Johnson & Johnson baby powder, and the floral scents of roses and gardenias. Participants used significantly more "enjoyment words" if true flower scents were present. The low-concentration floral odors increased feelings of enjoyment compared to air infused with synthetic perfumes or baby powders. Confronted by a stranger, participants who were exposed to floral odors were almost three times as likely to approach and touch the stranger compared to those subjects breathing synthetic odors. These findings were similar to Haviland-Jones's previous research when subjects were exposed to floral bouquets.

These clinical studies suggest that the ancient and current widespread use of decorative flowers, at home and in social gatherings, makes sense. At least since the Persians and the Egyptians, pleasant floral odors, even below perceptible concentrations, may have encouraged positive moods and socially responsible behaviors among people. Maybe from now on we will consider "healthy air" to be room or outdoor air that has been florally scented.

Now may be a good time to introduce a bit of caution. There are two kinds of modern aromatherapy. Flower-scented oils used in massages combined with other therapeutic techniques probably have positive effects on our health and moods and likely cause no harm. However, aromatherapist claims that by smelling certain essences you can be cured of specific conditions such as the plague, cancer, malaria, etc., are almost certainly false. Many unsupported claims are routinely made for scented products in human healing and welfare. Use caution and common sense when using these substances.

Flowers Make Us Smile!

When you present people with a flower or a bouquet, their first reaction is to bring the blossoms close to their face and smell them. While they are inhaling the pleasant aroma, their lips part and they flash a knowing, toothy smile, the kind referred to by researchers as a genuine or Duchenne smile. Psychological research is yielding tantalizing glimpses into our long associations with flowers. Flowers evoke positive psychological responses, promote happiness, decrease social distance, enhance our living and work spaces, and may play a role in improving our long-term memories.

Öhman, Dimberg, and Öst in their 1985 study used photographs of snakes as possible fear stimuli, and pictures of flowers for possible neutral stimuli. However, they found that flowers were not neutral at all. Subjects viewing the floral images produced zygomatic muscle activity (smiles), which they reported as positive responses. The researchers may have been some of the first to experimentally study the human response when viewing or being given flowers.

Human and Flower Coevolution? Who Is in Control?

Selfishly, we believe that humans are in control of everything that happens. We believe we manage plant and animal domestication. Ten thousand years ago, inhabitants within the Fertile Crescent domesticated grasses, peas, olive trees, and many of the animals that feed us. We enjoy the fruits and seeds of animal-pollinated crops (apples, pears, pumpkins, cherries, etc.), contributing about 35 percent of the annual global human diet. We plant them, they grow and bear fruit, end of story, right? Well, maybe not. A number of scientists believe that flowering plants have more control over us than we think. Just who has domesticated whom? Perhaps it's time for a new look at human and flower ecology and coevolution.

One new thinker is Jeannette Haviland-Jones, discussed above. Haviland-Jones and her colleagues proposed that "plant-human coevolution has been based on the emotional rewards that flowers provide, just as companion animals provide an emotional reward and reduce stress." The idea that emotions play a role in evolution comes from one of the pioneers in the field of emotions research. The late Silvan Tomkins claimed, "Man is one of those animals whose individual survival and group reproduction rests heavily on social responsiveness and mutual enjoyment."

Haviland-Jones and her colleagues have proposed a new explanation of plant-human coevolution, for why we like, respond to, and care for cultivated flowers. Other researchers suggest that we enjoy flowers because of innate preferences for their perfect symmetry or an inborn love of all nature. Haviland-Jones believes that humans and cultivated flowers need one another. Flowers fill a positive emotional niche. In turn, flower seeds are collected, sown, grown, and protected by us. The reproductive fitness of plants was enhanced when they encountered and began to rely upon us for their care.

We humans depend upon wild and domesticated organisms for our health and happiness (often termed ecosystem services), but we rarely consider how animals (except pets) may depend upon us. This is true not just for large animals, but for the countless beneficial microorganisms (gut symbionts) that inhabit our bodies, without whose chemical secretions and other benefits we could not survive.

Does this type of coevolution occur in nature? Recently (2000), Otto von Helversen found that certain bat flowers had floral scents containing sulfur compounds. These mimicked the sex pheromones of the bats themselves, ones used in sexual recognition during bat sex parties, during which the flowers are visited and pollinated.

Or think of highly domesticated animals, especially our pet dogs and cats. A lot has happened in the thirty thousand or so years that humans and dogs have roamed together. Wolves were camp followers and began early to read our emotions, understanding our human ways. Maybe you have read the pouplar book *Inside of a Dog* by Alexandra Horowitz? Quickly, on an evolutionary time scale, wolves became dogs. One of a domesticated dog's "duties," like that of flowers, is to ensure our happiness and reduce our stress levels. In contrast, we haven't created wildy different honey bee breeds, but simply given them comfy wooden boxes, surrogate bee trees, to live inside, while we go about robbing their honey. We have, however, drastically modified almost all garden flowers from their wild ancestors.

Flowers, whether living in pots or flower beds, have taken on a new cultural and evolutionary role as our companion plants. Plenty of us, millions of gardeners and floral caretakers, water, feed, and care for them. We transport flowering plants around the world, tending to their needs, then harvesting their precious fruits and seeds. But, who is in charge, really? Is this coevolution a mutualistic dance, or are flowers simply exploiting us? Are we too naive to understand this truth? Perhaps it is the flowers who have led us along garden paths, using their seductive petaled beauty, since they were first intentionally grown, tended, and admired in ancient gardens. Have flowers induced new behaviors in humans and other species, leading to their increased seed production and dispersal, and hence the replication, survival and spread of "emotive" genes into subsequent generations of new plants? I think that flowers may have done some or all of these things as part of human cultural evolution.

The Sick Rose?

About 350,000 flowering-plant species have been described today. With the number of unrecognized species in herbarium collections and in the wild, the number of extant flowering plants could be as high as 425,000 species. Even the bookkeeping for plants already described by botanists is debated. The most floral diversity can be found in rain forests of the earth's equatorial belts. As recently as 1950, 15 percent of the earth's surface was clothed in verdant rain forests. Today, half of all rain forests have literally gone up in smoke, with losses of more than two hundred thousand acres every day. Every acre of these richest of all habitats may hold 750 kinds of trees and 1,500 flowering plants. Some estimates are that we are losing 137 plant and animal species each day, a staggering 50,000 annual extinctions due to tropical deforestation alone. Half of all the world's plants and animals live in these rain forests.

Given the above figures, it should not come as a surprise that we have lost many of our flowers even before they are discovered, appreciated, or used (e.g., vincristine for childhood leukemia). At least 80 percent of the developed world's diet originates from tropical agricultural plants. About three thousand edible fruits are found in rain forests. The Western world uses only two hundred of them, while indigenous cultures have used over two thousand. The Center for Plant Conservation at the Missouri Botanical Garden in St. Louis estimates that globally we have already lost more than 90 flowering-plant species to extinction. At the time of writing (2016), about 20 to 25 percent of the 350,000 flowering plants species worldwide (some 70,000 to 88,000) appear to be critically endangered, endangered, or vulnerable, and this number could easily double over the remainder of the century, with many species lost, if present downward trends continue. In the United States and Canada, the IUCN categories of critically endangered, endangered, and vulnerable roughly correspond to G1 and G2 designations in NatureServe parlance, which is our local (US) classification. Recent estimates by researcher Anne Francis calculate that the G1 and G2 combined numbers for the United States and Canada include about 16 percent threatened species of our native flowering plants. As terrifying as the loss of 20 to 25 percent of all flowering plants species would be, it's important to remember that plant conservation can be a bit more hopeful than is the case for threatened insects and other animals, since plants, through intensive cultivation, seed banking, cryopreservation, and tissue culture, can be preserved in much higher numbers than that dire estimate would imply. Through a combination of these methods and an experimental approach to them, we *could* save virtually all species of wild plants and our crops that are in existence now. We certainly should have that plant conservation ideal as our global long-term goal.

What will plant losses be like in another twenty-five or fifty years? Will unbroken tracts of rain forests exist anywhere? In the United States, forty-two hundred species have federal or state endangerment status. Humans are the culprits. Biologist Edward O. Wilson stated that rampant anthropogenic species extinctions happening now are what future generations are most likely to remember and least likely to forgive us for. What were we thinking, and why didn't we care? Where was our biophilia?

Flowers are only an ephemeral link in the life history of a flowering plant, but the critical first step for what follows. You need a flower to make a fruit with seeds representing the next generation. Conservationists, environmentalists, and land managers need to recognize when a link in the conservation process breaks. Botanists find out why a link is broken, and then conservation biologists apply various remedies to fix it. These conservation measures can be as simple as enacting protective laws, removing an introduced herbivore, or protecting critical remaining plant habitats, or as complex as eliminating a disease agent or reintroducing a rare plant, and its pollinators, to its former homelands.

Many examples of rare and endangered plants appear around the world. These include most of the native flowering plants in Hawaii, especially the lobelioids that are dependent upon curved-bill avian pollinators such as the crimson 'I'iwi that we met in an earlier chapter. Broken relationships are also to be found in the low reproductive rates in the rare lady slipper orchids (*Calypso* spp.). Slipper orchids are pollinated by bumble bees in American peat bogs or montane habitats such as those in the Colorado Rockies. The white flowers of bear grass (*Xerophyllum tenax*) are stolen by plant poachers in the Pacific Northwest; thus like some rare orchids, they are threatened by overharvesting.

The yellow Missouri bladderpod (*Physaria filiformis*), a threatened species, is confined to hilltop glades in the Ozarks and endangered by encroaching housing developments. Across the plains of Canada and the Midwestern US corn belt, weedy plants, milkweeds in the genus *Asclepias*, are being plowed under or slammed with herbicides and other "chemical chain saws" alongside irrigation ditches. To many farmers, these are only noxious weeds to be dug out or sprayed upon every encounter. Fortunately, these antiquated views are changing. For migrating monarch butterflies, and scores of bees, wasps, and other pollinators, native milkweeds are their essential food resources. For the monarchs, each clump of milkweed is a nectar refueling site, a way station on their multigenerational, two-thousand-mile migrations from the Canadian prairies, across America's heartlands, over the Gulf of Mexico, to their eleven-thousand-foot-high winter roosts among the branches of oyamel firs in the mountains of Michoacán, Mexico. The 2014/15 winter saw the lowest number of overwintering monachs ever. Monarch migrations are on their way to becoming an endangered epiphenomenon, unless we act now.

In Missouri, Mead's milkweed (*Asclepias meadii*), studied by botanists Peter Bernhardt and Retha Edens-Meier, is threatened by an introduced fungus that attacks the dainty milkweed blossoms. Fungal diseases turn the delightful flowers of campions (*Silene*) into spore makers instead of pollen makers. Many beautiful flowering plants have been brought to the threshold of extinction because they are no longer reproducing or are now suffering drastic declines in the number of seeds produced on the plants. You simply can't make seeds without flowers, or without the help of pollinators in most cases. Unmanaged pollinators are often better and less expensive pollinators than human surrogates in the form of conservation biologists and their hordes of ever-willing volunteers. The rural Chinese women and children now climbing among fruit tree branches dabbing pollen on stigmas with paintbrushes is not a viable economic model nor should it ever be for any part of the world.

Some species such as the beautiful Franklin (*Franklinia alatamaha*), a small tree first collected in 1765 by John Bartram as seeds from specimens growing along the banks of the Altamaha River in Georgia, are now extinct in the wild. Patriotically, the genus *Franklinia* was named after Benjamin Franklin by a Bartram cousin in 1785. The lovely *Franklinia* has large, fragrant, white flowers much like *Camellia* flowers, but sweetly scented, reminiscent of a honeysuckle. Today, you rarely find the plants growing in cultivation, and gardeners complain that the plant is susceptible to a root-rot disease and difficult to cultivate. *Franklinia* lives on only in captivity behind garden gates, and frozen in liquid nitrogen canisters within US national seed banks.

Can Humans Heal Nature?

Dangling from a rope, in climbing gear, a young conservationist rapels backward down a two-thousand-foot-high sea cliff along the Nā Pali Coast of Kaua'i in the Hawaiian archipelago. He moves carefully toward isolated individuals of a strange, unworldly looking plant. Like a pollinator, he delivers pollen (but purposefully), powdery grains stored in a glass vial and applied with an artist's watercolor brush. The rare plants look like cabbages atop baseball bats. This rare Hawaiian plant is *Brighamia insignis* (alula), a critically endangered plant in the bellflower family. Broad, succulent leaves form a rosette atop tapering stalks three to sixteen feet tall. Brought to near extinction by the powerful hurricane Iniki (1992), browsing by feral goats, and human disturbance, it is now literally a cliff-hanger. There may be only five populations totaling forty-five to sixty-five specimens left in the wild. Alula's fragrant, showy, yellow flowers have a strong honeysuckle-like fragrance. They bloom at night, offering nectar deep within three- to five-inch-long floral tubes.

Historically, *Brighamia* plants appear to have been pollinated by a native Sandwich Islands moth, the green sphinx moth (*Tinostoma smaragditis*), once believed to be extinct, but which now occurs only in isolated, small populations far from its host flower. Without its moth, *Brighamia* must be hand-pollinated to produce any seeds. Ironically, although protected under the US endangered species act, *Brighamia* has become an almost-commonplace European potted houseplant after becoming a darling of plant collectors. Drastic rescue efforts in Hawaii have worked for *Brighamia*. Specimens are not only being hand-pollinated, but seedlings raised in greenhouses are now being reintroduced into former habitats. And two introduced hawk moths (*Manduca quinquemaculata* and *M. sexta*) seem to be substituting for *Brighamia*'s endemic moth pollinator. Humans, however, can't step in as surrogate pollinator superheroes for every imperiled flower around the world. We must strive to protect habitats, flowering plants, and their coevolved animal pollinator guilds by changing a few human bad habits.

Around the world thousands of wildflower species are threatened with extinction. Many are now extinct. Flowering plants should be protected for their own sake. If an economic rationalization must exist to conserve flowers, we needn't look farther than our own home gardens. Many endangered blooms around the world are ancestors of our most beloved garden and cut flowers. If flowering plants are truly our sidekick companion plants, then we must think about caring for them and their wild relatives. The daily news or NGO annual reports need not be filled only with depressing statistics. Dedicated scientists, naturalists, students, citizen scientists, and volunteers are busily planting, transplanting, and caring for rare plants. Conservation ideas are spreading, and people are now coming to the aid of flowering plants, fellow riders on our planet, a singular but fertile pale blue dot in the vast cosmos. Some plants, once facing extinction, now have bright futures due to the actions of concerned people.

By planting native wildflowers or heirloom varieties in pollinator-friendly private and public gardens, by not using insecticides or herbicides, and by joining grassroots public campaigns and organizations such as the North American Pollinator Protection Campaign, the Pollinator Partnership, Monarch Watch, Make Way for Monarchs, the Xerces Society, and others devoted to protecting native plants along with their pollinators, all of us can make significant efforts to conserve flowers and their animal pollinators. These may be conservation baby steps, but combined across the globe, they can quickly afford lasting protection. We can become plant stewards, starting right in our homes, backyards, and parklands.

We can all help by buying organic flowers, especially those certified as green by various agencies. We can support local flower producers who raise their crops without contaminating insecticides, fungicides, and fertilizers, which ultimately pollute our groundwater and soils. Buying organic flowers helps ensure safe working conditions on flower farms, enabling living wages and other benefits, along with promoting social and environmental justice, truly caring for the workers along with their flowers.

The relationship between flowers and people has been a long and wondrous mutual journey. Flowers arose during the early Cretaceous period while dinosaurs looked on, munching their leaves, flowers, and fruits. Our distant hominid ancestors learned to recognize flowers as the harbingers of spring and their luscious fruits that followed. The tastiest and most nutritious of human and wildlife foods are fruits, berries, and seeds. Natufians living in the Middle East over ten thousand years ago laid their dead upon floral biers. We still honor and gift one another with vibrant blooms. Flowers scent the air and our bodies. Our homes and offices are decorated with their cut stems and with potted plants. We garden with flowers and they soothe our minds and bodies. They inspire us. We write about flowers and choose them as subjects in our paintings and photographs. Whether flowers or people are in control of this relationship is perhaps debatable. Nevertheless, by caring for them, we learn that flowers sustain and feed us, enriching our lives.

If flowers heal us, shouldn't we also try to heal flowers? Can we meet the numerous environmental challenges, including desertification, deforestation, and other habitat alterations along with climate changes, ones of our own making? Will people heal nature? It's not all gloom and doom in our wildlands, parks, and cities. I'm optimistic that this generation and future ones can coexist with nature, that species losses can be slowed and eventually stabilized. All is not lost, there is abundant hope. Flowers and people need and depend upon one another for mutual survival.

ACKNOWLEDGMENTS

For Kay Richter, my life partner, for her unfailing support, for carefully reading and commenting upon the entire manuscript and offering her insightful advice on the text and photographs, I express my profound love, respect, and heartfelt thanks. Our relationship flowered along with this book. We enjoy sharing many experiences watching bees, birds, and bats visit flowers, while often photographing them together. Please know that *The Reason for Flowers* would not exist, could not have been written, without your untiring love.

To my literary agent, Judith Riven, go thanks for her encouragement while developing the *TRFF* book proposal, contract negotiations with Scribner, and during the writing stages of this book. I thank you, Judith, for believing in me and making this book happen.

I gratefully acknowledge Colin Harrison, my editor at Scribner, for his advice, guidance, and fine editing, his devotion to the craft, and for believing in the book. Thank you, Colin. Katrina Diaz at Scribner has my thanks for her assistance with book production, along with insights about chapter frontispieces and interior art. To Dan Cuddy, our production editor, and Steve Boldt, our copy editor, I share my gratitude, along with everyone at Scribner, in producing this elegant book in a timely fashion. My sincere thanks to senior publicist Gweneth Stansfield and Kara Watson for their combined marketing acumen. I thank those individuals who kindly penned jacket blurbs for me.

I especially thank those who read the entire manuscript and offered invaluable advice. They include: Colin Harrison, Peter Bernhardt, Retha Edens-Meier, Kay Richter, David Roubik, and Judith Riven. I sincerely thank Peter Bernhardt and Retha Edens-Meier of St. Louis University for their careful reading and Beth Rashbaum for hers of the early chapters. I particularly acknowledge Peter Bernhardt and Retha Edens-Meier for their diligence in botanical fact-checking. Peter's encyclopedic knowledge of Greek and Roman mythology, floral biology, the Australian biota, and all things botanical has been invaluable as has his collegiality as a fellow pollination biologist for many decades.

I am grateful to special-collections Missouri Botanical Gardens librarian

Douglas Holland, and MOBOT itself, for digital scanning and permission to reprint the antiquarian images.

I owe many thanks to my Tucson friend, fellow Malay traveler, illustrator, and artist Paul Mirocha, for his fine flower and pollinator renderings in my books. Thanks for the Stargazer, Paul, reminding us all to keep looking up.

For mentoring during my college years, my heartfelt thanks go to Claris E. Jones Jr. (CSUF, biology) and Robbin W. Thorp (UC Davis, entomology) as my graduate advisors in pollination and bee studies. Gene, you started me along this path on a lifelong journey of floral and pollinator discovery, starting with our 1972 O.T.S. Fundamentals of Ecology course. I fondly remember the cloud forest at San Vito de Java on the Costa Rica/Panama border, although I still have not developed a fondness for peanut butter sandwiches. A special thanks to Gene Jones, Karl Niklas, Peter Bernhardt, Amots Dafni, and the late Grady Webster and Herbert and Irene Baker, for being my botanical mentors and muses over the years. To Bayard Brattstrom, I express my appreciation for his friendship, and for the use of his Kay Sonagraph, when I took my first steps listening to bees sonicate flowers.

To my fellow pollination ecologists, melittologists, artists, and writers I especially thank: David W. Roubik, John Alcock, Gary Paul Nabhan, James Cane, Bryan Danforth, the late George Eickwort, Karl J. Niklas, Laurence Packer, Terry Griswold, John Ascher, Jack Neff, Gretchen LeBuhn, Jerome G. Rozen, Ron McGinley, Charles Michener, Mike Engel, Paul Cooper, William Schaffer, George Poinar, Justin Schmidt, the late Hayward Spangler, Robert Raguso, Daniel Papaj, Judith Bronstein, Annie Leonard, Wulfila Gronenberg, Avery Russell, Jake Francis, Felicity Muth, Sophie Cardinal, Ricardo Kriebel, Diana Jolles, Diana Cohn, Thomas Seeley, Scott Camazine, Paul Mirocha, Steven Thoenes, M. K. O'Rourke, Owen K. Davis, Chris O'Toole, Joseph Scheer, Michael Wilson, and Dató Makhdzir Bin Mardan for their camaraderie over the years, and providing the personal anecdotes and published information for many of the topics that I discuss.

My thanks are extended to Luca Turin, the "emperor of scent," for his musings on floral scents and the modern perfume industry, and for supplying us (the Gronenberg laboratory) with pure deuterated molecules for testing. Thanks to Rick Schoelhorn of Proven Winners LLC and to Jianping Ren for their insights into the world of horticultural flower breeding, methods, and field trials. A big thanks to Conrad Labandeira of the Smithsonian Institution, for information about fossilized insect pollinators and for his insights into their suspected floral relationships.

I thank the flower booth workers and shop owners whom I met and interviewed during a visit to the Los Angeles Flower Market, especially Garcia and Martin.

I am grateful to Israeli archaeologist Dani Nadel, for his friendship during a recent Tucson sabbatical visit and information on the Mt. Carmel Natufian flower burials he's excavated. Thanks to psychologist and professor Jeannette Haviland-Jones of Rutgers, for sharing with me her published and unpublished research on the roles of flowers in keeping us mentally healthy, and smiling. I thank Rhiannon Rowlands for her comments on Greek deities and their flowers.

My sincere thanks to Hollywood film director and producer Louie Schwartzberg and line producer Grady Candler, for the opportunity to work alongside them on the Disneynature feature film *Wings of Life* and for Louis's technical advice, helping me create floral time-lapse images. For pleasant Sonoran Desert interludes taking DSLR stills, and capturing other floral time-lapse sequences, I thank fellow photographers, cinematographers, and Tucsonans Keith Brust and Thomas Wiewandt, for their enduring friendships and photographic advice over the years.

I thank my partners in pollinator and flowering-plant conservation, especially Gary Paul Nabhan, Retha Edens-Meier, Laurie Adams, Paul Growald, Vicki Wojcik, Orley Taylor, Mark Moffett, Rogel Villanueva-Gutiérrez, Gordon Frankie, Gary Krupnick, Matthew Shepherd, Mace Vaughan, Peter Bernhardt, Bonnie Harper-Lore, and Peggy Olwell, for keeping me informed about what they and others are doing to conserve and protect the worlds' flowering plants and their pollinators.

To all, and especially to those who have made important differences and contributions to my life and learning, I express my heartfelt gratitude and thanks. I can't possibly name everyone. But, as in all efforts, a performance if you will, like the solitary endeavor of writing a nonfiction book aimed for a science-appreciative readership, any and all omissions, errors, or misstatements of facts, are entirely my own, and I take full responsibility for them. I hope you, gentle reader, are inspired to go outdoors, to appreciate and explore the largely hidden world of flowers and their animal go-betweens. Inhale deeply, while letting the flowers' secret weapon—their beauty, forms, colors, and scents—be your guide.

Finally, I wish to acknowledge and thank my daughters, Marlyse and Melissa, for making my life complete and for our shared experiences among the ochre landscapes, native wild flowers, bees, and other pollinators of Arizona's Sonoran Desert. May you never tire of these natural splendors.

APPENDIX 1: FLOWER STATISTICS

US Customer Trends on Buying Flowers	
Percentages based on personal consumer purchases of fresh flowers, flowering houseplants, green plants, and bedding/garden plants. Data from the Society of American Florists for 2005.	
What Are Consumers Buying?	
Outdoor bedding/garden plants	46%
Fresh flowers (cut)	34
Flowering/green houseplants	20
Who's Buying?	
Women	79%
Men	21
For Fresh Flowers (Cut) Only	
Women	65%
Men	35
For Whom Are They Buying?	
Self	63%
Gift	37
For Fresh Flowers Only	
Self	33%
Gift	67
Why Are They Buying?	
Calendar occasions	14%
Noncalendar occasions	86
For What Calendar Occasions Are They Buying?	
Christmas/Hanukkah	30%
Mother's Day	24
Valentine's Day	20
Easter/Passover	13
Thanksgiving	6
Other	7
For What Noncalendar Occasions Are They Buying?	
No special occasion	50%
Home decoration	13

Birthday	5
Sympathy/memorial	5
Anniversary/love	3
Get well	2
Other	22
US Flower Industry Overview	
Industry Segments	
Retail florist shops (2011)	15,307 stores
Estimated average annual florist sales, per retailer (2011)	$362,318
Floral wholesalers	530
Domestic floriculture growers (in top fifteen states)	5,419
Fresh-flower growers	280
Potted flowering-plant growers	1,014
Foliage growers	790
Bedding/garden plant growers	1,537
Fresh-greens growers	142
Potted herbaceous perennial-plant growers	1,241
Where Do US Flowers Come From?	
Top Flower-Exporting Countries (to USA, by Value, 2012)	
Colombia	78%
Ecuador	15
Mexico	2
Other	2
Thailand	1
Guatemala	1
Netherlands	1
Note: Imports account for about 64 percent of fresh flowers sold by dollar volume in the United States. Statistics from the Society of American Florists.	
Top Fresh-Flower (Cut and Live Plants) Growing States	
California	76%
Washington	6
New Jersey	4
Oregon	4
Hawaii	2
North Carolina	2
Florida	1
Note: Data as of May 2013 from the Society of American Florists.	

APPENDIX 2: COOKING WITH FLOWERS: SELECTED RECIPES

Cheese-Stuffed Sonoran Squash Blossoms

10–12 freshly picked male blossoms from pumpkin or zucchini squash
1 cup all-purpose flour
1 egg yolk
1 cup water, tap or sparkling
½ teaspoon salt
⅓ cup goat cheese, at room temperature. Ricotta or Mexican Cotija
    cheeses can be substituted for the goat cheese.
2 tablespoons cream cheese, at room temperature
2 teaspoons heavy whipping cream
1 green onion or chive, diced
¼ teaspoon ground black pepper and/or smoked paprika powder
¼ teaspoon ground cumin (optional)
2 tablespoons chopped fresh basil or cilantro leaves
Canola oil or other vegetable oil for frying

Carefully wash and drain the blossoms. Remove the central stalk. In a medium bowl, whisk the flour, egg, water, and salt until smooth. In a small bowl, blend and mix the goat cheese, cream cheese, whipping cream, green onion, ground spices, and chopped basil or cilantro until smooth. Season with salt and pepper. Spoon 2 teaspoons of the cheese filling into each of the opened blossoms. Close the petals by twisting and gently pinching them closed. Fill a 10–inch, heavy skillet about one-third full with the cooking oil. Bring the oil to 350–375 degrees F. Dip the stuffed squash blossoms into the flour-and-egg batter to thinly coat. Fry quickly for about 2–3 minutes, turning once with tongs until crispy and golden. Drain the blossoms on a paper towel. Serve with your favorite marinara sauce for dipping. Allow 30–40 minutes for preparation and cooking. The fried squash blossoms can also be added to a mixed-greens salad.

Candied Flowers

Candied flowers make a delightful garnish to many dishes and are delicious.

1 egg white
100-proof vodka
Superfine granulated (not powdered) sugar
Violet, borage, pansy, Johnny-jump-up, or rose petals
Wire cake rack or similar support
Parchment baking paper
Fine, soft artist's paintbrush

In a small bowl beat the egg white to a froth. Add 2 or 3 drops of vodka and mix. Put some of the sugar in a shallow bowl. The flowers wilt quickly, so pick and candy a few at a time. Cover the cake rack with the parchment paper. Hold the flowers one at a time by their stems. Dip the brush into the egg-white mixture and carefully paint all of the petals and other surfaces, front and back. Gently dust the surfaces with the fine sugar. Set the flowers aside to dry. Place the finished flowers in a warm place, or in a food dehydrator set on low heat. Store the brittle blossoms in an airtight container until used.

Flower Butter

1 cup flower petals (whole or diced) from any edible flowers
½ pound unsalted butter
¼ teaspoon flavoring, such as almond extract

Mince the cleaned flower petals and mix into the softened butter. Add the almond extract. Cover with plastic wrap and let sit at room temperature for several hours. The butter can be stored and used for up to 2 weeks if refrigerated, or as long as 3 months if frozen. Flower butter can be formed or pressed into butter molds.

APPENDIX 3:
AFTER BRINGING THEM HOME:
CARING FOR YOUR CUT FLOWERS

How many days flowers last when displayed in a vase, whether they came from your garden or local market, depends on the care they were given previously by growers and distributors, and what you do for them at home. Once cut from their parent plants, blooms need a great deal of care to maintain freshness and appearance, their so-called vase life. Their stems are often dipped in a citric acid solution to inhibit bacterial growth, and they may be hydrated for six to twenty-four hours in water. They may be stored in buckets of cold water (e.g., thirty-four degrees Fahrenheit for roses) along with chilling during shipment and once at your local florist shop. A rose, with an average cut life of twenty-one days, should have ten to fourteen days of vase life in your home or workplace.

Use fresh water, commercial flower food, and the following tips to enhance your enjoyment of cut flowers. Commercially available flower food contains sucrose (sugar), which gives the flowers a source of energy to make up for the loss of leaves. An acidifier brings the water's pH closer to that of the natural cell sap and helps stabilize the color of your flowers. Flower food also contains a bacterial inhibitor to help retard the growth of bacteria (cloudiness) in the water. Bacteria and fungi can plug up the water-transporting cells in the flower stems.

Here are some helpful guidelines based upon my experience and research by the staff at Grower Direct. An extensive table of vase life and ethylene sensitivity can be found on the author's website.

Some Do's and Don'ts of Fresh-Flower Care

Do's
- Always use a clean vase and pure water. Change or top up water daily if possible!
- When first placing flowers in water, use warm (100–110 degrees F) water, since this will be absorbed (along with the plant food) better than cold water.
- Always use commercial fresh-flower food (packet of white powder). Use the recommended amount of food; don't overfeed your blooms.
- After purchase, cut off at least one inch of the flower stems with a sharp

310

knife. Slanted cuts are best. This can be done with the stems submerged in a bowl of water (for purists!).

- Remove any flowers that look less than completely fresh. This will help keep the remaining flowers in the display looking great longer.

Don'ts

- Never use a homemade substitute for flower food, including aspirin, Viagra tablets, soda pop, bleach, or copper pennies. They don't work, or not as well as the commercial food packets.
- Avoid sodium, fluoride, and minerals in water. Sodium in soft water is toxic to roses and carnations. Fluoride may be great for preventing dental cavities, but it is harmful to *Gerbera*, *Gladiolus*, and *Freesia* blooms. Hard (mineralized) water can also shorten the life of cut blooms.
- Never remove all the leaves from the stems.
- Never place your flowers near fresh fruit (especially apples) or cigarette smoke. Both produce ethylene gas, which will shorten floral life.
- Never place flowers in direct sunlight or other sources of excessive heat. This is why florists store their flowers in cold rooms.
- Don't use commercial flower food in lead-crystal or metal vases. The acid in the flower food will react with the metal.

APPENDIX 4:
ONLINE RESOURCES FOR WILDFLOWER AND POLLINATOR CONSERVATION ORGANIZATIONS

North American Pollinator Protection Campaign (http://pollinator.org/nappc//index.html)

The Pollinator Partnership (http://www.pollinator.org)

The Xerces Society (http://www.xerces.org/pollinator-conservation/)

Monarch Watch (http://www.monarchwatch.org)

Make Way for Monarchs (http://makewayformonarchs.org/i/)

Bat Conservation International (http://www.batcon.org)

Center for Plant Conservation (http://www.centerforplantconservation.org/)

IUCN World Conservation Union (http://www.iucn.org/)

Center for Biological Diversity (http://www.biologicaldiversity.org/)

Plant Conservation Alliance (http://www.nps.gov/plants/)

United States Botanic Garden (http://www.usbg.gov/plant-conservation)

Lady Bird Johnson Wildflower Center (http://www.wildflower.org/organizations/)

The Smithsonian National Museum of Natural History Department of Botany (http://botany.si.edu/)

USFWS Endangered Species Information Gateway (http://fws.gov/endangered)

Missouri Botanical Garden (http://www.missouribotanicalgarden.org/)

Canadian Botanical Conservation Network (http://www.bgci.org/canada/Canadian_botanical_couser/)

Society for Conservation Biology (http://conbio.org/)

NOTES AND SOURCES

Suggested Readings

From the volumes in my scholar's library are a few dozen flower and pollinator books that I consult often as references in my research as a pollination ecologist studying flowers, bees, and other pollinators. Some of these are highly technical scientific works, while others are intended for a scientifically engaged and curious audience. I offer these suggested readings for your own journey of discovery into the world of flowers, their pollinators, and the people who love them.

Cathy Barash, *Edible Flowers: From Garden to Palate* (Golden, CO: Fulcrum Publishing, 1995), 250 pp.

Peter Bernhardt, *The Rose's Kiss: A Natural History of Flowers* (Washington, DC, and Covelo, CA: Island Press/Shearwater Books, 1999), 267 pp.

———, *Gods and Goddesses in the Garden: Greco-Roman Mythology and the Scientific Names of Plants* (New Brunswick, NJ: Rutgers University Press, 2008), 239 pp.

Stephen Buchmann and Gary Paul Nabhan, *The Forgotten Pollinators* (Washington, DC, and Covelo, CA: Island Press/Shearwater Books, 1996), 292 pp.

Stephen Buchmann and Banning Repplier, *Letters from the Hive: An Intimate History of Bees, Honey, and Humankind* (New York: Bantam Books, 2005), 275 pp.

Retha Edens-Meier and Peter Bernhardt, eds., *Darwin's Orchids: Then and Now* (Chicago: University of Chicago Press, 2014), 419 pp.

Loren Eiseley, *How Flowers Changed the World* (San Francisco: Sierra Club Books, 1996), 32 pp.

Knut Faegri and Leendert van der Pijl, *The Principles of Pollination Ecology* (Toronto: Pergamon Press, 1966), 248 pp.

Theodore Fleming and John Kress, *The Ornaments of Life: Coevolution and Conservation in the Tropics* (Chicago: University of Chicago Press, 2013), 588 pp.

Gordon Frankie, Robbin Thorp, Rollin Coville, and Barbara Ertter (with Mary Schindler), *California Bees & Blooms: A Guide for Gardeners and Naturalists* (Berkeley, CA: Heyday, 2014), 296 pp.

Roy Genders, *Scented Flora of the World* (London: Robert Hall, 1994), 560 pp.

Jack Goody, *The Culture of Flowers* (Cambridge: Cambridge University Press, 1993), 462 pp.

E. Buckner Hollingsworth, *Flower Chronicles: The Legend and Lore of Fifteen Garden Favorites* (Chicago: University of Chicago Press, 2004), 302 pp.

Stephen Kellert and Edward O. Wilson, eds., *The Biophilia Hypothesis* (Washington, DC: Island Press, 1993), 484 pp.

Gretchen LeBuhn, *Field Guide to the Common Bees of California: Including Bees of the Western United States* (Berkeley: University of California Press, 2013), 175 pp.

David Lee, *Nature's Palette: The Science of Plant Color* (Chicago: University of Chicago Press, 2010), 409 pp.

Charles Michener, *The Bees of the World* (Baltimore: Johns Hopkins University Press, 2007), 992 pp.

Andrew Moore and Anna Pavord, eds., *Flower Power: The Meaning of Flowers in Art* (London: Philip Wilson Publishers, 2003), 96 pp.

Cathy Newman, *Perfume: The Art and Science of Scent* (Washington, DC: National Geographic Society, 1998), 157 pp.

David Roubik, *Ecology and Natural History of Tropical Bees* (Cambridge: Cambridge University Press, 1989), 514 pp.

Amy Stewart, *Flower Confidential: The Good, the Bad, and the Beautiful* (Chapel Hill, NC: Algonquin Books, 2007), 306 pp.

Luca Turin, *The Science of Scent: Adventures in Perfume and the Science of Smell* (New York: Ecco, 2006), 207 pp.

Paul Williams, Robbin Thorp, Leif Richardson, and Sheila Colla, *Bumble Bees of North America: An Identification Guide* (Princeton, NJ, and Oxford: Princeton University Press, 2014), 208 pp.

Pat Willmer, *Pollination and Floral Ecology* (Princeton, NJ: Princeton University Press, 2011), 778 pp.

Chapter Sources

The following bibliography is a mix of citations including books, scientific-journal and magazine articles, edited volumes, and website URLs. They include some but not all of the bibliographic sources used during my research and writing. Primary scientific articles can be located using keyword searches with the Google Scholar search engine. Reference librarians will be glad to assist in your bibliophilic searchers. The main sources have been shortened. The complete source list can be found on the author's website.

Chapter 1: Attracting Attention

Pollen as a floral reward in angiosperms: Pat Willmer, *Pollination and Floral Ecology* (Princeton, NJ, and Oxford: Princeton University Press, 2011), 154–89.

Nectar as a floral reward in angiosperms: Ibid., 190–220.

Other floral rewards: Ibid., 221–33.

Oil-producing flowers: Stephen Buchmann, "The Ecology of Oil Flowers and Their Bees," *Annual Review of Ecology and Systematics* 18 (1987): 343–69.

Euglossine orchid bees and neotropical orchids: David Roubik and Paul Hansen, *Orchid Bees of Tropical America: Biology and Field Guide* (San Jose, Costa Rica: INBio, 2004).

Charles Darwin and orchids: Retha Edens-Meier and Peter Bernhardt, eds., *Darwin's Orchids: Then and Now* (Chicago: University of Chicago Press, 2014).

The ecology of floral scents: Robert Raguso, "Wake Up and Smell the Roses: The Ecology and Evolution of Floral Scent," *Annual Review of Ecology, Evolution, and Systematics* 39 (2008): 549–69.

Electrostatic charges on bees: Eric Erickson and Stephen Buchmann, "Electrostatics and Pollination," in *Handbook of Experimental Pollination Biology*, eds. C. Jones and R. Little (New York: S & AE Division of Van Nostrand Reinhold Company, 1983), 173–84.

Floral pigments and color: David Lee, *Nature's Palette: The Science of Plant Color* (Chicago and London: University of Chicago Press, 2010).

Ultraviolet floral patterns as cues for bees: Eugene Jones and Stephen Buchmann, "Ultraviolet Floral Patterns as Functional Orientation Cues in Hymenopterous Pollination Systems," *Animal Behaviour* 22, no. 2 (1974): 481–85.

Ultraviolet signaling by plants and animals: Robert Silberglied, "Communication in the Ultraviolet," *Annual Review of Ecology, Evolution, and Systematics* 10 (1979): 373–98.

Color vision in insects: Adriana Briscoe and Lars Chittka, "The Evolution of Color Vision in Insects," *Annual Review of Entomology* 46 (2001): 471–510.

Chapter 2: Flowers and Their Ancestors

Early nonflowering plants and angiosperms: Karl Niklas, *The Evolutionary Biology of Plants* (Chicago and London: University of Chicago Press, 1997).

What were the earliest angiosperm flowers like?: Peter Endress and James Doyle, "Reconstructing the Ancestral Angiosperm Flower and Its Initial Specializations," *American Journal of Botany* 96, no. 1 (2009): 22–66.

The first flowers: Peter Bernhardt, *The Rose's Kiss* (Washington, DC, and Covelo, CA: Island Press/Shearwater Books, 1999), 221–33.

The origin of angiosperms: James Doyle, "Molecular and Fossil Evidence on the Origin of Angiosperms," *Annual Review of Earth and Planetary Sciences* 40 (2012): 301–26.

Ancient scorpion flies as early pollinators of flowering plants: Scorpion flies may have been pollinating seed ferns, conifers, and other gymnosperms during the Jurassic as early as 167 mya. For more see Doug Ren et al., "A Probable Pollination Mode before Angiosperms: Eurasian, Long-Proboscid Scorpionflies," *Science* 326, no. 5954 (2009): 840–47.

Darwin's abominable mystery: William Friedman, "The Meaning of Darwin's Abominable Mystery," *American Journal of Botany* 96, no. 1 (2009): 5–21.

Earliest bees from Burmese amber: Bryan Danforth and George Poinar, "Morphology, Classification, and Antiquity of *Melittosphex burmensis* (Apoidea: Melittosphecidae) and Implications for Early Bee Evolution," *Journal of Paleontology* 85, no. 5 (2011): 882–91.

Earliest flowers were tiny: A representative paper on a small Cretaceous "charcoalized" flower from New Jersey clay pits. Also, from an unpublished plot of floral diameters over time by Dr. Bryan Danforth. William Crepet and Kevin Nixon, "Two New Fossil Flowers of Magnoliid Affinity from the Late Cretaceous of New Jersey," *American Journal of Botany* 85, no. 9 (1998): 1273–88.

Pollination in the earliest/basal angiosperms, the ANITA group: Leonard Thien et al., "Pollination Biology of Basal Angiosperms (ANITA Grade)," *American Journal of Botany* 96, no. 1 (2009): 166–82.

The first flower?: G. Sun, David Dilcher, S. Zheng, and Z. Zhou, "In Search of the First Flower: A Jurassic Angiosperm, *Archaefructus*, from Northeast China," *Science* 282, no. 5394 (1998): 1692–95.

Ecology of tropical bees: David Roubik, *Ecology and Natural History of Tropical Bees* (Cambridge: Cambridge University Press, 1989).

Flowers, fruits, pollination mutualisms: Theodore Fleming and John Kress, *The Ornaments of Life: Coevolution and Conservation in the Tropics* (Chicago and London: University of Chicago Press, 2013).

Chapter 3: The Pollinators

An early warning on pollinator declines: Stephen Buchmann and Gary Paul Nabhan, *The Forgotten Pollinators* (Washington, DC, and Covelo, CA: Island Press/Shearwater Books, 1996).

Flies, the second most important order among anthophilous insects: B. Larson, Peter Kevan, and David Inouye, "Flies and Flowers: Taxonomic Diversity of Anthophiles and Pollinators," *Canadian Entomologist* 133, no. 4 (2001): 439–65.

Monarchs at risk?: Lincoln Brower et al., "Decline of Monarch Butterflies Overwintering in Mexico: Is the Migratory Phenomenon at Risk?," *Insect Conservation and Diversity* 5, no. 2 (2012): 95–100.

Deep flowers for long tongues: Joseph Arditti et al., "'Good Heavens What Insect Can Suck It': Charles Darwin, *Angraecum sesquipedale* and *Xanthopan morganii praedicta*," *Botanical Journal of the Linnean Society* 169, no. 3 (2012): 403–32.

Yucca flowers and their pollinating moths: Olle Pellmyr, "Yuccas, Yucca Moths, and Co-evolution: A Review," *Annals of the Missouri Botanical Garden* 90, no. 1 (2003): 35–55.

Bumble bees of North America: Paul Williams, Robbin Thorp, Leif Richardson, and Sheila Colla, *Bumble Bees of North America: An Identification Guide* (Princeton, NJ, and Oxford: Princeton University Press, 2014).

Conserving our bees: Laurence Packer, *Keeping the Bees: Why All Bees Are at Risk and What We Can Do to Save Them* (Toronto, Canada: HarperCollins, 2010).

Giving good vibrations: Stephen Buchmann, "Buzz Pollination in Angiosperms," in *Handbook of Experimental Pollination Biology*, ed. C. Jones and R. Little (New York: Scientific and Academic Editions, Van Nostrand Reinhold, 1983), 73–113.

The ecology of buzz pollination: Paul De Luca and M. Vallejo-Marín, "What's the 'Buzz' About? The Ecology and Evolutionary Significance of Buzz-Pollination," *Current Opinion in Plant Biology* 16 (2013): 1–7.

Every third bite of our food: Alexandra Klein et al., "Importance of Pollinators in Changing Landscapes for World Crops," *Proceedings of the Royal Society B, Biological Sciences* 274, no. 1608 (2007): 303–13.

Ecological services from insects: John Losey and Mace Vaughan, "The Economic Value of Ecological Services Provided by Insects," *BioScience* 56, no. 4 (2006): 311–23.

Pollination by birds: Theodore Fleming and John Kress, *The Ornaments of Life: Co-evolution and Conservation in the Tropics* (Chicago: University of Chicago Press, 2013).

Pollination by bats: Theodore Fleming, Cullen Geiselman, and John Kress, "The Evolution of Bat Pollination: A Phylogenetic Perspective," *Annals of Botany* 104, no. 6 (2009): 1017–43.

Human as pollinators: Uma Partap and Tang Ya, "The Human Pollinators of Fruit Crops in Maoxian County, Sichuan, China," *Mountain Research and Development* 32, no. 2 (2012): 176–86.

Chapter 4: Pleasure Gardens Ancient and Modern

European gardens, history: Tom Turner, *European Gardens: History, Philosophy and Design* (London: Routledge, 2011).

Ancient Egyptian gardens: Lise Manniche, *An Ancient Egyptian Herbal* (London: British Museum Press, 2006).

Gardening through the ages: Tassilo Wengel, *The Art of Gardening through the Ages* (Leipzig: Edition Leipzig, 1987).

Garden plants and Greco-Roman mythology: Peter Bernhardt, *Gods and Goddesses in the Garden: Greco-Roman Mythology and the Scientific Names of Plants* (New Brunswick, NJ: Rutgers University Press, 2008).

Gardens of ancient Pompeii: Annamaria Ciarallo, *Gardens of Pompeii* (Rome: L'Erma di Bretschneider, 2000).

Gardens of Monticello and Mount Vernon: Peter Martin, *The Pleasure Gardens of Virginia: From Jamestown to Jefferson* (Princeton, NJ: Princeton University Press, 1991).

Attracting native pollinators: Xerces Society, *Attracting Native Pollinators: The Xerces Society Guide, Protecting North America's Bees and Butterflies* (North Adams, MA: Storey Publishing, 2011).

Pollinator gardening: Xerces Society and Smithsonian Institution (anonymous), *Butterfly Gardening: Creating Summer Magic in Your Garden* (San Francisco: Sierra Clubs Books, 1998).

Moonlight gardens: Peter Loewer, *The Evening Garden: Flowers and Fragrance from Dusk till Dawn* (Portland, OR: Timber Press, 1993).

Chapter 5: Flowers for Eternity

Neanderthal flower burials: Ralph Solecki, "Shanidar IV, a Neanderthal Flower Burial in Northern Iraq," *Science* 190, no. 4217 (1975): 880–81.

Natufian flower burials: Dani Nadel et al., "Earliest Floral Grave Lining from 13,700–11,700-y-old Natufian Burials at Raqefet Cave, Mt. Carmel, Israel," *Proceedings of the National Academy of Sciences of the United States of America* 110, no. 29 (2013): 11774–78.

Mummy garlands and collars: Lise Manniche, *An Ancient Egyptian Herbal* (London: British Museum Press, 2006).

Grecian burial customs: F. Retief and L. Cilliers, "Burial Customs, the Afterlife and the Pollution of Death in Ancient Greece," *Acta Theologica* 26, no. 2 (2006): 44–61.

Roman burial practices: http://ancienthistory.about.com/od/deathafterlife/a/RomanBurial.htm.

The lotus flower in art and culture: Riklef Kandeler and Wolfram Ullrich, "Symbolism of Plants: Examples from European-Mediterranean Culture Presented with Biology and History of Art: JULY: Lotus," *Journal of Experimental Botany* 60, no. 9 (2009): 2461–64.

Flowers in Bali and the culture of flowers: Jack Goody, *The Culture of Flowers* (Cambridge: Cambridge University Press, 1993).

Mexico's Day of the Dead: Stanley Brandes, *Skulls to the Living, Bread to the Dead: The Day of the Dead in Mexico and Beyond* (Malden, MA: Wiley-Blackwell Publishing, 2006).

Victorian mourning: Sonia Bedikian, "The Death of Mourning: From Victorian Crepe to the Little Black Dress," *Omega: Journal of Death and Dying* 57, no. 1 (2008): 35–52.

Death and dying in America: Jessica Mitford, *The American Way of Death Revisited* (New York: Vintage, 2000).

Chapter 6: Best of Show

Flower sex and other secrets: Ruth Kassinger, *A Garden of Marvels: How We Discovered That Flowers Have Sex, Leaves Eat Air, and Other Secrets of Plants* (New York: William Morrow, 2014).

Garden flowers and their lore: E. Buckner Hollingsworth, *Flower Chronicles: The Legend and Lore of Fifteen Garden Favorites* (Chicago: University of Chicago Press, 2004).

Luther Burbank: Peter Dreyer, *A Gardener Touched with Genius: The Life of Luther Burbank* (Santa Rosa, CA: L. Burbank Home & Gardens, 1993).

Debunking tulipmania: Anne Goldgar, *Tulipmania: Money, Honor, and Knowledge in the Dutch Golden Age* (Chicago: University of Chicago Press, 2007).

Nudging mother nature: J. Mol, E. Cornish, J. Mason, and R. Koes, "Novel Coloured Flowers," *Current Opinions in Biotechnology* 10 (1999): 198–201.

Pollinators and gardeners beware: Livio Comba et al., "Flowers, Nectar and Insect Visits: Evaluating British Plant Species for Pollinator-Friendly Gardens," *Annals of Botany* 83, no. 4 (1999): 369–83.

Make mine a single: Sarah Corbet et al., "Native or Exotic? Double or Single? Evaluating Plants for Pollinator-Friendly Gardens," *Annals of Botany* 87, no. 2 (2001): 219–32.

RHS Chelsea: Brent Elliott, *RHS Chelsea Flower Show: The First 100 Years, 1913–2013* (London: Frances Lincoln, 2014).

Gardens across America: Thomas Spencer and John Russell, *Gardens Across America, East of the Mississippi: The American Horticultural Society's Guide to American Public Gardens and Arboreta, vol. 1* (Boulder, CO: Taylor Trade Publishing, 2005).

Chapter 7: Arriving by Jumbo Jet

At the Miami airport: Amy Stewart, *Flower Confidential: The Good, the Bad and the Beautiful* (Chapel Hill, NC: Algonquin Books, 2007).

The Dutch floral trade: Niala Maharaj and Gaston Dorren, *The Game of the Rose* (Utrecht, Netherlands: International Books, 1995).

Various statistics on flowers grown in the United States and exported: US Department of Agriculture, Economic Research Service, www.ers.usda.gov/.

Data on US imports of cut flowers is contained in the various yearbooks: US Department of Agriculture, Economic Research Service, "Floriculture and Nursery Crops Yearbook," www.ers.usda.gov/.

Buying patterns and statistics: Society of American Florists, www.safnow.org/.

The florist industry: Florists' Review Enterprises, *A Centennial History of the American Florist* (Topeka, KS: Florists' Review Enterprises, 1997).

Flowers for the holidays: Leigh Schmidt, *Consumer Rites: The Buying and Selling of American Holidays* (Princeton, NJ: Princeton University Press, 1995).

Per capita spending on flowers: Flower Council of Holland, www.flowercouncil.org; and United Nations COMTRADE database, http://comtrade.un.org/.

Chapter 8: Eating Flowers

Saffron, thistles, and Roman capers: Peter Bernhardt, *Gods and Goddesses in the Garden: Greco-Roman Mythology and the Scientific Names of Plants* (New Brunswick, NJ: Rutgers University Press, 2008).

How Rome tamed the artichoke: Gabriella Sonnante et al., "The Domestication of Artichoke and Cardoon: From Roman Times to the Genomic Age," *Annals of Botany* 100, no. 5 (2007): 1095–1100.

Rose water and rose recipes: Eleanour Rohde, *Rose Recipes from Olden Times* (Mineola, NY: Dover Publications, 2013).

Essential oils from spices, and pathogens: M. Tajkarimi et al., "Antimicrobial Herb and Spice Compounds in Food," *Food Control* 21 (2010): 1199–1218.

The spice routes: Gary Paul Nabhan, *Cumin, Camels, and Caravans: A Spice Odyssey* (Oakland: University of California Press, 2014).

More than garnish: Cathy Barash, *Edible Flowers: From Garden to Palate* (Golden, CO: Fulcrum Publishing, 1995).

Edible flowers: Rosalind Creasy, *The Edible Flower Garden* (Boston, MA: Periplus Editions, 1999).

In hot water: Kevin Gascoyne, *Tea: History, Terroirs, Varieties* (Richmond Hill, Ontario, Canada: Firefly Books, 2011).

Honeys and beekeeping: Stephen Buchmann and Banning Repplier, *Letters from the Hive: An Intimate History of Bees, Honey, and Humankind* (New York: Bantam Books, 2005).

Also from the hive: Justin Schmidt and Stephen Buchmann, "Other Products of the Hive," in *The Hive and the Honey Bee*, ed. Joe Graham (Hamilton, IL: Dadant & Sons, 1992), 927–88.

Chapter 9: A Little Dab behind the Ear

The sense of smell: Wolfgang Meyerhof and Sigrun Korsching, eds., *Chemosensory Systems in Mammals, Fishes, and Insects (Results and Problems in Cell Differentiation)* (Berlin: Springer, 2009).

Floral scents and bees: S. Dötterl and N. Vereecken, "The Chemical Ecology and Evolution of Bee-Flower Interactions: A Review and Perspectives," *Canadian Journal of Zoology* 88, no. 7 (2010): 668–97.

Flowers and their scents: Roy Genders, *Scented Flora of the World* (London: Robert Hale, 1994).

Desert trumpets: Robert Raguso et al., "Trumpet Flowers of the Sonoran Desert: Floral Biology of *Peniocereus* Cacti and Sacred *Datura*," *International Journal of Plant Sciences* 164, no. 6 (2003): 877–92.

The ecology of floral scents: Robert Raguso, "Wake Up and Smell the Roses: The Ecology and Evolution of Floral Scent," *Annual Review of Ecology, Evolution, and Systematics* 39 (2008): 549–69.

The making of perfumes: Cathy Newman, *Perfume: The Art and Science of Scent* (Washington, DC: National Geographic Society, 1998).

Unguents, perfume, and eyeliner: Lise Manniche, *Sacred Luxuries: Fragrance, Aromatherapy and Cosmetics in Ancient Egypt* (Ithaca, NY: Cornell University Press, 1999).

Perfume and the science of smell: Luca Turin, *The Secret of Scent: Adventures in Perfume and the Science of Smell* (New York: Ecco, 2006).

Is this how the nose works?: Chandler Burr, *The Emperor of Scent: A True Story of Perfume and Obsession* (New York: Random House, 2004).

Perfumes of the world: Luca Turin and Tania Sanchez, *Perfumes: The A–Z Guide* (New York: Penguin Books, 2009).

Chapter 10: The Secret Language of Flowers

Flower lore: Hilderic Friend, *Flowers and Flower Lore*, 6th ed. (Whitefish, MT: Kessinger Publishing, 2010).

The language of flowers: Louise Cortambert, *The Language of Flowers with Illustrative Poetry; to Which Are Now Added The Calendar of Flowers and the Dial of Flowers*, 10th ed. (London: Saunders & Otley, 1846).

Flower masquerades: J. Grandville, *The Flowers Personified: Being a Translation of Grandville's Les Fleurs Animées*, trans. N. Cleaveland (New York: R. Martin, 1849).

Floral meanings: Gretchen Scoble and Ann Field, *The Meaning of Flowers: Myth, Language and Lore* (San Francisco: Chronicle Books, 1998).

Language of the flowers: Marina Heilmeyer, *The Language of Flowers: Symbols and Myths* (Munich: Prestel, 2006).

Flower legends and lore: E. Buckner Hollingsworth, *Flower Chronicles: The Legend and Lore of Fifteen Garden Favorites* (Chicago: University of Chicago Press, 2004).

Ancient Olympic games and flowers: http://www.olympic.org/documents/reports/en/en_report_658.pdf.

Flowers in other cultures: Jack Goody, *The Culture of Flowers* (Cambridge: Cambridge University Press, 1993).

List of US state flowers: http://en.wikipedia.org/wiki/List_of_U.S._state_flowers.

Bluebonnets not billboards: Lewis Gould, "First Lady as Catalyst: Lady Bird Johnson and Highway Beautification in the 1960s," *Environmental Review* 10, no. 2 (1986): 76–92.

Chapter 11: Flowers on the Page

Flowers of the Bible: Amots Dafni and Salah Khatib, *Plants, Demons and Miracles: Folklore of Plants of the Bible Lands* (forthcoming).

Flowers of purgatory: Dante Alighieri, *The Divine Comedy: Inferno; Purgatorio; Paradiso* (New York: Everyman's Library, 1995).

Ancient Chinese poems: Qu Yuan, *The Songs of the South: An Anthology of Ancient Chinese Poems by Qu Yuan and Other Poets* (New York: Penguin Classics, 2012).

Ancient Japanese poetry: Marc Keane, *Songs in the Garden: Poetry and Gardens in Ancient Japan* (Ithaca, NY: MPK Books, 2012).

Robert Herrick: Robert Herrick, *A Selection from the Lyrical Poems of Robert Herrick* (FQ Books, 2010).

William Wordsworth: William Wordsworth, *William Wordsworth: The Major Works: Including the Prelude* (Oxford: Oxford University Press, 2008).

Tennyson's poems: Alfred Tennyson, *The Major Works* (Oxford: Oxford World's Classics, 2009).

Flower fairies: Cicely Mary Barker, *Flower Fairies: The Meaning of Flowers* (London: Warne, 1996).

Sonnets and flowers: Jessica Kerr, *Shakespeare's Flowers* (Chicago: Johnson Books, 1968).

Chapter 12: Flower Power: The Meaning of Flowers in Art

Flower art of ancient Egypt: W. Stevenson Smith, *The Art and Architecture of Ancient Egypt* (New Haven, CT: Yale University Press, 1999).

Western art: Bruce Cole: *Art of the Western World: From Ancient Greece to Post Modernism* (New York: Simon & Schuster, 1991).

Flower power: Andrew Moore and Christopher Garibaldi, eds., *Flower Power: The Meaning of Flowers in Art* (New York: Philip Wilson Publishers, 2003).

Dutch still-life paintings: Tanya Paul and James Clifton, *Elegance and Refinement: The Still-Life Paintings of Willem van Aelst* (New York: Skira Rizzoli, 2012).

Sensual blooms: Barbara Lynes, *Georgia O'Keeffe Museum Collection* (New York: Harry N. Abrams, 2007).

Psychedelic flowers: Andy Warhol, *The Philosophy of Andy Warhol (From A to B and Back Again)* (Fort Washington, PA: Harvest, 1977).

Panchromatic flowers: Ansel Adams and Andrea Stillman, eds., *Ansel Adams: 400 Photographs* (Stockton, CA: Ansel Adams, 2007).

Flower arrangement: F. Rockwell and Esther Grayson, *The Complete Book of Flower Arrangement: For Home Decoration and Show Competition* (New York: American Garden Guild and Doubleday, 1947).

Japanese ikebana: Sato Shozo, *The Art of Arranging Flowers: A Complete Guide to Japanese Ikebana* (New York: Harry N. Abrams, 1965).

Woven into rugs and tapestries: Louise Mackie, "Covered with Flowers: Medieval Floor Coverings Excavated at Fustat in 1980," in *Oriental Carpet and Textile Studies*, ed. R. Pinner and W. Denny (International Conference on Oriental Carpets, 1993), 23–35.

Magnificent glass impostors: Richard Schultes et al., *The Glass Flowers at Harvard* (Cambridge, MA: Harvard University Press, 1992).

Chapter 13: The Flower and the Scientist

Gregor Mendel: Elof Carlson, *Mendel's Legacy: The Origin of Classical Genetics* (Cold Spring Harbor, NY: Cold Spring Harbor Laboratory Press, 2004).

Casting their pollen into the wind: Karl Niklas, "The Aerodynamics of Wind Pollination," *Botanical Review* 51, no. 3 (1985): 328–86.

Flowers in the wind tunnel: Karl Niklas and Stephen Buchmann, "Aerodynamics of Wind Pollination in *Simmondsia chinensis* (Link) Schneider," *American Journal of Botany* 72 no. 4 (1985): 530–39.

Form and function: Karl Niklas, *Plant Biomechanics: An Engineering Approach to Plant Form and Function* (Chicago: University of Chicago Press, 1992).

Trumpet flowers and their moths: Robert Raguso, Cynthia Henzel, Stephen Buchmann, and Gary Nabhan, "Trumpet Flowers of the Sonoran Desert: Floral Biology of *Peniocereus* Cacti and Sacred *Datura*," *International Journal of Plant Sciences* 164, no. 6 (2003): 877–92.

Signposts for bees: Eugene Jones and Stephen Buchmann, "Ultraviolet Floral Patterns as Functional Orientation Cues in Hymenopterous Pollination Systems," *Animal Behaviour* 22, no. 2 (1974): 481–85.

Communicating in the UV spectrum: Robert Silberglied, "Communication in the Ultraviolet," *Annual Review of Ecology and Systematics* 10 (1979): 373–98.

How pollinators recognize their flowers: Lars Chittka and Nigel Raine, "Recognition of Flowers by Pollinators," *Current Opinion in Plant Biology* 9, no. 4 (2006): 428–35.

Artificial flowers and learning in bumble bees: Anne Leonard, Anna Dornhaus, and Daniel Papaj, "Flowers Help Bees Cope with Uncertainty: Signal Detection and the Function of Floral Complexity," *Journal of Experimental Biology* 214 (2011): 113–21.

Bees discriminate odors: Wulfila Gronenberg et al., "Honey Bees (*Apis mellifera*) Learn to Discriminate the Smell of Organic Compounds from Their Respective Deuterated Isotopomers," *Proceedings of the Royal Society B* 281, no. 1778 (2014), doi:10.1098/repr.2013.3089.

Chapter 14: Good for What Ails Us: Healing Our Bodies and Minds

Humans need nature: Edward O. Wilson, *Biophilia: The Human Bond with Other Species* (Cambridge, MA: Harvard University Press, 1986).

Tea and stress levels: Yi-Ching Yang et al., "The Protective Effect of Habitual Tea Consumption on Hypertension," *JAMA Internal Medicine* 164, no. 14 (2004): 1534–40.

Honey for dressing wounds: Peter Molan, "The Evidence Supporting the Use of Honey as a Wound Dressing," *International Journal of Lower Extremity Wounds* 5, no. 1 (2006): 40–54.

Efficacy of honey-coated bandages: Betina Lund-Nielsen et al., "The Effect of Honey-Coated Bandages Compared with Silver-Coated Bandages on Treatment of Malignant Wounds: A Randomized Study," *Wound Repair and Regeneration* 19, no. 6 (2011): 664–70.

Recovery from surgery: Roger Ulrich, "View Through a Window May Influence Recovery from Surgery," *Science* 224, no. 4647 (1984): 420–21.

Fear is in the air?: Denise Chen and Jeannette Haviland-Jones, "Human Olfactory Communication of Emotion," *Perceptual and Motor Skills* 91 (2000): 771–81.

Indoor air; wild or scrubbed: Jeannette Haviland-Jones et al., "The Emotional Air in Your Space: Scrubbed, Wild or Cultivated?," *Emotion, Space and Society* 6 (2013): 91–99.

The Duchenne smile: Leanne Williams et al., "In Search of the 'Duchenne Smile': Evidence from Eye Movements," *Journal of Psychophysiology* 15, no. 2 (2001): 122–27.

Flowers make us smile: Jeannette Haviland-Jones et al., "An Environmental Approach to Positive Emotion: Flowers," *Evolutionary Psychology* 3, no. 1–4 (2005): 104–32.

PHOTO AND ART CREDITS

Photographs © Stephen Buchmann, except for the following:
p. 7 Illustration by Paul Mirocha.
p. 21 Photograph by Oleksandr Holovachov.
p. 211 With permission from Missouri Botanical Garden.
p. 254 Photograph by Retha Edens-Meier. Used with permission.
p. 260 With permission from Missouri Botanical Garden.
p. 281 Photograph by Keith Brust. Used with permission.

My thanks to Dan Bach of Bach's Greenhouse Cactus Nursery for allowing me to borrow and photograph his plants. Thanks also to Dr. Christine Conte and Jo Falls of Tohono Chul Park (Tucson) for permission to photograph and film on the grounds of this exquisite biopark.

INDEX